MW00780335

STAND FOREVER, YIELDING NEVER

THE CITADEL IN THE 21ST CENTURY

To Peter, in hopes this brings some good memories.

STAND FOREVER, YIELDING NEVER

THE CITADEL IN THE 21ST CENTURY

JOHN WARLEY

'67

EVENING POST
BOOKS

Published by
Evening Post Books
Charleston, South Carolina

Editor: John M. Burbage
Designer: Gill Guerry
Cover Photo: Louis M. Brems, The Citadel

Second printing 2019
Printed in the United States of America

A CIP catalog record for this book has been applied
for from the Library of Congress.

ISBN: 978-1-929647-37-8

DEDICATION

*The publication of this history resulted from a discussion
among several members of the Class of 1967 on the night
before Pat Conroy's funeral in Beaufort, South Carolina,
in March 2016. The Class of 1967 sponsored the book as
a gift to the entire Citadel family on the occasion of our
50th reunion and the 175th anniversary of the founding of
The Citadel. With profound admiration and gratitude we
dedicate it to the boys of '67 who became men on the far side
of the world and didn't come home:*

Fred Joshua Carter
Glenn Richard Cook
Frederick Young Holjes
William Livingston McCormick
George Louis Miner
Thomas Duckett O'Connor
Richard William O'Keefe
John Thomas Orrico
George Thomas Taylor, Jr.
Bruce Richard Welge

*And to the memory of
our classmate Pat Conroy*

Epigraph

"It is, Sir, as I have said, a small college, and yet,
there are those who love it …"

Daniel Webster, The Dartmouth College Case

Lay her foundations deep,
In the soil where her soldier-sons sleep!
Lay them square,
Make them straight,
Take thought for the weight
They shall bear.
Lay them wide as democracy's creed,
Make them strong as democracy's need.

Opening stanza of an Ode composed by Colonel Oliver James Bond on November 24, 1920, to commemorate the laying of the cornerstone for the Greater Citadel.

Oh Citadel, though strife surrounds us,
We will ever be
Full conscious of the benefits
That we derive from thee.
Stand forever, yielding never
To the tyrant's Hell
We'll never cease our struggles for
Our mighty Citadel

Second verse of *The Citadel Alma Mater*

CONTENTS

INTRODUCTION **10**

CHAPTER 1
A Quarterback Returns to call the Plays **13**

CHAPTER 2
"A system of education at once scientific and practical" **20**

CHAPTER 3
Eight Stars, Thirty-Three Years **37**

CHAPTER 4
"The fundamental cornerstone of the Military College's Operation" **44**

CHAPTER 5
"There ain't no daylight in Vietnam . . . not a bit." **55**

CHAPTER 6
"Sir, it was the least I could do." **70**

CHAPTER 7
Is there Something Wrong with The Citadel? **92**

CHAPTER 8
The Summer of His Discontent **113**

CHAPTER 9
Grimsley Plans the Future as the Past Wears Thin **129**

CHAPTER 10
The Watts Era is Swept in by 140-mph Winds **155**

CHAPTER 11
If you build it, they might (or might not) come **169**

CHAPTER 12
Skirts Climb the Gates **187**

CHAPTER 13
A Year in Transition **196**

CHAPTER 14
Into the New Millennium **213**

CHAPTER 15
"We put the future of The Citadel on their backs . . ." **236**

CHAPTER 16
Planting the Flag — A Big Red One **254**

CHAPTER 17
LEAD 2018 . . . . **266**

CHAPTER 18
The Citadel Today, and Tomorrow **277**

ACKNOWLEDGMENTS **295**

ENDNOTES **297**

INDEX **323**

INTRODUCTION

Those who gather to celebrate The Citadel's 175th anniversary on Corps Day 2018 can take an extra measure of pride in the past half-century, for in those 50 years the college has reached an educational plateau many would not have foreseen in 1965 when General Mark Clark retired as president.

The factors accounting for this ascension are many. Perhaps most laudable in this march of progress is the school's relentless reaffirmation of the principles on which it was founded in 1842. We remain an institution of higher learning providing a practical education within a military environment. Life within the gates was and is rigorous, structured, infused with core values of honor, duty and respect. Leadership and promotion within the ranks is measured, as it always has been, by merit. Reveille and taps still begin and end each day.

But by every other measure, The Citadel is vastly different and, it must be said, vastly better. While holding fast to its most prized traditions, it has improved in areas critical to its continued success. The faculty — once an all-male, all-white semi-sinecure for retired military — mirrors those found in the best schools where academic excellence, terminal degrees, experience in the chosen field, and communication skills determine hiring and tenure. The curriculum is expanded in response to needs and trends in today's job market to include study options not remotely contemplated in the 1960s. For example, the college's Swain Department of Nursing now offers a Bachelor of Science in Nursing within both a cadet and evening studies environment. A recently added Bachelor of Arts degree in Intelligence and Security Studies is taught completely online.

The school's iconic architecture remains familiar to the tens of thousands of students and visitors who have passed through Lesesne Gate, but, in fact, millions of dollars in improvements and renovations have characterized the past half-century. Though we are still considered a state-supported college, many of the buildings have been built and maintained with private funds largely from alumni giving back to the school they credit for their successes.

Three of the four old barracks were razed and rebuilt to accommodate more stringent building codes, air-conditioning and modern communications. An entirely new barracks, Watts, was constructed. Sports facilities, from intramural to revenue, rival any to be found on campuses where we compete. Older facilities including long-suffering Capers Hall are scheduled to be modernized while new ones, such as Bastin Hall, the business school to be constructed on Hagood Avenue, promise expanded opportunities.

The Corps of Cadets has been diversified to better reflect the world our graduates enter. Applicants are better qualified, and those who come more likely to remain due to increased emphasis on leadership training during all four years. Cadets also are afforded the opportunity to study abroad. The Citadel has risen to a level of unprecedented excellence in its long history. For seven consecutive years the *U.S. News & World Report* ranked The Citadel as the No. 1 public college in the South offering up to a Master's degree, and No. 4 when private colleges are included. Its undergraduate engineering program ranks 19th nationwide for schools offering up to a Master's degree.

There have been high hurdles, missteps and setbacks along the way. A gradual reduction in the state's annual appropriation coupled with periods of declining enrollment have clouded the college's future more than once. For every institution of higher learning in the nation, education is much more expensive. In 1954-1955, General Clark's first year as president, the school's budget was $2.32 million. For fiscal year 2016, it reached $116.98 million. Leaving aside inflation, Clark's first budget would run today's Citadel for about a week, and if inflation is considered, for just over two months. As it has done with other challenges, the college addressed the funding issue head-on and with resolve, so that today its future is more assured than at any time since its founding.

Challenges went beyond dollars and cents. Racial integration in 1966 brought tensions that mirrored those in the South and the nation as a whole. The Citadel's history of having fired the first shot of the Civil War makes particularly ironic the modern emphasis on racial and cultural diversity. Hazing incidents spawned unwelcome publicity. We fought coeducation but embraced it when it became inevitable. Progress is seldom seamless here or elsewhere but we pressed forward toward the brighter future we now claim.

As you read the pages that follow, bear in mind that a history of the last 50 years for most colleges in America would be a recitation of dramatic expansion. In the mid-1960s, Ohio State University enrolled about 25,000 students. Today, it enrolls 60,000. Our neighbor, the College of Charleston, grew from a student body of less than 500 in the mid-1960s to its current population of over 10,000 undergraduates. Mark Clark's Corps of Cadets educated and trained 2,000 young men. Today's does the same for about 2,300 young men and women. We cannot double, triple or quadruple in size. We have neither the space nor the desire. We are committed to the educational model that has demonstrated its worth for generations, and to the mission that was reaffirmed by the Board of Visitors as recently as April 2015: "to educate and develop our students to become principled leaders in all walks of life by instilling the core values of The Citadel in a disciplined and intellectually challenging environment."

Also bear in mind that the greater Citadel includes more than the Corps of Cadets, though this book is focused on the Corps in recognition of its 175th anniversary. Meaningful and essential contributions to Charleston, the state and the nation have been made by the Citadel Graduate College, veterans programs, and collaborative efforts with the Medical University of South Carolina and the College of Charleston. The stories of those auxiliary components of the college deserve their own volume beyond the scope of this one.

The Citadel's journey from good to great did not occur by accident. Strong, visionary leadership brought it about. Alumni demanded it and contributed generously to its actualization. Faculties and administrations pushed standards ever higher and the Corps of Cadets responded. As we celebrate in March 2018 our 175th anniversary from the day those first 20 cadets reported to the Old Citadel at Marion Square, we marvel at how we got here and glimpse on the horizon possibilities yet to be fully formed. This book is about that journey, the march of the long gray line that has made The Citadel's storied history possible and assures its future.

Chapter 1

A QUARTERBACK RETURNS TO CALL THE PLAYS[1]

O n a spring day in 2005, Lieutenant General John W. Rosa, Jr., USAF, stood at a window looking out on a sight that never failed to inspire him: the majesty of the U.S. Air Force Academy cadet chapel, its 17 spires set against a bright-blue Colorado sky. On that day, he needed inspiration for a crucial career decision. In the distance rose the majestic Rocky Mountains where springtime promised rebirth and renewal. Maybe, thought Rosa, rebirth held the key for him as well: a renewal of his ties to Charleston, South Carolina, where he and his wife, Donna, met and married, and where his four years at The Citadel set him on the road to that window where he stood staring at the chapel.

He was 53 and superintendent of the Academy sprawling below and around him. Option 1 was to stay in Colorado Springs, continuing work he knew the Academy needed from the moment of his arrival in 2003. He had parachuted into a firestorm of sexual assault allegations that brought the Academy and the Air Force publicity that ends careers. Rosa's predecessor, Major General John R. Dallager, had been demoted from lieutenant general by just such a scandal, sending shock waves to the Pentagon and other service academies where the same problems existed but had yet to surface so publicly.

Rosa remembered the day at the Pentagon when he was summoned to the office of Air Force Chief of Staff General John P. Jumper. Rosa, at that time deputy director for operations for the Joint Chiefs of Staff and the military spokesman for the Pentagon, was nervous, assuming he had misspoken during a recent press conference. What did he say that was so egregious as to bring him to the attention of the top brass? He would know momentarily as the elevator lifted him to Jumper's office.

There was a problem, to be sure, Jumper told him, but it wasn't yet Rosa's. It depended on Rosa's willingness to accept assignment as superintendent of the Air Force Academy. Rosa's nervous twinge gave way to heady contemplation of a third star when only recently he received his second. Superintendent of the Academy was a three-star post and the man whose office Rosa just entered could make it happen. It would mean leaving his present Joint Chiefs of Staff J3 operations assignment at the Pentagon, a steady diet of post-9/11 war planning and 16-hour days. And it would mean he wouldn't go to his next slated assignment, the Pacific, to fill a two-star billet commanding and flying F-16s; a return to the cockpit, to the perfume of jet fuel and the sheer rush of Mach 2 with only an acrylic canopy between him and his Maker. He didn't get where he was that day by flying a desk, and adding to his 3,600 hours of flight time had its appeal. The irony of the meeting was lost on neither man: Jumper, a VMI graduate, asking Rosa, a Citadel man, to rescue the reputation of the illustrious Air Force Academy.

In addition to leaving the urgent J3 slot and the failed rendezvous with the F-16s, there was a third consideration. Service academy superintendent jobs are career minefields where the personal benefit-to-risk ratio weighs heavily on the perilous end of the equation. Dallager's demotion had ample precedent. Rosa wasn't a wealthy man, and a fall from grace could have disastrous implications for his family's economic security and his retirement.

As always, Rosa withheld this career decision until he talked it over with Donna. Her instincts had proven invaluable over the years, and he considered flag rank as much hers as his. They were inseparable since his sophomore year at The Citadel, where he arrived in the fall of 1969 as a recruited quarterback on a football scholarship. He played high school ball in Jacksonville, Florida, cheered on by three sisters and his parents, John and Elizabeth Rosa. His father had retired from the Navy as a master chief petty officer, the Navy's highest noncommissioned rank. Rosa credits him for early lessons in precision and high standards, telling a newspaper reporter in 2006 that living with a jet engine mechanic meant changing the oil in the family car is a four-hour project.[2]

In his knob year, he flirted with leaving The Citadel a dozen times, an inclination shared by his roommate for his entire four years, Paul Plunkett, a baseball catcher. But by the following year, he was flirting with Donna Kangeter, a pretty West Ashley girl as outgoing as himself. He enjoyed the respect of his teammates, according to his classmate and the center on the football team, Keith Roden: "John wasn't just our quarterback, he was our leader. When he spoke, the guys paid attention. But he never took himself too seriously, unlike some others I could name. More than once he left campus or returned in the trunk of a car." Roden's eyes animated when he recalled the time after graduation when he and many of his teammates traveled to

Tennessee for the wedding of Ed Barnwell, one of their linemen. "We all stayed at this motel with a pool. I can't tell you why — maybe one or two beers — but I strayed into John's room and put on the suit he planned to wear to the wedding. I was modeling it out by the pool when he came up behind me and pushed me in. He was laughing pretty hard, but I laughed harder when I broke the news I was wearing his clothes."[3]

As a sophomore, Rosa started at quarterback, getting his baptism by fire at Clemson, where he showed he could run Bulldogs Coach Red Parker's veer offense. Life was good. He was at the throttle of a team with talent and promise, he had made a certain peace with the military environment that had vexed him the year before, and win or lose he knew a beautiful girl awaited him after the game. With all that going for him, what could go wrong?

Spring practice went wrong. On April 2, 1971, during the annual spring game, he suffered a knee injury that required surgery and left him in a cast for 12 weeks.[4] The bum knee limited his playing time thereafter, but not his ambition. He began to think seriously about life beyond football. Upon graduation, he took a commission in the Air Force and never looked back . . . until that day at the window in Colorado Springs.

When he arrived at the Air Force Academy, Rosa found the tensions every bit as advertised. What had begun with a few former cadets claiming they had been raped at the Academy swelled to a platoon of 60 women.[5] Dallager and three other top officials purged in the wake of the scandal said they were unaware of this, which was in itself a problem according to the independent panel that investigated the allegations. A cadet-run victim hotline proved less than effective in forcing the accused to face courts martial, while the alleged victims endured insult after injury in the form of punishment for relatively trivial offenses. Many of the women lost their Air Force careers, while fellow cadets circled the wagons in an effort to discredit them. According to one panelist, Colonel John W. Ripley, a retired Marine, "It's very apparent to us that the system at the Air Force Academy has utterly failed the majority of victims."[6] Rosa was about to earn the third star he received with the assignment.

The key, he believed, was to instill in the academy's cadets a better sense of respect for others, one that came naturally to some but for others required much more. His "Values and Respect Program" grew out of 165 recommendations from a blue-ribbon panel. It changed the culture at the Academy and became a model for other institutions to emulate.[7]

While Rosa and the Academy sought solutions to the crisis, a new challenge arose: religious proselytizing by some on staff, in the faculty and among guest speakers. Colorado Springs is home to the well-known Focus on the Family radio broadcast organization and other Christian evangelical organizations whose members led some of the 19 faith-based groups at the Academy. A 16-member panel commissioned by the Air Force found no overt religious discrimination but a lack of sensitivity to the beliefs of non-Christians. The panel's chairman, Lieutenant General Roger A. Brady, made it clear that the appropriate boundaries for religious expression were an issue beyond the Academy gates and he praised the leadership for aggressively confronting the problem.[8]

On a day that saw Rosa wrestling with proselytizing, interfacing with faculty, handling issues with parents and cadets, and performing the endless duties of a man responsible for 4,400 young men and women, he arrived home to learn from Donna that The Citadel had called. A solicitation for money? "I don't think so," she said. "They want you back in Charleston … To be the president." For the first time John Rosa, senior private in the Class of 1973, entertained the thought that maybe he would be offered a chance to lead the school he loved in the city he loved.

The "maybe" had more to do with Air Force regulations than with anything in his resume. As an officer on active duty, he was prohibited from discussing civilian employment opportunities. But he was intrigued. In the days that followed, he recalls exactly one telephone conversation on the subject. He told William B. Sansom, Citadel Class of 1964 and head of the search committee, that his active-duty status prevented him from discussing the opening, but that he was sufficiently interested to approach the Air Force for permission to throw his hat into the ring. To do so, he contacted General Jumper, the man most responsible for his current assignment.

"No," Jumper said, which seemed to settle the matter. Jumper's opposition wasn't the only hurdle. Rosa had been a lieutenant general for fewer than three years, so by regulation would retire as a major general unless his retirement was blessed by the Secretary of Defense, in this case Donald H. Rumsfeld. This requirement was in place to discourage early retirement in the Armed Services' senior ranks.

The Citadel's effort to woo back its former quarterback as its new president seemed doomed. Jumper, having thrown into the Academy's fire the man who proved he could put it out, wasn't about to tamper with his own success. In the weeks that followed, Rosa appeared destined to serve the traditional five years at the Academy before retiring.

But Jumper had a change of heart, thinking he may have been too hasty with his refusal. Rosa wasn't asking to interview with a defense contractor or seeking some private enterprise payday, he wanted to make a contribution to education as he had done at the Academy. A worthy goal, in Jumper's opinion, and one justifying release. If the Secretary of Defense approved, as Jumper thought he would, Rosa was free to interview at The Citadel. "But John," Jumper said, "with your credentials I'd be surprised if you were not selected, so make damn sure this is something you and Donna want."

Which brought Rosa to that window staring at the chapel in scenic Colorado Springs. A man could do worse than have two such options, both of them attractive — the kind most men his age coveted: A soft landing at the Air Force Academy, which he had come to know and respect highly, or to his alma mater — home, Donna's home, with a chance to make a big difference in the institution that made such a difference in him.

The Citadel job held another potential for difference, a darker one. He would be going back to live and work among the men, then boys, who made his four years in Charleston some of the happiest of his life. Teammates, classmates and others with whom he had endured the rigors of the Fourth Class System, partied, swapped stories and bonded, would no doubt welcome him. Yet, the college president, as with any college president, must make decisions that inevitably do not meet with universal approval. He could expect criticism, second guessing, Monday morning quarterbacking — some of it from those same friends. Might he be poisoning the well from which the waters of his adolescence tasted so sweet?

But The Citadel needed him, and he knew it. He read up on the challenges facing the school, founded in 1842. A state-supported college, The Citadel's administrations and faculties watched that support melt away year after year. In the name of fiscal austerity, the Legislature ate its own seed corn, forcing higher education in South Carolina to do more with less. Deferred maintenance alone was enough to discourage even the most gung-ho president, as it had daunted the man whose resignation prompted the need for a search committee, Major General John S. Grinalds, USMC (Ret). Rosa estimated the deferred maintenance at $70 million when Rosa arrived, and by 2012 it had grown to $100 million.[9] The Citadel had abandoned its all-male admissions policy in 1996, and there was no reason to believe sexual tensions there weren't the same kind he dealt with at the Academy. Rosa had been back for Citadel reunions. He well knew that residual resentment of women at the Academy was prevalent among a large segment of Citadel alumni and classmates. Racial issues also lingered, complicated by the most hardened alumni who viewed the 140 years since the end of the Civil War as merely a lull in the fighting. The challenges awaiting him in Charleston seemed every bit as daunting as those that greeted him in Colorado Springs if he was offered and accepted the job. If …

Rosa turned from the window, his mind made up. He and Donna would fly to Charleston to be interviewed together. He had neither filled out an application nor submitted a resume. The Citadel would embrace them or not. The morning after the interview, The Citadel's Chairman of the Board of Visitors Colonel William "Billy" Jenkinson called to offer Rosa the presidency. He accepted with confidence that he and Donna had made the right decision. They were headed home.

Rosa is every inch a general officer, tall and trim with a year-round tan more common to tennis players than senior officers, though he prefers golf, sailing and riding his Harley. He exudes a commanding presence, which in his case should not imply reserve or aloofness. In casual conversation or over a beer he is affable, with a beguiling sense of humor. Still, you do not wish to cross him.

By the time Rosa attended his first Board of Visitors meeting in February 2006, he had met with cadets, faculty, staff, alumni, and each vice president and former president of the college. (Their advice: "Find a getaway retreat. You're going to need it.") In that same initial meeting, he noted a disengagement by third classmen as being outside the leadership team, which provided a segue into what would become a hallmark of his administration: Principled leaders are built year by year, following a logical and predictable roadmap to excellence. He would settle for nothing short of that goal, and it would start now.

By integrating the lessons of the Values and Respect Program begun at the Air Force Academy with the Krause Initiative (discussed in Chapter 15), all cadets would benefit and the college would thrive.

And it has. In addition to bragging rights afforded its seventh consecutive selection by *U.S. News & World Report* as the No. 1 public college in the South offering up to a master's degree, The Citadel maintains its nationally ranked engineering program (No. 19) and, by the metrics used in the rankings, the highest overall score nationally for public colleges in its category.

Rosa credits others with this achievement. He is still, at heart, a quarterback and college administration is a team sport. And Rosa is the driving force behind it. By consensus among Board of Visitors members, alumni and employers of graduates, his leadership has taken the school to the much-aspired-to next level. And his vision could not have come at a better time: In an era of shrinking educational budgets, identity politics and the dramatically shifting needs of the workforce, the need has never been greater for well prepared, principled leaders. They are at a premium, and The Citadel is a source of them.

As great a challenge as any for Rosa was the school's culture, which had changed radically during the decades before he arrived. To measure and assess those changes, step back to 1965 when General Mark W. Clark retired as Citadel president.

Chapter 2

"A SYSTEM OF EDUCATION AT ONCE SCIENTIFIC AND PRACTICAL"

As the focus of this book is on The Citadel since General Clark's retirement, the school's history will not be presented in the thoroughness explored by John P. Thomas, Colonel Oliver Bond and Colonel D.D. Nicholson, Jr., the school's first three biographers.[10] The founding in 1842 is sketched here to give context to that which follows.[11]

In the year 1799, an enslaved man named Denmark Vesey won the East Bay Lottery. Ticket No. 1884 paid out $1,500, and with his winnings he purchased his freedom for $600. By all accounts Vesey was bright, strong, energetic, ambitious and a skilled carpenter. At an age estimated at 55, and inspired by a horrific slave revolt in Santo Domingo, he plotted an uprising of his own in Charleston. At midnight on Sunday, June 16, 1822, he and his followers planned to rebel against the white population. Using arms and munitions stashed over time for the purpose, they planned to seize more weapons from various places in the city where they were kept with minimum security. But some slaves unsympathetic to Vesey's plot alerted authorities, who mobilized patrols and squelched the rebellion before it began.

Of 131 people arrested and tried thereafter, 52 were acquitted, 43 relocated and 35, including Vesey, executed. The nature of the rebellion is still debated. Evidence at trial pointed to an intent to murder as many of Charleston's white men, women and children as possible, and convictions relied on that evidence.

On the other hand, Vesey is hailed as a hero by those denying the murder plot and insisting he intended to lead his people in an exodus to Haiti.[12] One student of the Vesey uprising put at 9,000 the number of slaves that were recruited to participate.[13] If true, it made more realistic the goal of murdering every white person in Charleston, then the nation's sixth largest city with a population of about 25,000.[14] This also made it certain that the conspiracy would be foiled, as any secret shared by 9,000 would have leaks. As fanciful as the murder plot seemed, the idea of safely sailing 9,000 conspirators anywhere was equally fanciful. There is today in Charleston's

Hampton Park, adjacent to The Citadel campus, a handsome statue of Vesey that lauds him as a revolutionary and omits any reference to murder. The historical narrative on the statue's base cites the exodus to Haiti as a likely explanation for the insurrection.

Some link the college's birth to the Denmark Vesey uprising, but that is true only for the original building on Marion Square, known today as the Old Citadel. An important distinction should be made between the college and the building it occupied beginning in 1843. The original building, called the Citadel (but not *The* Citadel), was an armory where arms and munitions were stored under guard. It served no educational purpose whatsoever.

Fear of slave uprisings had for generations created extreme paranoia about the South's "peculiar institution," and in response to the Santo Domingo/Haiti slaughter of whites and Vesey's "near miss," the State Legislature authorized the construction of two buildings for the storage of weapons and munitions. The building in Columbia was to be called the Arsenal and the one in Charleston the Citadel, to be constructed on the site of a tobacco inspection warehouse no longer in use on Marion Square. Once finished and stocked with weapons and explosives, the facilities were to be guarded by a militia. It is ironic but not surprising that the revenue source for paying the guards was a tax on free Negroes such as Vesey.[15]

The Charleston facility wasn't completed until 1829, seven years after the terror that prompted its construction. When it was finally fit for occupancy, United States troops from Fort Moultrie moved in to guard the munitions. But in 1832, South Carolina passed the Ordinance of Nullification, the state's response to unpopular tariffs imposed by the federal government. The ordinance amounted to a state statute defying a federal one, creating a Constitutional crisis and raising tensions between the states and the national government to a level that risked civil war. President Andrew Jackson threatened to send an army to enforce the tariffs. As a precaution against having South Carolina's munitions in the hands of soldiers being ordered to use them against the people that owned them, the Legislature requested the removal of U.S. troops from the Citadel. When the federal force left late in 1833, a local militia replaced them.[16]

This Municipal Guard, intended to ease the minds of Charlestonians, generated much debate and little comfort. Eleven years had elapsed since the failed Vesey revolt, but locals remained fearful of weapons falling into the hands of more skillful, better organized conspirators. They were not in the least impressed with the quality of the militia. In a petition to the state's lawmakers, the locals denigrated the Municipal Guard, asserting, "Most of them are shopkeepers or retailers of spirituous liquors to the negroes." The militia took umbrage, responding that "the members of the Guard are employed in some occupation throughout the day, and when night comes are totally incapacitated from serving as sentinels."[17] Whether profiteers or merely exhausted merchants, over the next decade the Municipal Guard as constituted created more problems than it solved. Their odious conduct mirrored that of guards in Lexington, Virginia, where, since 1816, munitions had been stored in an arsenal that would eventually become Virginia Military Institute (VMI). Thus, both South Carolina and Virginia confronted the same problem: Contingents of bored security guards who routinely drank, disturbed the peace and made general nuisances of themselves to the growing irritation of the local population.

Virginia sought to solve its problem by establishing VMI in 1839,[18] and in 1842 the South Carolina Legislature passed "an Act to convert the Arsenal at Columbia, and the Citadel and Magazine in and near Charleston, into Military Schools." In his message to the Legislature proposing the conversion, Governor Richardson minced no words about the munitions guards who stood to be replaced by cadets:

> [W]e have but to contrast [cadets with] the indiscriminate enlistment of many of the most profligate, licentious and abandoned of society — men without local attachments — the indolent, intemperate and depraved — outcasts from society, and sometimes fugitives from justice, whose crimes impel to this last resource for employment; whose passions prompt to the first occasion of treachery or insubordination, and whose character, however temporarily subdued by the restraints of discipline, can never be reclaimed, or fitted for the duties and obligations of useful citizens.[19]

In admitting that there "are many honorable and distinguished exceptions to this general depravity of character," the governor had in mind members of the Washington Light Infantry (WLI), a venerable local militia formed in 1807 and comprised of many of the city's elite. So highly regarded was this unit that in 1824 it was designated as a special honor guard, the *Fusilier Francaise*, to escort the renowned Marquis de Lafayette into the city on his farewell tour of America.[20] The WLI rotated with other units as part of the larger militia maligned by the governor. When cadets replaced the militia in March 1843, to the WLI went the honor of handing over the keys to the building, the old guard giving way to the new. In 2002, some 159 years later, the WLI paid to have the gates from the Old Citadel refurbished for their installation in The Citadel's current Alumni Courtyard at the Holliday

Alumni Center across the street from Johnson Hagood Stadium.[21]

In founding military schools, both Virginia and South Carolina came to the same conclusion. For about what they were spending on "the indolent, intemperate and depraved" to guard their munitions, they could provide sorely needed educations for young men who would not otherwise get them.

At the time of its founding, The Citadel was one of five colleges in South Carolina. The others were the College of Charleston and Mount Zion College (in Winnsboro), both chartered in 1785; South Carolina College (later, the University of South Carolina), founded in 1801; and Beaufort College, chartered in 1795 but not opened until 1804.[22] Although each was in theory a "college," the term had a fluid and imprecise meaning in the early 19th century. One commentator described what was taught as "higher schooling," as the so-named colleges awarded their own degrees without objective standards by which to measure them.[23] The Citadel, for example, did not grant a Bachelor of Science degree until 1900.[24] The College of Charleston, which began as a private church institution, had "never been much more than an elementary school" until taken over by the city in 1837.[25] Beaufort College struggled to maintain enrollment in the early years but ultimately found its place as a prep school for Lowcountry families who wished to send their sons to South Carolina College or off to Harvard and Yale.[26] South Carolina College came the closest to what we might think of as a college today, offering a classical education taught by an internationally prominent faculty.

Whether deemed an elementary school, a prep school or a college, each of these shared in common an emphasis on Latin and Greek, the building blocks for what was considered a classic education. In the case of the College of Charleston, these languages were required until 1968, when students were able to opt out of the ancient tongues.[27] The real value of such educations had been questioned early. In 1836, Governor George McDuffie told the Legislature: "In my opinion, our system of school instruction should be more practical, having a more direct reference to the business and duties of active life. The common reproach against a classical education, that it tends to disqualify our young men from performing these duties, is not without some foundation."[28]

It should come as no surprise that a secondary school background in Latin and Greek and a reading of the classics in literature were open to a privileged minority of South Carolinians. Affluent children of professionals, successful merchants and wealthy planters attended private schools or were tutored at home, much as they had been in Jefferson's day two generations earlier. For the vast majority of the state's children, particularly those in rural areas, their only hope for an education, even a rudimentary one, lay in the public realm, which was a thin hope indeed.

The antebellum South as a whole had a poor record of providing schools for its children, but South Carolina's was particularly dismal. At the dawn of the 19th century, there was no compulsory primary or secondary public education in the state.[29] One generation removed from the Revolution, public opinion largely mirrored the British view that education was essentially a private matter with no obligation for the state to provide an education for its citizens.[30] Given such attitudes, it could be considered progressive that in 1811 the S.C. Legislature passed the Free School Act, a flawed effort to address a problem that most Northern states took seriously. Free Schools, also known as common schools, received funding from South Carolina but the districts where the money could be used were expected to supply the buildings, which they often failed to do. There was no superintendent of education, as most other Southern states had, and funds distributed pursuant to the act were loosely monitored. A stigma was attached to those attending Free Schools and among the poorer families: The children who might otherwise have attended were needed for manual labor or to work in the fields — constant sources of interruption of whatever schooling happened to be available. [31]

Attendance at Free Schools was voluntary, and it was assumed that they would be supplemented by private academies, which enjoyed a surge in popularity among the more elite after the Revolution. By 1830 there was at least one such academy in every district in the state,[32] and by 1860 there were 227 of them in South Carolina.[33] Private academies provided elementary and college preparatory work at a reasonable rate of tuition per quarter,[34] but these were hardly a substitute for publicly funded schools. In the decades leading to the Civil War, a minority of school-age children in South Carolina had ever attended any classes, and by 1860 no more than half had any formal education. Repeated efforts to strengthen or improve the Free Schools Act were defeated, so it remained failed legislation until 1868 during Reconstruction when black state legislator Robert Smalls of Beaufort pushed through a constitutional provision requiring South Carolina to educate its students of all races, and requiring them to attend.[35]

The presence of various educational options for the landed elite begged the question of how to educate a boy between 15 and 19 years old with little formal education (but literate) from families with modest means or none at all. Such boys had little if any chance of becoming wealthy planters owning vast acreage and slaves. For them, a classical education was a luxury they couldn't afford even if they somehow secured the primary and secondary educations necessary to comprehend the curricula and the means to finance one. In South Carolina alone there were thousands of such boys, and what they needed most was practical education. Their best chance to get ahead lay in supplying what the state most needed: engineers, teachers and citizen-soldiers.

Because this problem persisted to a greater or lesser degree throughout the antebellum South, state leaders from Louisiana to Kentucky found a way to address it: military schools. By the time the first shot was fired at Fort Sumter, 12 Southern states supported military academies. Another 70 flourished as private institutions, bringing combined military school enrollment to an estimated 11,000 students.[36] The most successful and enduring of these state-supported schools are The Citadel and VMI.

In her analysis of military schools in the antebellum South, Jennifer R. Green studied the biographies and correspondence of more than 1,000 cadets, including VMI matriculates, in the two decades from their foundings to the eve of the Civil War. From these personal records, supplemented by those of the institutions they attended, including The Citadel, she drew a detailed picture of military education and its primarily middle-class constituency:[37]

> After 1839, then, military schools offered one of the few sustained programs for engineering training in the antebellum nation. Overall, just less than 10 percent of all antebellum military academy matriculates and 14 percent of graduates became engineers. . . . As a result of such educational priorities, Southern military education successfully led non-elite alumni into "practical professions," . . . In addition to the alumni who entered engineering, military schools funneled 19 percent of their alumni into law, 17 percent into medicine (including dentistry, reflecting the moderate status of antebellum doctors) and nearly 30 percent into teaching.[38]

One statistic in particular demonstrates the degree to which military schools, including The Citadel, served middle-class families: "Of the more than 300 elite planters who lived in the South in 1850 and 1860, only one of them sent his son to a military school." [39]

This focus on the practical coincided precisely with the intent of those who founded The Citadel, as the Board of Visitors acknowledged in its first report to the governor: "The board have aimed at a system of education at once scientific and practical, and which, if their original design is carried out, will eminently qualify the Cadets, there taught, for almost any station or condition in life."[40] Edwin Heriot, a VMI graduate, in an 1850 speech at The Citadel entitled "The Best System of Practical Education," praised the college as the ideal place to educate "the mass — the working classes — the more exclusively industrial portion of the people."[41]

Green identified three characteristics shared by antebellum military schools: funding, discipline and curriculum.[42] The Citadel fit squarely within those parameters.

At the time that the Arsenal in Columbia and the Citadel in Charleston were converted into military schools, South Carolina spent $24,000 annually to pay the state militia guards who proved so disruptive to the civilian populations.[43] The same sum was appropriated in the 1842 act: $8,000 for the Arsenal and $16,000 for the Citadel. Thereafter, those guarding the arms and ammunition stored in the respective facilities would receive an education instead of a pay allotment. For the state, the conversion was, as designed, a fiscally break-even proposition.[44]

Regulations adopted by the initial Board of Visitors, modeled in large measure after West Point's, governed both the Arsenal and the Citadel. They authorized a combined maximum enrollment of 108 students, divided evenly between "beneficiary" and "pay" cadets.[45] A beneficiary cadet paid no tuition, his family unable to afford the $200 charged to pay for room, board, uniforms and instruction.[46] While that seems a paltry sum today, in the 1840s, $200 was the modern equivalent of more than $5,500,[47] far beyond the means of the average South Carolina family. Regulations required the 54 beneficiary cadets to be drawn from the state's 29 judicial districts, 34 of them for the Citadel and the remainder for the Arsenal, with a like number of pay cadets authorized for each institution. To be admitted from the judicial district they represented, beneficiary applicants had to show an acceptable level of literacy, meet certain physical standards and provide evidence of good moral character. Applicants recommended by commissioners of Free Schools received preference. All cadets admitted had to pledge to remain at the college for four years, after which they were free to pursue whatever career they chose.[48] This contrasted with the systems at other schools, notably VMI, where state-sponsored cadets committed to teach for two years following graduation as a way of repaying the state.[49]

Of the 34 beneficiary cadets authorized for the Citadel, 20 reported on March 20, 1843, which came to be known as Corps Day. After that first

Corps Day, seven additional beneficiary cadets were admitted. Only two pay cadets joined, for a total first year matriculation of 29, well below the 68 authorized. In a foreshadowing of a future trend in Columbia, the government withheld $4,000 of the $12,000 promised the Citadel, necessitating a smaller Corps than originally envisioned. Four years later, six cadets would comprise the first graduating class, three of whom — Charles Courtenay Tew, Charles O. LaMotte and John H. Swift — had reported with the original 20.

Discipline, a self-evident characteristic of military schools, took aim at a proclivity that would cause parents from Hawaii to Maine to nod in agreement: Boys in their mid- to late teens are prone to all kinds of mischiefs, distractions, dissipations and resistance to authority. Those predilections are exacerbated by, indeed sometimes caused by, too much idle time. Military schools offered a solution. By the kind of dawn-to-dusk, reveille-to-taps schedule imposed, cadets had little time to go astray (though most managed to fit that in occasionally).

In its earliest days, The Citadel's academic year began on January 1 and ran for what amounted to the full year. After exams in April and November, classes were suspended but cadets were still held to a stringent leave policy by which, with approval, they could be gone for up to 15 days.[50] When outbreaks of yellow fever persistently posed a health threat to the campus, particularly in the summer months, the academic year was adjusted to something closer to what we have today. The daily schedule, as set forth in regulations for 1849, bore vague resemblance to that of the modern era, anachronistic terms notwithstanding:

> Reveille: Will be regulated by the beating of the Picquet Guard.[51]
> "Peas Upon a Trencher" (the nickname in camp for the bugle call for breakfast. It came about 30 minutes after Reveille. A trencher is a wooden bowl): Signal for breakfast. 8 a.m., March to September; 7:30 a.m. the rest of the year.
> "Roast Beef": Signal for dinner, 1 p.m.
> Retreat: At sunset.
> Tattoo: 10 p.m., March to September; 9 p.m. the rest of the year.[52]
> Classes ("recitations"): 9 a.m. to 1 p.m. and 2 to 4 p.m. Monday through Friday.[53]

Saturday brought the inevitable inspections and on Sundays church was mandatory. Because there were no team sports, cadets competed on Saturday nights as members of debate societies, which pitted the Lowcountry's Calliopeans against the Upstate's Polytechnics in displays of mental and oratorical combat.[54]

Clearly, cadets meeting this schedule had little time for themselves, much less the enticements offered by Charleston, particularly in view of the fact that the superintendent's permission was required to attend anything off campus. In its first report to the governor in 1843, the Citadel's Board of Visitors acknowledged its success: "By requiring [the cadets] to account for every moment of their time, it prevents them from acquiring vicious habits and withdraws them from the allurements of dissipation."[55]

The Citadel's curriculum bypassed classic languages and courses in favor of practical applications. First-year students took "Arithmetic, Geography, English Grammar, History of South Carolina and Duties of a Private Soldier." The second year built upon and complemented the first: "Algebra, Geometry, Trigonometry, French, History of the United States, Bookkeeping, the School of the Company and Duties of Corporals." French was preferred as the contemporary language of engineers.[56]

The difference between a cadet's course of study and the other in-state offerings was dramatic. At the College of Charleston, for example, applicants for admission needed an accurate and minute knowledge of the Latin Grammar and Prosody, and the ability to translate Caesar's Commentaries, Virgil, Cicero's Select Orations and Sallust. The requirement for Greek was equally daunting: a thorough knowledge of Valpy's *Greek Grammar* (Anthon's edition) and be able to translate and parse, with readiness, any portion of Jacob's *Greek Reader*, the first two books of Xenophon's *Anabasis* and the first book of Homer's *Iliad*.[57] Such a proficiency in ancient languages would have been available only to those privately tutored or by attendance at elite private schools. None of the 20 boys who gathered on Marion Square that day in March 1843 had such advantages.

Once admitted, College of Charleston freshmen studied "Horace and Cicero, a continuation of Prosody and Greek Grammar, *Exempla Majora*, Professor Dalzell's *Collectanea Minora*, recitation of passages from Greek and Latin authors, Roman Antiquities; Euclid's *Elements* (the first six books); Algebra, English Grammar, and Exercises in Public Speaking. A Teacher of the French language will be provided for those who may choose to study that language."[58]

At Beaufort College, "the Languages must still occupy much of [a student's] attention — In a learned Education the knowledge of the Greek and Latin Languages cannot with propriety be omitted as long as they continue to be taught in all Colleges and Universities, and constitute in a great measure the Language of Science . . ."[59]

At South Carolina College in Columbia, the curriculum was no more accessible. In 1820 the college raised its minimum age for entry to 15 and applicants "were required to be able to translate more Latin and Greek. The juniors and seniors were required to study Tacitus, Cicero, Xenophon and Homer. Juniors and seniors were to recite twice per week in Latin and Greek, alternately . . ."[60]

To a student from Charleston, as three of the first six Citadel graduates were, the divide between college options was more like a chasm, the practical equivalent of the Ivy League on one hand and a community college on the other. But at the end of four years, Citadel graduates could find work as teachers, engineers, soldiers and in the professions of law and medicine.

John P. Thomas, the college's first biographer, put it eloquently:

The Board [of Visitors] thus devised an excellent course of study — one practical in character and well calculated to qualify young men for the duties of life — one conceived in the spirit of Milton, who called "a complete and generous education, what which fits a man to perform justly, skillfully and magnanimously, all the offices of a citizen, both private and public, of peace and war."[61]

A major dynamic of life at The Citadel was and remains today the tension between a cadet's voluntary sublimation to strict rules and regulations and his sense of independence and personal honor. Cadets felt duty bound to obey the rules. The college expected it, their parents expected it and they came to expect it of themselves. But at times this devotion to duty conflicted with his personal code, particularly where honor was at stake. Success as a cadet required him to reconcile those conflicts, and when he couldn't the result was often resignation or dismissal.

The source and nature of this personal code has been debated. Some historians have branded Southerners as militaristic by nature, a product of "geography, frontier conditions, incessant warfare, slavery and cultural notions of honor."[62] If true, the flourishing of military schools to serve such young men would seem a logical fit. But such forces also bred in Southerners a sense of bravery and personal independence. Valor, personal honor and fierce independence are qualities that do not lend themselves to the strict regimen demanded by the military, and where they conflict, as they often have, the results can be far reaching.

The Class of 1853 presents a vivid example. While exact details of the dispute are frustratingly scant, it is known that a senior, acting as adjutant, caused the dismissal of a highly regarded junior. The junior's classmates took exception and rallied around their man, whom they believed had been unfairly treated. The entire class, 27 members strong, issued an ultimatum to the administration: Re-admit their classmate or else. The "or else" was mass resignation. This threat violated paragraph 82 of the regulations stating:

> All combinations, under any pretext whatever, are strictly pro-
> hibited. Any cadet, who, in concert with others, shall adopt any
> measure under pretense of procuring a redress of grievances, or en-
> ter into any agreement with a view to violate or evade any regula-
> tion of the Academy, or shall endeavor to persuade others to enter
> into such concert or agreement, shall be dismissed.

Major Richard W. Colcock, the superintendent at the time, took a dim view of mutiny and warned the potential mutineers that they faced dismissal. Undaunted, the juniors walked out of the sallyport, called roll and disbanded. Twenty-seven men from throughout the state, from families in which no member had ever advanced so far in education, whose parents had sacrificed to support that advancement, who had studied to get within a year of graduation — all walked.[63]

Clearly, this ultimatum violated Regulation 82, and just as clearly, per-haps, the administration felt the need to enforce it or render it moot. Yet anyone who has been through the Fourth Class System with its adversities can identify with the juniors' action. Their honor and loyalty to their class-mate trumped the regulation. But taking the stand they did came with the obligation to accept the consequences. As significant as it must have been for the members of the Class of 1853 to lose their chance to graduate, the loss of an entire body presented significant difficulties for the school. It lost the revenue that the cadets' tuition represented. Public reaction must have been mixed, with some applauding the strict discipline for which the college sought to be noted, and others aghast that an accommodation could not be reached to avoid such dire ramifications.

Major Francis W. Capers became superintendent in 1853. His two prede-cessors, Captain William F. Graham and Major Colcock, both were West Pointers. Capers, by contrast, finished at the College of Charleston.[64] As the first superintendent from a non-military background, several years were evidently required for him to find his disciplinary footing. In addition to serving as superintendent, Capers taught mechanics and engineering. In 1856 he summoned cadet James Lide Coker to the blackboard for a computation. Capers challenged him, claiming Coker had borrowed the answer from a book. Coker took exception, feeling his personal honor had been impugned. A pointed exchange ensued.

Coker, who served as a second lieutenant by virtue of rank bestowed by Capers, resigned it that afternoon. He also wrote to General James Jones, chairman of the Board of Visitors, appealing for justice. Jones' reply encouraged Coker that it would all be put right. The next day, Coker appeared at the office of his professor, who demanded an apology. Coker believed no apology was due, and said so. Later that day, Capers suspended Coker for insubordination and violation of regulations. In the week following, the chairman of the Board of Visitors interceded. When he assured Coker that Capers meant no insult, Coker agreed to retract what he had said — provided Capers' comments to him were reported as part and parcel of the retraction. General Jones refused that condition, so the rapprochement fell apart. Coker, a senior, stood on principle and left.

Cadet Thomas Law, whose journal recounts the events, proved prescient when he wrote, "I think Major Capers' conduct (rather misconduct) has lost to the institution one who would be an ornament to its graduates!"[65]

The following year, Coker went to Harvard, where he studied chemistry,[66] a discipline that allowed him to develop a process to pulp Southern pine into paper. Building on that process, the company he founded, Southern Novelty Company, manufactured the paper cones and tubes used by textile producers. Today the company — Sonoco and still headquartered in Hartsville, S.C. — is a major international conglomerate with 2015 revenues of over $5 billion.[67] He also proved his dedication to higher learning by founding Coker College.[68] One can only imagine what he might have bestowed upon The Citadel had he not suffered an affront to his personal honor, or had the school shown a more flexible diplomacy in dealing with it.

Two years later, Major Capers had more disciplinary challenges. In March 1858 he appointed Thomas Law, a Citadel junior, an assistant instructor, an honor that had theretofore belonged to a senior. The seniors rebelled, demanding that the appointment be rescinded. Even Law, the beneficiary of the perceived slight, joined in the ultimatum. This collective challenge would appear to be a repeat of the 1853 class' violation of Regulation 82, yet Capers backed down and rescinded his order. Did Law rejoice at this unanticipated about-face by the superintendent? Hardly, recording in his diary his lack of respect for Capers' decision and Law's guilt in the whole matter.[69]

Less fortunate were members of the Class of 1859. A professor took exception to the manner in which 11 juniors had marched into his section and ordered them to repeat the process in a more military manner. Believing the order misguided, the cadets refused, resulting in their suspensions by Major Capers. Thirteen of their classmates, in solidarity with the suspended cadets, convened a meeting in violation of Regulation 82 and in further violation of Major Capers's order that they not do so. The result was the dismissal of 23 juniors — one cadet having reconsidered and 10 juniors having declined to disobey the superintendent.[70]

But no discussion of the tension between duty and honor would be complete without detailing the Cantey Rebellion of 1898, the mother of all Citadel revolts. Perhaps no crisis in the history of the college sets up as dramatically the inherent tension between institutional discipline and personal honor. Alumni from all eras are likely to find in it the push and pull each felt as a cadet walking a fine line between competing duties.

It began with a desire on the part of six cadets to attend a dance. By being absent without leave (AWOL), a dismissal offense, they risked all, but it was March 19, springtime in Charleston, and it takes little imagination to understand the lure of a dance to these cadets. The Citadel's future president, Oliver J. Bond, was then a lieutenant and the OC (Officer in Charge) that day. He called an unscheduled inspection, word of which reached the dance. Five of the AWOL cadets hastily returned to campus and were spotted trying to make formation undetected. They were put on report and subsequently expelled.

When the Corps learned that the late-arriving cadets had been put on report by Cadet Sergeant Major Samuel O. Cantey, who was not on guard duty or under any obligation to turn in the AWOL cadets, all hell broke loose. Here, in their midst, was one of their own who had gone above and beyond not to save a comrade but to act the part of a Judas. The Corps rendered a swift verdict: Cantey must go. In violation of the anti-collective action regulation previously noted, they petitioned Superintendent Asbury Coward that Sergeant Cantey be court-martialed for "conduct unbecoming a cadet and a gentleman" and for spying on fellow students.

The Corps smelled victory when Coward offered to reinstate the expelled cadets in exchange for a withdrawal of the court-martial petition. Given the experience of the Class of 1853, they should have left well enough alone. But while such a resolution would have undone the damage Cantey's report had occasioned, it left the Judas as a member of the Corps, a result viewed as an intolerable affront to the honor of those who condemned him. They pressured Cantey to leave, and when all efforts to rid the school of him failed, took matters into their own hands. On April 4, two months shy of graduation, 64 cadets signed a pact to remove Cantey physically from the barracks.

Half the signers stood guard against interference by others while the other half besieged Cantey's room. Superintendent Coward arrived, accompanied by the commandant, Lieutenant John McDonald. The superintendent ordered the cadets to disperse. The cadets refused. Tensions rose, and rose again when 30 armed Charleston policemen entered the barracks to curses and jeers of the cadets. School property rained down from the upper divisions shattering on the quadrangle. Over the course of an evening, the rebellion reached a crisis that could not be negotiated away.

In its report, the Board of Visitors charged that the cadets:

[D]id willfully and violently attempt to enter the room of Cadet Cantey, and being ordered to their quarters by the commandant, the superintendent and other officers of the Academy, did positively refuse to obey the same; and in insulting profane and vulgar language defied the said authorities and refused to retire to their rooms; throwing down and injuring public property of the Academy; violently swearing that they would put Cadet Cantey out at all hazards; and did create such riotous noise and continue in their mutinous and rebellious conduct against all entreaties of the superintendent and commandant; thus necessitating the calling in of a squad of policemen to be used if necessary to prevent further violence, including loss of life or destruction of property. All this to the great scandal and disgrace of the South Carolina Military Academy.

The Board of Visitors report named the 64 cadets who were ordered dismissed, giving them two hours to vacate the barracks. Among those departing were 13 of the 14 highest ranking senior cadets, including one who consistently won recognition as most distinguished in his class.[71] The dismissed cadets represented almost half of the Corps. (For an excellent exploration of the entire incident, see Alexander Macaulay's article, "Discipline and Rebellion: The Citadel Rebellion of 1898," South Carolina Historical Magazine, Vol. 103, No. 1, January 2002.)

Cantey's act violated one of the most sacred Citadel rules, all the more sacred because unwritten and because honored to a greater or lesser degree by every class since 1842: Loyalty to one's class and fellow cadets trumps loyalty to the administration and the rules. By honoring that code, cadets acknowledge an ancient truth: Shared hardship and deprivation bonds those who can persevere together.

A Citadel alumnus asked to identify the first baptism by fire in school history is likely to name the cadet battery that fired on the *Star of the West* on January 9, 1861, just weeks after South Carolina declared the Union dissolved. The merchant ship had been sent to resupply Fort Sumter, then occupied by Union troops under the command of Major Robert Anderson. The encounter enjoys a well-deserved place in The Citadel's history. We annually honor the best drilled cadet by awarding the Star of the West medal with the winner's name inscribed on the parade ground monument.

The name George Haynsworth, a senior from Sumter, South Carolina, is well known for having pulled the lanyard on gun No. 1, thereby firing what is often referred to as the first shot of the Civil War. He also claimed to have fired the last shots of the war, having skirmished with General Sheridan's Union troops near Williamston, South Carolina three weeks after Appomattox. He later became a judge, and was killed in his courtroom at age 46 when he intervened in a dispute.[72] Haynsworth's moment in history is captured on a mural in Daniel Library on campus, and his portrait hangs there as well. Accounts of the firing confirmed the presence of a large red flag flying over the cadet battery. This flag, depicted in the mural, displayed a white Palmetto on a red background with a crescent facing the tree. It became known as Big Red, and would be lost for nearly a century and a half until returned to the college in 2010.

Less well known, and years earlier, Citadel graduates had been active in the Mexican-American War. A member of the first graduating class in 1846, Lieutenant William J. Magill, fought with General Zachary Taylor as part of the 3rd U.S. Dragoons in Mexico. Other graduates served in the famed Palmetto Regiment from Veracruz to Mexico City, the first time U.S troops had fought on foreign soil. Four of those Citadel men did not return home. They included Corporal Eugene Wilder, Class of 1849, the first alumnus killed in action. Allen H. Little, a private, lost an arm in a battle in Mexico, but returned home to finish with First Honors in the Class of 1852. He died of his wounds two years later.

Rebellion reached its apex in 1861. In January, three weeks after the *Star of the West* incursion, the Legislature passed a law combining The Citadel and the Arsenal Academy in Columbia into "The South Carolina Military Academy." Though each retained a separate identity, as a unit they comprised the Battalion of State Cadets, subject to call at any time and relied upon as an integral part of the military establishment of the state.

Graduation for the Class of 1861 was canceled days before the firing on Fort Sumter "in consequence of the imminent collision."[73] Classes continued during the war but military service claimed many of the cadets. Some participated in the war locally by training Confederate forces in the Palmetto Guard. Others left to join what became known as the Cadet Company, attached to the 6th South Carolina Cavalry Regiment. In June 1864, this collection of hard-charging cadets distinguished itself in Virginia, taking a critical role in what turned out to be the largest cavalry engagement of the war. Fighting at Trevilian Station, General Wade Hampton of South Carolina selected the Cadet Company to lead a counterattack against Union cavalry under the command of General George Armstrong Custer. Hampton and the Cadet Company broke Custer's charge. The entire Corps fought in South Carolina in the Battle of Tulifinny Creek in present-day Jasper County late in 1864, the only engagement in the war in which the Battalion of State Cadets was deployed. (For a detailed account of the school's participation in the Civil War, see Gary Baker's book, *Cadets in Gray*.)[74]

When Charleston fell in February 1865, Union forces occupied The Citadel for the next 14 years. Those years coincided with Reconstruction, a turbulent era in the state's history. That the college emerged from it to rise again is a near miracle.

When the last Union soldier left the barracks in 1879, a campaign to reopen The Citadel began, led by graduates and the Washington Light Infantry. The campaigners bombarded newspapers with letters citing the contributions alumni had made to the state, which put pressure on the politicians in Columbia. Opponents claimed the impoverished state treasury simply couldn't support another college. In a decisive vote in the state Senate in 1882, Lieutenant Governor John D. Kennedy broke a tie in favor of the college, saving it by the narrowest of margins.[75] The Act reauthorizing it contained one significant change from the 1842 legislation. In the antebellum years, beneficiary cadets repaid the state by guarding munitions, but after the reopening there were no munitions to guard. Therefore, as recompense to the state, beneficiary cadets were required upon graduation to teach for two years in the Free Schools of the counties from which they came.[76]

At a celebration to mark the 1882 reopening, Governor Johnson Hagood, Class of 1847,[77] confidently predicted that in five years enrollment would be 400 cadets and the school would become the West Point of the South.[78] Five years later, the Class of 1887 consisted of only nine graduates. Three years later, 58 graduated.[79] The barracks on Marion Square reached maximum capacity 30 years later, well short of the Hagood projection.[80]

The decades following the reopening brought reminders that disasters other than war could threaten a college still trying to regain its footing. In 1886 an earthquake devastated Charleston,[81] and in 1892 a fire destroyed a significant portion of the barracks.[82] Yet The Citadel soldiered on. When war with Spain broke out in the Philippines and in Cuba in 1898, the call was answered by 32 Citadel men, but fighting ended too quickly for them to be deployed in combat.[83]

In 1900 the school published its first yearbook, *The Sphinx*. Debating clubs that had served in the 19th century as outlets for the combative tendencies of cadets gave way to the more modern outlet of college athletics. In 1901-1902, the "base ball" team consisted of nine players while the "basket ball" team had the luxury of two reserves. *The Sphinx* in 1903 complained that "[a]s football is not tolerated at this institution and not all of us are baseball players, several tennis clubs have been organized." By 1905 that had changed, with the Board of Visitors consenting to football but with games limited to inter-class matches because "The Citadel is not yet in a position to place a representative college team in the field."[84] In 1909, the band was organized using instruments borrowed from the state, and soon "became an institution in the school which it could ill afford to do without."[85]

Colonel Oliver Bond became president, or "superintendent" as they were then called, in 1908. Following his graduation in the Class of 1886, Bond was a member of the faculty until his elevation to the top spot. He served for 23 years as president, the longest tenure of anyone in that position.[86]

That same year the city relinquished its central police station on Marion Square, known as the City Station House, for use by the school. When remodeled, this added 40 percent more space, put to good use by relocation of the hospital and the library from the barracks to the new addition. A fourth floor was added to the barracks in 1910 and when, in 1911 the building known as the Meeting Street Extension was constructed, the Marion Square complex stood complete. It housed a maximum of 325 cadets.[87]

During World War I, the entire graduating Classes of 1917 and 1918 entered the Armed Forces, with nine alumni paying the ultimate price.[88] By the time the armistice was signed in 1918, the college had outgrown Marion Square and plans were underway for construction of the Greater Citadel along the banks of the Ashley River.

Chapter 3

EIGHT STARS, THIRTY-THREE YEARS

A s this history is written, the modern Citadel faces a challenge that would be well understood by Colonel Oliver Bond and his administration at the Marion Square complex: There was very little room left to grow. When the campus was relocated in 1922, hundreds of acres along the Ashley River portended limitless expansion, while today at the Greater Citadel, it's a challenge to find enough space for a parking garage.

The limitations of the old campus would have been apparent to anyone who spent the five minutes it takes to walk across Marion Square. The only space suitable as a drill field was used by pedestrians out front of the barracks. Between chatty casual strollers and ever-increasing traffic on King, Calhoun and Meeting streets, the noise coming through open windows made studying difficult. When World War I ended, overcrowding became severe with returning members of the Student Army Training Corps hungry for education. Marion Square had outlived its virtues as a college campus.

Hampton Park's history is as colorful as that of the city in which it is located. Once a pleasant wooded area in which to picnic or, in antebellum days, fight a duel, it became home to the popular Washington Race Course, a one-mile horse track, before becoming the site of the South Carolina Interstate and West Indian Exposition. The Exposition, with its elaborate "Ivory City" built on 250 acres, drew half a million visitors before failing commercially and closing in May 1902.

The area then became Hampton Park. Between the park and the Ashley River lay Rhett Farm, the 76-acre Revolutionary-era estate of John Gibbes. The city acquired the farm intending to make it an extension of the park. Streets circling it were laid out by Frederick Olmstead, the landscape architect famous for designing New York's Central Park. The Board of Visitors decided it was a perfect spot for the Greater Citadel and convinced the city to deed it to South Carolina provided the state agreed to finance construction of the buildings. The Legislature in 1919 appropriated $300,000 for the purpose.[89]

On November 25, 1920 (Thanksgiving), a crowd estimated at 5,000 marched through Hampton Park to witness the laying of a cornerstone of the first building. The honor went to Samuel T. Lanham, grandmaster of the Masons of South Carolina. The stone was set not at the barracks but at the west wing of the academic building, now Bond Hall. Colonel Bond's history of the event includes an extensive description of the football game played that day between The Citadel and the University of South Carolina, which by then had become what Bond called "ancient rivals." Late in the season, USC had not allowed a touchdown to any state team, so their fans could justify the $6,000 being paid to their coach — a sum that would buy about 10 minutes of time today when Clemson pays Dabo Swinney an average of $6.5 million per year. On the game's first play, USC kicked off to the Dogs and quarterback Jack Frost ran it all the way back for six points. Although Carolina won 7-6, it was a moral victory for the Bulldogs.[90]

On October 18, 1922, the new campus opened for public inspection. It consisted of Padgett-Thomas Barracks; the east and west wings of Bond Hall, which served as the academic buildings; a temporary mess hall; a powerhouse; a laundry; and a campus hospital. An unpaved road surrounded the parade ground.[91] Padgett-Thomas held 450 cadets, and by the 1925-1926 school year was near capacity at 438. Once Murray Barracks was completed in 1927, enrollment jumped to 722.[92]

Even before the new campus opened, the Board of Visitors appreciated the importance of raising the school's academic standards. South Carolina's system of public education produced some poorly educated college applicants and, simply put, The Citadel admitted too many of them. The solution lay in raising admission standards to those imposed for membership in the Southern Association of Colleges. Lack of this proved a handicap to graduates seeking advanced degrees. With the opening of the Greater Citadel, the higher standards were imposed, with the result that in 1924 the Southern Association of Colleges (later, SACS), admitted The Citadel on the same day it admitted Furman and Texas A&M.[93]   Thereafter, SACS reaccreditation became a decennial challenge that continues to this day.

Admitting more qualified students enhanced an academic reputation that had been on the rise in the decades since the reopening. As mentioned in Chapter 2, the first degree awarded pursuant to recognized academic standards came in 1900 with the Bachelor of Science distinction. At the time, the curriculum was limited to liberal arts, the sciences and civil engineering. As the founders had envisioned, civil engineering found a ready constituency both inside the gates with students and outside with employers. The

Citadel's program is the fifth oldest in the nation, and in 1910 the school began awarding degrees in civil engineering.

In 1930 rank-holding junior members of the Class of 1932 decided to honor their seniors by forming a precision drill unit that would perform at "hops," formal dances that were the social focus of the academic calendar. The unit that became the Junior Sword Drill consisted of the 12 highest ranked juniors. It was entirely cadet-initiated and operated without support from the college. Rank determined membership, without the intense competition known to later classes. Drill routines lasted eight minutes. The success and popularity of early units created expanded performance opportunities including drill competitions, gubernatorial inaugurations and parades.[94] As will be seen, the Junior Sword Drill evolved into a unit far from its original roots.

On January 20, 1931, the first edition of *The Shako*, the college's literary magazine, was published. The following year, a precision drill team formed. It is The Summerall Guards, which drill to a silent count known only to its membership, composed of 61 seniors. They select their successors in a demanding competition for juniors, who are called Bond Volunteer Aspirants. Each is evaluated for military bearing, physical fitness, personal appearance and qualities that lend themselves to the cohesive teamwork demanded by Guard performances. At Corps Day, Guards relinquish their rifles to Bond Volunteers, and the cycle repeats. The Summerall Guards have performed across the country, including the inaugurations of Presidents Eisenhower, Reagan, George H.W. Bush and Donald Trump.

The school newspaper first appeared in 1924 as *The Bulldog*. Its editor in 1953, Carmine Pecorelli, renamed it *The Brigadier*.[95] The first woman to edit the paper was Cadet Dena Abrash in 2000, and in 2017 modernity overtook it when the print version yielded to online publication.

In the fall of 1931, Colonel Bond retired as president of the college, succeeded by General Charles P. Summerall.[96] A former Chief of Staff of the Army, Summerall served as president for 22 years, the second longest tenure of any Citadel president, though his first year nearly became his last. At a hearing on the college's funding before the state Senate Committee on Finance in Columbia, Sen. Wylie Hamrick impugned the general's character by suggesting that the $19,000 deficit Summerall inherited from Bond's administration had resulted from overspending by the new president. Summerall stood, stated his unwillingness to tolerate such disrespect, and announced that he would resign, effective immediately.[97] Hamrick did his best to, in modern parlance, "walk it back," insisting he meant no insult, but Summerall wasn't buying it. "I understand the English language," he was reported to have said.[98]

The next morning back in Charleston, he did as he said he would do. As D.D. Nicholson phrased it in his history titled *Years of Summerall and Clark*: "Not since the 1886 earthquake had anything shaken Charleston as did Summerall's resigning."[99] Ardent pleas from the Board of Visitors, the mayor, alumni and parents persuaded Summerall to reconsider, but only a petition signed by every member of the Corps of Cadets convinced him to stay.[100]

As the Great Depression entered its third year, The Citadel faced a depression of its own. The $19,000 deficit about which Sen. Hamrick chided him may have accrued on Bond's watch, but it was now Summerall's to manage and eradicate. Hardships brought on by the Depression reduced the number of students who could afford college, including The Citadel, which saw enrollment slipping toward a mere 400. The facilities needed repair as deferred maintenance took a toll. The survival of the school was in doubt.

It was under those conditions that the battle-tested Summerall proved that The Citadel had hired the right man for a crisis. W. Gary Nichols,[101] in *American Leader in War and Peace*, sets out Summerall's steps to snatch victory from defeat:

Summerall began his campaign to save The Citadel by reducing his own salary by 45 percent and those of the faculty and staff by from 30 to 40 percent. He laid off many hourly wage earners, and cut the salaries of those who remained from 15 to 20 percent. He rationed the use of electricity and water; he had telephones, including his own, disconnected; and he ordered the use of lighter-weight paper to save money on catalog printing and mailing. He personally enforced every "decree" and made rounds to insure lights and radiators were turned off in the classrooms when they were not in use; if they were left on, he sent through the campus mail terse hand-written notes written in pencil on strips of foolscap to those who were responsible.[102]

Summerall's frugality paid dividends beyond the mere survival of the college. The pre-World War II era saw growth and progress. By 1940 the campus boasted a new chapel, mess hall and faculty apartments. Bond Hall doubled in size. Construction work on a new barracks promised continued expansion. All cadet rooms were refurbished and re-equipped. From the near-fatal enrollment of just over 400 that Summerall began with, the cadet population had grown to 1,196. Nor did Summerall neglect academic improvements, doubling the number of faculty members holding master's degrees and increasing Ph.D.'s by 50 percent.[103] Summerall could look back on his first decade of stewardship with justifiable pride, for the progress made in the face of the economic challenges he faced was little short of miraculous.

The World War II decade brought challenges of a different nature, but Summerall addressed it with the same discipline, tenacity and energy he brought to the 1930s despite the fact that he would be close to 83 years old by the time the decade ended. The college battles to be fought in the war years were less about money than logistics, for the school saw an influx of 10,000 soldier trainees during the war and hundreds of veteran students after it ended, almost all of whom had to be housed, fed and educated.[104]

Summerall was a no-nonsense teetotaler and a man without hobbies. That he must have possessed a wry sense of humor is shown by an endearing tradition that grew up around his birthday. It began in Summerall's first year as president, less than a month after his confrontation with Senator Hamrick and his threatened resignation. Perhaps the Corps conceived of it as a way of thanking him for remaining as their president.

Beginning March 4, 1932, when the general turned 65, and for every year thereafter, the entire Corps marched to Quarters 1, where the band played a birthday tribute and from which Summerall would emerge in his full-dress uniform, four stars gleaming from the epaulets.[105] Brantley Harvey, Jr., of Beaufort, a former lieutenant governor of South Carolina and member of the Class of 1951, remembers those well: "He always greeted us with, 'Gentlemen, this is indeed a pleasant surprise,' and he always managed to look surprised." The Summerall birthday tributes remain some of Harvey's fondest memories of his cadet days.[106]

One of Harvey's schoolmates from the Class of 1954 provided the coda to the birthday tradition. Carmine Pecorelli began his knob year when he was 25. A veteran of World War II, Pecorelli, known as "Peck," wanted the entire Citadel experience, and the only way to get it was to go through the Fourth Class System. Like Harvey, those annual trips to salute the general on his birthday held a special memory for Peck. In the spring of 1955, General Summerall, 88, entered Walter Reed Army Medical Center to be treated for what proved to be his final illness. He died there on May 14. Peck lived a few miles from the hospital, and on March 4 felt the need to acknowledge the general's birthday. He drove to the hospital and entered the general's room with a cake in hands. Summerall, looking up from his bed, greeted him with, "Mr. Pecorelli, this is indeed a pleasant surprise."

Summerall happened to have a visitor sitting at his bedside. He introduced Peck, then proceeded to relate the details of Pecorelli's World War II service and his cadet years. "He told that guy things about me that I had forgotten," Peck said. As Summerall aged, some in Charleston questioned his ability to function as president, but Peck has no doubts.[107]

By the time he retired in 1953, General Summerall's declining health had become evident in both the man and the college he administered. Needed construction lagged, enrollment fell far short of capacity and the athletic teams languished predictably near the bottom of conference standings. The college needed, figuratively and literally, new blood.[108]

When Summerall stepped down, the Board of Visitors appointed an interim president, Colonel Louis LeTellier, who famously described his status as "a phony colonel sandwiched between two four-star generals."[109] The second of those was, of course, General Mark Wayne Clark. In accepting The Citadel's offer to become its president, a position that paid Clark $12,000 per year, he said he was motivated by "an opportunity to do something worthwhile,"[110] as if commanding the 5th Army invading Italy in World War II and serving as commander-in-chief of the United Nations forces in Korea were not enough.[111] The college thrived under Clark's leadership, and he brought with him an international reputation.

The man dubbed by Winston Churchill as "the American Eagle" oversaw a decade of improvements to the campus, to the faculty and to the athletic programs.[112] Under his leadership, the Honor Code was systemized. He refurbished all the rooms in the barracks. He built a new laundry, and upgraded the mess hall and chapel with what passes for manna in Lowcountry heaven: air-conditioning. He remodeled Lesesne Gate to more accurately reflect the improvements being made within it. He developed a plan for recruiting students that doubled applications after his first year and doubled them again the next year. He insisted that winning sports teams improved morale and allocated money for better coaches and more athletic scholarships. In 1960 the football team rebounded from years of losing or mediocre seasons with a record of 8 wins, 2 losses and a tie (with Florida State), and went on to win its first bowl game ever in the Tangerine Bowl.

He also instituted the Greater Issues program, which brought nationally and internationally prominent speakers to the campus, not the least of whom was his old Army buddy President Dwight Eisenhower. Clark increased professors' salaries, gradually lifting the academics.[113]

The idea that General Clark would run away from a fight was foreign to anyone who knew him. When, on March 13, 1964, he announced his retirement as president of The Citadel, effective at the close of 1965's academic year, his legion of admirers assigned to the general the usual motivations:

fatigue, a desire for personal time, a sense of accomplishment. Clark himself, then 68, expressed the need to "lay down the cares and responsibilities of administering this vibrant institution." As was well known, his wife Renie was quite ill, and he worried about the stress on her of being the college's "first lady." She died on October 5, 1966, a mere 16 months after Clark retired.[114]

Yet just over the horizon, and not by far, Clark must have seen the battles ahead. Integration was one, and Clark was known to favor a segregated Corps of Cadets.[115] Vietnam was another, as by the time Clark retired the college had lost six graduates to that undeclared war. It is possible that integration and Vietnam were two battles too many for the old soldier, particularly with Renie struggling for her life.

Perhaps, he may have reflected, it was time to give way to a younger man with greater energy. As he noted, he had been in uniform for more than 50 years since entering West Point in 1913. He had paid his dues and then some, and he lived to enjoy 19 years of retirement before his death on April 17, 1984.[116] He is buried on the campus, the only person to be so honored.[117]

Clark's retirement brought to a close a remarkable era of progress and increased institutional prestige for which he could justly take a healthy measure of credit. But in a larger sense, it also ended an era that had its roots in the founding of The Citadel: all male, all white, mostly Southern, overwhelmingly conservative. Change was coming, and though the college seemed poised to build on the solid foundation Clark had laid, figuratively brick by brick, a cloud loomed that had drifted over Charleston as well as the rest of the country from faraway Southeast Asia.

Chapter 4

"The fundamental cornerstone of the Military College's Operation"

Engraved at the entrance to the National Archives in Washington, D.C., is the quote from Shakespeare's *The Tempest*: "What's Past is Prologue." It serves as a pithy reminder that, for institutions as well as individuals, memory of the past performs its most important function when it guides the future. This history, and those that preceded it and will follow it, aim to record what has been in hopes of informing what should be, bearing in mind that the corollary of Shakespeare's famous phrase is equally true: "Those who forget the past are doomed to repeat it."

As will appear in this chapter, where the Fourth Class System is concerned, there was for many years an institutional amnesia, lapses in our organizational memory that doomed us to repeat practices and habits that were flawed. The good news is that in the 50 years which are the focus of this book, memory and experience have come to enlighten the future. Progress came neither quickly nor smoothly, but the momentum of those changes over time have nonetheless brought us to The Citadel of today.

Essential to The Citadel's disciplined structure are regulations governing conduct, and readers unfamiliar with life on campus may find it helpful to have a basic understanding of how the system of rewards and punishment operates. Days and weeks are highly organized, with virtually every hour accounted for, putting free time at a premium. This is particularly true for those just entering from high school, called fourth classmen, freshmen or "knobs." The term "knob" is thought to have originated with the buzz haircuts traditionally administered to Fourth Class males on arrival (there is a less severe standard for Fourth Class women). The shaved heads reminded someone of a doorknob, and the term stuck.

The knob year is particularly challenging, and the rules and procedures by which it is administered is referred to as the Fourth Class System. Historically, it runs from a knob's first day on campus until Recognition Day, when the system ends and knobs are "recognized" by their first names. While the system is in effect, knobs are expected to follow a litany of rules designed to test and improve their ability to function under stress. Examples include squaring corners in the barracks, walking in the gutter along the Avenue of Remembrance, reciting college facts known as Knob Knowledge and saluting cadet officers. Within the common areas in the barracks, they are expected to "brace," an exaggerated form of attention in which the chin is pulled in toward the spine and the shoulders are squared.

Cadets of the upper classes who perform well, obey the rules and exhibit leadership can earn cadet rank and promotion. Cadets of all classes can receive demerits for infractions of the regulations or failure to meet expected standards. Small shortcomings, like unpolished brass, an unmade bed or arriving late to a formation, are punished by demerits. More serious violations can be punished by a combination of demerits, restriction to the campus, confinements and tours. A confinement is 50 minutes in a room in a duty uniform during a period that would otherwise be free time — usually a weekend. A tour is 50 minutes spent walking on the quadrangle at a pace of 120 steps per minute with a rifle at right-shoulder or left-shoulder arms. Tours are also walked during hours when a cadet would rather be doing something else. The most serious violations — absent without leave, conduct bringing disgrace upon The Citadel or honor violations, for example — can prompt suspension, dismissal or expulsion.

Ask any graduate to pinpoint the linchpin for leadership and the likely answer will be the Fourth Class System. A widely circulated report on the system, the Whitmire Report, called it the fundamental cornerstone of the Military College's operation.[118] No single aspect of Citadel life has been more discussed, feared, lauded, vilified, studied, revised, abused, second-guessed, defended, condemned or romanticized than the Fourth Class System.

Every knob has a favorite horror story, and somehow that story becomes the one he or she repeats most often after they graduate. And the older the graduate, the more cherished the memory. It is worn as a badge of honor, a way to tell those who followed that it was damn tough but getting through it proved you had what it took. Without the Fourth Class System, you might just as well enroll at Clemson. As much as knobs complain about it, they would revolt if it was taken from them.[119]

In fact, they did revolt. In 1955, the Class of 1959 reported. Its 849 matriculants comprised the largest freshman class in the history of the college. Bill Endictor, a knob, had spent weeks with his classmates learning the ropes, only to realize that no matter how much he learned, he would end up on the ropes by taps. But then a routine he was just getting used to changed

— radically. At 11 p.m., the public-address system switched on and into it the bugler played not the time-honored taps but "Rockabye Baby." In lieu of all-in check, an upperclassman entered Endictor's room and offered to tuck him in bed. What was this all about? Endictor wondered.

The mystery deepened the next morning. At breakfast, Colonel Reuben H. Tucker, the Commandant, who was seated at the Regimental Staff table, announced over the public-address system that the Fourth Class System had been suspended, effective immediately. He gave no reason, perhaps a holdover habit from his commands during World War II when he led the 504th Parachute Infantry, part of the 82nd Airborne, in some of the toughest combat of the war. Tucker had grown up hard, one of six children in Ansonia, Connecticut. He graduated from West Point in 1935. He was a man's man, described by a member of General Matthew Ridgway's staff as "a wonderful athlete and soldier. Fearless. Dedicated. A gung-ho combat officer, exactly the kind of fellow you want when you go to war."[120]

General James A. Gavin, who fought alongside Tucker in Italy, Belgium and Holland and who, at age 37, became the youngest major general since George Armstrong Custer, called Tucker "a tough, superb combat leader . . . probably the best regimental combat commander of the war."[121] Tucker's courage under fire became the stuff of Army legend. Ordered to seize the town of Altavilla, Italy, then occupied by well-fortified German troops, Tucker and two of his three battalions seized two hills that commanded the town by overrunning the Germans. The next morning, they withstood four counterattacks by a much larger German force supported by tanks and artillery. The bitter combat continued for two days. The commander of the 82nd, fearing Tucker would be surrounded and annihilated, ordered him to withdraw.

"Hell, no!" was Tucker's response. "We've got this hill and we're going to keep it. Send me my third battalion!"[122] For his leadership and heroism at Altavilla, Tucker received the Distinguished Service Cross.[123] But if Tucker's talents made him a natural leader of men in combat, they were less evident in administrative matters, where deficiencies cost him promotion. When Eisenhower promoted General Gavin to command the 82nd Airborne Division, the assistant division commander slot opened. Tucker seemed an obvious choice for the assignment and for promotion to brigadier general. But, as Gavin observed, Tucker "didn't give a damn about administration and paperwork. Ridgway and I talked about it and we decided we just couldn't promote Tucker."[124] As Citadel Commandant, paperwork and administration were Tucker's daily diet. In announcing the suspension of the Fourth Class System, Tucker ordered knobs to eat "at ease." Bracing would no longer be required or permitted. Endictor and his classmates listened in disbelief. Had anyone other than the Commandant made such an announcement, epithets of skepticism would have rained down. But here, straight from the horse's mouth, came word that the ordeal that had begun only weeks before was over.

As Tucker strode from the podium, Endictor noticed something others may have missed but that the Commandant surely did not: On the toe of each of his highly polished shoes someone had placed a large dollop of butter. As he exited the mess hall, Tucker burst through the screen door with enough force to tear off the hinges from their moorings. Endictor and his classmates walked back to their barracks in a daze. No one knew the reason for this drastic change, nor quite what to do about it. One rumor held that a serious hazing incident had occurred the day before, one last confirmation that the Fourth Class System was out of control. Another laid the blame at the unacceptably large attrition rate. Whatever the cause, the effect was the same: Knobs were suddenly and overnight just cadets.

There then occurred one of those galvanizing events that cement class loyalties forever, and a photograph exists to prove it. Instead of marching off to their 8 a.m. classes, the Class of 1959 marched to Bond Hall. They gathered under Colonel Tucker's open office window and began to chant, in unison, "We want the plebe system! We want the plebe system!" According to several who were present, a small group of about a dozen stood off to the side, reluctant to forego their newfound leisure. For the past hour, they might have been at Clemson. But the overwhelming majority made it clear that they had come to The Citadel to be challenged by the Fourth Class System and by God they were going to have it.

A rumor never confirmed held that Cadet Colonel John F. (Jack) Nelson, the Regimental Commander in the Class of 1956, appeared at Colonel Tucker's office and, once inside, tendered his best salute. He removed the three diamonds from his collar, symbols of his rank, laid them on Tucker's desk, and said, "If you are going to run the Corps, I don't need these." If true, Nelson led that day. By noon, the plebe system had been reinstated.

Yet no one doubts that there have been in every class abuses of the Fourth Class System and incidents of hazing. Military schools have no monopoly on these. As much and worse takes place in college fraternities every year, with civilian administrations at equal loss as to how to prevent it. Men and women between 18 and 22 are endlessly inventive in formulating rites of passage that often entail pain, discomfort or embarrassment and sometimes all three.

The most egregious abuses can be fatal. In 2014 a Clemson University pledge fell to his death from a narrow bridge as part of an initiation ritual. At

Penn State, 18 fraternity members were criminally charged in the 2017 death of a sophomore pledge forced to consume large quantities of alcohol in a short amount of time. In both cases, delay in reporting the tragedies and attempts to cover them up made terrible situations worse.[125] According to one study, at least one hazing related death has occurred on a college campus every year since 1970, but thankfully none of those involved The Citadel. That study defined hazing as "any activity expected of someone joining or participating in a group that humiliates, degrades, abuses or endangers them regardless of a person's willingness to participate." Major findings of the study included:

More than half of college students involved in clubs, teams, and organizations experience hazing.

Nearly half (47 percent) of students have experienced hazing prior to coming to college.

Alcohol consumption, humiliation, isolation, sleep-deprivation and sex acts are hazing practices common across student groups.[126]

The official policy of The Citadel is, and always has been, that hazing, in all its forms, is against regulations and will not be tolerated.[127] Indeed, South Carolina law makes it a misdemeanor.[128] When it is confirmed, punishment can range from tours and confinements to expulsion.[129]

The evolution of the Fourth Class System over the past half-century is arguably the school's single most important achievement. To understand that evolution, few more authoritative voices could be found than Colonel Joseph W. Trez, USA (Ret.). Trez's journey from New Jersey knob in 1965 to professor of military service in 1994 to Commandant in 1995 to the Krause Center for Leadership & Ethics in 2012 has given him a perspective unmatched in Citadel history. At times, that journey took him across an institutional landscape that more closely resembled a minefield, where a false step — on cadets, on parents, on a member of the Board of Visitors, on administrators — could blow away a distinguished career. Lessons gleaned from his 50 years of leadership laboratories in the Army and at The Citadel cannot go unheeded.

Trez's path to Charleston was not unlike many who migrate south from colder climates. He had been drawn toward the military in the 1950s, when the service academies pushed what amounted to recruiting films by TV shows such as "West Point" and "Men of Annapolis." In high school, he won a scholarship to visit Greece, where he saw first-hand Nazi devastations that pockmarked the land and its people. When he heard his youthful president, John F. Kennedy, assure the world that America would "pay any price, bear any burden," he decided he would be a soldier. He aspired to West Point but lacked an appointment. A brother-in-law who was a West Pointer urged him to consider The Citadel, which he described as "the West Point of the South." Trez came for a weekend visit in February 1965, and was hosted by cadet Tom Barr, O Company. Everything about the school, Tom Barr and Charleston impressed him. He went home to read up on the place he was now certain would be his future, including Calder Willingham's *End as a Man*.[130]

When Trez reported in August 1965, company assignments were still made by height. The tallest cadets were placed at opposite ends of the alphabet and the parade ground — A Company and T Company. Those assigned to R and B were slightly shorter, and those in C and N more so. Companies H and I housed the shortest cadets. This practice was instituted to create an optical illusion at parade. With the Corps of Cadets fully assembled on the parade ground, visitors in the bleachers in front of Padgett-Thomas must have wondered how all the cadets could be the same height. By having the taller cadets at the far ends of the field and the shortest directly in front of the visitors, the optical illusion of uniform height was achieved.

Trez landed in A Company. As he was hardly the first to learn, company assignment could be a critical determinant in the life of a knob. "There were 17 companies," Trez said, "and 17 different cultures." Because of the height criteria, the bookend companies, A and T, were populated by athletes who tended to foster a more laid back, relaxed approach to the military and the Fourth Class System. By contrast, the culture in companies comprised of shorter cadets, euphemistically called "duck butts," reflected a more aggressive attitude, attributed by some to the Napoleonic Complex. Companies like H and I, where the average height might be 5'5", were home to few varsity athletes, leading their ranks to prove their *macho bona fides* in other ways, Junior Sword Drill and Bond Volunteers chief among them. According to Trez, years after the height criterion was eliminated as a basis for company assignment, coaches continued to press the administration to assign recruited athletes to A or B, T or R companies in the belief that conditions would be more hospitable.[131]

Joe Trez is a tall, looming presence who after his sophomore year nearly opted for the priesthood. Instead, he married his high school sweetheart, Carmela Pinelli, a few days after graduation. His training as an infantry officer and Airborne Ranger prepared him for a tour in Vietnam, which he completed in June 1971. He returned to The Citadel in 1978 to get his MBA, and stayed on for another two years as assistant professor of military science. By the summer of 1994 he served as an infantry battalion and brigade commander, and chief of staff for the 7th Infantry Division at Fort Lewis,

Washington. As a full colonel in that position, flag rank seemed a bright and logical prospect.

Then he received calls from two members of the Board of Visitors whom he has declined to name, but their message hit home. The Citadel needed him. They listed the challenges: A woman named Shannon Faulkner had sued the school and was attending day classes with cadets; a black cadet had been shot on campus in a bizarre assault; race relations on campus continued to be strained by the Confederate battle flag and renditions of "Dixie"; and James Clyburn, then head of the Council on Higher Education and later a multi-term U.S. Congressman, had issued a report blasting the school's failure to eradicate vestiges of perceived racism.

Trez loved The Citadel. He answered the call.

As a cadet, Trez, like General Rosa (also an A Company man), learned leadership by observation, not instruction; by copying the attitudes and practices of those he admired and rejecting others. When Trez became A Company commander in the 1968-1969 school year, he ran his company in that same spirit. As a second lieutenant in the Army's infantry branch, he observed and experienced both styles of leadership: The harsh and punitive made infamous by Marine Corps drill instructors in fact and legend, and the more collegial, mentoring A Company style. To Trez, results overwhelmingly supported the latter, and nothing in his later career persuaded him otherwise.

Attributes of leadership have been identified best by, not surprisingly, proven leaders. Jack Welch, a legendary CEO of General Electric, said, "Before you are a leader, success is all about growing yourself. When you become a leader, success is all about growing others." Field Marshal Montgomery defined it as "The capacity and the will to rally men and women to a common purpose and the character which inspires confidence." The Roman writer Publilius Syrus reminds us that "Anyone can hold the helm when the sea is calm." Leaders must be prepared to stand alone. Winston Churchill wryly noted that "The nation will find it very hard to look up to the leaders who are keeping their ears to the ground."

From its founding, The Citadel has been a laboratory for leadership. The rank system gives authority, but until the 21st century did little to ensure that authority was exercised prudently and wisely. A widely held assumption by those outside the walls is that leadership is taught, an assumption only recently justified with the establishment of the Krause Center for Leadership & Ethics and changes to the school's curriculum.

A consensus of those who should know is that leaders are made, not born. If true, how does one learn the essential qualities of leadership? That question has vexed The Citadel and other institutions for longer than many graduates might suspect. General Rosa's experience mirrored that of generations of cadets: "We looked at the people ahead of us and said, 'I want to be like him, but not that one.'"[132]

The evolution of leadership training is one of the great Citadel stories of the 21st century. This is not to deny that it produced leaders in the prior two centuries — plainly and irrefutably it did. Those leaders fought wars, founded great companies and filled the law, medical, engineering and teaching professions with eminent men. How many of those owed their success to leadership training received at The Citadel? Perhaps as importantly, how many others might have benefitted from a four-year regimen that ingrained the fundamentals of principled leadership?

Knob year is a cadet's first exposure to a system that for years was relied upon to instill the art and the science of leadership, and for many members of cadre, their first opportunity to employ the lessons derived from that year. The Fourth Class System is thus critical to both. Its benefits and its detriments have been exhaustively studied and debated, as have the methods used to carry it out. Its rigors have waxed and waned with successive classes, and with few willing to admit to anything less than "Old Corps" hardships, deprivations and hazings. Once done with it, we all tend to embrace it as a rite of passage even while vowing eternal vengeance on some corporal or sergeant who made us miserable. But, as Rosa observed, that tends to mold incoming cadets with the same positives and negatives that molded the preceding class, and there have been documented cases where the negatives predominated. Principled leadership has been deemed too important to leave to such haphazard implementation. Hence the structured four-year program now in place.

The Fourth Class System is indisputably "adversative," a term generally understood to embody upper-class cadets in opposition to knobs. But the term is subjective, like the shine on your shoes or the alignment of your brass. Anyone determined to find fault can do so, and an adversative system that puts a premium on criticism rather than encouragement can quickly slide down the slippery slope into abuse. If, as some claim, The Citadel's Fourth Class System has been adversative to the point of abuse, it is a fool's errand to attempt to pinpoint when it began, when it ended and who was most responsible.

General Summerall had suspended the Fourth Class System between 1943 and 1946. How adversative was the system prior to World War II? The novelist and screenwriter Calder Willingham attended The Citadel from 1940-1941, a fact mercifully omitted from a review of *End as a Man* in *The New York Times*. In the book, an odious (literally and figuratively) freshman named Simmons draws the attention of upperclassmen who mock him, exhaust him with deep knee bends and push-ups, and beat him with a broom. The book's combination of hazing, a subtle homoerotic theme and language considered indecent by 1940s standards was enough to get its publisher sued for obscenity by the New York Society for the Suppression of Vice. Even allowing for outsized literary license, the book leaves no doubt that the Fourth Class System at what Willingham called "The Academy" crossed the line into abuse on more than one occasion. A critic reviewing it called it "one of the angriest, bitterest, most gruesome and powerful books I have read in a long time." He speculated that "A good many copies are doubtless even now being read with avid interest and considerable indignation at Virginia Military Institute and The Citadel." If there is a hero in the book, it is the school's staunchly principled president, General Draughton, who expels the son of one of The Academy's major financial backers. Perhaps Willingham had General Summerall in mind. Willingham went on to a successful career, writing the screenplays for *One-Eyed Jacks* and *The Graduate* (co-written), among others.[133]

When the Fourth Class System was reinstituted in 1947, some elements of the pre-war system inevitably remained. Class histories from the early 1950s show knobs — or "dumbsmacks," as they were at times called then — with some of the same apprehensions about what awaited them as did later classes. But those histories document a trend toward a gradually onerous system. Note how the tone changes with the distance from war:

1949: On September 19, we, as members of the Class of 1953, disposed of our civilian habits and began the long tedious climb of becoming Citadel cadets. Over 300 strong, we began our cadet career on the quadrangle of PT Barracks. … We were told that the usual processing was about to begin, but we never expected what would inevitably happen. During the afternoon of that "first" day, we were instructed in the "art" of marching and received our introduction to our new "Bible" — the Blue Book. General Summerall gave us a formal welcome on the parade ground in front of the chapel.[134]

1950: We'll never forget that sultry day in September, 1950, when we strolled wide-eyed under the great tower of Padgett-Thomas. In contrast to the environment we left behind old Lesesne Gate, we at once felt as though we were in a strange new world. A new civilization where buildings loomed mightier, where the very air seemed to carry an ordered freshness about it, where men walked properly erect. Ah, and what a joy it would be to step right into a society such as this! How we all yearned to get into one of those smart uniforms, to be instantly transformed into one of those men who carried himself with such confidence, such manliness! But, alas, we found it was not as easy as all that. We were, within an hour of entering The Citadel, thrust into shabby, ill-fitting fatigues. Where were those neat greys that we saw the other cadets wearing? How was it that we felt so awkward, so unlike a man? Immediately we began to feel as though we were different, as though for some reason we were being singled out. We were confounded by a new language, replete with such terms as "Ponderous gut", "Dumbsmack", and "Right Oblique." We had to perfect the various marching movements, we had to learn the art of shining brass, the rifle manual, military courtesy, and how to shine even more brass. And it seemed as though we'd never learn.[135]

1951: It was a warm sunny day of 19 September 1951 when the Class of '55, then 560 strong, arrived on a stretch of forbidding territory that for the next four years was to be their "home away from home." Too confused that day were all the prospective recruits to notice that glint in the noncoms' eyes or the austere dignity of that figure with the gold band on his hat. Two days of sweet talk and kind words burst into one nightmare of horror as the machinery of The Citadel's famed plebe system began operating. Orientation week could be aptly described as the week about which everyone remembers little but the one which nobody will ever forget. It is a new way of life introduced by more than a mere tap on the rear. We were whelped in chaos and weaned on harsh words. Our first steps were hard or easy, depending on whether we ran on the quad at port arms or marched at right shoulder.[136]

1952: Of course, our first year was the roughest, but it is the one which we remember most vividly. Who could ever forget that miserable day in September of 1952 when we got our first good look at The Citadel. Needless to say, we were a little apprehensive, and scared. We had heard many tales about this place called The Citadel, tales that sent cold chills up our spine. After the first day we thought those tales were just wild stories, that they had been dreamed up to scare us, but then it happened. In one great crescendo we realized how far wrong we had been, and Tuesday morning found the Class of '56 lower than the President's dog and the Commandant's cat. … Our first week at our new "home" was a week of living hell. Never before had so many been so confused about so much. Learning a completely new way of life was hard to all of us, but slowly we began to grasp a little of the intense training we underwent that first week. We somehow survived our first SMI, although we were scared to death of our TAC Officers and almost passed out from fright when he asked us where we were from or how we liked The Citadel.[137]

One explanation for the change of tone has to do with the veteran students who filled the classrooms (and the school's bank account) after the war. In 1947, the year the plebe system was reactivated, cadets numbered 1,046 and veterans 1,225. By definition, the vets had been to war and were largely over it, focused on getting an education and leaving the military behind. Some cadets resented the veterans, perceiving their presence as a negative influence on old values and traditions. As Alexander Macauley observed in *Marching in Step*, "It bothered many cadets that veteran students did not have to wear uniforms, undergo inspections and stand in daily formations. Members of the Corps also grumbled when veterans crossed the parade ground during drill periods, regarding such acts as proof of the latter's disdain for The Citadel's military customs."[138] Their presence on campus would have tempered the martial tendencies of cadets, young men several years their junior in age and a world away in maturity and experience.

But the early to mid-1950s saw a gradual decrease in the number of veteran students, a commensurate increase in the Corps, and the Fourth Class System once again returned to the rigors of its pre-war traditions. After General Clark became president, he "intensified the institutional emphasis on discipline and order, adding physical toughness to the mix of manly ingredients that elevated Citadel graduates above their contemporaries." The school boasted of having a plebe system second to none when measured by toughness, with Clark alleged to have raised the ante by claiming it to be the toughest in the world.[139] On Clark's watch, the Junior Sword Drill began competitive tryouts that lasted for 14 nights, each one a grueling three-hour test of endurance and conditioning. What had previously been an entitlement by virtue of rank now became a survival of the fittest.[140]

As this book reveals in subsequent chapters, studying and revising the Fourth Class System became a feature of several administrations, all of them concerned that knobs were being denied the big three: (1) adequate sleep, (2) sufficient nutrition and (3) adequate and concentrated study time. As we shall see, the past was prologue and history did repeat itself. But eventually we made transformational progress.

Chapter 5

"THERE AIN'T NO DAYLIGHT IN VIETNAM . . . NOT A BIT."

N o one who lived through the Vietnam War era would have been particularly surprised by the full-page advertisement in the *Washington
Evening Star* newspaper. Moved, yes, but not surprised. The ad listed the
names of those killed in action in Vietnam and was paid for by the parents,
relatives and friends of those soldiers, and it put to the President of the
United States a simple yet profound question: Why?

What is remarkable about the ad, aside from its poignancy, is the fact that
it was published on May 12, 1964, when the U.S. death toll was 132, a tiny
fraction of what it would become.[141] That question "Why?" was still being
asked nine years and thousands of lives later. Many ask it today.

Two sponsors of the *Evening Star* ad were Mr. and Mrs. J.D. Cordell, whose
son, Army Captain Terry D. Cordell, had graduated from The Citadel in the
Class of 1957. Cordell served as a cadet company commander, a member of
the Honor Committee and a Distinguished Military Student. His classmates
voted him "Best Senior Officer."[142] When his plane was shot down on Oct.
15, 1962, he was among the first U.S. officers killed in Vietnam in combat.[143]

On July 27, 1953, just over a month before Cordell and his classmates
reported, a peace treaty had been signed at Panmunjom ending the Korean
War. The new cadets must have felt relief at knowing an armed conflict that
had claimed 25 alumni lives was over and that, as far as they or anyone else
could see, no war awaited them upon graduation in 1957.

It is certain that Cordell had never heard of a small Southeast Asian country
called South Vietnam because that country did not yet exist. The French
and Vietnamese partitioned Vietnam in a 1954 armistice and, a year later,
the Republic of Vietnam, South Vietnam, was born. Captain Cordell's death
in a war that would ultimately claim no fewer than 58,195 members of the
American Armed Forces cast a long shadow over the campus and the country.
More than 80 Citadel alumni paid the ultimate price in Vietnam. The final
tally won't be known until all veterans of that war are gone because Agent

Orange, long-term disabilities and post-traumatic stress disorder (PTSD) still claim victims each year.

Hundreds of Citadel graduates served there, first as military advisors ordered by Eisenhower and later supplemented by Kennedy. We were also among the last to leave when POWs were released at the war's end. Vietnam touched or impacted the lives of all cadets who matriculated in the 1960s and became the defining event of their generation.

The logic of aiding the South Vietnamese, accepted by administrations from Truman through Johnson, was known as the Domino Theory, a term that originated in a 1954 speech given by President Eisenhower, who predicted that should Indochina fall to the Communists the rest of Southeast Asia would likewise fall, like a "row of dominoes."[144] Implicit and explicit in this theory was the bedrock conviction that such a takeover by Communists threatened the long-term security of the United States and its world leadership. Fears in the West, while exaggerated, were not unfounded. Communist China and North Korea had invaded South Korea, Khrushchev had promised to bury us, the Berlin Wall went up, and Russian-supplied missiles had been secreted to Comrade Castro just off our coast.

One man who believed wholly in the Domino Theory was General Clark, firmly convinced that Communism presented a threat here at home. In 1962, he proposed as a buffer against the Red Peril that local high schools mandate a six- to eight-weeks course in Communism for seniors.[145] Many shared Clark's view. At the College of Charleston, George Grice, its president, cited Communism or Fascism as the inevitable result of yielding to federal and state pressure to integrate his college.[146] McCarthyism is most closely associated with the early to mid-1950s, but its vestiges remained well into the 1960s.[147]

In the years before body bags arrived in large numbers at Dover Air Force Base, the word "Vietnam" was more likely to show up in a Sunday crossword puzzle than a Sunday editorial. All but a few Americans would have been surprised to learn that between 1955 and 1961, U.S. economic and military aid to South Vietnam exceeded $7 billion, a small sum measured against our ultimate expenditures there but a significant amount by any measure. More importantly, by November 1963 seventy-eight of the 16,300 U.S. military advisers had been killed, a portent of the grim years ahead.[148]

In the fall of 1963, members of the Class of 1967 made the time-honored trip through Lesesne Gate to begin their college careers. Outside those gates, it was not conflict in Southeast Asia that dominated the news but local unrest as Charleston emerged from one of the most contentious, strife-filled summers in its long history. And as with so much of that history, issues of race and equality were at the root of the conflict.

In June and July, the Charleston Movement, led by prominent black activists and aided by $10,000 from the NAACP, organized marches, boycotts and demonstrations that brought the city to the edge. They also brought the Rev. Martin Luther King, Jr., who led a sit-in. Cool heads prevailed, the most immediate grievances were addressed and in September 1963 Rivers High School in Charleston became the first public school in South Carolina to integrate.[149]

The Citadel Class of 1967 matriculated with 663 members, of which 372 would graduate in four years.[150] The city that welcomed them on that humid day was in many respects unrecognizable from Charleston today. White flight to the suburbs was well underway, with population on the peninsula down to 40,000, as it had been in 1850.[151]

Hampton Park, just outside the gates, suffered benign neglect from those with the power to improve it. King Street below Calhoun had a diminishing number of retail merchants sprinkled among vacant and often boarded-up buildings. King Street above Calhoun was far worse and off-limits to the sensible after dark. The College of Charleston, with its meager enrollment of 422 students — significantly smaller than the freshman class of cadets reporting — remained an educational enclave whose very existence was unknown to some at The Citadel. The city's iconic churches and landmarks endured, and the homes along the Battery and South of Broad still exuded elegance, but major sections of the Holy City awaited the renewal that came when a Citadel graduate, Joseph P. Riley Jr., Class of 1964, became mayor in 1975.

Once inside Lesesne Gate and the confines of the campus, the Class of 1967 spent the fall adjusting to barracks life, absorbed into a system they would curse at Thanksgiving and celebrate upon graduation. As they got to know each other, learned to salute, drew M-1 rifles, recited Knob Knowledge and memorized their laundry numbers, events at home and abroad would have profound impact on them by graduation.

Generals in the South Vietnamese Army plotted a coup against President Ngo Dinh Diem and Ngo Dinh Nhu, his brother and principal advisor. In early November, both men were assassinated, and by Thanksgiving, President Kennedy, whose government had been complicit in the murder of the Ngo brothers, would suffer the same fate.

On the afternoon of Friday, November 22, 1963, freshmen cadets shined up for parade. Their first holiday loomed, and most could not wait to get home. Television was prohibited in the barracks, but radios blared in all four battalions. Suddenly, news flashes from Dallas interrupted music by the Beatles. President Kennedy had been shot while riding in a motorcade. Governor Connally of Texas, in the same car, was reported to have been wounded. For a time, Kennedy's fate was uncertain. Then certain. In fourth battalion, a few cheers could be heard in the stillness following the announcement that the president had died, and a popular myth at the time held that a radio station played *Hit the Road, Jack* by Ray Charles.

Gallows humor reaches an art form at military schools, but on that day anyone so callous as to be heartened by Kennedy's death failed to comprehend that America's commander-in-chief was now Lyndon B. Johnson, a man destined to draft them, send them overseas (more than once), and throw them by the regiments into a war that many had, even then, recognized as unwinnable.

Parade was canceled. A somber, omnipotent voice over the loudspeaker announced a prayer vigil at Summerall Chapel, and hundreds of cadets of all ranks and classes made their way there to mourn the death of the young president.

As many older Charlestonians knew, Kennedy lived in Charleston for a time in the early days of World War II. In 1942, he was stationed in Washington, D.C. when his affair with the married Danish beauty Inga Arvad made a Walter Winchell gossip column. Joseph P. Kennedy, whose political career had been torpedoed by an extramarital affair, saw his hopes for his son's career about to suffer the same fate. To separate the lovers, Joe Kennedy had JFK assigned to the Charleston Naval Base. Arvad boarded a train in D.C. and followed him, and the FBI followed her because she had been under surveillance since being photographed with Hitler and Goering during the 1936 Berlin Olympics. JFK lived on Murray Boulevard on the historic Battery. He and the newly arrived Inga continued their affair for at least one memorably long weekend, when the FBI taped them "engaged in sexual intercourse on numerous occasions."[152]

The year 1965 proved pivotal in the war, for it was in March of that year that Johnson committed the Marines in Da Nang, raising the stakes for the country, the Class of 1965 and the classes to follow. Over Corps Day weekend, General Clark gave his final report to the Board of Visitors. He described 1964-1965 as "the best year this college has enjoyed in the 11 years I have been privileged to serve as presiding officer." He took particular note of the growth of the Corps of Cadets to its maximum capacity of 2,001, and obvious pride in the 76 Greater Issues speakers brought to the school, including the first woman, Clare Boothe Luce. He left the impression that the Citadel ship of state sailed in perfect trim, and that his successor would do well to steer her on the course Clark had charted.

But as cadets and their dates cheered The Four Seasons at the Corps Day hop, decisions being reached in Washington decided the fates of many reveling in the bloom of that Charleston springtime. Many of those decisions were being made by Robert S. McNamara, who wrote perhaps the best, most unflinching account of that era in his book *In Retrospect*. McNamara, Secretary of Defense under Kennedy and Johnson, is considered the chief architect of what came to be called "McNamara's War." Published years after the war ended and not long before its author's death, *In Retrospect* includes revelations shocking even today. Particularly surprising if depressing is how early "the best and the brightest" perceived the handicaps the United States faced in fighting that war, yet plowed ahead as if it were all somehow unavoidable.

If Vietnam proved a national train wreck, the crew driving the locomotive saw the wreck coming from miles off and accelerated. As early as November 1961, almost a full year before Captain Cordell or any other Citadel graduate died in Vietnam, McNamara posed questions that he shamefully admits were never answered:

> The dilemma Dean [Rusk, Secretary of State] and I defined was going to haunt us for years. … We failed to ask the five most basic questions: Was it true that the fall of South Vietnam would trigger the fall of all Southeast Asia? Would that constitute a grave threat to the West's security? What kind of war — conventional or guerrilla – might develop? Could we win it with U.S. troops fighting alongside the South Vietnamese? *Should we not know the answers to all these questions before deciding whether to commit troops?* It seems beyond understanding, incredible, that we did not force ourselves to confront such issues head-on. [emphasis added][153]

In early 1965, President Johnson told Senator Richard Russell, chairman of the Senate Armed Services Committee, that "there ain't no daylight in Vietnam. There's not a bit."[154] About the time newly graduated members of the Class of 1965 reported to their various officer-training courses, and The Citadel's new president, Army General Hugh Pate Harris, was familiarizing himself with the campus, President Johnson was telling McNamara that he saw:

> [N]o program from either Defense or State that gives me much hope of doing anything except just praying and grasping to hold

on during [the] monsoon [season] and hope they'll quit. And I
don't believe they're ever goin' to quit. And I don't see ... that we
have any ... plan for victory militarily or diplomatically ... [155]

Three years later when Johnson was chased from office, he was still pray-
ing and grasping, and still without a plan for victory, military or diplomatic.
Freshly minted lieutenants in the Class of 1965 would have been surprised
to learn that their commander-in-chief was about to order them into a war
for which he had no plan for victory. Two of those new officers were Frank
Murphy and Joe Missar.

Frank "Skip" Murphy had been captain of the 1964 football team, an-
choring the line at center. Joe Missar played beside him at guard, and when
they weren't on the football field they could often be found together hanging
out or taking advantage of senior leave privileges. Skip had served as a cadet
first lieutenant, made the Dean's List, and was selected for inclusion in *Who's
Who in American Colleges and Universities*. He was the better student, but Joe
was the better player, named to the All Southern Conference football team
on both offense and defense.[156] Joe fell first. A second lieutenant, USMC,
he died May 6, 1966 in combat in Quang Nam, South Vietnam. Skip fell
seven months later, on Dec. 7, 1966. According to Brian Neal, who was in
the armored personnel carrier with him, Skip's platoon had extracted a unit
from a firefight within the Michelin Rubber Plantation when an explosive
charge flipped the vehicle. Skip, standing in the turret, died instantly.[157]
Today, both Skip and Joe are remembered by a bronze statue in Johnson
Hagood Stadium just outside the Bulldog locker room.

When he was inaugurated in the fall of 1965, General Harris became the
third four-star general in succession to become the permanent president.
Harris had held a number of senior positions, most recently as Commanding
General of the U.S. Continental Army Command at Fort Monroe, Virginia.
By the time he retired in 1970, the school had been governed for 39 years
by West Pointers Summerall, Clark and Harris, interrupted by the one year,
1953-1954, when Colonel LeTellier served as acting president.

Changes in South Carolina's educational landscape presented to Harris
his first challenges as president. In a March 5, 1965 editorial, the *News &
Courier* noted studies showing that between 1955 and 1965, the percentage
of students educated at state-supported schools increased at USC and Winthrop, remained roughly the same at Clemson, but declined at The Citadel,
from 12.8 percent to 9.5 percent. The newspaper urged the school to change

with the times while maintaining its distinctive educational mission, suggesting that the institution of a graduate studies program would be a step in that direction.

Had it simply been a matter of establishing a graduate program (as was done in 1968), the pressure on The Citadel would have been mild compared to what developed, but the fact of the matter was that all the institutions of higher learning in the Charleston area — the College of Charleston, The Citadel and the newly established Baptist College at Charleston — came under enormous state pressure to formulate what many wished would become a combined Charleston University.

Predictably, The Citadel wanted no part of such a system, one sure to subsume its culture into a university bureaucracy. To avoid such a fate, the school would have to solve its two most pressing problems: under-utilization of its facilities and under-representation of South Carolina students at a state-supported college. These were the primary issues Harris sought to address.

Establishing a graduate division within The Citadel in 1965 was a bridge too far, but in October, before Harris had even been inaugurated, the Board of Visitors authorized him to organize night classes. A night school, to better use the college's facilities, had been suggested before. In 1962 General Clark offered to create one for the training of teachers in Communist history and propaganda.[158] In agreeing to night classes, the Board of Visitors mandated that they not interfere with cadet activities, that only undergraduate courses were to be offered, and that the public be fully informed as to the relationship between the night school and the traditional programs.[159] Harris told *The Brigadier* in November that the plan envisioned use of facilities when not required by the Corps and at times when cadets were "otherwise occupied." Courses to be offered included biology, chemistry, business administration, electrical engineering, English, history, mathematics, modern languages, physics and political science. Regardless of courses taken or credits earned, no one attending night school would be eligible for a Citadel diploma.[160] Students would be high school graduates qualified for college work, men and women, without regard to race, a significant guideline in 1965.[161]

Another badly needed reform was a forum for faculty members to exchange ideas and experiences. Under General Clark and the administrations preceding him, faculty members had paltry influence on college policies. Department heads enjoyed what were tantamount to lifetime appointments, and how much they sought or considered the views of those within their departments varied from some to none. Department heads held monthly meetings chaired by the vice president for academic affairs, a group known as the Academic Board. This Academic Board determined issues critical to the faculty as a whole, with authority on hiring, firing, tenure, pay raises and subjects taught, all subject to approval by the president.[162]

While this system was arguably adequate prior to 1963, its shortcomings became more apparent when the baby-boom generation began arriving at the college. A more collegial approach was needed. Recognizing these shortcomings, a small coterie of liberal arts professors decided the time had come to form a Citadel chapter of the American Association of University Professors (AAUP), an organization respected in higher education circles and renowned for its contributions to academic freedom and faculty tenure. Mindful of General Clark's opposition to any organization that evoked unionism, the coterie wisely delayed formation until after his retirement.

In Clark's final weeks as president, first-year instructor Rodney Grunes brought the issue of academic freedom front and center. Grunes had arrived in 1964 from Duke University on a one-year contract to fill a void in the Political Science Department left by a professor on leave. In the spring of 1965, weeks before the expiration of his contract and General Clark's retirement, he received a summons from the dean, Colonel Ralph Byrd.

The dean was irate, having received a report of a comment Grunes had made to cadets in his class; a comment the Colonel refused to repeat. "You know what you said," was all that Byrd would disclose beyond the fact that Grunes was at imminent risk of being fired. Grunes concluded that his offending remark had been, "I'll defect to Cuba before I'll fight in the Vietnam war." It takes little imagination to appreciate how General Clark, when apprised of the comment, reacted, but in view of his looming retirement, the close of the academic year and the end of Grunes' one-year contract, the matter was allowed to die.[163]

The Citadel's chapter of the AAUP, chartered in the first year of the Harris administration, brought the faculty closer to the strength exercised by professors at other campuses. Laurence W. Moreland, now a professor emeritus but in 1965-66 in his second year, recalls meetings as well attended (close to 100 faculty) and an immediate success. "There turned out to be a huge hunger on the part of the faculty for an opportunity to express their views on matters that affected their teaching and their careers." AAUP made a significant contribution to the college when the Southern Association of Colleges and Schools (SACS), the organization most responsible then and now for The Citadel's accreditation, demanded as a condition of certification a statement of academic freedom.

None existed, at least here. The Board of Visitors adopted the AAUP's "1940 Statement of Principles on Academic Freedom and Tenure" verbatim, adding only a rhetorical flourish that faculty was expected to act "consistent with the principles of Americanism."

Reminders of the war persisted. News came of the death of Major Sam Savas, a member of the Class of 1951, who served as a TAC officer from 1961-1965. He died in Vietnam from natural causes but this did not lessen the sense of loss felt by cadets and faculty. On November 20, 1965, *The Brigadier* published a speech given by Secretary of State Dean Rusk entitled "Our Vietnam Commitment" in which he said the government considered the real enemy in Vietnam to be China. Even our most successful sports team evoked images of war as the Rifle Team repeated as national champions.[164]

In the fall of 1966, Charles D. Foster became the first black cadet to enter the college. Three black applicants had been accepted, but only Foster reported to the campus. Clemson and the University of South Carolina had integrated three years earlier, in January and September 1963 respectively.[165] At civilian schools, these barrier-breaking students could be ignored and there is evidence they were.[166] But ignoring an incoming freshman is not in The Citadel's DNA. The system of knob indoctrination and training does not permit it, regardless of the race or sex of the person being braced.

The administration fully perceived the potential for problems stemming from Foster's admission. Assistant Commandant Lieutenant Colonel Thomas Nugent Courvoisie, "The Boo," made the chain of command aware that he held them personally responsible for knob Foster's health. By height, the basis of company assignment in 1966, Foster belonged in F Company, a notoriously challenging place for freshmen. By assigning him to G Company, he fell under the charge of cadet Captain William Riggs, the company commander; executive officer Leon Yonce; and First Sergeant Billy Jenkinson (who would later serve as chairman of the Board of Visitors).

Foster was hard to miss in a formation, for not only was he dark complexioned and well-muscled but he stood a head taller than the other G Company knobs. This proved a small price to pay for escaping the perils of F Troop. James A. Probsdorfer, regimental commander and thus the head of the chain of command responsible for Foster's well-being, said, "He impressed me with his ability to ignore all the chaos around him, stand firm, never wincing and always looking right through you. I admired him for his courage and considered him worthy of being a Citadel man."[167]

Foster must have wondered about the motivations of corporals or sergeants during the worst of sweat parties, push-up challenges and square meals. Undoubtedly, he experienced incidents of racial animus in his knob year and thereafter, but he bore up well and graduated in 1970.

By then a small number of other black cadets comprised part of the Corps. In 1967, Joe Shine became the second black to report, and whereas Foster had been an average student and cadet, Shine excelled in academics and leadership, attaining the rank of captain on regimental staff and the designation of Distinguished Air Force ROTC student.[168] One memorable incident involving Shine was reported in *The Brigadier*. A King Street bar familiar to legions of cadets, Raben's Tavern, refused to serve Shine when he ordered a beer with others seniors, insisting that Shine would have to move to the back room to be accommodated. To their credit, Shine's classmates walked out, precipitating a boycott of Raben's Tavern.[169]

The year 1967 began badly with the death of Major Leon Freda, the much-beloved leader of the band for 19 years. It was said he could play any instrument to be found in Band Company.[170]

Early in 1967, use of the college's facilities and a threat to the very nature of the school prompted General Harris to request a special meeting of the Board of Visitors. In a memorandum dated Feb. 11, 1967, Harris outlined his concerns about recent developments in higher education. While acknowledging that his worries could be seen as "yelling wolf," that risk was outweighed by what he described as "trends, requirements, attitudes and needs that may place The Citadel in jeopardy again as an essentially military college." The issues he was raising, he told the board, "today exist in each state that has a state-supported military college."

Harris cited changes already implemented at VPI (hereinafter Virginia Tech), North Georgia, Clemson and Texas A&M, where their respective Corps had become mere adjuncts to an essentially civilian environment. Private military colleges, Harris added, "are fighting for their lives to survive in the current environment and time frame," an obvious allusion to diminished enrollments brought about by the war.

A key component of the problem lay with the Defense Department's allocation of funds. Military colleges supplied 12 percent of the officers to the Armed Services but received only 3 percent of DOD's allocation of available funds for ROTC. An officer from schools such as The Citadel was a bargain, costing the DOD less than $5,000, compared to the $50,000 price tag at a service academy. With 25 percent of recent Citadel graduates in career service and, over the most recent decade, 50 percent on extended active duty, why should cash-strapped states including South Carolina continue to fund what the federal government needed?

Harris urged board members to lobby congressmen and any other source to force the DOD to contribute more to state-supported military schools, reasoning that "the state will be very hesitant to attempt to knock us off if there is considerable federal money and obligation involved." Harris praised S.C. Governor Robert McNair as very progressive and interested in the state's educational problems and needs. He appointed a committee to examine those needs and make recommendations. The Legislature will be shocked, Harris predicted, by the additional facilities required and totally discouraged by the cost. When confronted with the additional $80 million required, "they will surely ask a vital question, i.e. 'Do we need a military college in South Carolina?'" The Citadel's vulnerability stemmed from insufficient in-state students, 43 percent and holding, a "plateau of about 900 from South Carolina."[171]

Significant sums of federal money were available to states that were expanding educational facilities, but expanding The Citadel presented challenges. Expanding to serve more out-of-state students was a non-starter, and impediments to growing the in-state population included, among other things, the rigors of the Fourth Class System. Harris made it clear he supported that system, but insisted it should meet four criteria: (1) plebes must be allowed to eat three balanced meals a day; (2) they must be left alone during ESP (evening study period); (3) they must be allowed to sleep undisturbed between taps and reveille; and (4) hazing is prohibited.

Then Harris stated what must have struck some board members as heresy: "I believe that The Citadel cannot contribute its greatest service to the state of South Carolina unless there is an escape valve for those who would like to attend school here but do not agree with us as to the merits of the plebe system."

It is difficult to avoid the conclusion that Harris was proposing that a Corps of Cadets become a component of a larger institution, as had happened at Clemson, Virginia Tech and Texas A&M. He did not elaborate on what "escape valve" he had in mind, but whatever it was he was convinced it would help not only to attract more South Carolina students but in athlete recruitment and retention as well. Harris then put to the board three essential questions: Did they agree a threat to the school's continued viability existed, and if yes, should The Citadel's existing programs and curricula be changed to meet the threat, and if so, when should such changes be implemented? He closed with the recommendation that a study committee be appointed to weigh the issues carefully and assured them that no rush to judgment was then required.[172]

A month later, at the board's spring meeting, the chairman, General Edwin A. Pollock, USMC (Ret.), Class of 1921, appointed the study committee Harris had recommended. For a man not given to hyperbolic statements, Pollock's acknowledgement at the outset is remarkable. "This committee will probably be more important and far reaching than any ever convened by the Board of Visitors. The results of it might well mean *the continued success or death of The Citadel as we know it."* [emphasis added].

But Pollock didn't need to await the committee's findings to issue a few of his own, and he minced no words: "There is nothing wrong with The Citadel. We have no major problems at The Citadel." Then he took on Harris's escape valve. "Purely civilian-type day students will not be compatible with the military training at The Citadel, or with the Corps of Cadets. Our discipline and honor system would collapse. We would no longer be considered as a man's college but as a boy's school." On the subject of expansion, which Harris had insisted would be necessary to attract federal funds, Pollock said this: "Every military college in the United States that has expanded has removed itself from the standards of a distinguished and essentially military college. There are only two left: The Citadel and VMI." So much for Harris's escape valve, though Pollack did leave open the possibility of instituting courses leading to graduate degrees.[173]

The committee appointed by Pollock met for the first time on April 12, 1967, as the Education Action Committee (EAC). It passed a resolution requesting the Charleston County Education Committee to employ an outside research firm to study the needs of the Charleston area and share its findings with the committee. At its June meeting, the board adopted recommendations by the EAC that veteran students be admitted as had been done after World War II and Korea and that the college contract with the Medical University of South Carolina for use of Citadel professors and facilities for instruction of student nurses.

At its October meeting, the board approved establishment of a graduate program for awarding a Masters of Arts in Teaching (MAT), to begin the following fall. By instituting the night school, admitting veteran students, cooperating with the Medical University and initiating the MAT graduate program, The Citadel could justly claim to be making an effort to accommodate generally recognized educational needs in the Charleston area. The hope was that these accommodations would spare the school the more draconian suggestions being made to incorporate it into a university system based in the Lowcountry, a result the board viewed as anathema and the death of The Citadel.

In that same month, death almost came to three cadets stranded at sea and unable to steer because they ran out of gas off the coast. Search parties working for three days and nights eventually located and rescued them. According to an article in *The Brigadier*, they had with them only "four Pepsis, four pieces of bread and a little peanut butter" which, if true, may indicate that they polished off the beer early in the voyage. White slips charged them with "too long in water."[174]

In the spring of 1967, three weeks prior to graduation, South Carolina Lieutenant Governor John West gave a Greater Issues speech to the Corps. West graduated with the storied Class of 1942, whose members included two future Citadel presidents, Major General James A. Grimsley, Jr. and Lieutenant General George M. Seignious; U.S. Senator Ernest "Fritz" Hollings; media giant and philanthropist Alvah H. Chapman Jr.; and war hero Colonel Theodore S. Bell. West served as governor from 1971 to 1975 and thereafter as U.S. Ambassador to Saudi Arabia from 1977 to 1981.

In the audience that day sat West's son, a knob in K Company. West directed his remarks at the class about to graduate, insisting that they were "the most fortunate group of young people that ever lived." This was true, he said, because of the challenges they faced. West had been told the same thing in his senior year by one of his professors, who cited World War II, the "greatest struggle for survival that civilization has ever seen." The unnamed professor told West and his classmates what they undoubtedly knew, that "many of you will die, but your experience will mold character and provide opportunities beyond the human concept." His prediction came predictably true, as 19 members of the Class of 1942 fulfilled his prophecy in World War II. In his speech, West diplomatically avoided reminding the Class of 1967 that they too would die, as indeed 10 did within four years of graduation.

One month prior to West's address, *The Brigadier* carried an article entitled "6,766." The newspaper had received a press release issued jointly by the Teachers Committee for Peace in Vietnam and the Inter-University Committee for Debate on Foreign Policy claiming that 6,766 teachers — nursery school through college — had signed off on a condemnation of the war. The teachers favored an end to the bombing, a ceasefire, the inclusion of the National Liberation Front as part of any future Vietnam government and removal of all foreign troops from Vietnam as mandated by the 1954 Geneva Convention.[175]

The Brigadier reporter/editor, "TDG," expressed sarcastic appreciation for the teachers' concern about Vietnam, noting that it would "be more assuring if they would support the men who are dying to keep them free." After mentioning the recent death of John Fuller, Class of 1966, he dispensed with each point in the teachers' proposal in summary fashion. Withdrawing U.S. forces would leave in Vietnam only the South Vietnamese, the North Vietnamese and the Chinese fighters, raising the prospect of a Red invasion of *South America* [emphasis added]. He concluded thusly: "Next weekend they [the Inter-University Committee] plan to hold massive demonstrations in New York and San Francisco. As these two large, unarmed armies show their concern for the war they are afraid to fight, our small army will be at Goose Creek, showing our concern for the war we will fight to keep these 'citizens' free. If honor is the most cherished principle of the cadet's life, what indeed motivates these 6,766?"[176]

The juxtaposition of *The Brigadier* article and the West address exposes the essential tensions between The Citadel and much of academia in the late 1960s. TDG's response to the teachers was to impugn their patriotism, their courage and their motivations. Their very freedom (and apparently the freedom of some people in South America) depended upon folks like us, slogging it out in Goose Creek. For TDG and for the overwhelming majority at The Citadel, it was a matter of honor, with the clear implication that dishonor motivated the 6,766. Invoking honor in matters of war implicates a host of echoes from the Lost Cause, because in defeat and economic ruin, the South clung to honor as its last treasured possession. Its men had fought and died with honor; its women had borne their burdens and their widowhood with honor; the skill and daring of Confederate officers had honored their cause and their South.

The Brigadier published on September 23, 1967 listed 22 alumni deaths in Vietnam. One week later, that toll increased by one with the combat death of Major David Bruce Tucker, Class of 1961. In that his father, Major General Reuben H. Tucker, served as Commandant of Cadets, the pall over the campus was felt by the entire Citadel family.

But if Vietnam defined this generation, it is also true that Citadel alumni defined the U.S. effort in Vietnam, which was nothing short of heroic given the challenges they faced there. A statistic impossible to calculate is the number of men who came home because, in an otherwise luckless war, they had the good fortune to serve with or under a Citadel officer. By the mid-1960s, those who took commissions in the Army, Air Force and Marines knew where they were headed. No doubt for some, Vietnam loomed as a great adventure, a chance to serve their country while channeling an endless store of testosterone. For others, the call had more to do with following the examples set by their fathers and grandfathers, veterans of World War II and Korea. Some aspired to flag rank; all aspired to return home. Service in Vietnam made careers, broke hearts (here and there), turned boys into men, reduced men to invalids, cemented life-long bonds, rendered wives and children widows and orphans, drove some to drink and some to suicide, forced the battle-ruined to seek shelter under an interstate bridge and others a plot in Arlington. It remains the saddest chapter in America's military history.

Chapter 6

"Sir, it was the least I could do."

A full account of service in Vietnam by Citadel graduates would require a separate book — a thick one. The examples recited here represent an infinitesimal fraction of the whole. If the war produced cynics, and it did, it also produced heroes.

Myron Harrington, Class of 1960, had always wanted to be a Marine. His father had been a decorated soldier in World War I, and growing up in Decatur, Georgia, Harrington wanted nothing more than to emulate his dad's service. He planned to join the Marine Corps when he graduated from high school, but his father insisted he go to college first. They made a pact. Harrington would apply to one school and if rejected, his father agreed to let him join the Marines. If accepted, Harrington agreed to defer his service for college. His father thought his son's one application should be to North Georgia, but Harrington had another idea. In the *Decatur News* he had read about a war hero, a local boy named Walter Clark, who was awarded a Silver Star in Korea. Clark, a 1951 graduate of The Citadel, had led his platoon of mostly Spanish speaking Puerto Ricans in an assault on Hill 167 near Yu-hyon, defended by a superior Chinese force. With the cry of *"Arriba, Muchachos"* ("Go, boys!) Clark led his men up the hill into hand-to-hand combat. Wounded by rifle fire and grenades, Clark continued to exercise all the duties of command. His heroism inspired Harrington to make The Citadel the recipient of his all-or-nothing application. "I thought it was a safe bet because with my high school transcript there was no way they were going to let me in." But they did, so he went.[177]

At Thanksgiving in 1956, Harrington went home, and was enjoying a respite from the plebe system when his father suffered a heart attack and died. The next year proved difficult with the loss of his dad and the rigors of The Citadel. "I was not much of a student and a marginal cadet," Harrington acknowledges. "I don't remember holding rank but I do remember walking tours as a senior." After graduation, he realized his dream to be a Marine

Corps officer with a single career goal: to command Marines in combat, an ambition that in 1968 put him in charge of Company D, First Battalion, Fifth Marines, First Marine Division in Phu Bai, South Vietnam.[178]

Many consider the turning point of the war to have been the Tet Offensive, launched by the North Vietnamese and Vietcong on the evening of January 31, 1968, during the lunar New Year holiday. Communist forces staged surprise attacks on dozens of civilian and military command and control centers, including Saigon. Stanley Karnow, in his seminal, Pulitzer Prize winning book *Vietnam: A History*, wrote:

> Vietcong teams ... conducted house-to-house searches immediately after seizing control of Hue, and they were merciless. During the months and years that followed, the remains of approximately three thousand people were exhumed in nearby riverbeds, coastal salt flats and jungle clearings. The victims had been shot or clubbed to death or buried alive.[179]

In the center of Hue stood an ancient fortress called the Citadel, the highest point and the nerve center of the Communist forces. In response to what became known as the Massacre at Hue, three U.S. Marines battalions arrived from 12 miles away in Phu Bai.

Told by his battalion commander that Company D would take the Citadel at Hue, Harrington spent a restless night before the attack. "I resigned myself to the fact that I would either die or be wounded the next day. I made my peace with either." How ironic that his hardening at The Citadel in Charleston would now be tested halfway around the world. Early the next morning, with two platoons and a tank, he and his men advanced to the base of the fortress. Meeting no resistance, Harrington assumed the NVA had abandoned their high ground during the night. When he stepped out into the open, he learned otherwise.[180]

A fierce battle ensued which went on for several days. In Harrington's words:

> We were both in a face-to-face, eyeball-to-eyeball confrontation. Sometimes they were only 20 or 30 yards from us, and once we killed a sniper only 10 yards away. After a while, survival was the name of the game as you sat there in the semi-darkness, with the firing going on constantly, like a rifle range. And the horrible smell. You tasted it as you ate your rations, as if you were eating death. [181]

Like Walter Clark, whose heroism in Korea had inspired Harrington to apply to The Citadel, Harrington's bravery and command performance in Hue earned him a Silver Star. He was also awarded the Navy Cross, the citation for which reads in part:

> On the afternoon of 23 February 1968, Company D was attacking a well-entrenched North Vietnamese Army force that was occupying a fortified section of the wall surrounding the Hue Citadel. As the Marines maneuvered forward, they began receiving a heavy volume of small arms, automatic weapons, mortar and antitank rocket fire. Realizing the seriousness of the situation, Captain Harrington skillfully deployed his 3.5 rocket teams into advantageous firing positions. Continuously moving from one position to another, he pinpointed enemy emplacements and skillfully directed the fire of his men. After silencing four hostile positions, he requested supporting arms fire and skillfully adjusted 60-mm. mortar fire to within twenty-five meters of the forward elements of his company, while simultaneously adjusting artillery fire. Disregarding his own safety, Captain Harrington then fearlessly maneuvered to the point of heaviest contact and, rallying his men, boldly led a determined assault against the enemy soldiers. Shouting words of encouragement to his men, he skillfully maneuvered his unit forward and directed the Marines' fire upon the hostile emplacements. Largely due to his resolute determination and intrepid fighting spirit, his men overran the hostile positions and routed the North Vietnamese soldiers, accounting for twenty-five enemy soldiers confirmed killed. By his courage, superb leadership and unfaltering devotion to duty in the face of extreme personal danger, Captain Harrington upheld the highest traditions of the Marine Corps and the United States Naval Service.[182]

He attributes his survival to "the grace of God and my time at The Citadel, where I learned that failure isn't forever and success isn't guaranteed. The real story of The Citadel is what happens when people leave."[183]

Harrington continues to serve his country and his alma mater as a member of the Board of Visitors and by active involvement in a host of community benefits.

In 1963 the entire nation met Sam Bird, Class of 1961, when he served as the officer in charge of President Kennedy's burial detail. Years later, many who watched that television broadcast would read his remarkable story in a Reader's Digest article entitled "The Courage of Sam Bird," by B.T. Collins, who served under Bird in Vietnam, lost an arm and a leg to a hand grenade there, and went on to serve as chief of staff to the governor of California and deputy treasurer of that state.

Collins told Bird's story about as well as it can be told, with the kind of authenticity that could come only from someone who had been a brother-in-arms:

> If ever a man looked like a leader, it was Sam Bird. He was tall and lean, with penetrating blue eyes. But the tedium and terror of a combat zone take far sterner qualities than mere appearance. … Sam's philosophy was to put his troops first.
>
> On that foundation, he built respect a brick at a time. His men ate first; he ate last. Instead of merely learning their names, he made it a point to know the men. A lot of the soldiers were high-school dropouts and would-be tough guys just a few years younger than himself. Some were scared, and a few were still in partial shock at being in a shooting war. Sam patiently worked on their pride and self-confidence.
>
> Yet there was never any doubt who was in charge. I had been around enough to know what a delicate accomplishment that was.
>
> Half in wonder, an officer once told me, "Sam can dress a man down till his ears burn, and the next minute that same guy is eager to follow him into hell." But he never chewed out a man in front of his subordinates.
>
> Sam wouldn't ask his men to do anything he wasn't willing to do himself. He dug his own foxholes. He never gave lectures on appearance, but even at God-forsaken outposts in the Central Highlands, he would set aside a few ounces of water from his canteen to shave. His uniform, even if it was jungle fatigues, would be as clean and neat as he could make it.
>
> Soon all of Bravo Company had a reputation for looking sharp. One sultry and miserable day on a dirt road at the base camp, Sam gathered the men together and began talking about how tough the infantryman's job is, how proud he was of them, how they should always look out for each other. He took out a bunch of Combat Infantryman's Badges, signifying that a soldier has paid his dues under fire, and he presented one to each of the men. There wasn't a soldier there who would have traded that moment on the road for some parade-

ground ceremony.

That was the way Sam Bird taught me leadership. He packed a lot of lessons into the six months we were together: Put the troops first; know that morale often depends on small things; respect every person's dignity; always be ready to fight for your people; lead by example; reward performance.

On his 27th birthday, January 27, 1967, the men of Company B had planned a birthday party for Sam when they got an order for Bravo to lead an assault against an enemy regimental headquarters. Collins told what happened thereafter:

> Sam's helicopter was about to touch down at the attack point when it was ripped by enemy fire. Slugs shattered his left ankle and right leg. Another struck the left side of his head, carrying off almost a quarter of his skull. His executive officer, Lt. Dean Parker, scooped Sam's brains back into the gaping wound …
>
> Nearly a year later, in March 1968, I finally caught up with Sam. I was just getting the hang of walking with an artificial leg when I visited him at the VA Medical Center in Memphis, Tenn. Seeing him, I had to fight back the tears. The wiry, smiling soldier's soldier was blind in the left eye and partially so in the right. Surgeons had removed metal shards and damaged tissue from deep within his brain, and he had been left with a marked depression on the left side of his head. The circles under his eyes told of sleepless hours and great pain.
>
> The old clear voice of command was slower now, labored and with an odd, high pitch. I saw his brow knit as he looked through his one good eye, trying to remember. He recognized me, but believed I had served with him in Korea, his first tour of duty.
>
> Slowly, Sam rebuilt his ability to converse. But while he could recall things from long ago, he couldn't remember what he had eaten for breakfast. Headaches came on him like terrible firestorms. There was pain, too, in his legs. He had only partial use of one arm, with which he'd raise himself in front of the mirror to brush his teeth and shave.
>
> He had the support of a wonderful family, and once he was home in Wichita, his sister brought his old school sweetheart, Annette Blazier, to see him. A courtship began, and in 1972 they were married.
>
> They built a house like Sam had dreamed of — red brick, with a flagpole out front. He had developed the habit of addressing God as "Sir"

and spoke to him often. He never asked to be healed. At every table grace, he thanked God for sending him Annette and for "making it possible for me to live at home in a free country."

In 1976, Sam and Annette traveled to The Citadel for his 15th class reunion. World War II hero Gen. Mark Clark, the school's president emeritus, asked about his wounds and said, "On behalf of your country, I want to thank you for all you did." With pride, Sam answered "Sir, it was the least I could do."

Later Annette chided him gently for understating the case. After all, he had sacrificed his health and career in Vietnam. Sam gave her an incredulous look. "I had friends who didn't come back," he said. "I'm enjoying the freedoms they died for."

I visited Sam in Wichita and phoned him regularly. You would not have guessed that he lived with pain every day. Once, speaking of me to his sister, he said, "I should never complain about the pain in my leg, because B.T. doesn't have a leg." I'd seen a lot of men with lesser wounds reduced to anger and self-pity. Never a hint of that passed Sam's lips, though I knew that, every waking moment, he was fighting to live.

On October 18, 1984, after 17 years, Sam's body couldn't take any more. When we received the news of his death, a number of us from Bravo Company flew to Wichita, where Sam was to be buried with his forebears.

The day before the burial, his old exec, Dean Parker, and I went to the funeral home to make sure everything was in order. As Dean straightened the brass on Sam's uniform, I held my captain's hand and looked into his face, a face no longer filled with pain. I thought about how unashamed Sam always was to express his love for his country, how sunny and unaffected he was in his devotion to his men. I ached that I had never told him what a fine soldier and man he was. But in my deep sadness I felt a glow of pride for having served with him, and for having learned the lessons of leadership that would serve me all my life. That is why I am telling you about Samuel R. Bird and these things that happened so long ago.[184]

Noted historian and Kennedy biographer William Manchester said of Bird, he was "a lean, sinewy Kansan, the kind of American youth whom Congressmen dutifully praise each Fourth of July and whose existence many, grown jaded by years on the Hill, secretly doubt."[185] Bird's name has been added to the Vietnam Memorial, Panel 14E, Line 90, yet one more casualty of that war.

Ted Bridis came to The Citadel in the fall of 1963 on a football scholarship, a recruited linebacker on a championship team at Miami (Florida) High School. Following graduation from The Citadel in 1967, he married, had a son, and went to graduate school before joining the Army, which sent him to Vietnam in 1969. On February 22, 1970, a mortar round cost Lieutenant Bridis both legs and his right arm. For the next 43 years of his life, he refused to be defined by his injuries. His wife, Sallie, widowed when Ted died of cancer in 2013, described her husband's attitude to a newspaper reporter in 1982. "Ted is not haunted by the war. He's a happy man. He wants to forget it. It's over. Let's move on. That's his philosophy."

And move on he did. He completed a master's degree in engineering at the University of Miami and was employed as a civil engineer for the U.S. Coast Guard for 33 years. He was a certified rescue diver. He carried the Olympic torch when it passed through South Florida on its way to Atlanta in 1996 and represented the United States in the Paralympics Games in 2000 and 2004.[186]

As in all wars, there were moments of humanity that remain indelible for those affected. One such moment occurred in 1969 near Pleiku. Army Captain Michael Steele, serving as an advisor to an RVN (Republic of Vietnam) Ranger Battalion, happened upon his classmate, Army Captain Jim Probsdorfer, who was in charge of Mobile Advisory Team No. 71. At The Citadel, they had served together on regimental staff in 1966-1967. Steele needed a dozen machine guns serviced for an anticipated firefight with the Vietcong and two battalions of North Vietnamese regulars.

Together they drove to Pleiku, where they were directed to an ordinance depot commanded by Army Captain Thomas R. Dickinson, their classmate and yet another member of that same regimental staff. Three friends, classmates and now officers found themselves in the middle of a war with responsibilities none could have foreseen as college seniors a mere two years earlier.

Probsdorfer retired as a lieutenant colonel, had an exemplary second career at the Newport News Shipbuilding and Drydock Company, and went on to attain a Ph.D. Steele rose to the rank of lieutenant general, commanded the 82nd Airborne, and served as chairman of the Board of Visitors. Dickinson retired as a brigadier general, and, needless to say, Steele received not repaired machine guns but new ones.[187]

The Tet offensive put a different perspective on the war for millions of Americans. It presaged the violence to come in that year in Vietnam and the contentious rancor at home. If we were winning the war as Johnson, Westmoreland and McNamara repeatedly assured the American public, how could such coordinated attacks take place so close to areas that we had every right to feel were secured?

Ironically, by almost any measure, Tet was a military victory, with thousands of enemy casualties against modest American losses, but psychologically it was a disaster. Tet drove McNamara from the Department of Defense, and furor over the war drove Lyndon Johnson's decision not to seek a second term as president. A month later, Dr. Martin Luther King, Jr. was gunned down in Memphis. Robert Kennedy did not survive his victory in the California Democratic primary, falling victim to an assassin's bullet in Los Angeles. Chaos and tear gas ruled on the streets of Chicago as the Democratic Party nominated Hubert Humphrey for president. In a mock election held on The Citadel campus, 1,360 cadets cast votes giving Nixon a clear victory by a 2-to-1 margin.

As antiwar outrage grew louder, protests across the nation became the daily feature of the nightly news. Students with the most to lose by the war's escalation burned draft cards, occupied administration buildings, chanted "Hell, no, we won't go," pleaded to "give peace a chance," and lit candles at vigils. In April 1969, antiwar parades took place in cities from Seattle to Atlanta. In New York, a crowd estimated at between 50,000 and 100,000 marched from Bryant Park to Central Park in a downpour to demand an end to the war.[188] At Brown University, commencement speaker Henry Kissinger saw two-thirds of the graduates turn their backs as he rose to speak.[189] Soldiers began circulating radical underground newspapers in military installations across the country, including one at Fort Jackson, S.C. called *Short Timer*.[190]

By contrast, The Citadel continued as what has been called an "oasis of order,"[191] and remained a roost for hawks. In 1969, when mostly black hospital workers went on strike in Charleston, Governor McNair mobilized 5,000 National Guardsmen as a hedge against the violence that had erupted in other cities under similar circumstances.[192] During the 100 days before the labor dispute was settled, The Citadel fed and housed the National Guardsmen, with armored personnel carriers rumbling in and out of the gates during the final weeks of the 1968-1969 term.[193] Such support for the military at any other college is difficult to imagine.

Yet the reasons were obvious and understandable: (1) news coverage; (2) partiality to the military by Charleston in general and The Citadel specifically; (3) a Lost Cause mentality that equated military strength with honor and manliness.

In our internet, Googled era, fewer people recall the days when newspapers and nightly news reports on three networks served up the information ingested by most Americans. Televisions were not permitted in cadet rooms, and for members of classes in the 1960s, it was not unusual to go for weeks without seeing one. Increasingly gruesome images viewed at home by cadets' parents went largely unseen by their sons, for whom the stakes could not have been higher. Walter Cronkite, the most trusted man in America, famously turned against the war in February 1968, sending shudders through the Johnson administration and prompting the president to remark that "if I've lost Walter, I've lost middle America." Cronkite's about-face did not send shudders through the barracks, where cadets destined for that war studied.

The News and Courier and the *Charleston Evening Post* published news to cadets who read the newspapers, but always with the conservative bent that would be expected from an area as militarily dependent as Charleston was. Lastly, there were Citadel publications, *The Brigadier* and *The Shako*. Both reflected by and large the pro-government, anti-communist views of their readerships. As student protests escalated on other campuses, there would occasionally appear a verbal genuflection toward the First Amendment and the right of students in America to air their opposition. What did not appear was an analysis of that opposition — the substance of the protests rather than their form.

In theory, the Greater Issues Series would have been an ideal forum in which to present opinions contrary to the ones usually encountered in and around Charleston. General Clark initiated the series shortly after he became president in an era when McCarthyism was at its zenith and the Red Scare gripped America. Using his connections in Washington and the halls of power, he hosted President Eisenhower in 1954 and a series of generals and admirals thereafter, all of whom reflected Clark's staunch conservatism. Harris continued the series in more or less the same tradition. Any college wishing to make an emphatic statement in opposition to student protests would have secured S.I. Hayakawa as a commencement speaker. Hayakawa earned a reputation as the no-nonsense president of San Francisco State College when he confronted radicals on his campus like the Black Panthers, the Students for a Democratic Society (SDS) and the Third World Liberation Front, all demanding an immediate end to the war in Vietnam. He spoke at The Citadel's graduation in 1972 and was elected U.S. Senator from California four years later.

The man most responsible for Charleston's economic stake in the war machine was undoubtedly L. Mendel Rivers, a U.S. Congressman of South Carolina and member of the House Armed Services Committee. Rivers did for the Lowcountry what Lyndon Johnson did for Houston with the space program, turning pork barrel politics into an art form. It was said that in Charleston there were three rivers: the Ashley, the Cooper and the Mendel.[194]

In the 1960s, the military buildup in Charleston was little short of astonishing. In 1963 the Charleston Naval Base became home to the U.S. Navy Fleet Ballistic Missile Submarine Training Center, and to make certain that training could be applied locally, Rivers arranged for the construction of a dry dock for Polaris submarines at a cost of $16.5 million. Government largess escalated when Rivers became chairman of Armed Services in 1965. In that year, the Navy commissioned five ships at the Charleston Navy Yard and the following year the Charleston Air Force Base became home to 10 C-141 Starlifters, enormous transport planes that became a common sight in the skies over Charleston. In much the same way that Boeing and Volvo are doing for modern Charleston, the Navy Yard and Air Force Base attracted ancillary businesses such as DuPont, Lockheed McDonnell-Douglas and General Electric that further boosted the local economy.[195] As the war in Vietnam escalated, so did the military spending in and around Charleston.

By the mid- to late-1960s, many of The Citadel's ROTC instructors had served at least one tour in Vietnam. Most took justifiable pride in their service there. As late as 1969, platoons of cadets on physical fitness runs would sing out a cadence called by their tactical officer: "I want to be an airborne ranger, I want to live a life of danger, I want to go to Viet-Nam, I want to kill the Viet-Cong, all the way! Airborne!" Chants such as that reinforced the team spirit that a positive attitude about the war demanded. One can only imagine the reactions at civilian campuses by the late 1960s, but those reactions don't have to be imagined because Citadel graduates in law schools and medical schools serve as eyewitnesses. James T. Roe, regimental executive officer in 1967, entered Harvard Law School that fall. "Total culture shock," Roe recalls. "I came from a place where everyone supported the war to a place where hardly anyone did."[196]

News of more casualties in Vietnam brought the haunting sounds of echo taps with greater frequency, but in other ways life in and outside the barracks followed long-standing traditions. Seniors still frequented the Merchant Seamen's Club on East Bay. To "perch at the Merch" was to walk on Charleston's wilder side. It roared to life just about the time all-in checks were being conducted on campus, and admission at almost any hour was assured provided you could get past a formidable bouncer named Pompey (a/k/a "Tugboat"), who guarded the door as if activities inside were nefarious and illegal, which several were. In the wee hours, two members of the Class of 1966 and their dates stopped by for a nightcap. Pompey admitted the first couple but put up a meaty, forbidding hand to the second, reminding the cadet that shoes were part of the dress code. The cadet's explanation, that it had been a long evening, that they had consumed a goodly amount of alcohol, and that he could not remember where he left his shoes moved Pompey not at all. "No shoes, no Merch," Pompey said. The indignant cadet, not to be denied, returned to the car and removed whiskey bottles from two brown bags, tying the bags around his feet. He returned to the door triumphant, only to be told by Pompey, shaking his ample head, "Dem ain't no shoes."

Members of all classes shagged at Art's Seaside on the Isle of Palms, slipped downtown to drink beer at Big John's or across the Ashley River to Gene's Haufbrau Lounge, or walked the railroad tracks on campus to the Ark. Knobs continued to torment the lion in Hampton Park, happy to be dishing it out instead of taking it. Ordering a Long Island Ice Tea on Sunday at LaBrasca's remained a way to circumvent Charleston's loosely enforced alcohol laws.

One change met with sadness, and in some quarters anger followed with the reassignment of Lieutenant Colonel Thomas Nugent Courvoisie, USA (Ret.), "The Boo," from his position as Assistant Commandant to transportation and baggage officer. Few Citadel legends have matched The Boo's, protected and burnished by another Citadel legend, Pat Conroy, in his first book, *The Boo* (1970). A member of the Class of 1952, The Boo came to The Citadel in 1959 as assistant professor of military science. By 1961 he had been promoted to assistant commandant, a job which made him the lord high sheriff of the campus dispensing demerits, punishment orders and on occasion, forgiveness. In its dedication to him, the 1964 *Sphinx* lauded him as "a favorite with the Corps while representing the authority which must enforce its discipline."

With his ubiquitous cigar, his booming voice and his uncanny nose for B.S., The Boo sanctioned, restricted, confined, entertained, forgave and loved some 7,000 cadets in his eight-year reign as assistant commandant. A cadet's first encounter with him was like Kennedy's assassination or the landing on the moon — few forgot the time, place and nervousness they felt in his larger-than-life presence.

Infractions beyond tarnished brass required an ERW (explanation of report, written). This required the offender to explain to The Boo why there was a pet snake in his room during SMI (Saturday Morning Inspection), or why he wore a t-shirt to a formation when the uniform of the day was dress grays, or why he missed the formation entirely — all such explanations bounded by the limits of the cadet mantra, "Yes sir, no sir, no excuse, sir" on the one side and the honor code on the other. Most such ERWs were dry as toast, but creative ones might prompt The Boo to bring down upon the ERW his "Drop Dead" stamp. A cadet who appeared at his office to request a weekend pass was well advised to pass The Boo's smell test for legitimacy. Failure would bring the colonel out of his chair, around his desk, and his nose to within an inch of the supplicant's. The Boo's eyes would flash, he would shift his cigar from one corner of his mouth to the other, and he would growl in a voice that sounded like the meeting of tectonic plates deep within the earth, "Transfer to Clemson, Bubba. I'll approve it right now. I'll even pay your tuition. Now get the hell out of my office."

Cadets who toed the line, "played the game" as it was called, encountered The Boo less frequently. By the very nature of his work, most contact occurred with the misfits, the screw-ups, the out-of-steps — the boys he called his lambs. For all The Boo's ferocity, his lambs sensed he cared about them, and they were right. In some cases, he watched out for them to his detriment. For many in Jenkins Hall, the military heart of the campus and the "Tool Shed" to cadets, Boo's lambs constituted 90 percent of the discipline problems on campus. Unable to get rid of that many cadets, they got rid of The Boo instead.

Conroy said this about him:

> He was both dutiful and humane, stern and merciful, fierce and infinitely kind. The heart of a lion and the spirit of a lamb wrestled for primacy in his high-rulings over our destiny. He was the father of the Corps, the father who replaced the ones all of us had forsaken, and still needed, when we left our homes for college. Like all fathers, he was both prince and tyrant; like all fathers, there were times when he failed and betrayed us. But the mystique of Colonel Courvoisie lingers on indelibly at The Citadel, because all of us knew he could never quite stop loving us.[197]

About the time the Class of 1968 graduated, a crisis developed at the College of Charleston that carried potential ramifications for The Citadel. Most cadets and many Citadel alumni knew little about the College of Charleston, given its small student population, but all would have been surprised to learn that the college was essentially broke. Founded in 1770 as a private college, it was acquired by the city in 1837, making it the first college in the country to be operated by a municipality.[198] In 1949, the NAACP threatened a suit to compel integration. Fearing the college would be forced to accept black applicants if it depended on government funds, the city sold the school to the Trustees for $1, making it again a private institution in theory, but in reality, not much changed as the city continued an annual stipend and elected city officials continued their support through donations.[199] Eventually these sources of revenue dried up. Forced to rely on tuitions and a modest endowment to meet expenses, by the mid-1960s it was running a deficit and the endowment was being tapped to cover the shortfall.

By the spring of 1968, the endowment was gone and so were the president and the chairman of the Board of Trustees. That perfect storm of deprivation and departures produced a call to General Harris, requesting that The Citadel administer the College on a temporary basis until a permanent solution could be found. In Nan Morrison's *History of the College of Charleston*, she notes that, "When a uniformed delegation from the military college came to the College to renumber the rooms in a more 'uniform manner,' the only faculty members who did not start looking for other positions were the old guard, but they too were concerned."[200] At the request of Governor McNair, General Harris met with the College's Trustees, but by September he was able to report to the Board of Visitors that The Citadel would not be involved in any plans for the College.[201] The long-term solution for the College was to join the state system with state support, which it did in 1970.[202]

As General Harris completed his third year as president, he answered a survey sponsored by the American Institute of Management and conducted by one of its directors, Dr. Peter Sammartino of Fairleigh Dickinson University. The responses were to be anonymous, and General Harris omitted answers to several questions that might have identified him. Asked to list his "prime worries" as college president, he checked blocks for "inefficiency of administrators, skyrocketing costs and pressures of a 'rat race' schedule." His "secondary" worries included the inability of the institution to become "as outstanding as [he] should like it to be, inability to really control things, institutional politics, pressures from alumni and the community, inability to get rid of unworthy faculty members, the inability to attract outstanding students, unfavorable 'ragging' by outside press and student newspaper, wastage of money, time and energy that could be used for educational purposes."

Clearly, General Harris was at peace with his faculty and the Board of Visitors, as he listed as "no worry at all" unreasonable demands of professors and students, impending financial disaster, pressure from or interference by trustees and the difficulty of finding a commensurate position if he quit. He concluded the survey by noting that he was having a "wonderful time," had all the power he needed and that if anyone had too much power it was the state Legislature — a justified complaint in view of the school's annual jousts for adequate funding.[203]

In 1968, weary of letters from "bitter" parents who insisted their sons were being subjected to hazing, Harris did what good administrators do: He ordered a study. The Whitmire Report became the first organizational analysis of the Fourth Class System in the modern era.

Colonel James M. Whitmire, Jr., USAF, Class of 1938, served as a professor of Aerospace Studies and chaired the committee that produced the report that bears his name. The committee derived its authority from a January 30, 1968 letter from General Harris, requesting it to "review all aspects of the Fourth Class System and the Manual related thereto." Specifically, Harris asked the committee to consider in depth a system "which insures that the Fourth Classman has adequate time to prepare for his academic work, to eat three full meals a day and to sleep from Taps to Reveille" (Eat, sleep, study). Whitmire's committee was comprised of 10 cadets, three faculty members and two representatives of the commandant's department. Two members of the Committee, Whitmire and Don Bunch, were alumni. It met 17 times between February 2 and March 16, 1968, produced a 51-page report, and recorded 75 hours of meetings and hearings. It assumed the value of the Fourth Class System: "The Committee considers the Fourth Class System at the very heart of the Military College itself wielding a tremendous impact on the pride, morale and well-being of the entire Corps of Cadets." It declined to specify abuses, but their existence was implicit in the committee's work.

The study recited a laudable respect for positive leadership techniques, particularly when those techniques were exhibited by seniors, who the committee viewed as best able to influence those under them and also those with the biggest responsibility to exert that influence.

Specific recommendations included (1) automobiles not authorized for Fourth Classmen and (2) punishment PT ("group motivational activity") limited to 30 minutes after parade on Friday or the last scheduled activity on Saturday, supervised and led by seniors. Changes to two widespread practices addressed the "eat, sleep, study" priorities Harris had articulated early in his administration. To correct abuses in the push-ups inflicted on knobs, the committee recommended that the practice be restricted to open galleries within the barracks. No longer would upperclassmen ordering knobs to drop be able to extend the time in the leaning rest position with the result that the knob eventually dropped from exhaustion. Henceforth, push-ups must be administered at a normal cadence with a limit of 15 every 15 minutes. Any knob subjected to more than the prescribed number was obligated to report it to the upperclassman who ordered the drop.[204]

For alumni veterans of sweat parties, extended bracing and running the stairwells, this duty to report has the look and feel of a policy built to fail. Corporals and sergeants inclined to abuse such "disciplinary" tactics would surely be more inclined upon being told they could not legally do what they just ordered. That fictional "conversation" might go something along these lines:

> Knob: "Sir, the push-ups you have ordered exceed the limit as per the regulations."
> Corporal: "Oh? How's that?"
> Knob: "Sir, fifteen minutes have not elapsed since my last set of push-ups."
> Corporal: "Really? My mistake, wastewad. So what we need to do is kill a few minutes before you can legally perform the push-ups."
> Knob: "Sir, yes, sir."
> Corporal: "How many minutes do you figure we need to kill?"
> Knob: "Sir, five, sir."
> Corporal: "In that case, how do you feel about your ability to return to your room, put on your field jacket, overcoat and raincoat, run the fourth division in a complete lap and be back in front of me in five minutes? Think you can do that?"
> Knob: "Sir, no sir."
> Corporal: "Oh, I have faith you can, knob, so let's give it a try. Then the fifteen push-ups you give me when you get back here will be 100 percent okie-dokie."

This exchange is, of course, apocryphal, but it illustrates the futility of writing or fashioning regulations to curb the conduct of those bent on circumventing them.

The other area of abuse addressed by the committee was mess hall interrogations that, in some cases, required a knob to disgorge so much information during the meal that he had no time to engorge himself. As with push-ups, a majority of committee members seemed to believe the cure for abuse required a tweaking of the Knob Knowledge tradition that the cadets on the committee had experienced. The committee recommended that henceforth recited information must come from specified sources. Examples included the front page of the newspaper and *The Guidon*, the cadet handbook. Regurgitations of old standbys, "How's the Cow?" etc., were prohibited. Two committee members felt this woefully inadequate for real change. In the words of Don Bunch, the tennis coach and an alumni representative, the Fourth Class System should be left "at the doors of the mess hall," and all cadets allowed to eat in a relaxed environment.

The board heard Colonel Whitmire and received his report at its March 1968 meeting, which coincided with the quasquicentennial celebrations. At the board's May meeting, General Harris distributed a six-page memorandum reflecting on the recommendations made in the Whitmire Report. In general, he agreed with its findings and its proposed solutions. If complaints of abuse from parents and/or cadets had prompted him to commission the Whitmire study, those abuses had evidently diminished significantly, because Harris's letter states: "During this last semester, I have had no protest from any source that the cadets could not, in fact, study, sleep and eat a proper balanced meal."

He reserved two specific issues for further contemplation. The first was the adoption of the "detail system." According to Harris's research, a detail system whereby fourth classmen performed functions for upperclassmen existed until 1936, when General Summerall discontinued it. Harris acknowledged that such a system was currently practiced, entailing "precluded personal service" by knobs. In place of the system Harris declined to call a detail, he recommended one he termed "advisory and apprenticeship" [A&A]. Under A&A, a first classman would be obligated to assure "the general welfare of his protégée" knob. Curiously for a man of Harris's experience and background, he saw no need for the A&A he proposed to be formally reduced to regulations. He seemed to be suggesting something that in later years would be called plausible deniability. "It will not be written, and if there is any serious consequence of it, the cadets cannot claim that it was, in fact, condoned as a part of the written Fourth Class System. It will be immediately discontinued if abused."

The second Whitmire recommendation Harris took under advisement concerned whether to discontinue the plebe system prior to the end of the academic year, as was customary. To again borrow from more current terminology, Harris kicked that can down the road, deferring a decision "until I have had more experience with the changes which I have indicated to you we will accept."[205] As will be shown, he had less experience with those changes than he anticipated.

The Citadel's concern over attrition has always been driven by the fear that hazing and abuse constituted a prime explanation for departures, but in truth all colleges experience attrition in their freshmen classes. At times, financial issues drive the decision to leave. A senior from a small high school decides a large university is right for him/her, only to realize after days or weeks that it isn't. Homesickness or family disruption claims dropouts every year. According to the *U.S. News and World Report*, "Among public institutions, an average of 64.2 percent of full-time, first-time students who started school in fall 2013 returned in fall 2014, according to a report from ACT, which manages the standardized test by the same name."[206] An average national attrition for freshmen at public colleges of 35.8 percent is about double the average rate at The Citadel. Below are the rates of withdrawal at Day 270 over the 20 years beginning in 1973-1974 and the presidents for those respective years:

Academic Year	Withdrawals	Attrition Rate	President
1973-74	116	21.8% of 533	Duckett
1974-75	78	14.6% of 534	Seignious
1975-76	109	14.2% of 768	Seignious
1976-77	137	19.1% of 717	Seignious
1977-78	156	24.9% of 625	Seignious
1978-79	152	25.2% of 603	Seignious
1979-80	120	18.8% of 637	Stockdale
1980-81	167	24.5% of 682	Grimsley
1981-82	129	18.8% of 685	Grimsley
1982-83	88	13.7% of 641	Grimsley
1983-84	107	20.2% of 529	Grimsley
984-85	93	17.6% of 527	Grimsley
1985-86	88	13.4% of 657	Grimsley
1986-87	116	17.8% of 652	Grimsley
1987-88	94	14.6% of 646	Grimsley
1988-89	115	17.6% of 655	Grimsley
1989-90	101	18.9% of 535	Watts
1990-91	139	21.6% of 645	Watts
1991-92	126	20.3% of 622	Watts
1992-93	117	18.5% of 627	Watts

The academic year 1992-93 saw typical attrition, and a statistical analysis provided to the board is instructive. In the first 72 hours, 28 knobs withdrew. Of those, 19 assigned as a reason that they did not care for a military environment or a regimented lifestyle, which would seem to beg the question of why anyone who found a military environment or regimented lifestyle unsuitable would come to The Citadel in the first place. But they do, year after year, including some who have visited the campus prior to matriculation and presumably know what they're signing up for. Of the 28, four others left for medical reasons and the remaining five for miscellaneous other reasons.

After those initial 28 departures in the first 72 hours, 89 more left by the end of the academic year, bringing the total to 117. Of those 89, thirty-five cited incompatibility with the military environment/regimented lifestyle, 19 faced academic problems, 11 assigned medical issues, and for 12, financial considerations determined their decision to leave. The remaining 12 gave various reasons ("problem with cadre after reporting an infraction": 1; "changed to major The Citadel does not offer": 1; "resigned in lieu of facing Commandant's Board": 1; etc.).

The Citadel has always tracked attrition carefully, particularly freshmen attrition. There has been a tendency over the years to equate high knob attrition with overly zealous cadres or abuses within the Fourth Class System. At times, company comparisons have been made to identify those where the leadership may be falling short or the company's culture may be encouraging abuse. In its most recent rankings, *U.S. News and World Report* put The Citadel's freshman retention rate at 85 percent while at the College of Charleston it was 81 percent, at Charleston Southern 65 percent, and Coastal Carolina 64 percent.[207] As the national and regional statistics make obvious, many will leave every year for reasons unrelated to the Fourth Class System.

As the 1960s came to a close, so did Harris's tenure as president, and the circumstances of his departure remain murky. Statements made by Harris after he left office appear to conflict with the record while he was still in it. Recall that in the 1968 survey discussed earlier in this chapter, Harris reported having a "wonderful time." His relationship with the board was good, prompting his survey response that pressure from or interference by trustees was "no trouble at all." The record supports those responses. In January of that year, the board gave him a unanimous vote of confidence, praising his leadership and commending "his straightforward and uncompromising approach to the current educational program." In the board's view, he had "exceeded the normal requirements of his office."[208]

The good times appeared to extend into the following year. In September

1969, the board gave him the administrative equivalent of a standing ovation when it:

[E]xpressed exceptional confidence in the administration and person of General Harris and went on record by acclamation as favoring his remaining in the position of president of The Citadel until the latest date he would consider serving which the board understands to be July 1, 1972, and therefore the board determined that it should take no overt action toward securing a new president until near to that date.[209]

By declining to form a search committee, the board expressed its confidence that it had the benefit of Harris's services until at least July 1, 1972. But that is at odds with what Harris was reported to have told Ron Brinson of the *Evening Post* in an interview published September 4, 1970, shortly after Harris retired. There, Harris claimed he had informed the board when he was hired that he intended to remain for five years and had reminded the board of his time frame "as long as two years ago."[210] From where did the board get the impression in 1969 that Harris intended to remain until July 1, 1972? The date is of undeniable significance in view of the fact that the board went on record as delaying its search for a new president in reliance upon its understanding of Harris's intentions.

By May 1970, something clearly had changed. Harris abruptly ceased to be president, literally overnight, and the then-Dean, Major General James W. Duckett, SCM, became the president-elect. This change came five years after Harris arrived, lending credit to his *Evening Post* interview. But no search committee sought his replacement, giving credence to the board's assumption that he would be there two more years. There are no Board of Visitors minutes documenting Harris's resignation, if indeed he resigned, as seems likely.

The board minutes leading up to this change in leadership give no hint of dissension. At the March 20, 1970, meeting both General Harris, president, and General Duckett, vice president, were in attendance. Harris made numerous recommendations, all of which received positive response from the board. The closest thing to a controversy appears to have been a report by Harris of "a small minority activist group in the Cadet Corps" which had attacked *The Brigadier*. Harris expressed concern over the paper's "taste, appropriateness and liable (sic)." He requested "the board's support in the matter, which was given without dissension." Harris recommended the appointment of a committee to be called the "Committee on Customs and Traditions," and the chairman appointed such a committee. Following routine reports, selection of recipients of honorary degrees and financial resolutions, the meeting adjourned until the next scheduled meeting, May 29, 1970.[211]

The minutes for May 29, 1970 record as present General James W. Duckett, vice president, and General Hugh P. Harris, president. At the end of a meeting at which business seemed on the surface to have been routine, there is this:

> General Jennings stated that Major General James W. Duckett was elected president of The Citadel to be effective September 1, 1970 to succeed General Harris in executive session of the board on May 28, 1970, and moved that this action be approved. This was seconded by Colonel Figg and unanimously approved. Colonel Prioleau stated that in executive session concurrent with the election of General Duckett as president, a resolution was adopted to retain General Harris as special consultant to the President with full remuneration until January 1, 1971, and moved the action be approved which was seconded by Colonel Cuttino and unanimously adopted.[212]

What happened? No minutes from the May 28 executive session have been located and it is doubtful any were kept. In view of the cordial relationship that appears to have prevailed in the months leading up to the abrupt development, a logical inference is that some issue personal to Harris or a member of his family caused him to accelerate his timetable for retirement. Perhaps a health issue surfaced between the March and May meetings. If a personal concern, health or otherwise, drove his decision, he may have requested the executive session to avoid disclosure to a wider audience, and his desire for privacy is understandable. His severance package, four months at full pay, was hardly an insult, and would suggest he left on good terms. By way of farewell, General Duckett planned a reception for the Harrises at the alumni house on August 30, the day before Harris officially stepped down.[213]

If Harris' departure was on other than good terms, we are left to speculate about what caused the rift. Between the two board meetings, March and May, only two agenda items raise possibilities. The first is the Health Education and Welfare (HEW) inspection on March 31, 1970, forecast by Harris at the March board meeting. HEW reviewed the college for compliance with Title VI of the 1964 Civil Rights Act. By letter to The Citadel dated April 22, 1970, HEW reported its findings which, considering the time and place, showed progress. It noted that "Negro students are admitted to the college, and are being accorded most of the rights and privileges that are accorded other students . . ."[214] The area flagged by the investigators for improvement centered on affirmative action in recruitment of students, faculty members and employees. The board concurred in Harris's response to HEW. Given board makeup and traditional attitudes in 1970, the year Charles Foster graduated, it is unlikely the board was displeased with Harris's performance in affirmative action.

A second area of potential conflict involved a report given by Colonel Timmerman, the head of the Biology Department, on the future of The Citadel. In essence, Timmerman challenged the board to make changes in areas he called "non-vital" to the school's preservation of military education. These included admission of women, permitting female faculty, eliminating the requirement that faculty wear uniforms and doing away with fictitious military titles for professors. Harris reminded the board that he had previously reported on Timmerman's recommendations and did not agree with them. Given that coeducation was still a quarter-century away, the chances that Harris' opposition was out of step with his board would appear to be zero. He nevertheless recommended the matter be referred to the Education Action Committee for a report at the next meeting, but by that meeting, Harris was already a lame duck.

In short, the record discloses no frictions at the highest level that would account for Harris' departure on anything other than good terms. There is nothing to suggest he pressed his "escape valve" agenda, although he could have done so privately and off the record. We are left to assume either (1) Harris stuck to the five-year timetable he insisted to the *Evening Post* had been his intention all along and the board forgot or misunderstood his intention; (2) the board correctly gauged his retirement window of July 1, 1972, but some personal consideration caused him to accelerate his retirement; or (3) some off-the-record issue or issues arose that pitted him against the board.

A final oddity about the Harris departure is the presence in the Board of Visitors minutes of a certificate of appreciation for Harris. It praises him for "diversifying the curriculum, expanding the physical plant, introducing a graduate school, improving the facilities for the faculty, modernizing the campus services, introducing youth activities, initiating a faculty development program" and other accomplishments. The certificate is signed by the secretary of the board and the seal is attached, but it is not signed by Colonel John M.J. Holliday, the chairman. Presumably, Harris never got it.

In his *Evening Post* exit interview, Harris claimed to have authored, at the request of a colleague, a memorandum on his accomplishments. He listed

79 of them, including those itemized in the certificate of appreciation, which remains in the archives.[215]

The decade of the 1960s ended with a new president, persistent questions regarding The Citadel's role in the larger fabric of higher education in the Lowcountry, and cadet enrollment down to 1,770, or a mere 88 percent of capacity. If it was to survive with its traditional institutional values intact, major efforts in recruitment would be needed and the continued support of loyal alumni would be essential. The winding down of the war and eventual withdrawal of troops from Vietnam held out relief in the recruitment process, but exceptionally clear vision would be required to maintain and build upon the school's storied culture.

Chapter 7

IS THERE SOMETHING WRONG WITH THE CITADEL?

General Pollock's summary conclusion that "there is nothing wrong with The Citadel" seems at odds with a reality that could not be denied: The Corps of Cadets grew smaller each year, and by 1974 its future was legitimately in doubt with the barracks at 78 percent of capacity and a projection that at the then-current rate of decline, a mere 300 would report as knobs in 1976.[216]

The early 1970s were difficult years for the country. The war in Vietnam dragged on despite Richard Nixon's "secret plan" to end it. Protests continued as soldiers returning from Southeast Asia were scorned by some of the very people they felt they were fighting for. Henry Kissinger stayed in Paris to negotiate an honorable peace that to most of the country would ultimately look more like surrender. The public's cynicism over events abroad only worsened with Watergate and Nixon's resignation. Colleges banned ROTC and those that didn't saw their programs undersubscribed or shunned. Such a climate was unlikely to produce banner years at military schools, as General Duckett learned early in his administration.

As with the Harris departure, the record is murky on the particulars of Duckett's elevation to the presidency, but that may say more about the board's *modus operandi* of holding their cards close to the vest than about any intrigue or controversy surrounding his selection. However, from the board's failure to form a search committee in the wake of Harris's resignation it may be inferred that it viewed Duckett as an interim choice, an inference supported by the fact that in the spring of 1972 it asked Army Lieutenant General George M. Seignious to become president. That request had the backing of Governor John C. West, Seignious's classmate of 1942. As reported by Seignious, "[t]he South Carolina Legislature was extremely unhappy about 400 empty beds at The Citadel as a result of the anti-military feeling that was so rampant in our country, and some were threatening to close The Citadel." At the time, Seignious was director of the Joint Chiefs of Staff, having been chosen by the chairman for the position. Federal law required him to remain as director until June 1974, a restriction that forced him to decline The Citadel's offer.[217]

The overture to Seignious signaled the board's interest in finding new leadership. When rumors surfaced in the fall of 1972 that General William Westmoreland was being considered as the next president, board chairman Colonel John Holliday expressed amazement. "Gen. Duckett is our president and we are not considering anyone else," he said. When asked if Westmoreland had ever been considered for such a position, Holliday said, "Way back, about 20 generals were being considered before we decided on Gen. Duckett."[218] Colonel Holliday pointedly omitted consideration of General Seignious a mere six months earlier.

One of Duckett's first acts was to reorganize the Corps of Cadets from a regiment into a brigade, but tradition is a persistent thing. When Cadet Colonel Timothy C. Miller became Regimental Commander in 1972-1973, he sealed the status of James P. Johnson (1970-1971) and Terrence M. Potter (1971-1972) as the only two brigade commanders in the school's history.

Shortly after he became president, Duckett welcomed the Navy as a new ROTC alternative to the Army, Air Force and Marines.[219] He was also called upon to deal with a problem that had not theretofore surfaced at the college but would prove trying for him and his successors: Drugs. The unwelcomed November 4, 1970 headline in the *Evening Post* announced "3 Cadets Charged with Drug Sales," the contraband in question being amphetamines and the arrested offenders all seniors. State Drug Inspector Joseph Hodge commended the school for its strong approach to the problem. "If the cooperation received from The Citadel had been received from others," he noted, "the drug problem would not be as bad as it is today."[220]

As Dean Duckett, his focus had been necessarily academic. As President Duckett, that focus enabled the school to earn maximum accreditation from SACS, the Southern Association of Colleges and Schools, as well as from the Engineering Council of Professional Development.[221] He could claim with pride that if there was something wrong with The Citadel, it wasn't to be found in its academic offerings. His major hurdle remained: The future of the college depended upon recruitment of new students and retention of those already enrolled.

The challenge presented by falling enrollment was hardly unique to The Citadel. A 1973 *U.S. News and World Report* study found 600,000 college vacancies nationwide. Institutions with far larger resources scrambled to fill their dorms and classes. Recruiters from Skidmore College in New York visited 276 high schools in 12 states, including California.[222] Notre Dame employed 50 full-time recruiters. One who traveled to Europe in search of potential enrollees found 52 U.S. colleges already there and pitching their schools. During this same period, The Citadel employed one full-time recruiter and one half-time recruiter with no secretarial support.

If schools like Notre Dame struggled to lure students to civilian campuses, enticing them to enter The Citadel proved doubly difficult. In a 1972 letter to Board Chairman Holliday addressing recruitment, General Duckett lamented that the nation remains in an anti-military, anti-discipline era. Few would have disputed Duckett's assessment, and fewer still would have held him responsible for the anti-war zeitgeist during his tenure as president.

Not long after General Duckett became president, his administration confronted an issue that had vexed his predecessor. The easy ways around Whitmire's limitation on push-ups had been found and exploited, again prompting concerns over hazing. Duckett initially eliminated push-ups as part of the Fourth Class System, then reinstated them until the Commandant, Colonel William Crabbe, Jr., could oversee another review. The 1972 committee — comprised of cadets, administrators, academics and representatives of the Commandant's office — found itself in lock step with the Whitmire group as to the importance of the Fourth Class System in molding whole men — Citadel men. The "whole man" concept is attributed to General Clark, who used the phrase often as a shorthand for molding men of character in honor and in truth.[223]

As usual, the devil was in the specifics. The values held out as sacrosanct — eat, sleep, study — were still being infringed upon with a frequency unacceptable to the committee. To address the problem of newly empowered corporals with more zeal than judgment, the authority to punish, including push-ups, was limited to juniors and seniors on cadre. To boost morale, ranked cadets were given more responsibility and TAC officers were instructed to "let the Corps run the Corps."

A humorous illustration of this took place in 1969. Regimental Commander David Goble, currently The Citadel's head librarian, stood to address the Corps at the evening mess. Cadets being cadets, a chorus of turkey "gobbles" arose from the Corps as "Goble" stood at the microphone. A TAC officer at Goble's mess ordered him to call the Corps to attention. In Goble's judgment, that would have been a mistake, prolonging the harmless derision, so he stood his ground until the mess became quiet. Thereafter, the Commandant, Army Colonel James B. Adamson, informed Goble that the TAC wanted him busted for disobedience to a direct order. As told to Goble, the TAC had threatened to leave the school unless Goble was reduced in rank. Goble graduated as Regimental Commander, while the TAC's fate is unknown. If the Corps is to run the Corps, Goble and other cadets in authority must be able to make their own decisions, even when a commissioned Army officer would have made a different choice.[224]

While giving lip service to the minority recommendation of the Whitmire Committee — to leave the Fourth Class System at the mess hall doors — the committee declined to take that radical step. In short, the conclusions reached by the Crabbe committee did not significantly differ from those reached by Whitmire's, and attrition rates continued to follow traditional patterns. Within the Corps itself, just as many cadets felt the system had become too easy as it had become too harsh.

Declining college enrollment followed a national trend, but with local repercussions. Once again, an idea surfaced that The Citadel wanted no part of: a so-called "University of Charleston." The concern stemmed from the prospect that a university system purportedly making better use of physical resources and local expertise would sacrifice the school's uniqueness on an altar of theoretical efficiency. As noted earlier, the idea had been around for some time, with The Citadel keeping a wary eye on developments. But the proposal seemed to acquire added momentum when, in 1973, Charleston County's Legislative Delegation voted unanimously to call for a new state-supported university in the greater metropolitan area. In Columbia, the State College Board of Trustees, which administered the College of Charleston after it became state-supported, endorsed a "University of Charleston," envisioned as "an Oxford-type grouping offering graduate and undergraduate studies in the arts and sciences to include dentistry and medicine."[225] In fact, the General Assembly did pass legislation allowing state colleges to designate themselves as universities beginning July 1, 1992. The College of Charleston did so for the purpose of awarding graduate degrees, but the option held no appeal to The Citadel, which remained "The Military College of South Carolina.[226]

Smaller knob classes, uncertain state support and debates about the college's role in an anti-military era begged the question raised by General Pollock: Was there something wrong with The Citadel?

By 1974 that question seems to have been answered rather forcefully: Yes, there were many things wrong, and they didn't originate on Duckett's watch, according to critiques received by the Board of Visitors at its March meeting.

They reviewed a report from their own recruiters (by then there were three as opposed to 1.5 in 1972) and an assessment from Marine Lieutenant Colonel Harrison W. Kimbrell, Class of 1954.[227]

The report identifies them by name (Captain Hanna, Lieutenants Moore and Kennedy) and by qualifications: recent Citadel graduates who have "relatives in the Corps who represent a considerable portion of The Citadel's recent history." Their most obvious strength as observers came from their service as "front-line troops in the recruitment battle."

They reached their conclusions after many months of observation and discussion with cadets, alumni from multiple eras, faculty, staff and potential cadets. After establishing that, in their judgment, there was a market for those seeking a challenging military education (albeit a diminished market due to Vietnam), and that they, the recruiters, were effective salesmen for the school, they identified the weak link in the chain: The Corps of Cadets itself. Put in generic terms, they concluded that there was demand for the product, that they were competent and aggressive salesmen for that product, but defects in the product, the Corps, accounted for reduced applications and enrollment. In their words, "The declining enrollment at The Citadel is a direct result of, and in direct proportion to, the strength, pride, values, integrity and discipline in the Corps of Cadets."

When, in their view, did a "policy of adulterating, changing, and weakening the demands of our system" begin? Answer: the Harris administration.

What specifically, in their view, was wrong with "the product"? They itemized seven shortcomings: (1) the Honor System, which "has become weak, legalistic and held in contempt by too many cadets." (2) "The complete elimination of the rigor and ordeal of the Plebe System with a consequent loss of class solidarity, and pride in accomplishment"; (3) a non-functioning class system; (4) a double standard in the administration of punishment; (5) a "suitcase" leave policy that results in five-days-a-week cadets; (6) excessive civilian clothes privileges; and (7) sloppy, indifferent wearing of the uniform.

In the opinion of the recruiters, the school had become hopelessly conflicted, wanting and claiming an eliteness felt by prior generations while at the same time tolerating a "do your own thing" ethos. The growing plethora of civilians — "Special Students, Day Students, Veteran Students, Night Students in the MAT, MBA and undergraduate programs" — was reducing cadets to second-class citizens on the campus, leading inevitably to the fate suffered by Texas A&M, Clemson and Virginia Tech. The cure for this cancer (a metaphor employed earlier in the report) was to return to old values under new leadership.

Coupled with the report of the recruiters was Lieutenant Colonel Kimbrell's assessment. In his senior year, Kimbrell served as a cadet captain, DMS, a Summerall Guard, and was voted "most dignified" by his classmates. His was a significantly longer and more detailed analysis but even more blunt in its conclusions, beginning with his contention as to when the school began going to hell. "It is universally accepted that The Corps commenced its fall to its present level in the mid-1960s." In other words, once General Harris took over from General Clark, "The Corps decay of integrity began."

Kimbrell's claim of universal acceptance is open to question, as many members of the classes from 1966 to 1974 would have bristled at the notion that they were either parties to or victims of a decay of integrity. At the time of his assessment, Kimbrell was a TAC officer in the Commandant's Department. His class, 1954, graduated immediately prior to Clark's first year as president. According to the letter of board member Colonel Frank Mood transmitting the report and the assessment to the board, the recruiters and Kimbrell reached their conclusions independently, though they are remarkably similar. Kimbrell's assessment was entitled "The Diminished Citadel Image and the Cadet Enrollment Crisis."

To Kimbrell, night students then attending classes were the camel's nose under the tent and presaged the demise of the college as a military institution. The fates of Virginia Tech, Texas A&M, Pennsylvania Military Academy and Norwich awaited The Citadel unless this trend was arrested and consideration of increased access for civilians ceased. He claimed it was commonly acknowledged that empty beds in the barracks were a direct result of a weakened Corps, which had been allowed to abandon the values, policies and traditions of Generals Summerall and Clark. *"Integrity, excellence and discipline have lost their meaning."* Kimbrell listed nine culprits, several of which echoed those cited by the recruiters, including an ineffective honor system, a broken class system and liberal leave policies (a "four-days-a-week military college"). Unlike the recruiters, he came down hard on faculty "hostile to the existence of The Corps," labeling them "disciples of dissidence." Some of those disciples, Kimbrell alleged, had selfish motives, regarding "growth as progress, and with growth and progress they envision more students (not cadets), larger departments, more jobs and bigger salaries in a vicious cycle."

He had equally harsh words for administrators who "have demonstrated neither the character nor courage in setting the example."

When it came to Kimbrell's co-workers, the tactical officers, he offered a dual assessment: Many suffered from the same malaise infecting the Corps, and for the same reasons, while some, he admitted, "are here enjoying study, golf and hunting, displaying the same lack of interest and association with The Corps that many faculty do."

He refused to attribute declining enrollment to college-age youth "and its culture of dissatisfaction, its sexual permissiveness, its designed sloppiness and no draft status." For Kimbrell the problems and their solutions lay not with the character of those being recruited but rather within the walls of the institution. Too many faculty and administrators gave lip service to the school's mission without supporting it with actions and policies. Without naming names, he claimed that in the hiring and retention of faculty, the school had "perhaps not been parochial enough," insisting that "it is essential that only those of positive Citadel attitudes and appreciation for The Corps of Cadets be employed and continued."

In addition to echoing many of the recommendations made by the recruiters, Kimbrell believed that a revitalized alumni association was a key ingredient to renewal of the old Citadel values and surviving the economic crisis threatened by declining enrollment. He praised the Foundation but suggested fewer of its resources be directed to supporting the faculty. His silver bullet for lagging revenue was allocation by the Armed Forces of 300 additional four-year ROTC scholarships with the Army, Air Force and Navy programs each earmarking 100 for Citadel cadets. Between the school's historic contributions to the Armed Forces and several influential alumni in high office, Kimbrell seemed certain a financial crisis could be weathered with the additional scholarships.[228]

While the recruiters and Kimbrell went out of their way to avoid pointing fingers at anyone in the boardroom, the implications for the man in charge, General Duckett, were obvious, and that March meeting at which he was present must have caused him some discomfort. The problems being focused on had been identified for some time, with the office of the Commandant drawing fire from cadets and others. Duckett acknowledged as much in a 1971 speech to the Corps at the start of the spring semester.

"I know some of you are disenchanted by what you consider inconsistencies in the actions of the commandant, the chain of command, or the TACS." He then launched into a defense of his Commandant, Colonel Hood. "The Commandant has been accused of being insensitive and inflexible, of not listening, of not being in tune with the changes in the Armed Forces regulations or changes in the outside world." He then itemized some changes within the gates, expressed as rhetorical questions. "Colonel Hood eliminated release from quarters at 22:30, delayed Taps until 24:00 hours and strictly forbade visitors, meetings and drills during ESP so as to insure uninterrupted study time. Was this insensitive? ... You have noticed that you have more free weekends and less drill and parades. We will continue this policy. Is this insensitive? Colonel Hood has been the leading proponent in the adoption of the blazer for off-campus wear and for more liberal rules concerning its use. He is right now heading up a committee to review all the rules by which you live and to eliminate those that are not essential to the making of a Citadel man — in other words — to get rid of the Mickey Mouse. Is that insensitive or inflexible?"

Duckett obviously supported such changes, but these and others would draw the fire of the recruiters and Kimbrell three years later. And if these particular adjustments to "the rules by which you live" were not the culprits per se, they contributed to the slackness and malaise that explained declining enrollment.

Duckett's 1971 speech also alluded to the pride the Corps needed to feel in itself:

> Now what are the real gut issues at The Citadel? A half an inch of hair? No. If whether a girl likes you or not depends on sideburns — you haven't much else going for you. Enforcement of regulations which have a purpose? No. A reinforcement of pride in yourself and in your Corps? Yes. An increase in the Corps of new cadets who are fully qualified in every respect? Yes. Do we strive to reach all young men who would adapt to our unique system of a quality education in a proud military atmosphere? Yes. Do we continue our system at The Citadel to foster patriotism and love of God and country and make no apology to anyone for it? Yes.

He returned to this theme in 1974 as declining enrollment reached a crisis and critics contended that the Corps had lost its way. He agreed with the recruiters and with Kimbrell that only the Corps could save the Corps. Two months earlier, on January 25, 1974, Duckett had published an open letter to the Corps in *The Brigadier*. In it, he sought the Corps' help in procurement. "Proud as you are of your college, Corps, class and company, I am amazed that you cadets have not shouldered the burden of bringing your Corps up to strength." That seems a fairly remarkable statement coming from the college president, and it takes little imagination to anticipate the response from the typical cadet:

"Let me understand this. I'm expected to rise at 6:15 or earlier, meet all formations, attend all classes, maintain my personal appearance, carry out any command or leadership responsibilities that have been entrusted to me, make suitable progress toward graduation, and you are amazed that I haven't 'shouldered the burden' of filling the barracks? With all due respect, sir, I thought that was YOUR job."

In hindsight, some societal shifts have been blamed for drops in enrollment, calling into question Kimbrell's contention that the solutions were to be found inside The Citadel's walls. The end of the draft in 1973 played a major role in decisions by high school students as to whether to begin college immediately. Until then, enrollment in college assured deferment for as long as a student remained academically proficient. When military deferment ceased to be a factor, some with the means to do so spent a year abroad or traveling, postponing their higher education for a year or longer. Those without such means went to work to save money for college or opted for lower cost community colleges closer to home. Escalating tuitions and fees discouraged many. One college administrator noted a fundamental shift in the attitudes toward education among young people, particularly among upper and middle class white Americans, many of whom questioned the value of a college degree when weighed against not only its financial costs but four years of opportunity costs as well.

Everyone acknowledged that the war had taken a toll on the military as a career and therefore the number of young men who wanted to begin that career at a challenging military college. But that toll may have been underestimated by the school's recruiters, who pointed out that a mere 12 freshmen from each state were required to meet the recruiting quota. They chose to assume there were enough young men still interested because to assume otherwise, they said, would force the decision to "parade and retire the colors, disband the Corps and close the gates."[229] Which is, for all relevant purposes, what Pennsylvania Military Academy did when it opened its gates to civilians wide enough to keep them open. In a study performed for PMC by an opinion research firm and shared with Lieutenant Moore in 1971, only two-tenths of 1 percent of the high school seniors surveyed expressed a willingness to attend a non-service academy military college, throwing into doubt the ability of The Citadel to attract those 12 freshmen from Pennsylvania, let alone Idaho and Wyoming.[230]

Hindsight also lends some credibility to the recruiters and Kimbrell. In

October 1967, General Tucker, then Commandant, was conducting a tour for some dignitaries when a cadet company marched by. Tucker reported being aghast at what he and they witnessed: an officer with no head gear, many out of step, one or two with their caps on the backs of their heads "with great shocks of hair showing on their foreheads."[231] In 1974 The Citadel received 1,033 applications for the incoming class, a mere 117 more than VMI's 916. In that VMI's student body stood at 1,108 compared with a 34 percent larger enrollment at The Citadel,[232] mathematical extrapolation would suggest an applicant pool of almost 1,400. Many variables could explain why the applicant pool was so similar in spite of The Citadel's size advantage, but one potential explanation is the very laxness the recruiters and Kimbrell railed against.

If, as Kimbrell posited, the Corps suffered a slacking malaise, its sense of loyalty remained intact, as it demonstrated in 1973, the year The Boo suffered a major heart attack. After surgery and recuperation at North Charleston's Naval Hospital, he came home to his campus quarters. The rumor mill ground out reports that he was dying, as in fact he nearly did. For the five years prior to this life-threatening illness, he pined away in the obscurity of the baggage warehouse, invisible to the cadets he loved and, by his own sad account, forgotten by them as well. Or so he thought.

After a Friday parade, he learned otherwise. Marching off Summerall Field as they had done for decades, the men of First Battalion took an unusual series of turns, followed by the rest of the Corps. They marched between Third and Fourth, past the infirmary, then to The Boo's home, where their "eyes right" was returned by a crisp salute from a man whose doctors would have said should be in bed instead of standing at attention. Those same doctors would no doubt claim credit for the additional 33 years of life The Boo enjoyed, but they were only partly responsible. By this singular act of devotion and respect, the Corps provided the kind of medicine not found in hospitals: a balm for the spirit. Would The Boo credit the Corps with saving his life? We'll know when we get to that Lesesne Gate in heaven, which he always claimed he would be guarding.[233]

The year 1973 was also notable for something no one would have foreseen at the time, and it may be unprecedented at any comparable college football program. Red Parker had been hired away by Clemson at the end of the 1972 season. To replace him, The Citadel hired Bobby Ross, a 1959 VMI grad who captained the football team there in his senior year and was a member of two teams that won the Southern Conference championship in an era when VMI was a football powerhouse.

As scheduling would have it, The Citadel opened at Clemson in 1973, pitting the new coach against the old one. Clemson won 14-12, however by all accounts, the Bulldogs gave them all they could handle and more. But the remarkable back-story is the staff Bobby Ross had assembled. His assistants that year were: Cal McCombs, Citadel Class of 1967, who later coached as an assistant at the Air Force Academy before becoming head coach at VMI; Ralph Friedgen, who became head coach at Maryland for many years; Frank Beamer, who went on to win 280 college games as head coach at Murray State and Virginia Tech, and is the sixth winningest coach in Division 1 football; Jimmye Laycock, who became head coach at William & Mary in 1980 and as of this writing is still there; and Charlie Rizzo, who is still active with coaching stints at TCU, Rice and the University of Houston. Later, even as a head coach in the NFL with San Diego and Detroit, it is doubtful Ross had a more capable staff than he assembled in Charleston in 1973.

The 534 knobs who entered in 1974 made up the smallest class in years, and while still well above a number that would have confirmed the dire projection of 300 by 1976, it reinforced the conclusion that enrollment was heading in the wrong direction at an accelerating rate. Yet a mere one year later, applications were up almost 29 percent, to 1,426, and the incoming class numbered 762.[234] What had changed?

For one thing, there was a new president. Duckett tendered his resignation in January 1974, effective August 1, and the Board of Visitors elected Lieutenant General George M. Seignious, USA (Ret.), to replace him.[235]

Seignious's inability to accept the board's offer in 1972 didn't keep him from working on the school's behalf. His help took the form most needed: bodies in the barracks, and the tuitions that followed them. His Pentagon duties brought him into contact with representatives of the Iranian government. At the time, Iran spent billions of dollars on U.S. weapons and, aside from Israel, could be counted on as perhaps our most steadfast ally in the Middle East. Some of those billions went for ships, but the Iranian Navy lacked the personnel to operate them. That led to the idea of enrolling Iranian midshipmen in schools where they could acquire the education and skills then lacking. Seignious knew just the place to send them. Twenty-six of them enrolled in the fall of 1973 despite the fact that in the two prior years they had numbered only four. Twelve more arrived in 1974, and in 1975 the stream became a flood as 50 Iranian midshipmen became knobs.[236]

As welcome as their tuition was, the Iranians caused problems. For one thing, they knew little English. In engineering, business and naval science courses, professors found themselves teaching not only their subject matters but basic English as well. Colonel L.K. Himmelright, head of the Engineering Department, said, "You can't send a boy to engineering school who doesn't know English. I think a lot of them didn't even know what civil engineering was when they came here." He put the failure rate at 75 percent and recommended they take a year at an American prep school before coming to The Citadel.

But the Iranians had no trouble mastering American luxuries and dissipations, which created additional tensions. The midshipmen received an astounding $1,100 per month allowance, permitting them to live like minor Iranian princes, driving Jaguars, renting fine apartments in Charleston and enjoying a lifestyle that would never have been permitted in their own country. One apartment manager complained of loud parties and "hot and cold running women." "Spoiled" is a term reserved for only a few in the traditional Corps of Cadets, but these Iranians developed a spoiled sense of entitlement that seeped into their classrooms and the barracks. Based on his own observations and reports from his professors, Himmelright commented on their poor attitudes. "Many of the Iranians wouldn't study the assignments and expected the professors to do just about everything for them." Their lavish lifestyles and sense of elitism prompted a request to their government that their monthly allowance be reduced, after which they received $350 per month, with the rest escrowed in a Washington, D.C. bank.

And then there was the Fourth Class System. To say the Iranians were unprepared for it would be rank understatement. Corporals screamed insults at them, calling them "camel drivers." Worse, they insulted the knob's sister and mother, which in Iran was punishable by death. The Iranians brought a shy modesty that made the open communal showers in the barracks unnerving. The school's advisor to foreign students, Major Lynn DeMille, said, "The fact that they survived at all is remarkable."[237] On the other hand, many did more than simply survive. Some proved able students. Easa J. Sayadchi became the first Iranian cadet captain in 1978, serving on First Battalion staff with a 3.48 cumulative GPA.[238]

For all the problems that the Iranian students created in Charleston, it seems clear their government enthused over the program, inquiring as to how many of its students the school could accept in 1976. For the first time a concern was expressed that the number of foreign students might be rising to an unacceptable level. A contingent of more than 100 Iranians could impede the school's ability to accept all qualified South Carolinians, whose representation in the Corps still hovered around a disappointing 40 percent.

Some publicly questioned the school's education of foreign students at the expense of South Carolina taxpayers. By its March meeting, the board felt compelled to formulate a policy covering future admissions and dispersion within the Corps. Thereafter, foreign students from all countries were not to exceed three per company, with foreign students from any one country limited to one per company. Beginning with the class entering in the fall of 1978, foreign students from any one country could not exceed six. Graduation and attrition could be counted on to reduce the number to a more modest level, and no one would be asked to leave.[238]

In September 1979, four freshmen from Iran reported, bringing the number of Iranians in the Corps to 53. But on November 4, 1979, Muslim students in Tehran overran the U.S. Embassy, taking 54 American hostages. The Carter Administration took a number of actions in response, including freezing Iranian assets in U.S. banks and expelling diplomatic personnel. As 26 of the Iranians at The Citadel were present on diplomatic visas, they were deported.[239] In the fall of 1980, no Iranians matriculated and none in the upper classes returned. The captives in Tehran remained imprisoned for 444 days, and were released minutes after Ronald Reagan was sworn in as president on January 20, 1981.

With assurances from the highest echelons of the Army that he would receive a fourth star, Seignious faced a tough decision in returning to his alma mater. It came down to a host of personal considerations. He and his wife, Anne, had just purchased a new home on Hilton Head Island and their son Chip would be entering The Citadel in the fall of 1974. Anne was born in Charleston and they both loved the city as well as The Citadel. The Army's loss would be The Citadel's gain.

Seignious was a Citadel man to the soles of his highly polished shoes. In a personal memoir written for his 11 grandchildren, he said, "In 1938, I entered The Citadel in Charleston, South Carolina. This act changed my life to a degree that is still indescribable. Life at that institution became the centerpiece of my goals, my dreams, my character, my personality, my mind, my faith, my friends — in essence, my total being."

As a member of the famed Class of 1942, he rose to become battalion commander, earned gold stars, was voted by his classmates as Best Senior Officer and was the only member of his class to receive a regular Army commission upon graduation. He was known to his friends as "Obbe." The nickname, according to Seignious family lore, had been passed down from his grandfather, his namesake, who while in business attended a social event in Charleston and recited from memory the Book of Obadiah in the Bible.[240]

Following officer basic training at Fort Benning, Seignious was assigned to the newly formed 10th Armored ("Tiger") Division, which trained at Fort Benning and Fort Gordon. His unit deployed to Cherbourg, France in August 1944. Seignious served in the Plans and Operations Division's G3 section with the rank of captain. The 10th Armored Division was in the 20th Corps, of General George Patton's Third Army. Seignious saw combat duty when his unit crossed into Germany and captured Heidelberg, Brucksal and Crailsheim. On April 2, 1945, during a German counterattack at Unterowisheim, he braved intense fire to coordinate three combat teams in a successful repulse of the German forces, which earned him a Silver Star. The Tigers were fighting south to the Alps to link up with combat units coming north from Italy when the war in Europe ended.

He lived in Heidelberg as an aide to Lieutenant General Geoffrey B. Keyes. In early December 1945, Keyes invited Seignious to accompany him to dinner at General Patton's residence in Bad Homburg. Seignious declined, as he had planned to go pheasant shooting. Upon his return from the shoot, he learned from Keyes that Patton had been in a serious auto accident that morning and taken paralyzed to a hospital in Heidelberg. Mrs. Patton arrived, and Seignious became, in effect, her aide-de-camp:

> I accompanied her daily to prayers in a little and cold Episcopal church in Heidelberg where she would kneel on my heavy Army overcoat. She spent almost all of her waking moments by General Patton's side. On the 21st of December, as was General Keyes's custom, we stopped at the hospital to see General Patton and to pick up Mrs. Patton to take her up to the house for dinner. She declined that night, saying she thought she would just eat at the hospital mess hall and return to General Patton's side and read to him before he fell asleep. We departed and went to the house, but upon arrival the telephone was ringing and it was the head of the hospital saying that General Patton had taken a severe turn for the worst and that we may lose him. General Keyes and I hurriedly returned to the hospital. General Keyes went directly to General Patton's room and I went to get Mrs. Patton at the mess hall. She quietly took my arm and we went back to the room. Just as she arrived, he died.[241]

One year later, Beatrice Patton wrote to Seignious thanking him for "that Sunday you took me to communion and all the days that followed."[242] By then, Seignious had joined F.P. Seignious & Sons, the family cotton business in Kingstree, South Carolina. His father, Francis Pelmoin Seignious, founded the firm in 1926. It also employed his brother, Pel. In Summerall Chapel on April 5, 1947, he married Anne Ficken Padgett, a war widow whose infant son, Richard Padgett, would become a member of the Class of 1968. Seignious missed Army life, and shortly after being married he returned to active duty.[243]

In a remarkably short time, Obbe Seignious proved he was the right man for the Citadel job at the right time. At his inauguration as president, he asked the large crowd, which included former presidents Clark, Harris and Duckett, to imagine being present in 1843 when the old guard, the Washington Light Infantry, gave way to the new guard, the new cadets.

In your mind's eye picture a winter's night of uncertainty by the new guard and a trained, seasoned and confident old guard – and imagine with me the general orders passed to the new guard:

> **General Order No. 1** — You are to be men of learning, seek the truth.
> **General Order No. 2** — You are patriots, guard your state and nation's heritage and resources.
> **General Order No. 3** — You are men to be trusted, you cannot lie, cheat or steal.
> **General Order No. 4** — You are responsible, thus you are to be accountable for your deeds.
> **General Order No. 5** — You are special and have been given great opportunity to learn and develop, thus much will be expected of you.
> **General Order No. 6** — You are Citadel men, cherish and preserve it.[244]

Seignious unveiled his priorities to the Board of Visitors shortly after taking over. To the surprise of no one on the board, he listed low enrollment and uncertain finances as the major challenges. Key to the school's revival was his program named "Spirit of '76," a fund-raising effort that went hand-in-glove with the country's Bicentennial two years away. He acknowledged that renovation of the barracks was essential to providing a better living environment for cadets, beginning with Barracks No. 1. He came down hard on shaved heads and physical abuse, pointedly mentioning the Junior Sword Drill as a culprit. He updated the board on his efforts to secure more ROTC scholarships, Kimbrell's most immediate solution to the funding woes.[245]

Seignious reunited with his classmate, Governor John West, to pose for a photo with the actor Peter Falk when Universal Studios came to campus to film an episode of the popular TV series "Columbo" in 1974, shortly after Seignious assumed his presidency. West reportedly came to confirm the state's interest in luring the film industry to South Carolina.[246] As will be seen in Chapter 9, such "on location" productions can feature drama not found in the scripts.

Shortly after Seignious took over as president, Charleston Mayor Palmer Gaillard announced that he would not seek a fifth term. Many in the city couldn't remember a time when Gaillard wasn't mayor, and while the occupant of the Charleston's highest elected office was of only passing interest to most inside Lesesne Gate, it was of intense interest to Joseph P. Riley Jr., Citadel Class of 1964. Riley had been a cadet lieutenant in F Company, a Summerall Guard and a member of the Catholic choir. He sold ads for *The Sphinx*. By his senior year he served as Commodore of the Citadel Yacht Club. When asked what had drawn him to The Citadel, he cited its devotion to duty and honor. While he may have been a model cadet, he was not a perfect one, and even managed to run afoul of The Boo when he returned from a weekend leave on Sunday with a pass that expired on Saturday. For that oversight, a venial sin by Citadel standards, he was demoted and awarded tours. When The Boo sought to mitigate the punishment by forgiving the remaining un-walked tours, Riley kept walking, determined to fulfill the punishment order, duty and honor intact.[247]

Riley served six years in the South Carolina Legislature before declaring his candidacy for mayor. Charleston needed a visionary at the helm with as much unity of purpose as could be mustered. Scars from the city's civil rights struggles of the 1960s threatened to drive a wedge between the white and black populations. Elected and non-elected black politicians demanded a greater voice in the city's future. Residents of West Ashley and James Island, annexed by the city under Gaillard's administration, had competing agendas. A consensus among voters, black and white, was that the next mayor needed to be a unifier.

Joe Riley filled that need. His priorities for the city included economic development, historic preservation, better schools and housing, an attack on crime and more inclusive hiring practices at City Hall. He was only 32 when he beat three other candidates to become mayor. Charleston would have no other mayor for the next 40 years, a run unprecedented in modern American politics. At his victory party at the municipal auditorium, which was renamed for Gaillard, nine reelections couldn't have been foreseen by even his most ardent supporters, and certainly not by Riley himself.[248]

Like Riley, Seignious also brought a vision, and after a mere seven months on the job he reported to the Advisory Committee of the Board of Visitors the success of his efforts. The Spirit of '76 initiative, supplemented by a contribution from the Citadel Development Foundation, might produce as many as 150 scholarships, each in the amount of $1,976, to freshmen who would report in the fall as members of the Class of 1979. Among the 700 expected in the fall were 50 Iranian midshipmen who would receive Corps indoctrination and English-language training that summer. He reported on extensive efforts to secure the Kimbrell solution, but with the exception of the Navy, the Armed Services were convinced that they lacked the legal authority to allocate ROTC scholarships in a way more advantageous to The Citadel.[249]

By October 1975 the pessimism so evident 18 months earlier had been banished. Enrollment was up 44 percent, with 768 freshmen. Recruiting targeted at those who missed appointments to West Point proved especially effective, with 61 freshmen directly linked to those efforts. Freshmen attrition was down to 5.7 percent from the prior year's 6.3 percent and far below the 11.4 percent experienced in 1973. His April forecast had been spot on: Spirit of '76 had raised $176,000 from alumni and friends and $89,000 from development foundation, which provided scholarships to 148 incoming freshmen, most of whom were from South Carolina.

Unwilling to let the Armed Services have the last word on the Kimbrell solution, the college enlisted the aid of South Carolina's senior senator, Strom Thurmond, who agreed to sponsor a bill that would authorize the preferential allocation of ROTC scholarships.[250]

Early in his administration, Seignious was reminded that some time-honored Corps habits continued, like spray painting the campus of the next Bulldog opponent. In September, some spirited cadets (that Wofford College would have called vandals) did $750 worth of damage, and in November a cadre of nine cadets paid a social call on Furman to the tune of $650 and 100 tours. Whether due to such exuberance within the Corps or the talent of the football team, seasonal attendance at Johnson Hagood Stadium reached 110,000, double the 1974 crowds.

In what was decidedly not a Corps tradition, Cadet Bentley Adams III, Class of 1976, decided it would be a good idea to form a chapter of the National Organization for the Reform of Marijuana Laws (NORML) on campus, and he sued the school in Federal Court when The Citadel, not surprisingly, denied his request. The judge, ruling for Adams, relied on a case brought against Virginia Commonwealth University by the Gay Alliance of Students seeking to register as a student organization. In declining the organization's application, the VCU Board of Visitors denied it privileges extended to registered clubs, including inclusion in a student directory, use of VCU's facilities for meetings and activities, use of the campus newspaper, radio station and bulletin boards, eligibility to obtain VCU funding for its activities and other benefits. VCU claimed that, by registering the Gay Alliance, the school would be encouraging some students to join who might not otherwise join, would increase the opportunity for homosexual contacts and would tend to attract other homosexuals to the college.

The District Court ordered VCU to provide many of the benefits, but ruled the Gay Alliance had no constitutional right to registration as a sanctioned organization. The Fourth Circuit Court of Appeals disagreed, holding that the First Amendment's freedom of assembly and the equal protection clause entitled the Gay Alliance to registration.[251] Upon advice from the Attorney General of South Carolina, The Citadel Board of Visitors wisely decided in March 1976 not to appeal the Adams ruling.[252] While the Fourth Circuit's opinion in VCU was still months away, it would have doomed any appeal of Adams. His victory in court appears to have been pyrrhic, as the "Clubs" section of the 1976 *Sphinx* features Rod and Gun, SCUBA, Surfing, Flying, among others. But NORML is not listed.

The year 1976 began on the saddest of notes with the death of Anne Seignious, the president's wife, on the last day of 1975. Writing to his grandchildren about his wife 21 years after her death, Seignious said: "Even as I write this, I weep. I weep for my loss, the loss to all of you of the most beautiful person inside and out that God has created. If any of you, my progeny, achieve the quality of character, charm and grace, and the capacity to love that she had, you will become a great person."

Her death devastated him. As he confessed, "I almost lost interest in living."[253] He was 18 months into his presidency, but his heart was broken and, as one who knew him well then said, "the life went out of him."[254] Fortunately for Seignious and for The Citadel, he had recruited his dear friend and Citadel classmate Major General James A. ("Alex") Grimsley Jr., in 1975 to be vice president of administration and finance. As discussed more fully in Chapter 8, Grimsley's assistance proved invaluable.

The year 1976, which began on such a somber note with the report of one death, got worse in November with the report of four — all murdered by a knob named Harry De La Roche, Jr. in Montvale, New Jersey. While on Thanksgiving leave, De La Roche shot and killed his parents and two younger brothers. His lawyers employed an old criminal defense tactic: Put someone on trial other than the defendant. In this case, they sought to indict The Citadel's plebe system, claiming that their client feared a return to it and his father's wrath if he quit. De La Roche is currently serving four life sentences. Publicity in the Northeast was extensive, generally unfavorable to The Citadel, and freshman admissions from New Jersey and New York dropped precipitously in its wake. This gruesome crime and its aftermath are detailed in Alexander MacAulay's book, *Marching in Step*.

Things improved for Seignious and for the school in 1977. In May, Charleston hosted the Miss USA Contest, featuring uniformed cadets as escorts. With a television audience of millions, Seignious estimated for the board that the event was worth a million dollars in publicity.[255] A month after the pageant, Seignious married Dielle Fleischman, owner of Harrietta Plantation on the Santee River and a frequent attendee at Citadel functions.[256]

By September, trailers brought in to handle an overflow in the barracks offered further confirmation that the enrollment crisis was well past. At its December meeting, the board reviewed a 10-Year Master Plan prepared by Lucas & Stubbs Associates of Charleston. One remarkable possibility contemplated a new entrance to the college from an extension of Lockwood Drive across Citadel-owned marshland via something called the Citadel Parkway. If you have never heard of the Citadel Parkway, it's because it was never built, a possible outcome the planners acknowledged. As shown on the drawings, access to the campus would have come from the Ashley River side, through the area now occupied by the rifle range and across the old Washington Light Infantry field, now used for soccer.

In the spring of 1978, the Summerall Guards made their annual pilgrimage to Mardi Gras. It did not go well. Brian C. Klene, editor-in-chief of *The Brigadier*, reported in the February 17, 1978 issue that:

During the main parade, the Guards performed with beads and other paraphernalia draped over their shakos. To compound an already motley appearance, they took drinks from people in the crowd, and stopped to kiss girls on the street along the way. Before the parade began, their condition was so bad that the parade coordinator issued an ultimatum – sober up or leave. [in the next issue, Klene amended his reported slightly; the coordinator's ultimatum had actually come shortly after the parade began].

Seignious received numerous complaints from graduates at the parade, others watching on television and from the head of Mardi Gras. Commandant Colonel John Gibler, citing the difficulty of identifying the specific individuals involved, issued General Order No. 20 disbanding the Guards. This drastic action came on the heels of Ring Night the previous fall, when some intoxicated Guard seniors returning from leave did damage to the campus in excess of $1,000. Cadet reaction to the disbanding varied. Richard Sossamon, T Company: "It was a bad decision to punish the whole Guard unit"; Steve Acenbrack, Band: "Their actions merited what happened to them. They made us look like a bunch of clowns"; Keith Johnston, D Company: "The decision might serve as an example for the Guards to come, but will not affect this year's Guards that much." When the 1979 Bond Volunteers became Summerall Guards at Corps Day, they received their rifles, but not from their predecessors as was the custom.[257]

As director of the Joint Staff in Washington, the position Seignious left to return to Charleston, he had been deeply involved in the SALT (Strategic Arms Limitation Agreement) negotiations. While president of The Citadel, he served as an at-large delegate to the SALT II negotiations in Geneva, Switzerland. From the viewpoint of the school, he had done too good a job in mastering the subject, because when Harold Brown left as director of the Arms Control and Disarmament Agency (ACDA) to become President Carter's secretary of defense, Carter tapped our president to head the ACDA. "George, I need you for this job," Carter is reported to have said. As Seignious put it, "A soldier has no alternative but to salute and say, 'Yes, sir,' to the Commander-In-Chief. It really broke my heart to leave The Citadel."[258]

Douglas A. Snyder, Class of 1982 and a future chairman of the Board of Visitors, hated to see him go. "He would drive into the barracks in his golf cart and talk to cadets," Snyder recalls. Snyder's time as a cadet spanned three presidents, with Seignious the most personally engaged.[259]

In October 1978, Seignious reported his presidential appointment to the Board of Visitors, and in December he requested a leave of absence without pay pending his confirmation by the Senate, his resignation as president to be effective not later than April 1, 1979. Major General Wallace E. Anderson, Class of 1934, vice president for Academic Affairs and Dean of the College, became acting president.[260]

Shortly after General Anderson became acting president, the board instituted a common-sense change in the diploma policy. Charles T. Porter, Jr., in his last year of medical school at MUSC, wrote to Chairman William F. "Buddy" Prioleau, Jr., to lament his ineligibility for a Citadel diploma despite having spent three years as a full-time undergraduate veteran student. He matriculated in January 1972, earned Gold Stars with a cumulative GPA of 3.82 and left The Citadel under honorable circumstances to enter medical school, from which he would graduate in the top 10 percent of his class with a GPA of 3.36. Under the board's existing policy, students (cadets or non-cadets) who left school after three years to enter law, dental or medical schools did not receive Citadel diplomas. Porter pointed out the short-sightedness of this policy. "I now find myself in the peculiar situation of having graduated from medical school but not from college."

In a memo to General Seignious recommending the policy be changed, General Anderson acknowledged that it presented "an old issue that has not been decided to the satisfaction of all concerned." In May 1979, the board adopted Anderson's view. Henceforth, a Citadel bachelor's degree would be awarded to anyone (1) completing three years as an undergraduate; and (2) honorably discharged before enrolling in an accredited law, medical or dental graduate school from which he/she graduated; and (3) lacked a baccalaureate degree from any other collegiate institution.[261]

As the decade of the 1970s drew to a close, those most responsible for planning The Citadel's future could only speculate on "what ifs." What if Anne Seignious had lived to fulfill her time as the college's first lady? And what if Obbe Seignious had not been laid low by her death and had not been tapped by the President for national service? "He planned to be there for a decade," according to Richard Padgett, Class of 1968, who was Anne's son and Obbe's step-son.[262]

And what if his immediate successor had been Alex Grimsley instead of a Vietnam war hero, former prisoner of war, recipient of the Medal of Honor, and a graduate of the U.S. Naval Academy?

Chapter 8

THE SUMMER OF HIS DISCONTENT

For the first time in memory, Major General James A. Grimsley Jr. had nothing to do. It was June 1980 and Grimsley had just left what he had described to his wife and family years before as his "dream job." A long, hot summer loomed ahead and Grimsley couldn't imagine not spending it as he always had: working.

In 1975 he had been offered that dream job by his old friend and Citadel classmate, Lieutenant General George Seignious, the new president. After nearly 30 years on active duty with the Army and the moves and relocations that came with it, what could be better than a return to his beloved alma mater as a vice president? Back to South Carolina and to Charleston, where he had spent happy years as a cadet. As a member of the famed Class of 1942, he had many "brothers" from the long gray line, but none closer than George Seignious, a man he liked, admired and respected. Here was a rare opportunity to contribute to his school. As vice president of administration and finance, he could employ to maximum advantage the sound judgment tempered by experience that were the legacy of a distinguished military career. This job, thought Alex Grimsley, had it all.

And from 1975 to 1979, it proved to be the dream job he had envisioned when he accepted Seignious' offer. With that job came more responsibility than he had anticipated, brought about by circumstances he could not have predicted. As related in Chapter 7, Seignious had been dealt a blow by the death of his wife, Anne, on the last day of 1975, a mere 18 months into his presidency. His zest for the job diminished, an understandable byproduct of grief. Grimsley felt called upon to help out his old friend in the same way Seignious had helped Grimsley. "I was kind of running The Citadel for him [Seignious], which by his admission he knew," he said.[263] The arrival of Vice Admiral James Bond Stockdale as president changed everything.

James Alexander Grimsley, Jr. was born in Florence, South Carolina on November 14, 1921. His father, James A. Grimsley, Sr., worked for Railway Express and his mother, Anne Darby Grimsley, taught music. Known as

Alex, he set his sights on The Citadel early. An uncle, James Spann, a member of the Class of 1931 and editor of *The Sphinx*, came to Florence shortly after graduating to work for the highway department as an engineer. But the Depression was in its early years and the highway department cut back, letting go the recent hires. Grimsley's family took Spann in until he could find work. Space in the household being what it was, 10-year-old Alex was forced to relinquish his bedroom to Spann and move in with his sisters, about which he was "none too happy." But he got to know Spann and admired his Citadel yearbooks, with photos of officers attired with Sam Browne belts and riding boots. Grimsley decided "that's for me."[264]

A deeply religious man, Grimsley's beliefs were formed early as a member of St. John's Episcopal Church in Florence where his mother played the organ for half a century. When the Diocese of South Carolina approved formation of a Young Peoples Service League in 1923 to involve Episcopal youth in activities sponsored and supported by the church, St. John's organized a local chapter which chose Alex as its president in 1938-39.[265]

At The Citadel, Grimsley rose to the rank of cadet captain, commanding C Company in his senior year.[266] He nearly lost that command due to an incident that occurred one Friday afternoon prior to parade. In those days, several rooms in the barracks served as classrooms; regulations prohibited noise, room visitation or congregating on the galleries between 1 p.m. and 3 p.m. because some classes were still being held. As often happens over time, the rule was honored in its breech on Friday, when the barracks buzzed with preparation for parade and pre-weekend anticipation. On the Friday in question, a sergeant-of-the-guard (SG) was in the process of writing up cadets for unauthorized presence in rooms and playing radios — technical violations that would not have been tolerated Monday through Thursday. Grimsley confronted him and told him, in so many words, to find something else to do.

Grimsley knew he had no authority over the SG, who by virtue of his duty assignment had the right to enforce the regulation. He put Grimsley on report for interference in the performance of the SG's duty, and when the Commandant's punishment order came down, Grimsley took the long fall from Friday's hero with the cadets to Monday's goat with the administration. In a personal memoir written for his family, Grimsley relates it this way: "Despite my straight-forward (I thought), eloquent (I thought), soldierly (I thought) written explanations of my actions to the commandant, he ordered me reduced to cadet private and to walk four weeks' worth of tours. And this only two months before graduation — I was crushed!" Grimsley credited some swift intervention by classmates Seignious, Regimental Commander

Alvah Chapman and Maxwell Anderson for retaining his rank, but not even these three celebrated classmates could spare him a springtime of confinements prior to graduation.[267]

Grimsley's confrontation with the SG is a common one. Officers-of-the-guard (OGs or SGs) are empowered with authority they may lack on any other day of the year. Such empowerment is not always used wisely. In 1964 a senior private in Fourth Battalion who had made himself particularly unpopular among fourth classmen, became OG. He had never held rank and never would. His day as OG gave him the power to settle some scores, and he used it. While the knobs in T Company were in class, he inspected every room, finding a long list of violations from "dust on press" to "improper alignment of shoes." Had he contented himself with merely turning in a stack of white slips at the end of his tour, he would not have aroused the anger he provoked. But in each room he left evidence of his inspection.

Knobs returned from class to find their laundry bags emptied onto the floor, their T-shirts and underwear strewn across the room, their beds unmade and their desks rearranged. The knobs fought back with a secret they learned from the OG's roommate: The OG had a deathly fear of bugs. That weekend a knob returned from Sunday leave with 400 very much alive crickets in a canister he purchased from a fishing bait shop in North Charleston. That night, the knobs of T Company set their alarms for 3 a.m. The barracks was utterly still when they silently made their way to the OG's room on the fourth division. No doors were locked in those days, but by a simple combination of a stick and some webbing, a bolting device could be constructed which allowed someone on the outside to prevent a door from being opened by someone inside the room.

The knobs had constructed such a bolting device and had practiced its swift deployment. At a signal, one knob opened the OG's screen door, a second opened the wooden door and a third stepped over the threshold with the canister. He opened the canister, freeing the crickets, which made a collective swooshing sound as they scattered across the floor, onto the beds and into the presses. As soon as the wooden door was closed and the bolting device applied, a scream came from the room, followed by a heavy thud as the OG leaped from the top bunk. As he stepped on crickets, more screams and curses issued forth as he crossed the room to the light switch. But the lights did not come on; the knobs had flipped the circuit breaker at the fuse box on the gallery.

The wooden door shook in his effort to get out, but the bolting device had been skillfully placed. The knobs scattered. Message delivered. Mike

McCarter, a knob who participated in the great cricket caper, lived on the third division in a room directly below the OG. He recalls hearing random chirping in his room for weeks after the raid.[268]

Grimsley went on active duty in June 1942 and saw combat in World War II. He left the service when the war ended to try his hand at the civilian life. But jobs in a lumber yard at $27.50 a week and later, as a manager of a local gas utility in Florence, left him uninspired. Like his buddy Seignious, he missed the army life, and returned to active duty in 1948. After two years at Fort Jackson, he reported to the 307th Infantry Regiment of the 77th Infantry Division in Europe. That assignment reunited him with yet another classmate, Ted Bell, who like Grimsley served as a company commander in the 307th.

Grimsley's last combat deployment took him to Vietnam, where fragments from an exploding artillery shell left him with limited use of two fingers on his left hand, a nuisance when he played the piano, always by ear as he never learned to read music. By the time he left the Pentagon to accept Seignious' offer to return to The Citadel, he had been awarded two Silver Stars, four Bronze Stars, four Legions of Merit and three Purple Hearts.

When Seignious resigned as president in 1979 to become the director of the U.S. Arms Control and Disarmament Agency, Grimsley lost the close personal relationship that had been such an incentive for him to return to The Citadel. And he had a new boss: Vice Admiral James Bond Stockdale, USN (Ret.). In the words of Grimsley's younger son, Major General Will Grimsley, "Stockdale and Dad were oil and water." Not only did Alex Grimsley find himself at odds with Stockdale over policy issues and management styles, but by the end of the 1979-1980 school year, he was the lone Citadel graduate in the upper echelon of the administration. His dream job had evaporated almost as unexpectedly as it had arrived.

The year of Admiral Stockdale's abortive presidency has been subjected to conjectures, explanations and suppositions.[269] Looking back, points of consensus are few, but there are some. First, as a man and a sailor, Stockdale enjoyed virtually universal admiration. A 1947 graduate of the U.S. Naval Academy, he made his reputation as a Navy test pilot before earning a M.A. in International Relations at Stanford. While at Stanford he took courses in philosophy, including Comparative Marxist Thought. According to his wife, Sybil, he fell in love with the subject and read philosophy in his spare time.[270]

In an age worn cynical by the Vietnam war and the Arab oil embargo, genuine heroes were in short supply, but Stockdale was just that: an American hero. Having endured seven and a half years as a POW, he returned home to universal acclaim and a Medal of Honor, the citation for which leaves no doubt about his bravery in the most trying conditions:

> For conspicuous gallantry and intrepidity at the risk of his life above and beyond the call of duty while senior naval officer in the Prisoner of War camps of North Vietnam. Recognized by his captors as the leader in the Prisoners' of War resistance to inter-rogation and in their refusal to participate in propaganda exploita-tion, Rear Adm. Stockdale was singled out for interrogation and attendant torture after he was detected in a covert communica-tions attempt. Sensing the start of another purge, and aware that his earlier efforts at self-disfiguration to dissuade his captors from exploiting him for propaganda purposes had resulted in cruel and agonizing punishment, Rear Adm. Stockdale resolved to make himself a symbol of resistance regardless of personal sacrifice. He deliberately inflicted a near-mortal wound to his person in order to convince his captors of his willingness to give up his life rather than capitulate. He was subsequently discovered and revived by the North Vietnamese who, convinced of his indomitable spirit, abated in their employment of excessive harassment and torture toward all of the Prisoners of War. By his heroic action, at great peril to himself, he earned the everlasting gratitude of his fellow prisoners and of his country. Rear Adm. Stockdale's valiant leader-ship and extraordinary courage in a hostile environment sustain and enhance the finest traditions of the U.S. Naval Service.

In his book *In Love & War*, co-authored with his wife, Sybil, Stockdale recounts years of torture, deprivation and isolation in Hanoi while she kept the family together. In Washington, she very effectively spearheaded the ef-fort to raise the plight of the POWs. Even among those who were critical of his tenure at The Citadel, his service to America cannot be sullied.

The second point of consensus is that he was never a fit for The Citadel, a fact he himself acknowledged after he left. Apropos of the adage that you only get one chance to make a first impression, The Citadel's first impression on the Stockdales could hardly have been worse, and it wasn't the school's fault. From the moment the Stockdales stepped onto the campus, the architecture reminded him of the waking nightmare he had endured in Vietnam.

"The Citadel barracks and French Indochina prisons are architectural first cousins and their high, whitewashed exterior walls identical," he wrote. "I could feel my handcuffs behind me cutting into my wrists after the long Jeep ride, sense Pigeye's rough touch as he dropped my blindfold. I was looking into the cell blocks off Heartbreak Hotel courtyard, Hoa Lo prison, Hanoi [the 'Hanoi Hilton']."[271] The college's very appearance made a first impression that foreshadowed the trouble which ensued.

The school's innocent and coincidental evocation of the worst years of Stockdale's life fairly prompts the question of why he would accept the presidency when offered. It wasn't as if he needed a job or couldn't find another. He had been offered the superintendency of the Naval Academy, a job he wanted, but accepting it would have required him to remain for 18 more months in a job he didn't want at the Pentagon. Instead, he chose to become president of the Naval War College.

Prior to leaving the Pentagon, he was promoted to Vice Admiral, his third star, but assignment to the War College foreclosed a fourth star because the path to that exalted military plateau, commander of a carrier division at sea, was a long way from Newport, Rhode Island, home of the War College.

In addition to his administrative duties, he taught a course, Foundations of Moral Obligation, designed by and co-taught with a philosophy professor from Columbia University named Dr. Joseph Brennan.

Philosophy may have been an academic passion for Brennan, but for Stockdale it had become, thanks to his POW experience, a matter of survival.

He wrote:

"The remarkable and eternal applicability of what the ancients had to say about the human predicament occupied hours and hours of my thoughts in solitary in prison. There was something very comforting in knowing, thanks to my excursions into philosophy at Stanford, that being cast in a role that was scripted for a lifetime of uphill fighting against hopeless odds was not an exceptional human fate in the broad scope of history. In fact, a legitimate school of philosophical thought, Stoicism, was built on learning to play that role with integrity and dignity." (emphasis added)

Stockdale had been president of the War College for three years when, in the spring of 1979, he received the first overture from The Citadel. By his own admission, he knew virtually nothing about the school. His memoir makes it clear that his primary motive in accepting its offer was a negative: His military career had peaked and he feared the Navy's "up and out" system that put "productive men out to pasture prematurely." At first blush, The Citadel offered an aging test pilot a soft landing in education, a field in which he excelled. His research revealed that average freshmen SAT scores were significantly below those entering service academies. To Stockdale, The Citadel's need to attract and retain a better caliber of student explained the school's interest in an experienced and acclaimed educator. "So we [Stockdale and his wife] went into South Carolina . . . with our eyes open. What we thought of as our logical conclusion was that a good old school had gone through the wringer in the 1960s and had come out with a shattered academic profile that needed somebody like me to upgrade it."

References to a "good old school" with a "shattered academic profile" reinforce an impression received by some that a goodly amount of hubris accompanied the Stockdales on their trip from Rhode Island to Charleston, an impression supported by Admiral Stockdale's account of his tenure. Shortly after being named the new president, he delivered a well-received speech to a joint session of the South Carolina Legislature, carried live on statewide television. In it he promised to inculcate cadets with "my brand of leadership, which entailed being simultaneously a moralist, jurist, teacher, steward and philosopher." At the time, he thought his message had resonated with the Board of Visitors, but he later said, "Little did I know that the people who called the final tune on The Citadel, those very rednecks who tilled the land and ran the general stores and had been brought up at their mothers' knees to look up to The Citadel as the very symbol of South Carolina manhood, were not even listening yet."

Even allowing for some justifiable bitterness on Stockdale's part, such a statement reveals a level of contempt for the Board of Visitors, the people who "called the final tune," and for South Carolinians in general.

There is also the matter of his selection as president to consider. When called by Board Chairman Colonel Buddy Prioleau, Stockdale understood his selection to have been unanimous. In fact, it was not. Stockdale later said that knowing a certain number of board members had reservations about him or preferred other candidates might have impacted his decision to come.

In extending to Stockdale the offer to become The Citadel's 15th president, the Board of Visitors felt they had found the perfect man for the job. The initial indications boded well. According to the chairman, Stockdale acquitted himself well in the September board meeting, his first president's report was well received and he seemed to get along well with the members.[272]

Whatever optimism Prioleau took from that first meeting disappeared quickly, as it soon became apparent that Stockdale possessed little patience for board politics and even less ability to navigate them. Additional strains developed with Sybil Stockdale's involvement in board business.[273] A strong and effective woman in her own right, and a dedicated life partner to her husband as she had so amply demonstrated to the entire country during his POW confinement, she nevertheless played a role in his administration resented by some board members, and it was never clear she felt any real commitment to the college. In all likelihood her perceptions were molded by that first visit to the campus, arrived at via a drive through a "rather shabby neighborhood," presumably Hampton Park. "Is this *it*?" [emphasis in original], she had asked upon seeing the school for the first time. At that moment, Admiral Stockdale said he knew how she would feel about being "suddenly boxed in in such a harshly structured arena after expecting the tree-lined walkways weaving through the soft and traditional architecture of places like Annapolis and West Point."[274]

Such a rose-colored view of Annapolis is understandable given Stockdale's affection for his alma mater, but few visitors to West Point leave judging its architecture to be "soft and traditional." Some would go so far as to call it bleak and severe, especially in January with a brisk wind off the Hudson. The inference to be drawn from this telling visit was that both Stockdales felt they had landed in a Southern backwater, and their view of the campus was unfortunately seen through those eyes.

Another reality that doomed Stockdale's tenure was his relationship with Alex Grimsley, the man who had, in effect, been running the college prior to Stockdale's arrival and who would replace him when he left. By most accounts Stockdale kept his own counsel, perhaps by nature but reinforced by years in isolation. Being "oil and water" with Grimsley, the man most familiar with the school, its traditions and its alumni, inevitably led to mistakes that Stockdale might have avoided.

Upon his arrival, Stockdale found some paperwork in the files of his predecessor, General Seignious. Included were letters from angry parents complaining about treatment their sons had received; treatment that included hazing. Even more worrisome to him were memos from Dr. George Mood, the school's physician, medically confirming the parents' complaints. Taken together, Stockdale confronted what seemed irrefutable evidence that the "eat, sleep, study" safeguards were not effective in many cases.

To address these issues, Stockdale and the board decided to review the Fourth Class System with, at least from Stockdale's perspective, a view toward total overhaul.

Francis P. Mood, Jr., Class of 1960 and a future chairman of the Board of Visitors, was asked to chair the study. As a cadet, he had been an exemplary leader, rising to the rank of cadet Lieutenant Colonel as Third Battalion Commander. He wore Gold Stars, was a member of the Junior Sword Drill and Summerall Guards, and was voted by his classmates "Most Likely to Succeed." As chairman of the Honor Committee, he also had a reputation for probity.[275] In his book *The Boo*, Pat Conroy named him as one of two cadets that, "by acclamation of their peers . . . were considered to be the most outstanding in character, determination and moral stamina."[276]

There was never any question about where Mood would attend college. His uncle Julius Mood had been First Captain (equivalent to today's Regimental Commander) in the Class of 1916. Two more uncles, Rogers Mood and Dan Mood, graduated in the Classes of 1918 and 1921, respectively. Francis Mood, Sr. finished in the Class of 1923, and there is every reason to believe his dedication to honor matched his son's, as Frank Mood, Sr. served on the Honor Court all four years.[277] Frank Mood, Jr.'s enormous contributions to his alma mater over several decades have been recognized. In 1985 he received an honorary Doctor of Laws Degree and in 2000 he was awarded the Palmetto Medal. His service on the Board of Visitors totaled 12 years.

Another study of the Fourth Class System was a thankless task given the charged atmosphere during Stockdale's year as president. From the outset, Mood's committee faced a challenge that neither the Whitmire study in 1968 nor the Crabbe evaluation in 1972 had to deal with: Any proposed changes to the Fourth Class System in 1980 were viewed as watering down the system to accommodate women, the first of whom would not enter for another 15 years. But with the service academies having admitted women in 1975, and the women's movement gathering steam in the 1980s despite the defeat of the Equal Rights Amendment in 1982, a challenge to The Citadel's and VMI's all-male policy seemed inevitable. Many alumni and cadets saw a tough, high-octane plebe system as the best insurance against the admission of women.

At the outset, the Mood Committee acknowledged that "*many of our Committee's findings have been found before.* Materials and recommendations from previous studies and the comments from faculty and staff who have previously registered their thoughts on this subject confirm this. The conclusion, thus, must be reached that previous recommendations were either not implemented or, having been implemented, ignored." [emphasis in original]. Unlike the Whitmire Committee, the Mood Committee recommended steps designed to dissuade a high school senior from coming to The Citadel by mistake — the question begged by the attrition statistics previously recited. In the view of the Mood Committee based on interviews and letters from parents and alumni, these seniors were "unprepared for or unwilling to endure 'the system.'" As a remedy, the committee suggested purging college publications of "misleading and over-glamourized references" to Citadel life; stress to parents the importance of an indoctrination visit and assure those visits portray "the positive side of this college in a realistic light."

Among the committee's other recommendations: terminating the Fourth Class System at Corps Day, involve TAC officers more directly in operations of the Corps, eliminate rank for sophomores and implement a partial rank rotation system for juniors and seniors, eliminate racking and, as the minority report in Whitmire had suggested, leave the Fourth Class System at the mess hall doors "with the exception of instructions in good manners."

One recommendation seemed directly aimed at the troublesome report from Dr. Mood at the infirmary. It was his 1978 letter to Colonel John Gibler, the commandant, detailing the nature and frequency of knob injuries, that had so concerned Stockdale on his arrival. The Mood Committee's solution was to require the company commander or executive officer to accompany to the infirmary any knob admitted there for heat exhaustion, overexertion or similar ailment, with the officer expected to explain the circumstances.

Another significant recommendation of the Mood Committee was for the school to initiate a core curriculum program on ethics and leadership. Here was an acknowledgement that these two critical disciplines were not being taught, and should be. More than a decade would pass before they would be.

The Mood Report raised concerns about two venerable institutions within the Corps, the Junior Sword Drill and the Bond Volunteers. Particularly as to the Junior Sword Drill, those concerns foreshadowed a pattern of conduct that would eventually result in a disbanding of the unit. In the committee's view, the worst abuses of the plebe system were becoming de rigueur within the units. Physical challenges inherent in trying out for the units became a test of strength, endurance and manhood, the trial-by-fire aspects of the Fourth Class System having little to do with drill prowess. Because members of the units selected those who succeeded them, a practice known as "roaching" became prevalent, as those eligible to try out performed duties for and curried favor with those who would soon be their judges. Worse, perhaps, those associated with the units either as candidates or members were perceived within the Corps as favored by the Commandant's Department on matters of promotion and punishment, creating at least the appearance of a double standard with its obvious implications for morale. The committee recommended the unit selection processes be examined.

The Mood Committee was candid in admitting that there were those, particularly among more senior cadets, who feared the committee intended to gut the Fourth Class System. With reforms, a tough system would be made easier, thereby destroying the very challenges and hardships that made the plebe system worth going through and its survival such a source of pride for those espousing this view. Such a taming would sound the death knell for the school.

The committee rejected this logic and the cynical prediction that came with it. "In our study we have sought to differentiate between toughness for toughness' sake and toughness with a higher purpose. We subscribe to the latter and firmly believe the dire predictions about the viability of The Citadel, under a system that forbids purposeless harassment, are invalid." The committee closed by endorsing an apropos quote attributed to General MacArthur when he was superintendent of West Point: In treatment of the fourth class, "Severity, yes, but administered in the tradition of a proud gentleman rather than a common thug."

Stockdale criticized the Mood Report for not going far enough and perceiving it to be a usurpation of his authority as president. Many of the reforms Stockdale was known to favor would eventually be adopted, but at the time he faced a rising tide of criticism, primarily from alumni, that he was softening the plebe system in the mold of the service academies. Once he left, General Grimsley's administration returned to the familiar, or in the words of a memorandum issued by his commandant, Colonel Floyd Brown, "Back to basics."[278]

The three studies of the Fourth Class System performed in 1968, 1972 and 1980 all embody consensus on three critical elements of the freshman year: A knob needs to eat, sleep and study, and abuses that prevent those needs from being met are wrong and cannot be tolerated. Arguing against this principle is a little like coming out against world peace, and few would dispute it, even among the most rabid alumni. The problem was effective enforcement among young men determined to prove their masculinity, their macho bona fides, by gaming the system. Stockdale acknowledged this truth in his May 1980 report to the board: "You have by now read the Mood Committee recommendations for the Fourth Class System. If you saw how our current Reg Book had to be changed to incorporate these recommendations, you would laugh. There were almost *no changes* [emphasis in original]. The only significant ones were to put corporal punishment under the control of the cadet company commander and to restore order in the mess hall. The key will be enforcement."[279]

Stockdale might have been correct in his judgment about enforcement, but within the Corps and the alumni, the perception persisted that he simply disliked the Fourth Class System and wished to radically change it. His criticism of the Mood report would seem to support that perception. At one point, Stockdale eliminated the requirement that knobs walk in the gutter on the Avenue of Remembrance.[280] One is left to wonder how this tradition could possibly cross the line into abuse and hazing, and if such an innocuous practice somehow offended Stockdale's sensibilities, it is easy to conclude that his sensibilities had been heightened to those closer to Mother Teresa's than to those of a flag rank general officer. Perhaps, given his brutal treatment as a POW, that heightening was understandable, but it did not serve him well at The Citadel.

The cadet on the spot during Stockdale's year was Regimental Commander Fred Whittle, who came to The Citadel via a vocational technical high school in Taunton, Mass. He graduated as class valedictorian with plans to become an electrician until he received a tri-fold brochure informing him about a Southern college with a zero tolerance for drugs and an honor system that didn't abide cheating. It spoke to him. In an interview 37 years after he graduated, Whittle cited the cadet prayer as a source of personal inspiration: "Preserve us faithful to the ideals of The Citadel, sincere in fellowship, unswerving in duty, finding joy in purity, and confidence through a steadfast faith . . ." Idealism, to be sure, but a standard to be aspired to. Whittle forged an enviable, stellar Citadel career, and in his last year of that career fate placed him at the head of a chain of command that answered to an authentic American hero. In all probability, each man recognized the leadership qualities in the other.

Whittle "deeply admired" Stockdale, and may be one of the few who maintained a correspondence with him after the admiral left Charleston. In one such letter, Stockdale acknowledged that he and The Citadel were "a bad match." According to Whittle, Stockdale was a loner who sought mostly his own counsel and was affected considerably by his POW experience. Given his history, he had what may have been an understandable aversion to Asians and gave instructions that they were not to be selected as parade ushers. His POW experience gave him virtually no use of his left leg, which he was unable to straighten. In the chapel, they had to cut a pew so that he could sit. "He was a man of Old Testament faith, with the deepest blue eyes." He told Whittle that the purpose of education was to teach a person how to deal with failure, a cornerstone of Stoic thought.[281]

Another Stockdale admirer was William C. "Billy" Mills, Citadel Class of 1971. In 1979, Mills served as the first alumni fund director of what was then known as the Citadel Development Foundation, now The Citadel Foundation. He loved his job and resisted Stockdale's initial efforts to lure him from it. In November 1979, when Stockdale had been president for a few months, he met with Mills to learn what it would take for him to become his aide. Mills listed as his conditions directly reporting to Stockdale with an office close by and access to staff meetings, to which the admiral agreed. Mills was transferred from development foundation that day. For the remaining 10 months of Stockdale's tenure, no one in The Citadel family was closer to James and Sybil Stockdale than Billy Mills.[282]

If Whittle admired Stockdale, it would be fair to say Mills' opinion of him bordered on worship. Mills attended Stockdale's funeral at the Naval Academy on July 23, 2005, and eulogized him at a memorial service held July 31, 2005 in Summerall Chapel. In that eulogy, Mills paid tribute to Stockdale as a man of love, humor and integrity. "To Admiral Stockdale there was no grey in an issue or situation of moral imperative, it was black or white, right or wrong."[283]

Stockdale's POW experience and his black-or-white view of the moral imperative explains his interest in *Billy Budd,* the Herman Melville novel that Stockdale required Whittle and his chain of command to read. Written at the end of Melville's career and his life, and not published until 33 years after his death, *Billy Budd* is a story of an innocent young sailor falsely accused of helping to plot a mutiny on board the British man-of-war *HMS Bellipotent.* Its captain, "Starry" Vere, a fair and intelligent officer, summons Billy to his cabin for a confrontation with Billy's accuser, Claggart, the ship's master-of-arms. Confused and momentarily enraged by Claggart's false accusation, Billy strikes Claggart, killing him. Vere has come to love Billy like a son and knows to a moral certainty that Claggart's allegation is a lie, but the maritime law requires Vere to sentence Billy to death, which he does. Billy is hanged. Vere and the crew feel Claggart got what he deserved and Billy did not, the triumph of evil over good, making it a perfect case study for the moral imperative.

In sessions scheduled by Stockdale to discuss *Billy Budd*, the chain of command may have felt that they were merely engaging in the kind of philosophical musings for which Stockdale was known.[284] In his joint address to the S.C. Legislature prior to assuming his duties as president, Stockdale had quoted Plato, Epictetus and Heschel. But according to Mills, who sat in on the sessions, Stockdale's purpose in the *Billy Budd* exercise was to evaluate The Citadel's ranking system. By Stockdale's reasoning, the cadets who showed the most insightful understanding of the moral imperative presented by the novel were most deserving of higher rank, and whether those cadets actually carried that rank informed Stockdale as to the quality of leadership evaluation being practiced at the school. In a post-mortem, Stockdale told Mills he planned to revamp the ranking system, but Stockdale's abrupt departure made those plans moot.[285]

Tensions between Stockdale and the Board of Visitors surfaced early and only grew worse as the academic year wore on. In October 1979, he touched one of the third rails of Citadel dogma by positing the admission of civilian students into cadet classrooms and cadets attending classes at civilian campuses in Charleston.[286] As had presidents before him, Stockdale saw himself as the ultimate authority on punishment orders issued by the Commandant and approved by him. And as a long line of his predecessors had learned, the board had a different view. When a cadet company commander sought to intimidate a knob by pointing a pistol at his head, Stockdale ordered him dismissed. The Board of Visitors reversed his decision based on "certain procedural errors."[287]

James Rembert, a revered professor of English for 40 years at the school, had served as the faculty adviser to the Honor Committee for five years prior to Stockdale's arrival. He recalls needing the president's signature on a form. He sought Stockdale out in the president's office to get it. Stockdale greeted him cordially and asked him to sit down. As this was his first occasion to engage Stockdale on an Honor Committee matter, Rembert explained that the form was an allegation of an honor violation brought by the cadet who signed the form, which had then been presented to the Honor Committee chairman for his signature. The president's signature was now required to make certain he was aware of the allegation, as such a serious charge often precipitated a call from the accused's parents, and it was in everyone's best interest that the president be aware of the allegation.

Rembert stressed that at this point nothing had been proved and that the charge had yet to be investigated, as would be done in the normal course. Stockdale demurred, asking why he should sign it. Suppose, suggested Stockdale, the allegation didn't seem right to him, or that his intuition told him the charge was not well founded. Rembert explained that the form merely initiated the process and that it was impossible to know whether the charge had merit because no one had done the investigation that would follow upon completion of the form. Stockdale said, "But I am the president," implying that his subjective judgment of the merits should end the inquiry. Rembert repeated his explanation of the process, assuming Stockdale had not grasped it.

As Rembert tells it, Stockdale retreated to a wall in his office on which hung photographs, citations and certificates attesting to Stockdale's long and storied service. "He stared at that wall for a long time and kept repeating, 'But I am the president. But I am the president.'"

Rembert finally decided to bring the matter to a head by saying, "Sir, presidents come and go but the Honor Code remains." That same afternoon, Rembert received a written request from Stockdale asking him to recommend two advisors to the Honor Committee. Rembert recommended Michael Barrett. Shortly thereafter Stockdale sent Rembert a two-word memorandum. "Barrett selected."[288] Rembert's five-year tenure as adviser to the Honor Committee ended that day.

Rembert's experience highlights a tension that was resolved only by Stockdale's resignation: Who would run the college? The admiral viewed it as his job and he implied, perhaps tellingly, it was his job alone. "I had to get out and try to hammer this place [The Citadel] together with my bare hands, just like I did as a fighter squadron skipper on aircraft carriers and as boss of the underground organization in prison." Stockdale took no part in deliberations by the Mood committee studying the Fourth Class System, but clearly, he viewed it as a usurpation of his authority. "What we had was a committee doing what a *leader* should do, and I was supposed to be that leader." [emphasis in original][289]

Stockdale exacerbated his relationships with the board and alumni by replacing the commandant. Colonel John K. Gibler was by all accounts a smart, decent, professional Army officer well suited to the job of commandant. Significantly in the context of Stockdale's administration, he was a Citadel grad, Class of 1952. His replacement raised more than a few eyebrows because Colonel Arthur H. Blair, USA (Ret.), was a former head of the English Department, hardly a rich or traditional breeding ground for the top disciplinarian on campus. He was also a West Point graduate, and his appointment in place of a Citadel graduate was, in the eyes of many, yet another manifestation of Stockdale's determination to remake The Citadel in the mold of a service academy.

In what may have been the proverbial straw on that weary camel's back, the board commissioned a study by Price-Waterhouse to recommend a reorganization plan that would have resulted in an admissions department committed to attracting a higher academic caliber of students, something Stockdale had made plain was one of his priorities. When the board delayed approval of the plan, Stockdale wrote out his resignation: "I hereby resign my office as President of The Citadel."[290] He had not yet even been inaugurated.

His decision may have felt spontaneous to those affected, but he and Sybil had agreed months before. "Either I was to be given real presidential powers as the leader of the college before the start of the next academic year or we were leaving."[291]

Will Grimsley remembers well the August Friday when Stockdale resigned. Alex Grimsley's younger son had graduated from Davidson that spring and spent the summer at home working and preparing to go on active duty in September. His parents were away from the house when the phone began ringing incessantly. First, it was The Citadel, trying to reach his father. Next came *The News and Courier*. "Suddenly, we had chaos," Will remembers. "The Citadel wanted Dad to come back."[292]

In the hindsight afforded by the 37 years that have elapsed since those frantic Friday phone calls summoning Alex Grimsley back as interim president, it seems clear that the school could not have chosen better. For the next nine years, Alex Grimsley set a standard for administration, governance and foresight. When he retired in 1989, the Board of Visitors designated him as President Emeritus, an honor shared by only Summerall and Clark. The boy from Florence, who had given up his bedroom for a 1931 Citadel graduate, had left his mark on his school.

But what left its mark on Alex Grimsley came near the end of the 1979-1980 school year, just prior to the summer of his discontent. He had endured the "oil and water" relationship with Stockdale, he had persevered as the last Citadel alumnus in the Stockdale administration, and he had watched his "dream job" go up in the smoke of unrealized hopes for himself and his alma mater. There seemed little left to do but pack his things and exit Lesesne Gate.

Fred Whittle had other ideas. Whittle liked Stockdale, but he loved The Citadel, and Alex Grimsley's imminent departure affected him. The Grimsleys, Alex and his wife Jessie, were family, the "finest quality example of a devoted couple." Whittle's class dedicated *The Sphinx* to him that last year, but that wasn't enough. Whittle saw a chance to lead the Corps in a fitting tribute, and he seized it. On a Wednesday before Grimsley departed, Whittle ordered the Corps to take an indirect route to evening mess. At Whittle's command, in the uniform of the day, the Corps marched past Grimsley's quarters. Whittle halted them long enough to tell General Grimsley, "We salute you."

"Carry on," Grimsley replied before taking the Corps' review. [293]

Years after his retirement, Grimsley never failed to choke up when he related the parade in his honor. "He didn't wear his emotions outwardly," said eldest son Jim Grimsley, Citadel Class of 1968, "but he couldn't hide his pride in that gesture."[294]

Chapter 9

GRIMSLEY PLANS THE FUTURE AS THE PAST WEARS THIN

Not long after Alex Grimsley's return as president, Paramount Pictures approached the college in hopes that the $200,000 they brought with them would induce the board to allow *The Lords of Discipline* to be filmed on campus. This adaptation of Pat Conroy's book of the same name could be expected to evoke the same controversy the book had occasioned within The Citadel family and beyond. It drew on Conroy's senior year when Charles Foster became the first and lone African-American cadet to matriculate at a thinly disguised Citadel called Carolina Military Institute. Foster's character, named Tom Pearce, is brutalized by The Ten, a secret organization unmasked by Conroy's alter ego, Will McLean. The Fourth Class System is portrayed in the book as an ordeal in which the weakest knobs are encircled by the pack, determined to drive out those judged to be undeserving of becoming "Institute Men." The book was widely condemned by many within the alumni community as grossly exaggerated, and lauded by others as fiction based on fact. Small wonder that a film based on the book would divide equally along those lines. At the same September 18, 1981 meeting in which the Board of Visitors adopted Copen Blue as the official Citadel blue, it said no to Paramount. Chairman Colonel George C. James, writing for the board, cited as justification for the rejection the anticipated filming schedule having "an undue adverse impact on college activities, academic routine, and cadet time at a critical time during the school year."

Pat Conroy, living in Rome at the time, saw James's explanation for what it was: a cover for the real reason. He responded to the rejection with a withering letter to Frank Jarrell, the *Post-Courier* staff reporter who had been keeping him apprised of developments in Charleston. In his response, Conroy aired some long-standing grievances with his alma mater, peppering his prose with ridicule and sarcasm as well as some self-deprecation. He advised the board to "loosen up" and questioned its qualifications to pass judgment on his book. "Can you imagine the Board of Visitors judging the merits of a novel?" he asked rhetorically. "I'll bet I could take every novel read by every member of the Board of Visitors for the last 20 years and fit them all comfortably in a cigar box." His letter was published on October 25, 1981, five days before the board was asked to consider a revised proposal from Paramount. Conroy must have assumed the outcome would be adverse, as his was hardly a letter designed to win over the board members. And he took their cover story head on. "If the board could simply admit that they did not like the contents of the book, that they thought the book was unflattering to The Citadel and that the movie would bring discredit to the school, their position would be sound and even admirable."

Presumably, then, Conroy admired the board for turning down Paramount's revised proposal. The motion to reject the revised offer acknowledged that "[t]here is great sentiment on both sides of the question as to whether or not we accept Paramount's offer," but James, in his official statement, made no mention of support within the Citadel community for allowing the film to be made on campus. Nor did he mention Conroy by name, alluding only to "the authors of the book and the screenplay." But he did come clean on the reason for spurning $200,000. "We do not propose to utilize The Citadel campus for the filming of a picture which presents the school in a distorted, unrealistic and highly uncomplimentary manner."[295] *Brigadier* editor-in-chief Dan Alfaro supported the board's decision as one that "deserves applause," predicting "there will be other Pat Conroys, other novels and other proposals to film a movie on campus. Hopefully, those making decisions for this school will do so keeping in mind that The Citadel is above temporal glamour."[296]

Grimsley was thrilled to be back. It had only been a year since he was "pretty much running the college" for Seignious and a mere five months since cadets had given him a spontaneous farewell parade. When Stockdale resigned, the board brought him back as interim president, but by December 1980 the "interim" had been removed. His inauguration as the 16th president received widespread positive publicity. The Charleston papers published a special supplement, states and cities across the country ran stories, the *State* in Columbia blessed the choice in an editorial, and South Carolina Educational Television (SCETV) produced a special half-hour program seen across South Carolina.[297]

In January 1981, five months after Grimsley's return, the Academic board unanimously recommended that the college adopt the academic honor designations familiar to students at most civilian schools. Beginning with 1982 graduates, students with a GPR of 3.50-3.69 on all work counting for the degree would be designated as *cum laude*; those achieving a GPR of 3.70-3.89

would be designated *magna cum laude*, and those finishing with a GPR of 3.90-4.00 would earn *summa cum laude* distinction. George Meenaghan, Grimsley's successor as Vice President for Academic Affairs and Dean, presented the recommendation to the Board of Visitors at its February 1981 meeting, and it was approved. Previously, students earning a cumulative GPA of 3.5 had been awarded General Honors and those with 3.60 or higher General High Honors, but those recognitions lacked the universal acclaim accorded the Latin designations.[298]

At the same February 1981 meeting, the board adopted another recommendation of the Academic Board by changing the name of the Department of Mathematics to the Department of Mathematics and Computer Science.[299] To modern readers, the growing influence of computers is a given and the college's experience mirrored society's as a whole. Three years later, Lieutenant Colonel Charles E. Cleaver, Ph.D., head of the recently renamed department, told the board in a report that "the computer science market has been wide open for several years" and that "knowing how to spell the word 'computer' could almost get you a job." Cleaver's department wrestled with a problem that would persist for a generation and still persists: the trend away from mathematics and toward computer science. In the prior semester, of the 259 students who had declared a major in his department, 217, or 84 percent, "are mainly interested in computer science," a trend he said was "typical of what other schools are experiencing."[300]

Early in Grimsley's administration, the college struggled with issues of racial assimilation that continued until the end of the Watts administration, when the admission of Shannon Faulkner largely shifted the focus of the public and institutional lens from race to gender. A 1979 assessment by the U.S. Department of Health, Education and Welfare (HEW) gave failing desegregation grades to 11 South Carolina colleges, including The Citadel. To stimulate improvement, the federal government brandished its biggest stick: loss of federal funds. The South Carolina Plan for Equity and Equal Opportunity in Public Colleges and Universities, an affirmative action plan, required endorsement by the state schools affected. In April 1981, the board expressed its support for the principles articulated in the plan but vehemently objected to Appendix K, which would have eliminated the requirement that members of the Board of Visitors be Citadel graduates. In declining to endorse the plan, the board said:

> [W]e are the most integrated educational institution in South Carolina. There are no closed doors of The Citadel campus. As

an example, we have no social fraternities. ... The provision of the Plan as it applies to the recomposition of the Board of Visitors, is incompatible with The Citadel and the fact that the very nature of this institution requires that it be governed by persons familiar with its background, its traditions and its mission. The Citadel encourages any qualified Citadel graduate, minority or otherwise, to declare for election to the board, and will be welcomed if elected.

As to the possible or threatened loss of federal funds, the board expressed "complete confidence in our Washington delegation, and others in authority."[301] The "others in authority" turned out to be alumni serving in the General Assembly and on the CHE board, whose opposition to Appendix K and its potential impact on the Board of Visitors forced a compromise. The final legislation authorized the governor to appoint one additional member to every board overseeing a South Carolina college, but as to The Citadel, that member was required to be an alumnus. Exercising that authority, Governor Riley appointed Alonzo Nesmith, Class of 1979, the first African-American member of the Board of Visitors.[302]

A year after Grimsley's return, the board approved a 10-year plan for the school. Entitled "The Citadel Goals for 1981-1990," it addressed every aspect of college life (hereinafter the "Grimsley Plan" or the "Plan"). And unlike the tenures of Seignious and Stockdale, Grimsley's tenure extended long enough — virtually the entire decade — to see most of those goals met. The Grimsley Plan is an excellent snapshot of the school at the start of the Grimsley era and established criteria by which his administration would be measured.

The prologue identifies two unique features of the college worth reciting:

> The Citadel ... is recognized by the S.C. Commission on Higher Education as the only specialized four-year college in the state. It is also recognized by the U.S. Department of Defense as one of only four essential military colleges in the nation. These facts attest to The Citadel's unique educational process and underline the unusual opportunity afforded all members of the Corps of Cadets in their pursuit of higher education.

The prologue continues:

> Complementing its role as a military college, The Citadel offers

other educational programs to benefit the community. The college accepts male veteran students in undergraduate, daytime classes; offers numerous programs in the evening courses to men and women students (non-cadets) leading to a baccalaureate degree and to the Master of Arts in Teaching, Master of Education, Master of Business Administration, and Specialist in Education degrees ... Summer school courses are open to all qualified students, both men and women.

Under "Goals and Objectives," these sentences appear:

The Corps of Cadets will continue as an all-male organization of approximately its current size. The size and scope of the Evening College will increase modestly commensurate with the need and the extent permitted by available personnel and facilities.

Some specific goals deserve mention:

(1) instituting a bachelor of science in mechanical engineering "if current studies confirm existing impressions." (The school began awarding these in 2014 and by 2017 it was the second most popular undergraduate major).
(2) participation in a consortium with USC's Ph.D. program in education.
(3) if justified by need, an MBA focused on international business and economics. (MBA now offered through the Tommy and Victoria Baker School of Business at The Citadel).
(4) courses or a major in national security policy and administration. (M.A. now offered in Intelligence and Security Studies).
(5) other possibilities included a Master of Arts in social sciences with emphasis on military heritage (M.A. in Social Sciences now offered); Master of Science in Biology (Consortium) (M.A. in Biology now offered); Master of Arts in English (Consortium) (M.A. in English now offered); Master of Science in Applied Mathematics and Computer Science (M.S. in Computer and Information Sciences now offered).

The Plan committed the school to an honors program, established in 1987.

Shifting its focus to the Corps of Cadets, the Plan called for the institution of a leadership training program for fourth classmen. This initiative would demonstrate the need for structured training for all four classes, leading eventually to the Krause Center, but an important first step was taken here.

Where faculty was concerned, the Plan called for hiring and rewarding active scholarship and an expectation of terminal degrees. It also committed the school to the increased hiring of African-Americans and women as faculty members. Programs designed for faculty development included hosting visiting professors, employing adjunct faculty, grants for additional study and sabbaticals, endowed chairs and realistic workload policies.

To assure proficiency, graduating seniors would be administered Graduate Record Examinations (GREs), or comparable standardized tests. Applicants were to be admitted based on higher SAT/ACT scores, high school GPAs, class standing and on extra-curriculars. Recruitment of students was to continue to be nationwide, consistent with The Citadel's status as a national asset, and recruiting efforts "to obtain black candidates for the Corps will continue to be emphasized and increased."

To furnish academic support the Plan committed to improving the quality of the library, archives and museum. To enhance support for academic departments, it called for a study of an integrated multi-purpose learning center designed to provide remedial instruction, instructional enrichment, a language laboratory, audio and visual assets for various courses, and the production of instructional materials. The computer facilities and capabilities would gradually be upgraded pursuant to a 10-year plan to modernize them. Student services were to be expanded to assure the retention of cadets and graduate students and to enhance their learning environment. The Plan called for the establishment of "acceptable and reasonably attainable goals for minority recruitment" of administrative personnel.

In terms of bricks and mortar facilities, the Plan acknowledged that the decade ahead would require "relatively little major new construction." It envisioned additions to the library, Mark Clark Hall and LeTellier Hall and construction of a faculty/club center and a new varsity athletics center to be named Seignious Hall. Renovations to existing facilities included Bond, Thompson and Alumni Halls, Johnson Hagood Stadium and faculty housing.

The Plan reaffirmed the school's commitment to excellence in intercollegiate sports without specifying how that excellence would be achieved. Intramural sports were acknowledged as essential to the "whole man" concept and would be "continued and vigorously supported."

Lastly, the Grimsley Plan dealt with the college's relationship to the Charleston Higher Education Consortium. It began by reaffirming the policy of "restricting Citadel day classes to male Citadel registrants," but agreed to cooperate with Consortium member institutions whenever it was in the best interests of all to do so. Areas singled out as having the potential for mutual benefit included library acquisitions and computerized search capability, use of physical facilities to avoid duplication, sharing expense and services of faculty and staff in positions "no single school might be in a position to fill," and development of new graduate programs leading to consortial degrees (i.e. degrees granted by two or more cooperating institutions).[303]

On January 28, 1982, General William Westmoreland, former commander of U.S. forces in Vietnam, gave the Greater Issues speech in McAlister Field House. Westmoreland attended The Citadel from 1936-37 before matriculating at West Point, a history that allowed him to remind his audience that "I was a 'rat' at this West Point of the South for one year followed by being a 'plebe' at the Citadel of the North."[304] If any of the 500 in attendance came in anticipation of hearing a post-mortem on Vietnam, they left disappointed. His subject was America's preparedness in the event of a first-strike missile assault by the Soviet Union, predicting that by the end of the decade such an attack could overpower the United States. He voiced skepticism over the disarmament talks in which Seignious had become so immersed, reinforcing the military's view that our nuclear stockpiles were gravely depleted, though he did concede that both sides probably had enough to deter the other from a war.[305]

Had Westmoreland known what the nation was to learn in the year ahead, he undoubtedly would have spoken of the heroism of Arland D. Williams, Jr., Class of 1957. But for months following the crash of Air Florida Flight 90, the identity of "the man in the water" had not been confirmed. On January 13, 1982, Williams and 73 other passengers boarded a Boeing 737 with a crew of five on a bitterly cold day in Washington, D.C. A steady snowfall and the need to clear the runways at Reagan Airport (then Washington National Airport) resulted in a delayed departure. Shortly after takeoff the plane began shaking violently, according to a surviving passenger, Joe Stiley. It climbed only a few hundred feet before plunging downward at a point within sight of where a terrorist plane would strike the Pentagon 19 years later. It struck the 14th Street Bridge, killing four commuters idling in heavy traffic stalled by the snow. The plane plunged into the Potomac, where the water temperature had reached 33, one degree above freezing. Ice caked the banks of the river, and only in the channel did water flow in a state of semi-slush.

Five passengers and one crew member, a stewardess seated at the back of the plane for takeoff, surfaced. They clung to the plane's tail section, the only debris not submerged, as a crowd began to gather on the banks of the Potomac. An inflatable raft launched from shore proved useless, locked in ice so thick it couldn't be broken. Maximum survival time in water that cold is put at 30 minutes, so by the time a rescue helicopter arrived on the scene 20 minutes after impact, the lives of the freezing victims were very much in doubt. The chopper hovered over the tail, dropping life vests and a floatation ring. The man in the water passed these to others. On two occasions, he passed rescue ropes that could have been used to save himself. When five of the six crash survivors had been safely brought to shore, the chopper returned to the tail, which by then had sunk further, taking with it the man in the water, the only casualty of the crash to die from drowning.

Twelve days after the crash, *Time Magazine* published an essay by Roger Rosenblatt entitled "The Man in the Water." The essay does not mention the man's name, still unknown. Here is an excerpt from that essay:

> He was there, in the essential, classic circumstance. Man in nature. The man in the water. For its part, nature cared nothing about the five passengers. Our man, on the other hand, cared totally. So, the timeless battle commenced in the Potomac. For as long as that man could last, they went at each other, nature and man: the one making no distinctions of good and evil, acting on no principals, offering no lifelines; the other acting wholly on distinctions, principles and one supposes, on faith.

Arland Williams came to The Citadel from Mattoon, Illinois, where he was known as Chub, a nickname that followed him to Charleston. He majored in Business Administration, served on the Salute Gun Battery his junior year, and rose to the rank of sergeant in O Company his senior year. He was likely a quiet, unassuming cadet, as General Claudius Watts, a corporal in O Company and a class behind Williams, has no personal recollection of him.[306]

Eighteen months after the accident, President Reagan presented the Coast Guard's Gold Lifesaving Medal to Williams's mother in an Oval Office ceremony. Reagan said, "Virtually everyone in the United States knows of his heroism, knows of his deeds, but very few if any knew his name." It took months of investigation by the Coast Guard to establish conclusively that Williams was the man in the water. That investigation revealed that he had been initially trapped in the rear section of the plane by a jammed seatbelt.

The Coast Guard's citation stated, "By not grabbing the rescue line and occupying valuable time in what probably would have been a futile effort to pull himself free, other survivors who might have perished if they had been in the frigid waters much longer, were saved. Mr. Williams sacrificed his own life so that others may live."[307] In 1983, The Citadel's own Fritz Hollings spearheaded a campaign that in 1985 resulted in the 14th Street Bridge being renamed the Arland D. Williams, Jr., Memorial Bridge.[308]

The Citadel honored Williams as well. In 1982, he received the Algernon Sydney Sullivan Award. Funded in part by gift from his mother, the board in 1985 established the Arland D. Williams Endowed Professorship of Heroism within the Psychology Department.[309]

During President Reagan's commencement address in 1993, he paid tribute to Williams:

> But for me, there is one name that will always come to mind when I think of The Citadel and the Corps of Cadets. It is a name that appears in no military histories; its owner won no glory on the field of battle. ... Many of you here today know his name as well as I do, for his portrait now hangs with honor —as indeed it should — on this very campus: the campus where he once walked, as you have, through the Summerall Gate and along the Avenue of Remembrance. He was a young first classman with a crisp uniform and a confident stride on a bright spring morning, full of hopes and plans for the future. He never dreamed that his life's supreme challenge would come in its final moments, some 25 years later, adrift in the bone-chilling waters of an ice-strewn river and surrounded by others who desperately needed help. But when the challenge came, he was ready. His name was Arland D. Williams, Jr., The Citadel Class of 1957. He brought honor to his alma mater, and honor to his nation.

Reagan spoke eloquently of the times in life when proof of character is offered up in a moment of crisis:

> But such occasions, in fact, are rather rare — far rarer, I suspect, than the confident eyes of one's early 20s can quite perceive. Far more often than we can comfortably admit, the most crucial of life's moments come like the scriptural "thief in the night." Suddenly and without notice the crisis is upon us and the moment of

choice is at hand — a moment fraught with import for ourselves, and for all who are depending on the choice we make. We find ourselves, if you will, plunged without warning into the icy water, where the currents of moral consequence run swift and deep, and where our fellow man — and yes, I believe our Maker — are waiting to see whether we will pass the rope. These are the moments when instinct and character take command, as they took command for Arland Williams on the day our Lord would call him home. For there is no time, at such moments, for anything but fortitude and integrity.[310]

At its September 1982 meeting of the Board of Visitors, General Grimsley was able to report Corps enrollment of 2,058, or 98 more than the 1960 accommodated by the barracks. He attributed the "over-strength" to a higher return and retention rate in the upper classes, reduced knob attrition and an excellent training cadre. For knobs, space in alcove rooms was maximized and larger two-man rooms housed three. Upper classmen resided in trailers and Thompson Hall. All South Carolina counties were represented in the freshman class. Knob attrition stood at 21, a mere 3.3percent compared with 6percent (49 knobs) the prior year, an improvement Grimsley attributed to a higher caliber of matriculates, a better training cadre and better leadership techniques. A full one-third of the Corps pursued Business Administration as a major.[311]

He also introduced Ambassador Jack R. Perry, holder of the John C. West Chair of International Affairs. As Diplomat in Residence, Perry was one of many distinguished senior members of the State Department's Foreign Service who taught and gave lectures, both on campus and within the Charleston Consortium.[312] That endowed chair and the speaker series begun in 1999 constituted part of Governor West's enduring legacy to the college.

Another strong benefactor's generosity made possible Seignious Hall, a long-sought home for varsity sports. The $1.5 million facility contained locker and weight rooms, offices, a laundry and equipment needed by trainers. While named in honor of Seignious, funding was made possible by a $1 million gift from Hugh Daniel, Class of 1929. In 1976, Seignious had joined the board of Daniel International (nee Daniel Construction Co.), founded by Hugh's brother Charles, who attended The Citadel for two years before he answered the call to serve in World War I. Soon after Seignious joined, Fluor International sought to acquire the Daniel company, a move Hugh opposed. Prior to the crucial meeting at which the issue would be decided,

Hugh suffered a stroke. At Hugh's request, Seignious made the case to the board against acquiescing in the Fluor takeover. The vote went against Daniel Construction Co. and Seignious, but Hugh, in a gesture of loyalty and respect, insisted the varsity facility be named for Seignious, who was on hand for the dedication in November.[313]

As *The Brigadier* went to press on November 19, 1982, senior cadet Louis Venable sought to set the world record for bent knee sit-ups, vowing to remain in Deas Hall until he reached his goal of at least 50,000. He estimated he would need 25 hours and a few bathroom breaks, the prize to be recognition in the Guinness Book of Records.[314]

In February 1983, the Curriculum Study Committee under the chairmanship of Colonel Isaac "Spike" Metts notified the faculty of the Committee's intent to establish an Honors program, an idea which received support from the Advisory Committee the following month.[315] Implementation required $70,000, half of which the school sought from the state. The Honors program would furnish superior students with a challenging curriculum and was perceived as an essential third leg of an academic triad, the other two being a Core Curriculum for average students and remedial help for those needing it (math and writing labs, counselors, tutors, etc.)[316] The delay in implementing it stemmed not from opposition but from competing priorities. Major Jack Rhodes, associate professor of English, served as director of the program.[317] To publicize this important addition to academic opportunity available at The Citadel, the college sent pamphlets detailing the Honors program to all South Carolina high school guidance counselors and all teachers of advanced placement subjects. Recruitment efforts aimed at students focused on about 5000 with high SAT scores.[318] It was not until the fall of 1987 that 15 entering freshmen were selected to be the first participants. They averaged 1243 on their SATs and ranked in the top 3.5 percent of their classes.[319] After the first semester, Honors students averaged a full grade point higher than non-Honors. An exceptional academic performance in the first semester by one student earned him a spot in the program thereafter, while two were dropped due to grades. Honors classes were opened to others on a space-available basis.[320]

In October 1983, the price of freedom again came home to us when we learned of the deaths of two deployed alumni three days apart. First Lieutenant Charles J. Schnorf, USMC, Class of 1981, embraced the full Citadel experience, serving as a sophomore corporal, a junior first sergeant, and in his senior year as a cadet major, the First Battalion Executive Officer. He was a member of the Summerall Guards and earned scholarships from both

Naval ROTC and the CDF. He was the recipient of the National Sojourners Award, presented to the cadet who "demonstrates and encourages the ideals of Americanism within the Corps of Cadets." Following graduation with a degree in business administration, Schnorf was commissioned as asecond Lieutenant in the Marine Corps. He completed officer basic and artillery training at Fort Sill before being assigned to Camp Lejeune. In May 1983, he deployed with the 24th Marine Amphibious Unit to Beirut, Lebanon, as part of the Multinational Peacekeeping Force based there.[321] On October 23, 1983, a truck driven by a suicide bomber exploded outside the barracks where the Marines were housed. In the deadliest single day loss of life experienced by the Marine Corps since Iwo Jima, 241 perished. First Lieutenant Schnorf was one of them. The bomber was Iranian and the attack, claimed by a group calling itself the Islamic Jihad, was believed to have been ordered in Tehran. Iran denied responsibility, but in 2004 its government built a monument to the bomber of the barracks and to the bomber of the Drakkar Building, where 58 French paratroopers were killed on the same day.[322] In 1977, when Schnorf reported for his knob year, the Corps of Cadets included a significant number of Iranians, but by the time he graduated in 1981 there were none. In 1992 a new obstacle course on campus was dedicated to Schnorf.[323]

Army Captain Michael F. Ritz, Class of 1977, was attached to the 82nd Airborne deployed to Grenada, the small island nation 100 miles north of Venezuela. A growing Soviet-Cuban influence had been a source of concern for months leading up to mid-October, when Communist rebels executed the Prime Minister and other officials to impose a government they called the Revolutionary Military Council. On the island at the time were over 600 U.S. medical students, giving rise to the possibility they would be taken as hostages in a replay of the Iranian hostage crisis. President Reagan ordered Operation Urgent Fury, a combined assault that began on October 25, 1983. On Day 2 of the invasion, near Calliste, a Cuban force ambushed a patrol from the 325th Infantry Regiment. Ritz commanded B Company and in the fire fight was killed in action. The students were saved, the deposed government returned to authority, and by November 1 order had been restored to the island. At The Citadel, Ritz, born in Munich, Germany, served as a cadet officer and played on the soccer team. Grenada remains a free nation today in part due to his sacrifice.[324]

In March 1984, the visiting SACS team arrived on campus for the on-site inspections required for recertification every 10 years. By letter dated June 7, 1984, the school received the SACS recommendations for improvement, many of which dealt with the contents of publications and clear delineation of the programs within the Corps from those of the Evening College. Grimsley responded by letter on August 28, 1984. He diplomatically agreed with most of the suggestions and said, in so many words, "we're working on it." But to one recommendation he was adamantly opposed, and said so. Dr. Henry Ashmore, author of the SACS letter, recommended that the Commandant report to the Vice President for Academic Affairs rather than directly to the president, as had long been Citadel policy. Grimsley let Ashmore know that such policy was not about to change. He stated that "even on activities related to academic performance of cadets, [the recommended change] would create a number of problems and inevitably draw the Vice President for Academic Affairs into disciplinary and military life concerns. Presently, the Vice President has input into such matters at the policy level, but the recommended change would draw him into operational aspects that would dilute his role." SACS reaccreditation followed the exchange.

In April, General Clark died. As would be expected, tributes poured in from all over the world. Billy Graham, then in Europe and unable to make the funeral, sent a letter of praise read by the former chaplain, Sidney Crumpton. A crowd estimated at 1,250 filled Summerall Chapel. Cadets served as pallbearers as Clark was laid to rest between the chapel and hall that bears his name. Amidst full-page photos of the pomp and ceremony, *The News and Courier* printed a letter that showed Clark's human side. Perhaps reprinting it here will give comfort to parents of cadets who hear from their sons and daughters only sparingly. Clark wrote:

> Following the capture of Rome and during the flight of the Germans toward the Arno, I had received a great many personal messages in which my friends and various distinguished persons had said some pleasant things about the accomplishments of the Fifth Army. Naturally, I had appreciated the messages, but I had kept looking for a letter from my son, Bill, who was a cadet at West Point. I had long since realized that he didn't write very often, but I had assumed I would hear from him after he read about the fall of Rome. Sure enough, I got a letter after a certain length of time. I opened it with considerable pleasure. I suppose that, after all is said and done, a man is most interested in what his son thinks of his accomplishments. In that light, the letter was rather interesting. It said:
> Dear Dad:
> It is June here and very pleasant (that was enlightening because it

was June in Italy, too). My studies are going along OK and I have very good marks this time. I have been made a cadet sergeant. We licked Navy at baseball yesterday. I took a blonde from New York to a dance last night and we had a wonderful time. Sorry I can't write more, but I have to make a formation.

Love, Bill

P.S. By the way, I see from the newspapers that you're doing alright, too.[325]

As a tribute to Clark, the board agreed to contribute $1,000 "to be specifically characterized as initial construction money for a building on The Citadel campus to house the Mark Clark Museum."[326] Today, 33 years later, no such museum exists. In fact, thousands of Clark's letters, photographs and memorabilia languish in the archives, which lacked even an archivist for five years after Jane Yates retired in 2011. In 2016 the school hired a bright, energetic archivist named Tessa Updike. She is methodically working to master what is there. Also in 2016, The Citadel Museum reopened on the third floor of the Daniel Library. As it stands, it is a small but impressive collection that will eventually be expanded. Just the recreation of a cadet room in the Old Citadel is worth a tour. Head librarian David Goble, Class of 1969 and the Regimental Commander who insisted on the "Corps running the Corps" as related in Chapter 4, is committed to preserving the college's rich heritage with additional collections.

General Grimsley summarized 1983-1984 as "an excellent year." He was particularly pleased with increased financial management and accountability, crediting their success to the system of quarterly program and budget reviews which he instituted in 1978 and the hiring of a fully qualified internal auditor in January 1984. The year was indisputably a good one for 1984 graduates. Dr. Tucker Weston, president of the Association of Citadel Men, put the unemployment rate for the class at "zero."[327]

The Business Department sought accreditation from the American Assembly of the Collegiate Schools of Business (AACSB). Dr. Robert King, head of the department, told the board that "no action is contemplated to establish a School of Business Administration," yet that was precisely what was done under General Grinalds' reorganization in 2002. The department faced other challenges to become accredited. An insufficient number of its faculty was engaged in research and publication — only six of 25 "would be judged satisfactorily in this category." Salaries presented another hurdle to accreditation. The average full professor at The Citadel made $4,300 less annually than those at the average AACSB accredited college. Dr. King's description of the department's equipment is a time capsule of sorts for technology in the mid-1980s. Not only did every classroom within the department have an overhead projector and mounted projection screen, but there was also a departmental movie projector, slide projector and opaque projector. The departmental office housed a CPT word-processor, a computer terminal, and an Apple IIe computer. There were some electric typewriters and "some marginally operational manual" ones, along with "modern electronic desk calculators."[328]

In the fall of 1985, two acts of violence were linked to the college, the first one a fatality. A Citadel Army TAC, Captain James M. Watson, brutally murdered his 31-year-old wife by shooting her 20 times in their James Island home. An accessory to the crime was also apparently the motive. The couple's 21-year-old baby sitter knew of Watson's plan months in advance.[329] In March 1986, a jury of seven men and five women took two and a half hours to convict Watson of murder. He was sentenced to life in prison, ineligible for parole for 20 years.[330] His lover pleaded guilty to failure to report a felony and received a five-year suspended sentence, three months of community service and a year of probation.[331] As General Grimsley reported to the board in June, the school "suffered no adverse public attention" in the matter, though news reports at the time consistently reported Watson's employment.[332]

The second violent impact took place on the football field. The team traveled to Johnson City, Tennessee to play East Tennessee State University, a rival it had not beaten in 20 years. Entering the game with a record of 2-3-1, the Dogs were hungry to get back to .500.[333] In the first quarter of a game the Bulldogs would ultimately win, tragedy struck when sophomore linebacker Marc Buoniconti tackled ESTU running back Herman Jacobs. Following the impact, Buoniconti did not move. Trainer Andy Clawson and team physician Dr. Buddy Wallace rushed onto the field "within five seconds," Citadel Athletic Director Walt Nadzak told *The News and Courier*.[334] As they cut away Buoniconti's jersey and pads, head coach Tom Moore approached to check on his player. "I knew it was bad. He turned as blue as our helmets. He nearly died." Moore returned to the sideline, went behind the bench, and puked.[335] According to Marc's father, all-pro and National Football League Hall of Fame linebacker Nick Buoniconti, his son's injury was like that suffered by Darryl Stingley, the New England Patriots wide receiver paralyzed by an infamous tackle by the Oakland Raiders' Jack Tatum. Stingley spent the rest of his life in a wheelchair, and the apprehension within The Citadel family and no doubt Buoniconti's family was that a similar fate awaited Marc.

On the Monday following the injury, an air ambulance from the University of Miami's Jackson Memorial Medical Center flew to Johnson City to transport Marc back to Florida. In November he underwent successful surgery to fuse the ruined vertebra in his spine at C-3. Dr. Barth Green, the chief surgeon and an internationally recognized expert in spinal cord injuries, put his chances of recovery at three-to-four percent. General Grimsley and Colonel George James, chairman of the Board of Visitors, traveled to Miami to express their concern.[336]

As Marc began his rehabilitation, his father teamed up with Dr. Green to found The Miami Project to Cure Paralysis. Operating from the Center of Excellence at the University of Miami Miller School of Medicine, it has become the premier investigative research program for brain and spine injuries. In 1992, Marc's family established the Buoniconti Fund to Cure Paralysis, the fundraising arm of the Miami Project, which has raised half a billion dollars for research.[337]

In an act that would engender bitterness for two decades, Buoniconti sued The Citadel, trainer Andy Clawson and Dr. Wallace for damages in excess of $16 million. The case came to trial in 1988. Buoniconti's lawyers claimed that their client should never have been allowed to play against ETSU because a neck injury had kept him out of contact practice in the week leading up to the game. They also claimed liability based on a horse collar and strap that Clawson had fashioned as a way to keep Buoniconti's head from excessive backward movement. For his part, Clawson defended his equipment as an accepted precaution against neck and head trauma as well as the decision to allow Buoniconti to play. Besides, the school contended, the real source of the injury was an illegal spear tackle. No penalty was called on the play, but at trial dueling experts disputed the legality of the hit. The trial ended with an $800,000 settlement paid by the school's insurance company and a jury finding of no liability on the part of Dr. Wallace.

Joel Thompson, Class of 1987, played linebacker with Buoniconti. On a visit to Buoniconti's condo in Coral Gables, Thompson was surprised to see Marc's Citadel blue home jersey hanging in a closet. It inspired Thompson to explore a reconciliation. "Marc, I love The Citadel," he said. "And I love you. Is there any way we can get you guys back together?'" When Buoniconti expressed cautious receptiveness, Thompson took the lead. He called their teammates, organized meetings and approached the Board of Visitors. In 2006, The Citadel welcomed Buoniconti home at Corps Day. "They rolled out the red carpet for me," Buoniconti said.

Six months later, on Friday, September 29, 2006, the Alumni Association presented Buoniconti with an honorary Class of 1988 ring at a moving ceremony at the Holliday Alumni Center.[338] The next day, at half-time of the game against Chattanooga, the school retired his number, 59, and presented him with the framed jersey he had been wearing when he tackled Herman Jacobs.[339] He received a standing ovation from the crowd of more than 12,000. The pep talk he gave the team before the game may have been the difference in a contest that ended 24-21 in the Bulldogs' favor. "This weekend has totally exceeded all my expectations, all my hopes and dreams," he said.[340]

Marc Buoniconti and Herman Jacobs were destined to meet again. As part of The Citadel's reconciliation with Marc, it began an annual event to raise money for The Miami Project. The next year Marc decided to look up Jacobs and invite him. He found him managing a fast-food restaurant across the street from Middle Tennessee's stadium. When Buoniconti asked Jacobs what his dream was, he learned Jacobs had an ambition to become a chef. That knowledge prompted Marc to invite Jacobs to Miami, where they visited Johnson & Wales, the culinary training school. Jacobs subsequently applied, was accepted and received a scholarship, but he had no place in Miami to live. Marc offered his place, and the two lived together for six months. When Marc's nurse took time off for an illness, it fell to Jacobs to lift Marc into his wheelchair each morning. The two men who had collided violently in 1985 had become mutually dependent. Buoniconti cheered from the audience when Jacobs received his diploma from Johnson & Wales in 2010. They remain great friends.[341]

In an interview with the Associated Press in 2010, Buoniconti said he has "never been more optimistic about walking again than I am right now."[342]

Following conclusion of the 1985-1986 academic year, President Grimsley and the board took stock, finding a solid basis for optimism. In his report to the board, Grimsley sought to put the midpoint of his administration into historical perspective by reciting what he believed to be the three formative periods of the college's modern era: (1) Summerall's tenure from 1931 into the early 1950s; (2) General Clark's presidency ending in 1965; and (3) the current Citadel. A major contributor to his bullish view of the future was The General Mark W. Clark Campaign for The Citadel Tomorrow, which had been launched the previous October with a fundraising goal of $27 million. He reported the kickoff "in a formal banquet setting with a great deal of fanfare orchestrated with traditional Citadel elements providing entertainment, color, and a disciplined patriotic ambiance with 429 important members of Citadel constituencies attending or participating. The occasion was hailed as the most ambitious and successful event of its kind ever staged at The

Citadel." Thus far $15.5 million had been raised in a campaign expected to last 3 to 5 years. Two years later, he told the board that the unparalleled success of the effort, with over $25 million in gifts, pledges and bequests, had "ensured the future of the college."[343]

Grimsley also reported on his activities as president. In addition to his administrative duties at the college, he found or made time in the prior 12 months to give 82 public presentations, serve on 21 public boards or commissions, and host at Quarters 1 with his wife, Jessie, 48 official functions attended by over 6,000 invitees. Grimsley's successors kept equally ambitious schedules, a testament to those given the highest responsibility.

A review of state and national publicity found no negative articles. In a story reprinted by several other publications, *The Washington Post* hailed "An American Sparta," noting, "A Citadel graduate gains far more than honor. In South Carolina, the ring is an important calling card, opening doors for jobs or bank loans. In a state steeped in military tradition and military bases, Citadel men are considered the cream of the crop."

Assimilation of black cadets was given an equally positive perspective. "Chip Lilliewood, 21, a black senior from Columbia, S.C., said racial tension at The Citadel melts in the uniformity of campus life. He said he expects to tap the influential alumni network after graduation. 'I'm sure there will be a few good old boys,' he said. 'But for the most part, those guys are going to help.'"[344]

This kind of press would be especially valued in light of the Nesmith storm that broke a few months later. One of the school's most regrettable episodes, it occurred in October 1986 when five white juniors decided it would be a good idea to dress as Ku Klux Klansmen and intimidate Kevin Nesmith, a black knob whose older brother happened to be a Citadel graduate and the first black member of the Board of Visitors. At 1 a.m., the hooded juniors entered Nesmith's room yelling obscenities. Nesmith's roommate, Michael Mendoza, awoke and confronted the intruders. A scuffle took place and the juniors fled, leaving behind a towel traced to the cadet wearing it and a small charred paper cross one of the five had crafted in his room. According to a news report of the incident, Nesmith was largely unaware that anything had happened, awaking as the intruders left, but not even that much exposure is certain. Isaac "Spike" Metts, faculty advisor to Nesmith at the time, insists that "Kevin slept through the whole thing."[345]

The black community expressed outrage. At a football game in November, 40 black members of the Corps of Cadets remained seated in protest when the rest of the Corps stood for the playing of "Dixie". The NAACP and local black ministers called for the offending cadets to be expelled and for Grimsley to be fired. On Saturday before The Citadel played East Tennessee State at Johnson Hagood, some 200 mostly black demonstrators gathered at Jerusalem Baptist Church on Rutledge Avenue. Dr. William Gibson of Greenville, national president of the NAACP, told those assembled at the church that "What went on there was no prank, nothing you can write off by saying 'boys will be boys.' I'm here to tell the general, 'You all have opened a whole can of worms — a bad can of worms — and the top won't be put back on as easily as it came off.'" His listeners included Nesmith's mother and brother, Amelia and Larry Nesmith, as well as state Senator Herbert Fielding. Led by a car with a loudspeaker on the roof, the crowd marched to Lesesne Gate as taped speeches by Dr. Martin Luther King, Jr. blared through Hampton Park. At the gate, they sang civil rights songs and chanted "Five cadets must go." From there, they proceeded to the Alumni House, where the chant changed to "Grimsley must go." Charleston police and State Law Enforcement agents guarded the route as a helicopter circled overhead. Chief Reuben Greenberg, taking no chances on security, said, "We just want to make sure we don't have some individual who wants to right all the wrongs of slavery or some yo-yo who wants to fight the Civil War again." The march ended outside the stadium while inside Grimsley received a 13-gun salute before the game.[346] Despite demands from the Nesmiths, the NAACP and local black leaders for the expulsion of the cadets involved, General Grimsley imposed stiff punishment orders consisting of 195 tours and restriction to the campus for the rest of the school year.

The Nesmith incident generated negative publicity for the college across the state and in national publications. Kevin Nesmith and the NAACP sued the five disciplined cadets, The Citadel, General Grimsley and two college administrators for $880,000, accusing the school of "racial terrorism."[347] The case settled in 1989 for an undisclosed amount, by which time Nesmith was a sophomore studying at South Carolina State, having left The Citadel soon after the incident that prompted the lawsuit.[348]

Reaction to the Nesmith incident varied predictably on the outrage scale, from those at the far-right end who viewed it as little more than a benign practical joke to those on the left who felt it confirmed a deep-seated racism endemic within the Corps. Heightening racial tensions during this period were the playing of "Dixie" at parades and football games and the waving of the Confederate battle flag at Johnson Hagood Stadium. To most members of the Corps, these were traditions that gave emotional vent to the school's most fundamental virtues: manliness, pride and patriotism. To the black minority, the message conveyed was quite different: slavery, oppression, subjugation. Through the second half of the 1980s and well into the 1990s, these competing narratives created the kind of tensions experienced in the rest of South Carolina and the nation.

Some months after the NAACP marched to the stadium, Mayor Riley weighed in with his thoughts on the controversy. His letter, entitled "Our Heritage and Our Future," is worth reprinting in its entirety:

> The pride that many have in the Confederate flag and "Dixie" should be easily understood and honored. The negative feelings that many have about some uses of the Confederate flag and "Dixie" should be easily understood and honored as well. I believe we can do both — and we must. For we must not only look to our past, we must build our future, together.
>
> The Confederate flag (battle flag) connotes at least two symbols. It became, in this century, a symbol of resistance to integration, resistance to the abolition of the repressive Jim Crow laws and, most unfortunately, a symbol of racial bigotry largely aided and abetted by the Ku Klux Klan. All people of good will, white and black, must admit that the use of the Confederate flag in this fashion or as a reminder of racial segregation and the resistance to the New South is improper and should be avoided.
>
> On the other hand, the flag is a reminder to many of those who fought and died gallantly, not so much to preserve slavery, although unquestionably many of those involved in the battle were seeking to do so, but rather as a battle then almost 100 years old about state sovereignty and independence. It is also the flag of a nation defeated in war and a people who suffered through a bitter occupation and a long period of economic deprivation. For grandsons and granddaughters, great-grandsons and great-granddaughters of those who fought in the Civil War, to wish to have ways to remember the bravery of their ancestors is understandable.
>
> In my opinion, this is best done, not by waving the Confederate battle flag above the Statehouse in an obviously controversial gesture, but rather in furling the flag and giving it places of honor in our museums and historical exhibits. One of the most moving and quiet expressions of honor for the valor of those who fought for the South in the Civil War is in the Lee Chapel at Washington and Lee University. There, inside the chapel, over the tomb of Robert

E. Lee, hangs the Confederate battle flag and the other flags of the Confederacy. It is done with honor, quality and respect. My belief is that those who fought for the South in the Civil War and lost would much prefer their flag to be treated with this respect and honor rather than having it fly as a pennant on the third rung of any flag pole.

"Dixie" was written as a minstrel walk-around by a Northerner and was popular around the country before the Civil War. As a matter of fact, President Lincoln asked the White House Band to play "Dixie" the week before he died.

Just as with the Confederate flag, "Dixie" has been appropriated by the Ku Klux Klan and others as a symbol of resistance to racial integration and racial progress. At Ku Klux Klan rallies as well as meetings held to protest civil rights advancements, you would always have a war-whooping rendition of "Dixie." It became the fight song, if you will, against racial progress. It is for that reason and understandably so, I believe, that you will seldom see a black person during a war-whooping rendition of "Dixie." While many white people are standing and cheering, our black friends are often sitting quietly, if not nervously, wishing the time would quickly pass. For they know that some of those who are cheering are doing so because deep down in their hearts, they wish that the racial progress that we have achieved had never occurred.

Yet "Dixie" does not have to be and should not be appropriated to those war-whooping circumstances. To me, "Dixie" is a hymn best played and sung softly, quietly and with melancholy. I have been greatly moved when hearing it played or sung in this fashion, perhaps no more so than a year ago when I heard and saw a very talented black woman sing it in that fashion. In that context, it is not a song of slavery or bigotry, but rather a lyrical and poetic song of years past. That is where "Dixie" belongs and how "Dixie" should be played and sung, as a ballad at concerts and other settings where black and white citizens together can enjoy its beauty and feel its nostalgia, without the attendant whooping and hollering.

Among such talk about our Southern heritage, we should emphasize the over-arching Southern quality of good manners. We are proud of that aspect of our heritage and our lifestyle. Good manners dictate that we should attempt to put ourselves in our friends' and neighbors' shoes, and that we not do things intentionally to make them uncomfortable, uneasy or sad.

Removing the Confederate battle flags from our public buildings and putting them in our museums and shrines, and taking "Dixie" out of the fight song environment and putting it into concerts, will be big steps toward the fulfillment of this aspect of our Southern heritage. And most important of all, it will remove yet another barrier to black and white Southerners achieving social and economic progress together.[349]

Six months after Riley's letter was published, David Wilson reported as a member of the Class of 1991. Wilson, an African-American, grew up in Charleston and attended Burke High School. His mother, a nurse at Roper Hospital, instilled in him and his older siblings a strong work ethic. At an early age he washed cars and shined shoes at car dealerships along Morrison Avenue near his home. When Harold Arnold, Citadel Class of 1963, bought Sentry Buick located next to David's home, Arnold appreciated at once Wilson's energy and drive, but also recognized that Wilson was legally too young to be working there. So, Wilson went back to shining shoes. When he turned 15, Arnold offered him his old car-washing job back. Wilson accepted, and Arnold became both his employer and his mentor. They developed a close and lasting friendship. Later, as Wilson advanced in rank and Arnold in age, they often discussed who should be answering to whom with "yes, sir."[350]

At The Citadel, Wilson served as a cadet officer, was a member of the Gospel Choir, wrestled and was elected president of the Afro-American Society. He made the Dean's List and the Commandant's List. He joined the South Carolina National Guard.

Upon graduation, Wilson was commissioned as a second lieutenant in the Army. He completed Artillery Officer Basic Training before being assigned to Camp Hovey in Korea. In 1996, while stationed in California, his future in the Army — indeed, his entire future —became uncertain when he was diagnosed with stage 4 kidney cancer. At the time, four out of five people afflicted with that disease died from it. He was told he had 90 days to get his affairs in order. Ninety days later he celebrated his victory over the disease. He went on to a stellar career, earning a Bronze Star and a chest full of notable military decorations. On April 13, 2017, he became the first African-American Citadel graduate promoted to the rank of general while on active duty.

As the site for his promotion ceremony, he chose Mark Clark Hall. Present that day were the people Wilson generously acknowledged for their contributions to his success. His wife, Patricia, his daughters Victoria and Rebecca, Harold and Martha Arnold, and others. Presiding over the ceremony was another South Carolinian, also African-American, Lieutenant General Stephen M. Twitty, the First Army's commanding general and a 1985 graduate of South Carolina State University. In his extensive remarks, Twitty noted the full room and celebratory atmosphere. Wilson's understated humility came through in his remarks. He quoted an African proverb: If you want to run fast, run alone. If you want to run far, run with others. Citadel graduates present along with the entire room of attendees gave him a standing ovation.

In the fall of 1988, the board adopted a Core Curriculum to go into effect beginning with the 1989-90 school year. When implemented, each student would be required to complete four semesters of English, a two-semester sequence in the History of Western Civilization, two-semester sequences in Biology, Chemistry or Physics for at least 16 credit hours in science, a two-semester sequence in math (the nature of which differed depending on whether the student was a B.A. or B.S. candidate), one semester in the social sciences (Political Science, Psychology, Business Administration), and two years of the same foreign language except for those students pursuing pre-professional disciplines such as Civil or Electrical Engineering and teacher preparation in English and Physical Education.

Tensions between the academic side of the college and the Commandant's Department surfaced with this statement in the description of the Core Curriculum: "Current efforts toward providing our entering students an adequate introduction to the academic aspects of college life are inconsequential when compared with those designed to introduce those same students to the cadet lifestyle." To remedy the perceived imbalance, the Vice President for Academic Affairs was charged with establishing a Freshman Academic Orientation Program "to ensure that entering Freshmen understand their roles as college students; are aware of the academic opportunities provided by The Citadel's 14 academic departments; are familiar with campus facilities and services; and are fully informed concerning their responsibilities and expectations as students."[351]

In a gesture that foreshadowed his retirement announcement the following January, General Grimsley pledged $1,000 per year for life with a $15,000 bequest at his death to establish "The President's Award for Teaching Excellence." The board accepted the gift with deep appreciation and unanimously renamed it "The Major General James A. Grimsley, Jr., Award for Teaching Excellence."[352]

At the January 1989 meeting of the Board of Visitors, Grimsley announced his retirement, effective June 30, 1989, giving the board six months to find a replacement. As would be expected at the end of nearly a decade as a successful president and an additional five years as a vice president and dean, tributes arose from numerous sources. A March 1989 concurrent resolution from the South Carolina House and Senate cited nine accomplishments during his administration and they present a yardstick by which to measure his administration against the goals set out at the beginning of it.

— "The steady upgrade in the Corps of Cadets, the centerpiece of The Citadel, in performance, appearance, leadership and caliber." Though this conclusion is perhaps the most subjective of the nine cited, there is some empirical support for it. The entering class in 1988 recorded an average GPA of 2.07 for the first semester, the highest in nine years. The Honors Program initiated in 1987 produced dividends, with Honors students averaging about a grade point higher than non-Honors.[353]

— "The increased application rate during the past five years by quality young men, nationwide, seeking admission." Applications for the class that entered in 1983 totaled about 2,000 and had been cut off for both in-state and out-of-state by the time the board met in March. The next year, applications were up again, necessitating an earlier cutoff date. Applications continued their upward climb in 1985, 1986 and 1987, permitting greater selectivity. With this trend came caution due to limited space in the barracks. Gone were the days of 700-plus knob classes, as there was simply no place to house them. In 1989, Corps strength stood at 1,987, and even at that level 19 cadets could not be billeted in the barracks. The cap on freshman admissions for the fall of 1989 was put at 550.

— "Recognition of The Citadel by the State Commission on Higher Education as first among all state institutions in overall student retention, in the graduation rate of student athletes, and in the retention rate of black students."

— "National recognition in 1986 and 1988 by *U.S. News and World Report* for its overall academic programs and its educational philosophy."

— "After six years of detailed analysis and review, adoption of a strengthened academic core curriculum affecting every student, regardless of course of study."

— "Upgrade of the physical plant with over $12 million in construction and renovation projects completed and over $45 million in projects underway plus those planned for which funding has been approved."

— "Successful completion, two years ahead of schedule, of the $27-million

Mark Clark campaign, the first in the college's history."

— "Development of sound financial management procedures, based on quarterly program and budget reviews, which have assured prudent yet flexible stewardship of available resources."

—"Steady upgrade of the intercollegiate athletics program, one competitive across the board in eleven varsity sports, while ensuring that the program operates within the context of The Citadel as a liberal arts, military college."

In March, board member Colonel George James chaired the presidential search committee consisting of fellow members Prioleau and Fulghum, Citadel Alumni Association president Dudley Saleeby, Jr., Colonel Mahan representing the faculty, and Ben Hagood as the community representative. The committee targeted June 30, 1989, for a decision.[354] There followed some parliamentary maneuvering seemingly designed to aid one unnamed candidate(s) at the expense of another. At the May meeting, board representatives Prioleau and Fulghum sought an executive session, out of which came a motion to require a quorum of 12 members for the presidential vote, with nine needed for election.[355] The board again went into executive session at a May 19 meeting, with no action taken.[356] On June 5, the board rescinded its May resolution establishing the 12 member quorum and proceeded to pass a new resolution that changed the regulations to require nine affirmative votes to elect the president. On June 18, the board again changed course, rescinding its June 5 resolution requiring nine affirmative votes to elect the president. By this time, it seems apparent, that no one candidate could command the nine votes needed.[357]

The board's annual meeting on June 23, 1989, lasted all day. The reason was obvious: a board divided as to the next president. Again a parliamentary maneuver surfaced. "[f]or the election of the 17th President of The Citadel, for the first five ballots, a majority plus one of the members present and voting is needed to elect the president, but that the candidate with the fewest votes on the first ballot be dropped if no one receives a majority plus one on the first ballot." [emphasis in original] The board adopted this rule by "a three-quarter vote of all voting members present." The minutes are silent as to the number of votes conducted after the adoption of the new rule, concluding only with the statement that after ballots were cast, "Lieutenant General Claudius E. Watts, III, USAF, was elected by unanimous vote."[358]

The board's practice was to declare winners by unanimous vote. To do otherwise evokes the joke about the hospitalized chairman who received a card from his board wishing him a speedy recovery "by a vote of 5 to 4." The practice of unanimity had been criticized by Admiral Stockdale as leaving him with the false impression that he was taking over an institution at which he was universally wanted.

On June 23, 1989, the board came within a single vote of doing something it had not done since the 19th century: elect a civilian as its president. But for a change of heart by a board member on an unknown ballot, Frank Mood would have been president.[359] There was further irony in the outcome. Mood had been one year behind General Watts as a cadet. "Bud Watts was my hero," Mood said.[360]

The Grimsley era ended a decade of progress, while challenges seen and unseen loomed for the new administration. Barracks and buildings showed their age, awaiting "repair or replace" decisions. Financial stability remained elusive as the State Legislature furnished less support annually and the school's endowment languished. Racial tensions persisted in the wake of Nesmith, the Confederate flag and "Dixie". But before any of those challenges could be met and overcome, the school would need to survive an uppercut from a force of nature known only by its first name: Hugo.

Chapter 10

THE WATTS ERA IS SWEPT IN BY 140-MPH WINDS

Lieutentant General Claudius E. Watts III, USAF (Ret.), had been the school's 17th president for all of 36 days when Charleston found itself in the bull's eye of Hurricane Hugo, a category 4 storm that did more damage than any single event since the 1886 Earthquake. To the ancient Chinese blessing, "May you live in interesting times," Watts might well have responded, "Did they have to be THAT interesting?" If he were a man given to omens, he must have pondered his timing in assuming the presidency on August 16, 1989.

At least General Watts was on familiar ground. He graduated from The Citadel in the Class of 1958. His father, Claudius E. Watts, Jr., had been a member of the Class of 1932. Raised in Cheraw, South Carolina, Watts III was both a student and an athlete, having been an all-state football player at center and linebacker. He flirted with Davidson Colege, where the football coach made it plain he would be welcome, but The Citadel had offered too much to turn down. As only the second recipient of the Star of the West Scholarship, his college education was paid for and he could walk on to the football team, which he did. Two separations of the same shoulder ended his playing career, enabling him to focus his time and talents on cadet life and academics. He excelled at both, serving as a battalion commander and chairman of the Honor Committee.

Nearly 60 years later, he recalled being pulled from class and ordered to report to General Clark's office. When he arrived he found Clark seated with an attractive woman who was visibly upset and had been crying. Clark introduced her to Watts as the mother of a cadet who had just been before the Honor Committee, alleged to have been stealing money from his classmates. At Clark's request, Watts explained to the distraught woman the committee's procedure, its requirement for a unanimous verdict by secret ballot and her son's failure to deny the allegation. Clark confirmed that pursuant to its regulations the school had no choice but to expel him, and the fact that the cadet's father was a Congressman was of no consequence. Clark's firm stance on principle impressed Watts and influenced decisions he made in a long Air Force career.[361]

The Fulbright Scholarship awarded to Watts took him to the London School of Economics after graduation. By the time he retired from active duty in 1989 as Comptroller of the Air Force, he had distinguished himself as a pilot, an administrator and a general officer.

Modern weather forecasting is a science, but as recently as 1989 it was still very much an art. A hurricane's likely track was as much guesswork as analysis. Hugo originated off the coast of West Africa in early September. It followed the familiar progression from tropical depression to storm to hurricane, and by September 14, a week before it would make landfall in Charleston, it packed eye winds of 150 mph. It ravaged St. Croix, skirted St. Thomas and left 30,000 people homeless in Puerto Rico. When the National Weather Service issued a hurricane watch on September 20, some 400 miles of coastline — between Fernandina Beach, Florida, and Cape Hatteras, North Carolina — went on alert. This did little more than confirm what everyone could see on a weather map — half of the east coast was at risk, but precisely where would it hit? Watts knew where to go for the most accurate updates, and while the news from his contacts at the Charleston Air Force Base was grim, its weather service's forecasts leading up to landfall were, in his words, "spot on."

He formed a Crisis Action Team (CAT) with the commandant, Colonel Art Richards, as its commander, and the dean and vice presidents as members. It didn't take them long to identify the major concerns: the cadets, the physical plant (including vehicles and generators) and the school calendar, which was destined to suffer, like Charleston, a major disruption.

Once Watts knew that Charleston and The Citadel were in the storm's crosshairs, he mulled his first major decision: release the Corps on the 20th or wait until the morning of the 21st? Complicating the decision was the timing of announcements by public officials including Governor Carroll Campbell, who did not urge residents of the barrier islands to evacuate until the evening of the 20th. Watts worried about sending 1,800 cadets out at night toward largely unknown destinations. He decided to wait until morning. At 6 a.m. on the 21st, the National Weather Service issued a hurricane warning, but it still could not narrow the impact area from the 400 miles previously put on watch. At 7 a.m., Watts released the Corps. Charlestonians in general and cadets in particular appreciated the danger. They clogged I-26 all the way to Columbia in an effort to get to higher and less exposed ground. Watts said he later learned that cadets had been expecting to be released on the night of the 20th, and many stayed awake in anticipation of just that. "I learned a lot from that," Watts said.

With the cadets gone and the storm bearing down, Watts weighed ordering professors, staff and others living on campus to evacuate. Instead, he set up shelters in Deas Hall and Jenkins Hall. With the shelters open and the campus otherwise evacuated, Watts spent the night of the 21st in Mark Clark Hall. Sometime around 5 a.m., after Hugo had done its worst, he walked out onto the parade ground. General Grimsley joined him. As they surveyed the downed trees and chaotic landscape, Grimsley could only say, "I'm so sorry."

Watts was sorry too, but to him fell the job of prioritizing needs and marshalling resources. Downed trees strewn across the roads would have made it impossible for fire equipment to respond, so clearing them was a high priority. Fortunately, the National Guard offered its assistance with cranes, front-end loaders and generators. Communication with the world outside the gates would be key to recovery. With local radio and TV off the air, news came from a radio station in Jacksonville. For reasons no one could explain, three phones on campus still functioned: Watts's phone in Quarters 1, a phone in the Public Safety Office and a lone pay phone.

Then there was the matter of the football team and the band, both safely in Annapolis for Saturday's game against Navy. The Bulldogs won 10-7, but now that the game was over where would they go? Watts told them to return to Charleston. They bunked on cots in Deas Hall. The team did double duty the next week, spending chunks of the morning cleaning up Stevens Barracks, where roof leaks had allowed water to accumulate. This was nasty work, as soggy wool uniforms had to be hauled to the laundry in Seignious Hall. In the afternoon, they practiced. The storm left Johnson Hagood Stadium unplayable, so games against South Carolina State and Western Carolina were moved to USC's Williams-Brice Stadium in Columbia.

National Guard generators allowed the mess hall to feed those who had remained during the storm: the football team and band members, the National Guard and even some people from the neighborhood who, like the campus, had no power.

While the ultimate cost of Hugo to the school would require years to tally, the immediate consequences were readily apparent. Eleven academic days lost, the first semester extended into January, cancellation of spring break, and major relocation issues for the engineering and science labs in Bond Hall, which suffered heavy damage.

The damage inflicted by Hugo on The Citadel exceeded $6.2 million, including $300,000 to the beach house on Isle of Palms. The Insurance Reserve Fund, which covers state-owned buildings and facilities, paid out $4.5 million. Donors contributed about $200,000, and FEMA, which would become infamous years later with the Katrina fiasco, eventually paid its share. Statewide, South Carolina suffered $6 billion in damage, a full third of that in Charleston County.[362]

In November, the Board of Visitors held its first post-Hugo meeting. Dean Meenaghan reported the resumption of classes on October 9 without incident. He described the damage to academic facilities as "rather severe, particularly to physics and business administration." Student and faculty attitudes were described as good.

And the news wasn't all bad. *U.S. News and World Report*'s annual ranking placed The Citadel at No. 7, with high ratings for academic reputation, quality of the faculty, and the ability to retain and graduate its students.

More good news came with recognition of Colonel Thomas W. Mahan, Ph.D., professor of education and psychology, as South Carolina's "Professor of the Year," in part to recognize his role in designing an innovative program, Project Challenge, aimed at the special needs of those attending Burke High School, which abuts Johnson Hagood Stadium. Mahan, the program director, began the project in 1988 as a pilot effort aimed at Burke ninth-graders. The idea was to use cadets to improve academic and leadership skills for a group just entering high school. He ran the program "out of pocket" before seeking funding from the Jesse Ball duPont Fund, which donated $50,000 to the school for Hugo relief. It came through again, this time to the tune of a $151,000 grant to support Project Challenge. The program's reach had been extended to 10th-graders in 1989, and with the duPont funds Mahan hoped to expand the program to include 11th-graders. Cadets and graduate students were expected to help with curriculum development and tutoring. The program was not designed for the gifted, but rather for a mix of accelerated and at-risk students selected based on test scores or recommendations from parents or administrators.[363] This outreach success presaged the community involvement that would become a hallmark of The Citadel in the 21st century.

Audits of the college and the athletic department for the fiscal year ending June 30, 1989 were unqualified. And, for the first time, contracts let pursuant to the school's ongoing Minority Business Enterprise efforts exceeded that program's goal.

Watts listed for the board his priorities beyond the obvious need to recover from Hugo. He expressed concern about some who failed to appreciate the seriousness of the Honor Code, about over-indulgence in alcohol by cadets, and about what he called the "sanctity of ESP."[364]

And while he may not have voiced it to the board, Watts had a different message for members of his Presidential Advisory Committee (PAC), composed of senior cadet leaders in the Class of 1990. He sought their help in solving a problem of increasing urgency: race relations within the Corps. Specifically, the presence of Confederate flags and the playing of "Dixie" at football games were driving a wedge between black and white cadets. Watts urged the class leaders to find a way to bridge the divide. Two of those leaders were roommates. Sanford "Sandy" Key served as Regimental Religious Officer and Charles Wallace II as Regimental Activities Officer. Significantly, Wallace is African-American, played football and enjoyed the wide respect of his classmates. He knew first-hand the offense taken by his black teammates and shared it. Key and Wallace joined forces to make a change.

Inspired by the Star of the West mural on display in Daniel Library, Key saw a flag everyone could rally around: Big Red, the flag flying over the shore battery manned by Citadel cadets on January 9, 1861. He found a shop in West Ashley that could make a prototype. With that in hand, he and Wallace approached their Regimental Commander, Clay Ludlum, who in turn sounded out Lieutenant Colonel Harvey Dick, the assistant commandant, the commandant and ultimately President Watts. All agreed that a spirit flag patterned on Big Red would be a worthy successor to the Confederate battle flag in the stands at Johnson Hagood. The red flag lacked grommets by design; by substituting sleeves, transom rods could be inserted to permit waving them at games. Selling the spirit flag to the Corps fell to class president Chris Sexton and to Scott Moore, both members of the PAC and acknowledged leaders of the class of 1990. The flag made its debut at Homecoming 1989, and while the 50 spirit flags sold through the Cadet Store did not eliminate Confederate flags in the stands, they did outnumber them. To cement its commitment to their flag, the Class of 1990 erected a flagpole at the north end of the parade ground, where Big Red was hoisted for the first time on May 10, 1990.[365] Two years later, the board unanimously voted to replace the Confederate battle flag with Big Red as the school's official spirit banner.[366]

In the spring of 1990, baseball provided a stellar finish to Watts's first academic year as president. Chal Port's Bulldogs wrote their names at the top of the page of Citadel sports history by advancing to the College World Series in Omaha. For a team predicted to finish sixth in the Southern Conference when the season began to win not only the conference championship but the NCAA Atlantic Regional tournament was phenomenal. At one point during the season they won 26 straight games. To get to Omaha, they had to get past the University of Miami, host of the 1990 Regionals in Coral Gables. Miami entered the tournament as the top seeded team, ranked No. 4 nationally. In the decisive game, the Dogs faced Miami's ace, Oscar Munoz, on their home field in front of a home crowd. Brad Stowell, the fourth pitcher in the Bulldogs' rotation, pitched the game of his life, allowing just four hits over eight innings, while his teammates pounded out nine hits and three earned runs against Munoz. By beating Miami 4-1, the Dogs avenged a bitter 16 inning loss to the Hurricanes in the opening round of the 1979 Regionals and punched their ticket to Omaha. Left fielder Anthony Jenkins, Class of 1990, was named the tournament's most valuable player, getting 9 hits in his last 10 at-bats and scorching tournament opposition pitchers, going 8-13 over four games. In earning the trip, the Dogs became the first military college to ever qualify for the College World Series and the first Southern Conference representative since 1949, when Wake Forest was still a conference member. Les McElwee, Class of 1953 and executive director of the Brigadier Club, called it "the biggest accomplishment in sports The Citadel has ever had. I can't think of anything that ranks higher than this."[367]

In Omaha, LSU ended the dream season by defeating the Bulldogs twice, but between those losses the Dogs beat Cal State-Fullerton 8-7 in 12 innings for its first ever College World Series win. When the last out came in the elimination game against LSU, 14,614 fans gave the Dogs a standing ovation.[368] Port was named Coach of the Year in the Southern Conference (for the fifth time) and *The Sporting News* national coach of the year.[369] By the time he retired in 1991, Port had posted a record of 641-386-2, remarkable for a program with limited scholarships. The ever-quotable Port said, "We just try to find guys who like to play baseball and march."[370]

Home games during the dream season of 1990 were played at College Park, the home of the Charleston Riverdogs that opened in 1939 at the corner of Grove Street and Rutledge Avenue. Prior to its construction, another stadium stood on the same site. That prior stadium hosted College of Charleston baseball games as early as 1906[371] and served as the home field for the Bulldogs football team before Johnson Hagood was built. The facility, which holds 4,000, filled to capacity when Elvis Presley played there in 1956.[372] It took a hit from Hugo and was made playable just before the start of the 1990 baseball season. It was late in the season before lighting was restored.[373] The tired old ballpark would have required major renovation to keep pace with the modern facilities being built by competitors. Given that reality, Mayor Joe Riley's presentation to a joint meeting of the college's Athletic, Building

President Dwight Eisenhower visited The Citadel on April 12, 1955 and is seen in this photo with Citadel President, Gen. Mark Clark.

The original Citadel campus at Marion Square as seen in 1935.

Three former The Citadel Presidents attended the dedication of the new Padgett-Thomas Barracks on Friday September 24, 2004. From left are: Lt. Gen. George Seignious (retired Army), Maj. Gen. James A. Grimsley, Jr. (retired Army), and Lt. Gen. Claudius Watts III (retired Air Force). The $28 million building replaces the original campus landmark that was built in 1922.

The Citadel's new campus in the early 1920s.

Citadel presidents Gen. Hugh Harris (left) and Maj. Gen. James Duckett in 1974.

Gen. Mark Clark and Vice Adm. James Stockdale, President of The Citadel in 1979.

Pat Conroy stands with 'The Boo', after they both received their honorary degrees from The Citadel. Conroy, a former The Citadel graduate and a nationally known author, wrote his first book titled *The Boo* about Courvoisie and his own experience at The Citadel.

Cannons are fired during the parade to honor 20 years of women at The Citadel, March 2017.

Conclusion of Recognition Day, March 2017.

The Citadel Color Guard, 2017.

Damage to The Citadel campus after Hurricane Hugo.

The flag believed to be the one that flew over Morris Island when The Citadel cadets fired upon the supply ship *The Star of the West* is on loan for four years from the State Historical Society of Iowa.

Official press
conference,
1995.

Outside the gates, protesters hold up a banner reading "Save the Males," 1995.

Citadel President
Maj. Gen. John Grinalds.

Shannon Faulkner (second in line from left), The Citadel's first female cadet,
marches with her squad.

Cadets on the Quad.

Petra Lovetinska leads cadets in parade.

The Post and Courier

Cadets leave barracks in formation.

The Post and Courier

Nancy Mace (left) enjoys a moment with fellow cadet Petra Lovetinska after becoming the first female graduate of The Citadel in 1999. Lovetinska graduated in 2000.

Citadel President Lt. Gen. John W. Rosa

Citadel President Lt. Gen. John W. Rosa hands the Silver Shako trophy to the Bull-dogs after their 21-3 win over VMI at Johnson Hagood Stadium in 2017.

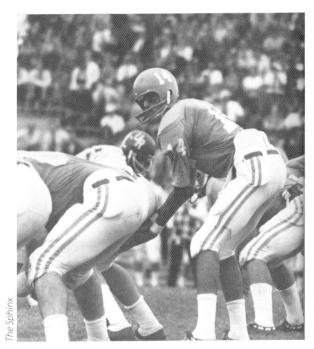

John W. Rosa
as Bulldog
quarterback,
1971.

Lt. Gen. John Rosa speaks at the 2018 graduating class ring ceremony.

ROTC Seal Training
on the Ashley River.

Padgett- Thomas
Barracks, 2004.

Construction of Watts Barracks begins, 1995.

Graduates toss their caps after commencement in 2017.

and Grounds, and Long Range Planning Committees was arguably more significant to the future of the baseball program than the team's appearance at the College World Series, because at that meeting the mayor made known his desire to build a baseball stadium on land owned by the college, and he wanted The Citadel to joint venture the project with the City of Charleston.

Putting a ballpark on acreage formerly owned by Trident Tech was the mayor's best idea for that property, but it was not his first. Previously, he had envisioned a convention center and basketball arena, and the fight over that proposal produced one of the rare rifts between the mayor and his alma mater.

The rift can be traced back to October 24, 1986, when the Board of Visitors approved a master plan for the college prepared by the director of the physical plant, Robert C. Collins, and Resident Engineer Boyd L. Wood. Included in the master plan was a renovation of McAlister Field House estimated to cost $7.9 million.

At its meeting on October 30, 1987, the Board of Visitors voted to authorize a contract with Ruscon Corporation for $6.9 million to make the repairs, but conditioned a notice to proceed on an additional vote by the board. The following month, the board examined a description of the improvements to be made and heard an opinion from Walt Nadzak, the athletic director, that with such improvements the school would enjoy "a good, solid facility" which, when combined with the facilities available in Seignious and Vandiver halls, would "provide a first-rate on-campus centralized athletic complex for all sports."

Following Nadzak's conclusory remarks, the board considered a letter from Mayor Riley in which he apologized for injecting himself "at this late date and making a difficult decision even more so." He felt compelled to do so, he told them, because he believed "The Citadel and the City of Charleston may have a once-in-a-lifetime opportunity." He asked the board to delay proceeding on the Ruscon contract for 60 days while the city and the school explored a joint venture to build a 9,000- to 10,000-seat coliseum and multi-purpose facility on the land formerly owned by Trident Tech. Board member Colonel Leonard Fulghum was not impressed, and moved that the board proceed with the Ruscon repairs. Despite a second on his motion by Colonel James Leland, it was defeated, after which the board voted to grant the 60-day extension. But the extension was conditioned on Ruscon holding firm the prices quoted in its successful bid on the project, and those prices were not guaranteed after December 8, 1987, only 24 days away. If Ruscon refused to guarantee its prices after December 8, the chairman was instructed to call the board back to consider its options.

In December, things got complicated. The board met on December 7, one day before the Ruscon prices would no longer be assured. Colonel George James wanted to get on with it. He moved that Ruscon be given a notice to proceed but that The Citadel continue to work with the city to explore the feasibility of Riley's proposal. Following a second by Colonel Fulghum, that motion was defeated. Colonel David Boyd then moved that the joint venture with the city be further explored by consultation with the South Carolina Budget and Control Board to make certain that the $7.9 million earmarked for McAlister renovations could be shifted and augmented as necessary to construct the coliseum, and to also restore McAlister to a useable facility. This was all to be determined within two weeks, and if it proved unfeasible, the McAlister renovations were to be re-bid. Following a second by Colonel William Prioleau, the motion passed. After the meeting adjourned, Ruscon notified Board of Visitors Chairman Colonel William Risher that Ruscon would guarantee its bid prices for an additional two weeks, until December 22, 1987.

With Ruscon's deadline in mind, the board reconvened on December 22. Mayor Riley again appeared in support of the arena. Board members voiced opinions pro and con, as did General Grimsley. Few opposed the arena in concept but several questioned whether the school would benefit as much from having it as it would from the refurbishment of McAlister. Despite Riley's assurance of funding sources for both projects, some members expressed doubt. After a full and lengthy discussion, Colonel Prioleau moved that the board " ... authorize the expenditure of available funds essential to restore McAlister Field House to a useable facility and proceed with final plans to construct a joint use facility [the arena] on land provided by The Citadel, using remaining funds available from the McAlister Field House Renovation Project, plus City of Charleston Revenue Bonds, plus an additional appropriation from the State of South Carolina."

Col. Padgett seconded the motion, which passed by a majority vote.

The city's argument in favor of the joint use facility leaned heavily on a study by KPMG Peat Marwick confirming the need for the facility and estimating its cost at $20 million. Concerns within The Citadel as to the soundness of this estimate led it to commission its own external study by Enwright Associates and HOK Sport. That study estimated the cost at $31.6 million if the arena was built with a convention center component or $25.8 million if the convention center component was omitted. Thus the competing studies varied by as much as $10 million, and that difference would potentially have to come from The Citadel.

At a January 29, 1988 meeting of the board, Colonel Boyd briefed members on the Enwright study, which caught Riley by surprise. Riley said he had just seen it, then repeated the arguments he had advanced on December 22 in support of the KPMG study and the project. Opponents, sensing their advantage, moved to reconsider the board's December 22 vote in support of the arena project. The motion passed by majority vote. The board then debated the motion being reconsidered, to push ahead with the arena project, and it was defeated. Without the competing proposal from the city, the decision to proceed with Ruscon was foregone. The board voted to award the Ruscon contract for $6.9 million and to give the notice to proceed.[374]

The board's action outraged Mayor Riley. After the meeting, he sent Chairman Risher a letter that showed a side of Riley seldom seen in print and unprecedented in Riley's relationship with his college. It began:

> I cannot adequately express to you my deep disappointment at the shabby treatment that I and the City were given today by the Board of Visitors of The Citadel. I have been stabbed in the back before, but never by a group that had so little reason to do so. For this city to have been refused by the Board of Visitors the opportunity to have our experts review your information [the Enwright study] and to respond is unforgivable. All I wanted or needed was a couple of days.

Two days later, Risher and Leonard Fulghum met with Riley, and in a letter dated February 1, 1988, Riley reminded Risher of the city's past contributions:

> I reiterate that this city, the city that made the land available for The Citadel campus to be built on the Ashley River in 1920, the city which built Johnson Hagood Stadium for The Citadel and then transferred it to The Citadel a decade later, the city which has never refused any request of The Citadel, the city which provides the stadium for The Citadel's baseball team and parking for its football stadium, and police and fire protection, etc., etc., that this city deserves the opportunity to address the apparent variances between the cost estimates, and an opportunity to discuss the issues that concerned the board on Friday.

Then Riley added language which he must have known would appeal to anyone with Risher's love for the school:

> We often talk about The Citadel Man and what we try to teach our cadets. There are two things I learned in my four years at The Citadel: the first is you don't give up, even under great adversity; the second is the brass plaque at the entrance to Padgett Thomas Barracks, quoting Robert E. Lee, which says, "Duty is the sublimest word in the English language". For my city, I cannot give up for it is my duty to work as hard for it humanly possible.

Risher replied on February 3 in a letter designed to end any hope of a jointly ventured basketball arena/convention center:

> In accordance with the resolution adopted at the BOV meeting Friday, 29 January 1988 at which you were present, the contract with Ruscon was signed and the notice to proceed was given. This action commits The Citadel to the McAlister Field House conversion project, already approved and funded by the state of South Carolina, and removes from further consideration any alternative which would involve rollover funding from this source. This is not only a *fait accompli*, but it represents the considered judgment of the BOV as to the best interest of the college.

But Joe Riley didn't get elected and reelected mayor 10 times by a conservative Southern city as a liberal Democrat by taking no for an answer. In his February 1 letter, he had put Risher on notice that lesson No. 1 learned at The Citadel was "don't give up," and he didn't. On Sunday, February 7, 1988, the board met for four hours in emergency session. Chairman Risher acknowledged the presence of the news media and stated that this was the first time in his memory that a meeting had been called at the request of at least three board members, as provided for in the by-laws.[375]

Riley and the city were present in force, as were Robert B. Russell, a Citadel graduate and the founder of Ruscon, and Robert B. Russell, Jr., Ruscon's president. Also on hand at Riley's behest was Robert Dove, a former Citadel professor and parliamentarian of the U.S. Senate. Helping fill the room were lawyers from all sides and a large contingent of Citadel alumni supporting the arena, three of whom had come from Atlanta and claimed to represent 1,000 alumni in Georgia who supported the mayor's proposal.[376] This meeting had few, if any, precedents in the board's 146-year history.

According to Kerri Morgan, the *Post-Courier* reporter who covered the meeting for the paper, Riley and Russell "almost had words." At issue was the board's vote at its January 29 meeting to sign the Ruscon contract and issue the notice to proceed. Riley cited the board's vote on December 22 to pursue the joint venture with the city and insisted that based upon it the city had taken steps to pursue funding. The board's vote on January 29 to proceed with Ruscon, Riley contended, amounted to a reconsideration of the December 22 vote, and such a reconsideration violated Robert's Rules of Order, rendering it illegal and void. He cited a rule in Robert's restricting the reconsideration of any approved motion to the day of the motion's approval. Dove, the parliamentarian, agreed.

But since Russell also attended The Citadel, it can be presumed that he too learned to never give up. Ruscon claimed to have already contracted for $3 million in work on McAlister based on the notice to proceed and therefore faced liability to subcontractors if the project didn't go forward. Ruscon reminded the board that the repairs were scheduled to begin the following day.

Risher, as chairman, ruled the board's vote on January 29 to proceed with Ruscon valid, which prompted a motion, duly seconded, to reject Risher's ruling. That motion was defeated by a vote of 7 to 6. Thus, by a single vote, the board authorized the needed repairs and improvements to McAlister. As a nod to the city, it then voted unanimously to form a committee to pursue the arena project with the city, a project doomed to fail because no one believed in putting two basketball arenas within a mile of each other. But a baseball park? That was a different matter, and in the spring of 1990, with baseball fever high in Charleston over the Bulldogs first trip to the College World Series, Riley was back with a proposal to use the Trident Tech acreage for a baseball stadium.

Riley's initial proposal called for The Citadel to deed the Trident Tech land to the city for construction of a new stadium; for the city to provide parking near the proposed stadium; and for the city to maintain College Park in a condition sufficiently suitable for baseball practice and for games where schedules conflicted. By letter to the board dated September 5, 1990, Riley fleshed out his plan. In exchange for the 7.8 acres formerly owned by Trident Tech and now to be conveyed by The Citadel to the city for construction of a baseball stadium, the city would develop a nine-acre tract to provide approximately 900 parking spaces for football games and other activities. The city also promised to convey its reversionary ownership rights in the 2.9 acres across from Johnson Hagood Stadium then occupied by the South Carolina

National Guard. Lastly, the city would convey to The Citadel ownership of College Park and its parking area, an area measuring approximately 5.6 acres. Because the land on which the new baseball stadium was to be built had originally been landfilled, the deal was to be contingent on the necessary governmental approvals. The board did not vote on Riley's proposal, but received it for information.[377]

Weeks before the Class of 1994 reported and a year after Hugo, a storm of a different kind erupted in the Middle East when Iraq invaded Kuwait. Saddam Hussein's forces overran its neighbor in 48 hours, prompting the United Nations Security Council to condemn the attack and issue an ultimatum in the form of Resolution 660, which demanded unconditional withdrawal of all Iraqi forces. Leading a rare coalition of world powers, the U.S. launched Operation Desert Shield, massing troops and equipment in Saudi Arabia in anticipation of Iraqi defiance of the ultimatum. When the January 15, 1991 deadline passed with Kuwait still occupied, the United States and its allies began Operation Desert Storm on January 17, 1991.

Multilateral forces retaking Kuwait consisted primarily of U.S. troops assisted by those of Saudi Arabia, the United Kingdom and Egypt. In a little under six weeks, the combat ended. Iraqi forces withdrew, leaving in their wake hundreds of oil fields on fire. With the call-up of reserve units, 22 Citadel cadets left classes for deployment, including six professors and college staff members.[378]

Brief as the conflict was, it lasted long enough to claim the life a Citadel alumnus, Army Captain Mario J. Fajardo, Class of 1984, killed in action on February 26, 1991, two days before the end of combat operations.

Fajardo was one of approximately 250 alumni who served during Operations Desert Shield and Desert Storm (often called the "First Gulf War"). His family came to the United States from Ecuador when he was 12. During telephone calls from the Gulf, he told his parents he planned to marry after the war and give them a grandson. In his last letter home, he said, "I'm proud to serve this country which has given me, an immigrant, so much opportunity." And then, in what some might read as a foreshadowing of his fate, he added, "I have no regrets. I would do it all over again." At The Citadel, he majored in electrical engineering and fought with the 82nd Airborne in Kuwait. He died disarming an Iraqi mine.[379]

Late in the fall of 1990, sophomore quarterback Jack Douglas made a fourth-down plunge over the University of South Carolina's goal line with 22 seconds left on the clock to seal a 38-35 Bulldogs victory over the Gamecocks before 63,000 stunned fans in Williams-Brice Stadium. USC came into the game with a 4-1 record and the fourth-ranked defense in the country yielding just 235 yards per game. Douglas and fullback Everette Sands each ran for more than 100 yards, Douglas threw for another 125, going 7 for 9, and their wishbone put up almost 400 yards in combined offense.[380] *News and Courier* sportswriter Ken Burger called it the "greatest football victory in modern times."[381] The win helped cement Coach Charlie Taaffe's popularity among fans, making especially bitter his sudden termination before the start of the 1996 season. It would be another 25 years before the Dogs could duplicate that upset over USC.

One senior celebrating on the Williams-Brice turf that day was Morris DeRhon Robinson, whose story is about as unlikely as the game's outcome. Robinson played tackle well enough to aspire to a professional career, and he achieved one . . . as an opera singer. Upon graduation from The Citadel in 1991 he joined 3M Technologies, where he enjoyed success in the corporate world until a lifelong passion for music took over, inspiring him to train his prodigious bass voice for the stage at the Metropolitan Opera and other internationally famous opera venues. He returned to campus in 2017 to deliver the commencement address, "the first African-American to ever address the Corps of Cadets."[382] His rendition of the alma mater, sung at the end of his talk, shook the foundations of McAlister Field House.

At a board meeting in the spring of 1991, Watts reported on his initiation of courses for real estate appraisers and tax assessors. In response to the Savings and Loan crisis of the 1980s, federal regulations mandated that appraisers be certified. A bill pending in the General Assembly would have required this specialized training and none existed in the state, prompting the South Carolina Real Estate Commission to request that The Citadel create and teach a certification program. General Watts agreed, provided the program was self-sustaining and at no additional expense to the college. Under the umbrella of the office of Professional and Career Development, the program began modestly enough, with six students enrolled and tuition totaling $900, but by the end of the year 201 students had generated $18,500, a clear growth trajectory. Five years later, Lewis Spearman, the project's head, reported that The Center for International and Regional Development had devoted 2,320 hours to instructing 2,267 students in 110 courses, generating in excess of $400,000 in revenue. The South Carolina Department of Revenue claimed the program had saved the state over half a million dollars. Demands by the state and local governments for additional courses to be provided assured a positive cash flow for the recently recertified Center for International and Regional Development, into which the program was to be merged. This program, begun under the Watts administration in 1991 with six students, not only filled vital needs in the state and localities but also generated needed income for the school.[383]

In the spring of 1991, the school found itself in the national media spotlight for all the right reasons. Charles Kuralt arrived with a film crew for a CBS Sunday Morning segment on the Persian Gulf War. And the school hosted a 20th Century Fox crew filming "For the Boys," starring Bette Midler and James Caan, who plays Midler's son, with the college providing the setting for his graduation before being sent to Vietnam.[384] This spate of positive public relations would soon be seen as the good old days as the coming battle over coeducation intensified.

Chapter 11

IF YOU BUILD IT, THEY MIGHT (OR MIGHT NOT) COME

The Grimsley Plan, which was adopted at the outset of his administration, had forecast that the 1980s would require "relatively little major new construction," but by the time General Watts assumed the presidency it was obvious that the 1990s would demand just that. All the barracks showed their age, but particularly Padgett-Thomas, No. 2, the original campus building completed in 1922. Moreover, in the half-century since Stevens, No. 4, was constructed in 1942, city codes had been revised to require more stringent protections against fires and earthquakes. The school confronted costly major renovation unless it decided to rebuild.

In November 1991, the Board of Visitors wrestled with repair vs. replace options for all the barracks. Engineering reports showed the only salvageable features of the existing structures were the outer walls and the columns supporting the first and second divisions. Seismic requirements dictated major foundation work along with remaining walls tied into an interior frame system. It took little imagination to envision four giant "money pits." Cost estimates by the engineering firm Davis and Floyd, Inc., showed replacement to be several million dollars cheaper than renovation.

The board pored over studies that justified replacement. Repair of the existing facilities was put at $47.08 million while for $44.09 million barracks 1, 2, and 3 could be rebuilt on their present footprints and a new barracks constructed on the site of the old mess hall. The sensible choice mandated replacement, which the board approved, to include demolition of Stevens Barracks, which as of this writing still stands.[385]

A year after his team's trip to the College World Series, Chal Port retired after 27 years as head baseball coach. He cited his health, his need for family time and increasingly restrictive NCAA rules for his decision. Port's teams won seven regular-season Southern Conference championships, and he was voted Coach of the Year six times. He went out as he had come in, speaking frankly. He didn't care for the controls creeping into college baseball.

"The NCAA tells me when to practice. The city tells me where to practice. And the Corps tells me who can practice." He admitted recruiting wasn't his strong point, and the recruiting wars were getting fierce. His proudest achievement: Only three of his players failed to graduate.[386] And his players loved him. He could be intense without ever losing sight of the fact that it was only a game. Pitcher John Flock, Class of 1967, tells of the game when the Dogs were being pounded by a very good Clemson team. By the middle innings, the game in which Clemson would ultimately score 27 runs had long been decided. Port went to the mound and signaled to the bullpen for Flock to come in as the relief pitcher. As Port handed Flock the ball, he told him to look back to the bullpen. "Tell me who you see back there," Port said. Flock looked back. "There's no one there, coach." Port smiled at him and said, "That's right, and there ain't gonna be. Good luck."

The shooting of Cadet Berra Lee Byrd, Jr., in March 1992 proved to be one of the more bizarre episodes in the history of the college. Byrd, dressed in salt and pepper with a pass to leave campus, was walking in the parking lot toward a friend's car. Suddenly, he felt a piercing pain in his chest. "I thought I was having a heart attack at first, but then I looked down and saw a hole in my uniform." A bullet entered his chest just above the heart and exited from his back. He didn't hear the shot, and he wondered if more were coming. He staggered toward the mess hall and was able to call out for help.

Cadets Robert Brodie and Ricky Freeman, standing outside Padgett-Thomas, heard the call for help and responded. While Brodie left to summon a nurse, Freeman applied pressure to the wound. Byrd, an African-American sophomore from Gaffney, spent days in the hospital, did not require surgery and recovered. No bullet was ever found despite intensive searches by cadets and the Charleston Police Department. After Byrd's release from the hospital, Charleston Police Detective Captain Robert H. Roberts interviewed Byrd and told reporter Edward Fennell of the *Post-Courier* that the interview produced "no new information as to suspects or motives." Roberts did acknowledge that "rumors are flying and run the gamut, but none have basis in fact."[387] The Board of Visitors offered a $1,000 reward for information leading to the apprehension of the person who fired the shot and doubled it to $2,000 in June.[388]

Following his release from the hospital, Byrd went home to Gaffney, where his family urged him not to return to The Citadel. His father wanted him to go to Clemson. But Byrd was determined to come back. "If it was a racial thing, I wasn't going to run," he said. His family eventually relented. He received letters of support from people across the country commending

170

him on his courage, and some of those letters came from Citadel alumni. He returned for the 1992-1993 school year and graduated in 1994 with a degree in Business Administration. As he would later learn, his shooter also graduated that day.

Byrd admitted to harboring some bitterness over the way the investigation was handled and what he felt was some damage to his reputation.[389] In the course of investigations by the school, the local police, South Carolina law enforcement and the FBI, he was asked a host of personal questions, from drug usage to his sex life to any enemies he may have had. They probed him on whether he had financial problems, whether he was dating a married woman or a white woman. He submitted to two polygraphs, one of which he failed when asked if he knew why he was shot. Colonel George B. Stackhouse, head of Citadel Public Safety, said that Byrd "was as fine a young man as we had, but we needed to know if he had done anything unintentionally to anger anyone, and I'm sure he felt victimized. That's the way investigations work. It's the frustration of anyone who is innocent."[390]

By the time Byrd received his diploma in 1994, his assailant was no closer to being identified than he had been on the day of the shooting. Given Byrd's ethnicity and ongoing tensions over "Dixie" and the Confederate flag, there was a rush to judgment in some quarters that he was the victim of racial violence. The fact that the day of the shooting, March 12, was the first day of the long Corps Day weekend fueled rumors and conspiracy theories. One rumor was advanced by a former black cadet that Byrd had sought admission to a secret black fraternity on campus, Omega Psi Phi. That former cadet, not named in news reports, took a lie-detector test and concluded from the questions asked by the FBI that it suspected a fraternity member as the shooter. One imaginative theory had Byrd shooting himself. Some thought the Klan must have been involved.

The NAACP sent letters demanding a federal investigation into what it called a "practice of discrimination," citing Byrd's trauma in support of its allegations. Byrd's father expressed no doubt that the incident involving his son was racially motivated.[391] Ironically, these charges of racial animus came during the time one of Byrd's classmates, Norman P. Doucet, Jr., served as the first black Regimental Commander.[392]

A full four years later, the FBI decided to reopen the investigation initially begun in the fall of 1992. It mailed 1,500 questionnaires to people who might have had information, including many former cadets. By appealing to the school's Honor Code, the FBI may have solved the case because David A. Burdock, Jr., the former roommate of George F. Cormeny, III, would have had a tough time with the question, "Do you have any knowledge regarding this incident?"[393] He was present in the room when it happened, and he came forward. That led the FBI to Cormeny, then enrolled at Trinity Episcopal School for Ministry in Ambridge, Pennsylvania.[394]

Cormeny admitted responsibility. For reasons never clear, he carried a 9mm handgun into his room on the fourth division of Padgett-Thomas. He said he unknowingly and unintentionally chambered a round by not first checking to see if the pistol held a clip. "Pointing the pistol out the window and thinking it unloaded, I pulled the trigger. To my indescribable horror the pistol fired. With that shot I knew my days at The Citadel were over. Seconds later the situation went from fright to sheer terror when I heard a scream in the distance. I saw a fellow cadet running across the parking lot screaming. It was Berra Byrd."[395]

Cormeny's expiation included a telephone call to Byrd, identifying himself as "Trip" Cormeny, a Citadel classmate. He told Byrd he'd been on the road all night from Pittsburgh and that he needed to see Byrd. Sometime later, he knocked on Byrd's door in Greenville.

The two had never met. Byrd recalled that Cormeny said, "Berra, I've come to tell you that I'm the one who shot you." Byrd listened in stunned disbelief as Cormeny described the accident, his stupidity and his regret. He apologized and said he had found God. When Byrd asked if he had come forward voluntarily, Cormeny admitted that his roommate had turned him in. Cormany asked for Byrd's forgiveness and expressed a desire to be friends.[396]

Cormeny's contrition following confession was total. In a letter sent to and published by the *Post and Courier*, he acknowledged that "the last four and a half years of living with this secret and the pain I caused Berra, his family and The Citadel have been unbearable." On what he described as "the worst day of my life," he panicked after he heard Byrd screaming for help. "I waited in my room for the expectant rush of people. No one came. Inexplicably, no one had heard the explosion . . . I panicked. I have no excuse, only an explanation. That panic led me to make the most foolish decision yet in a long line of foolish decisions. I did not come forward."

In an effort to man-up after the fact, Cormeny appeared before the Board of Visitors on October 25, 1996. He confessed to a lack of integrity in the entire matter and apologized for the shadow he cast upon the school. Board minutes from that meeting state only that he "appeared before the board and offered an apology for the offense and for bringing discredit to The Citadel by not coming forward at the time of the incident. The board offered no judgement."[397] The *Post and Courier* account of the meeting quoted the chairman, Colonel James Jones, as hoping Cormeny could forgive himself and accepting Cormeny's apology on behalf of the Board of Visitors.[398]

Byrd and his father sued Cormeny, his roommate Burdock, and the person or store that sold Cormeny the gun. Cormeny was prosecuted for possession of a firearm by a person under 21 and carrying a weapon into a public building. He pleaded guilty and was sentenced to 30 nights in the Charleston County Jail on work release, 400 hours of community service and probation for 18 months.[399]

In assessing the Byrd-Cormeny tragedy, it is hard to avoid drawing comparisons with the Buoniconti-Jacobs nightmare. In both incidents, strangers collided in a near-fatal instant that largely determined their futures. Berra Byrd had planned a career in the military, but the shooting left him with a collapsed lung and a broken arm and the military, where things were orderly and regimented, no longer appealed. He was working in a bank when Cormeny knocked on his door. More than that, he couldn't help but wonder why. Why had this happened? Was it random, or had he been targeted by someone or some group that might one day come back to finish the job? The FBI's investigation proved critical in that regard, because at last Byrd had some answers. After Cormeny came forward, Byrd could be certain the attack was not racially motivated, could count himself unlucky for having been hit and very lucky that the bullet had not struck two inches lower.

Twelve years elapsed between the Mood Report and the next attempt to assess and reshape the Fourth Class System. In January 1992, General Watts reviewed the findings of the Lane Committee, tasked with another study of this much-studied element of cadet life. He reiterated his support for academics as the top priority. Pursuant to the Lane Committee's recommendations, he eliminated square meals in the mess hall, meaning knobs were no longer required to sit at rigid attention and lift their food from plate to mouth at right angles. Hell Night, morning PT for freshmen and push-ups in the barracks were likewise banished. He retained the sophomore rank system for corporals but banned them from knob rooms.[400]

At its June 1992 meeting, the board reviewed a document with far reaching implications for the financial health of the college. George A. Brakeley, III, president of Brakeley, John Price Jones, Inc. of Stamford, Connecticut, reported to General Watts the results of his firm's study of the school's fundraising organizational structure. In reaching an assessment that must have shocked some board members and come as no surprise to others, Brakeley conducted 50 interviews with 39 individuals identified in the report. His bottom line conclusion:

> With four different entities actively asking for money for The
> Citadel without any kind of obvious coordination or reference to
> each other, with no common ground, and seeming to lack any
> rhyme or reason, it is hardly surprising that the prevailing at-
> titudes among alumni and friends are, at best, confusion, and, at
> worst, anger —and, most likely on the part of some, a knee-jerk
> reaction not to give *anything* to any part of The Citadel. Com-
> plaints about the profusion of fund-raising appeals from the Col-
> lege abound, not surprising in view of the fact that the "typical"
> alumnus or friend probably gets solicited, one way or another, 12
> to 15 times a year. [emphasis in original]
>
> Moreover, only a very few of the people with whom I spoke
> have any real understanding for which entity is soliciting for what
> purpose, let alone their relative priorities. The vast majority of the
> recipients of these requests, it appears, simply don't know enough
> to be able to differentiate one soliciting agency from another, and
> their animus is thus directed toward the College generally.

Brakeley minced no words in identifying the consequences of the school's
chaotic, hodgepodge approach to fundraising:

> By any comparative standards, The Citadel is a startlingly
> undercapitalized institution, even if one counts CDF's corpus,
> the income from which is limited as to use. What is missing is a
> significant amount of endowment the income from which can be
> used at your discretion for whatever the priorities of the moment
> are, be they operational, academic, athletic or capital in nature; or
> which supports *directly* such vital needs as scholarship support and
> academic chairs. [emphasis in original]

Brakeley supported his conclusions with some hard numbers. Over the
four years ending in 1990 for which he was provided data, fundraising efforts brought in an average of $3.3 million "For an institution of The Cita-
del's size, that's not bad on the face of it." The problem, in Brakeley's view,
stemmed from the fact that the college *per se* realized only 43.5 percent of
that amount. The Citadel Development Foundation (CDF) accounted for

30.6 percent of the $3.3 million, the Association of Citadel Men 2.3 percent, and the Brigadier Club 23.5 percent, resulting in the balance of 43.5 percent, or $1.44 million being raised by the college itself. Brakeley compared that to other schools during the same period: Washington & Lee, $10.1 million; Randolph-Macon, $3.5 million; Rhodes College, $8.6 million; Presbyterian College, $5.3 million; Wofford College, $6.1 million; VMI, $3.9 million. As a percentage of alumni giving to the school, The Citadel fared much better, "right up there with the national leaders," but when measured by the average size of the annual gift, "The Citadel falls well below any kind of national average." Brakeley's bottom line? "The Citadel has a tremendous amount of fundraising potential that it is not coming close to tapping with its present structure and methodology."

As any good consultant would, Brakeley proposed solutions for the problems he identified. His major concern was the structure of the CDF as it related to the all-important annual fund drive.

> The Annual Fund, currently administered by the CDF, is as extreme an anomaly as I can imagine. On the surface it appears to be generally like every other annual fund in higher education, replete with class agents, reunion year giving, direct mail, telephoning by class agents, et al. Yet, so far as I know, it is absolutely unique in American higher education, with the following specifics:
> It is the exclusive "property" of a legal entity which is completely at "arms-length" from the College *per se*;
> Monies given to CDF for the Annual Fund are narrowly restricted as to use;
> The usefulness and availability of those funds to the College for current, urgent priorities are very, very limited, and;
> The vast majority of alumni have no idea whatsoever that the three circumstances above exist, let alone what they mean.

With the reminder that some annual fund donors eventually become capital donors, Brakeley recommended establishing the position of Vice President for College Relations (or External Affairs) to allow the school to speak to the outside world with one voice. The annual fund campaign would move from the Foundation to the college's Development Office or, in the alternative, the CDF could perform the functions of the Development Office under a contract with the college.[401]

A month after the board received the Brakeley report, the executive committees of the CDF and the Board of Visitors met in what the heads of each agreed was an historic occasion. General Watts briefed the gathering on the circumstances that prompted him to hire Brakeley's firm and reviewed the recommendations contained in its report. Emmett I. Davis, Jr., speaking for the CDF, recited the Foundation's historic support for the college and insisted the annual fund needed to remain within its jurisdiction, though he expressed the organization's openness to a contract for services, which Brakeley had cited as an alternative to moving the annual fund campaign to the college's Development Office. This appealed to the board, whose chairman, Colonel James Jones, promised a written statement of the desire for the CDF to establish an umbrella organization to oversee and coordinate all fundraising. Both entities agreed that the Brigadier Club would not fall under the umbrella being contemplated.[402]

The CDF's effort to protect its turf is understandable in light of its demonstrated competence in raising money and investing it wisely. Founded in 1960, the CDF owed its existence to Dr. Tucker Weston and some other alumni visionaries in the Association of Citadel Men. While it is a separate legal entity apart from The Citadel, without the college there would be no need for it. As originally envisioned, CDF's mission was academic enrichment. In support of that mission, it contributed annually to the college an amount equal to 5 percent of the fair market value of managed assets as of December 31, less operating expenses of the Foundation. Obviously, as prudent investment increased the assets under management, the value of the 5 percent contribution grew accordingly, and between 1961 and 1993, annual contributions totaled $22 million. The growth of the endowment had been impressive. In 1971, some 10 years after it was established, the CDF's endowment stood at $450,000. By 1993 it exceeded $75 million.[403]

Additionally, CDF from time to time provided timely loans to the school for expenses outside its mandate of academic enrichment. For example, it loaned the college money to help construct Seignious and Vandiver Halls.[404] But loans must be repaid, and as General Watts and the Brakeley report highlighted, the school consistently required funds to meet a variety of expenses that other schools met using funds raised by the school itself and unrestricted in their use. The paltry sums available to The Citadel's administration for such needs ($1,443,000 in 1990) served as the basis for Brakeley's contention that the college was a startlingly undercapitalized institution.

The goal of consolidating all fundraising under one umbrella organization took a giant step forward in 2000 when CDF and the college's Office of

Institutional Advancement merged to form The Citadel Foundation (TCF). As the college prepares to celebrate its 175th anniversary in 2018, the total endowment exceeds $281 million.[405]

Not long after Berra Byrd was shot, Patricia Johnson, Elizabeth Lacey and Angela Chapman applied for admission to the day program for veterans studying engineering. Seventy-eight male veterans were then enrolled in the program. Although accredited courses could be taken elsewhere, The Citadel offered the only accredited engineering degree in the Lowcountry. Based on the school's all-male policy, the three female veterans were denied admission.[406]

In June the women sued. Rather than risk a court-ordered admission of women to day classes with cadets, the board shut down the program. In its September 3, 1992 resolution, the board cited the possible loss of its exemption under Title IX of the 1964 Civil Rights Act and the "substantial annual federal funding" to which a "traditionally and continually" all-male school like The Citadel was entitled by virtue of that exemption. Beginning with the spring semester in 1993, civilians of either sex would no longer be admitted to day classes. The board promised to help those currently enrolled to transition to the Evening College and to classes offered elsewhere and expressed its expectation that those being displaced by the board's action would ultimately have the opportunity to receive a Citadel degree.[407]

In furtherance of the board's pledge to help those veteran students affected by its September 3 decision, calls immediately went out to the 78 veterans informing them of a meeting the following day, September 4. Forty-seven veterans attended. At a follow-up meeting on September 8, at which 45 veterans appeared, Colonel Metts reiterated the college's commitment to help them transition to the Evening College or to other local colleges and universities using cross-registration agreements. Veterans benefits and financial aid would be continued through the spring semester, and all were urged to see their faculty advisors to determine their specific course requirements.

Termination of the veterans program angered the faculty. At a special meeting of the Faculty Council on September 10, 1992, the Council deplored the decision to terminate the program, urged the school to honor what it called the "moral contract a college assumes when it admits a student," and expressed regret that the faculty was not consulted in the decision-making process.[408]

Meetings with the veterans continued. By September 22, it had been determined that with one exception all lower division coursework was available from either the Evening College or at local institutions. The exception, a social science core course, was then added to the Evening College curriculum. In the days that followed, General Watts met with the Veteran Student Council president, Edward S. Kappler, and with all department heads to underscore the school's commitment to those being displaced. Spring registration was set for November 16, 1992. At a November 5 meeting, the administration addressed veteran concerns over costs of tuition, books and parking. The question was again posed as to accreditation of the Evening Program and the nature of the diploma graduates would receive. A rumor among the veterans held that fifth-year Citadel students would be allowed to wear their uniforms to day classes but otherwise be civilians. If true, the veterans were willing to wear their service uniforms to put themselves on an equal footing with the fifth-years. Not true, said the school. Fifth-year Citadel students could return to the Corps or enroll in the Evening College.[409]

Canceling the veterans program rendered the women's lawsuit moot, but it spawned another, this one by two male veterans required to seek other classes to fulfill their degree requirements. The male plaintiffs, Wesley Waters and Ted Blumstein, claimed they quit full time jobs to enter the day program. Not all classes they needed for a degree, they argued, were available through summer or evening schools, and only The Citadel's day program offered all required courses and an accredited degree. Dawes Cooke, The Citadel's attorney, disputed the hardship claimed by the veterans, insisting that the Evening College program would be accredited by the time the two plaintiffs graduated.[410] By the time the veterans sued, Cooke had earned his spurs in Citadel litigation, having represented the college since the Buoniconti and Nesmith cases in the mid-1980s. The veterans' case was but Round 1 in a series of litigation brawls that The Citadel fought in and throughout the 1990s and beyond. In the school's corner for each of those stood M. Dawes Cooke, Jr., a mild-mannered partner with the Charleston law firm of Barnwell Whaley Patterson & Helms, LLC. Routinely named to South Carolina's list of Super Lawyers (ranked #1 in 2014-2016), Cooke has represented the college in every piece of significant litigation for over three decades. Catherine Manegold, who covered the Shannon Faulkner case for the *New York Times*, said that "[c]lients and adversaries tended to think of him as both likeable and fair." During Faulkner's first deposition, Manegold described him as "persistent and skillful and flawlessly polite." Mark Brandenburg, class of 1990, worked with Cooke at Barnwell Whaley before Brandenburg was hired as The Citadel's in-house General Counsel in 2005. In Brandenburg's opinion, "you cannot overstate the significance of Dawes's work for the school." The board agrees, having awarded him an honorary degree in 1993.

In mid-September 1992, as the Bulldog football team upset Arkansas and embarked on the best season in the history of the college, *Sports Illustrated* published an article by Rick Reilly entitled "What is The Citadel? For some athletes, it was a place of nightmares." Many familiar with the facts found Reilly's reporting a nightmare. In detailing alleged trauma inflicted on athletes during what Reilly described as "the bloody and tortuous year of 1991," he credited every grievance story as gospel while reserving his considerable talent for sarcasm for anyone disputing them. An article that equates your uniforms to "the sort you might get at a good Army surplus store" telegraphs an agenda.[411]

Better press arrived in the form of another inclusion in *U. S. News and World Report*'s annual ranking, the fourth consecutive year in which "America's Best Colleges" gave the school high marks. It ranked in the top 10 percent of regional colleges and universities nationwide, a pool of 558 schools. It rated 13th overall among the 147 colleges in the South, the only regional comprehensive school ranked in South Carolina.[412]

The challenging year 1992 closed on a winning note thanks to the football Bulldogs, who won a school-record 11 games and finished the season tied for the No. 1 ranking in the final NCAA Division 1-AA poll. Led by quarterback Jack Douglas, running back Everette Sands, offensive linemen Carey Cash and Lance Hansen, and safety Lester Smith, the team won its first Southern Conference Championship since 1961, along the way notching memorable road wins over Arkansas and Army. After finishing the regular season 10-1, the Dogs hosted two NCAA 1-AA playoff games, beating North Carolina A&T for its first playoff win ever. Youngstown State ended the Bulldogs' season, then lost the title game 31-28 to Marshall, the only team to beat the Dogs in the regular season. Coach Charlie Taaffe was named National Coach of the Year by Sports Network and South Carolina Coach of the Year by the South Carolina Association of Sports Writers.[413]

Corps Day 1993 marked the school's sesquicentennial. The elaborate celebration began with Mayor Joe Riley delivering a Greater Issues speech on Tuesday, March 16. In addition to a full complement of activities on campus, special events at the Old Citadel highlighted the milestone. The Washington Light Infantry staged a changing of the guard, thereby reenacting the occasion in 1843 when the WLI, as the militia protecting munitions stored at the Old Citadel, turned over the keys to officials representing the newly formed college, thus beginning the great educational tradition that continues today.[414] A plaque commemorating the occasion was unveiled to acknowledge the role that the old fortress played in that tradition. On Thursday evening, McAlister Field House was the site of the first of two Citadel Tattoos, a legacy from the famous Edinburgh Tattoo, where the Regimental Band and Pipe Band performed in 1991.

On Friday, Dr. Jagdish Mehra, Distinguished Visiting Professor of Physics, lectured at McAlister, followed by Governor Carroll Campbell's address as part of the Greater Issues series. That night, the Bo Thorpe Orchestra performed to set the tone for the Grand March and Sesquicentennial Ball that followed. No guest present would have forgotten the 40-by-80-foot replica of Padgett-Thomas Barracks built for the occasion.

On Saturday, the 1994 Summerall Guard gave its first performance at a parade to honor Palmetto Award recipients Jack Douglas and Jerome White. Visitors got their first look (and taste) of the new mess hall. The week was capped off that evening at McAlister with the second Citadel Tattoo, a unique extravaganza featuring the "Regimental Band, the Cadet Chorale, the 1993 Summerall Guards, the Touchdown Canon Crew, the Pipe Band, the Regimental Staff, the Cadet Rifle Legion, the Chapel Color Guard, the 1994 Junior Sword Drill, the Gospel Choir, a 50-state flag detail and the Sesquicentennial Color Guard." An international flavor was added with the addition of the Royal Canadian Army Cadet Pipes and Drums.[415] It was a banner evening that set a standard for the next 150 years.

The spring of 1993 also marked the beginning of the Shannon Faulkner experience, discussed in Chapter 12. While she became the focus of news stories and talking heads, the business of the college continued apace. As related in Chapter 9, former President Reagan delivered the commencement speech in May. In the weeks that followed, the college received over 300 requests for copies of Reagan's remarks.[416]

The academic year 1992-1993 ended with a recommendation from Colonel William "Billy" Jenkinson, who would become Board Chairman in 2002, that focus for the coming year center on (1) discipline and drinking; (2) racial sensitivity; (3) cadet knowledge of the current litigation; and (4) the need to increase the number of applicants.[417] By the fall of 1993, the first of those priorities was being addressed. The Commandant, Army Colonel Roy F. Zinser, Jr., Class of 1968, instituted a random urinalysis drug test on campus. He pulled an unannounced inspection of 120 cadet cars (no contraband found). He disbanded the Junior Sword Drill for violations of Citadel policies and JSD by-laws. In its place, first sergeants and above who were not members of JSD were designated as an Honor Guard for Parents Weekend and to perform the Sword Arch at the Ring Ceremony.

The Watts administration took a step forward in leadership training when it acknowledged, in October 1993, that there was "no specific program or formal process" for leadership training.[418] True, but a more accurate statement would have been that there was *currently* "no specific program or formal process," because there had been when the school was founded. The original curricula, going back to the 1840s, instructed fourth-classmen in "the Duties of a Private Soldier;" instructed third-classmen in "the School of the Company, and Duties of Corporals;" second-classmen in "the School of the Battalion, and Duties of Sergeants;" and first-classmen in "Evolutions of the Line, and Duties of Commissioned Officers."[419]

Colonel Zinser organized a Leadership Development Program mandatory for all cadets. As envisioned, each class would be instructed on a level appropriate to its status, and its structure bore obvious similarity to the college's original curricula quoted above. Knobs would attend the "school of the cadet"; sophomores, "school of the corporal"; juniors, the "school of the NCO"; and seniors, "school of the officer." Zinser modeled the program on the Army's Leadership Assessment Program (LAP) then being used to teach leadership at West Point, modified to fit the needs of The Citadel. As a warmup to the program he had in mind, earlier that month he scheduled four-hour blocks of instruction for each class. Included in the lessons were examples of leadership successes and failures, tutorials on "how to" and "how not to." As part of the training, the entire Corps heard from legendary Charleston Police Chief Reuben Greenberg on the vital issues of respect for authority and the importance of accountability. Three months later, on January 12, 1994, the first Leadership Training Day took place, a forerunner to the more extensive leadership training that would be implemented in the years to come.[420]

Despite best efforts to maintain a "business as usual" mindset, litigation challenging the all-male admissions policy distracted the administration, as General Watts acknowledged to the board in January 1994. But regardless of the future gender composition of the Corps, the barracks reconstruction project was key to accommodating whomever was admitted. Groundbreaking for the new barracks, on the site of the old mess hall, was held on May 13, 1994.

Negative publicity related to the still-unsolved Berra Byrd shooting, the *Sports Illustrated* article, and litigation over the all-male admissions policy spawned a public relations effort to highlight the stories that weren't being told in the press and media. In addition to the high *U.S. News and World Report* rankings, the college could boast of some impressive graduation rates: 60 percent of Citadel students graduated in four years, far better than the 38 percent at Clemson, the next highest four-year graduation rate among South Carolina colleges.[421] Additionally, 70 percent of cadets enrolled as freshmen graduated in four years, whereas the national average at public colleges during the same time period was 48 percent. Rates were even more impressive for black cadets and black recruited athletes. Black cadets graduated at a rate of 67 percent, compared with 26 percent at public colleges, and the rate for recruited black athletes at The Citadel was 68 percent vs. 32 percent at public colleges and universities. For football recruits at colleges that awarded football scholarships, The Citadel's graduation rate was consistently among the top four, a group that included Duke University. Thirty percent of Citadel graduates went on to professional schools in business, law, medicine and the ministry. When the Corps of Cadets was combined with The Citadel College of Graduate and Professional Studies (formerly the Evening College), over a third of the school's enrollment were women.[422]

Lawyers defending the all-male admissions policies at both VMI and The Citadel confronted the issue that ultimately proved decisive — both were state supported schools, although as General Watts observed, the level of state support in South Carolina had fallen so far that it was more accurate to describe The Citadel as "state assisted" rather than "state supported." In General Clark's first year as president, 1954-1955, the state furnished 43 percent of the school's operating budget.[423] By the time the courts wrestled with Shannon Faulkner, that share had dropped to 28 percent and falling.[424]

Under such circumstances, it was natural to contemplate what would be required to convert The Citadel to a private institution. A preliminary in-house estimate done in May 1994 at the request of General Watts demonstrated just how ambitious that undertaking would be. The largest expense, not surprisingly, would have been the purchase of the buildings, put at $58.7 million. Equipment added $10.95 million; library books: $6.34 million; land: $2.63 million; changes to accounting system for private accounting standards: $25,000; repayment of institutional bonds to the state: $2.13 million. These costs would be one-time only, but they totaled $80.76 million. To that figure must be added the recurring contribution from the state, which in 1994 was expected to total $16.47 million. The endowment required to generate $16.47 million annually was reckoned at $329.3 million, assuming a 5 percent return on endowed funds. In 2017, that corpus is about $50 million above where it stands today, an ambitious yet attainable sum given the current fundraising expertise within TCF, but in 1994 it would have been a deal killer. Equally daunting would have been the tuition hike needed. An in-house estimate put that figure at $311 per in-state student and $765 per out-of-state cadet for each $1 million needed.[425]

In June 1994, Zinser left to take over the G-3 slot of the Cadet Command at Fort Monroe, Virginia. Replacing him was Colonel Joe Trez, who arrived back in Charleston as commandant and Professor of Military Science. One of his first calls was to Robert Foley, the commandant at West Point. Foley sent Trez information on the Cadet Leader Development System that had been instituted there and, in Foley's view, had changed the culture of West Point in a very positive way. After reviewing the CLDS materials from Foley, Trez planned a week-long retreat at Charleston Air Force Base with the 1994-1995 cadet leadership. The retreat was not focused on hazing, but rather on what Trez viewed as the top priorities: academics and the elimination of alcohol abuse. "We had Kevin Jarrard as Regimental Commander and excellent senior leadership. By the end of that week key pieces were in place for a great year," Trez said.

It all went south quickly. On the Monday knobs reported, the screaming in the barracks reached a fevered pitch. Anxious parents lingering at the sally ports and by their cars were treated to profanity-laced commands aimed at sons for whom the college experience was only minutes old. Trez witnessed it in frustration and amazement, shocked and embarrassed by the display playing out in view and earshot of those paying the tuitions. "Two weeks at Charleston Air Force Base wasted," he told himself.

For Trez, the news was about to get worse. Shortly before knobs reported in 1994, Judge Houck had ruled in the Shannon Faulkner litigation that The Citadel could require her to shave her head like all other knobs. Her lawyers had objected, displaying for the judge World War II images of women in concentration camps with shaved heads. Newspapers across the country followed the controversy, including the *Washington Post*, which ran an editorial and by-line updates.[426] Those did not go over well at the Pentagon, which in Trez's words "went ballistic." The Army brass decided it wanted its active duty colonel in Charleston to have nothing to do with the Faulkner conflict, so it issued an ultimatum, a Hobson's choice: retire or relinquish the role of commandant. Trez chose the latter. Colonel Roger Popham, USA (Ret.), Class of 1959, became commandant and Trez remained on active duty for the 1994-95 academic year as PMS.

He retired the following summer, at which point he resumed the job of commandant just in time to land at ground zero when Shannon Faulkner was ordered admitted. But the experience that "shocked and embarrassed him" in 1994 led to a change in schedule the following year, the year Faulkner reported. Instead of throwing knobs into the cadre maw as soon as they exited their parents' vehicles, they would report on Saturday, two days early, with Saturday and Sunday set aside for briefings and orientations. The "system" would begin the following Monday, which was the day Faulkner took ill and reported to the infirmary.

Trez was committed to the CLDS and determined to make it a success. By his own admission, he failed. Asked the reasons, he lists (1) West Point's superior technology, and (2) Citadel alumni resistance. To the more vocal alumni, the use of a West Point model translated into watering down The Citadel's system to accommodate women. The same reaction greeted the findings of the Lane Committee study of the Fourth Class System ordered by General Watts. The findings of that committee largely mirrored those of the Whitmire and Mood Reports, but came at a time of heightened threat to the all-male admissions policy. Resistance to change also came from within the Corps. Trez reported finding copies of *The Lords of Discipline* in almost every room, with too many cadets clinging to that fiction as a standard for the system they perceived themselves to be a part of.[427]

The year 1994 closed with reaffirmation of The Citadel's accreditation for 10 years by the Southern Association for Colleges and Schools (SACS). The SACS Committee made 41 recommendations for improvements, many of which had been identified by the college's Institutional Self-Study initiative that precedes SACS reviews. A majority dealt with issues related to the College of Graduate and Professional Studies. More than a few of these recommendations can fairly be described as academic esoterica, suggested rewiring of the organizational diagrams of who reports to whom. Others identify weaknesses that, once corrected or implemented, make for a stronger institution. For example, in response to what the Committee perceived as a lack of a coordinated process for evaluation of undergraduate programs and relating those evaluations to departmental and institutional goals, the school tasked the Dean of Planning and Assessment to "develop and implement a formal, coordinated, coherent assessment program keyed to departmental and institutional goals." The Committee also found wanting the school's efforts to evaluate undergraduate instruction and urged the adoption and implementation of a plan. The Citadel responded by reporting that in the fall of 1993, the Faculty Council had selected the CAFETERIA student evaluation of instruction software package developed by Purdue University. During the 1994-1995 academic year, the Faculty Council and the Academic Board were expected to assess results to determine how much weight they would carry in "faculty evaluations for merit, probationary reappointment, promotion and tenure." Another area of concern focused on faculty compensation, with the college urged to conduct formal annual reviews of faculty salaries. In response, the school charged the Vice President for Academic Affairs with the responsibility for conducting future formal annual reviews of faculty salaries, with results to be shared with the faculty, the President, and the Board of Visitors. For some shortfalls cited by the Committee, funding remained an issue for the school. The library's need for added space for student seating and future collections required a major capital expenditure of $1.9 million, the source of which awaited a decision from the state on whether requested revenue bonds would be issued.[428]

Colonel Mood reported on the hiring of Dr. Barbara A. Zaremba to head the newly established Department of Special Services, a counseling office designed to deal with learning disabilities and attention deficit disorder (LD/ADD). This effort had been mandated by federal law, the Rehabilitation Act of 1973 and the Americans with Disabilities Act of 1990. It served both cadets and those enrolled in the graduate and evening programs. In the fall of 1995 it counseled 234 students, and by the spring of 1996 that number had risen to 256, with seven of those students having attained Gold Stars, 17 on the Dean's List, and 40 achieving a GPR of 2.5 or better.[429]

Days before Shannon Faulkner reported, the board was presented with a document long in the making: "Toward the 21st Century, The Citadel Strategic Plan." As the name implies, it was intended to serve as a roadmap for navigating the way forward. Draft No. 4 of the plan, presented to the board that day, contained a section entitled "Guiding Assumptions." One of those assumptions was, "The Citadel's daytime program will remain military and single-gender." By the time Draft No. 5, the final draft, was approved five months later, Faulkner was gone but that assumption remained: "The Citadel will continue to provide a program that will remain military and single-gender."[430] The assumption remained valid for another six months, until the Supreme Court ruled against VMI, and The Citadel Board of Visitors voted to abandon its all-male policy. In August, four women would report, and this time two of them would remain and graduate. A new era began. See Chapter 12.

In March 1996, General Watts notified the board of his intent to retire effective August 31, 1996.[431] While the Supreme Court's decision was then still three months away, he could sense the way the tide was turning. Like his predecessors, he had planted his flag firmly on the side of an all-male Corps of Cadets, and to his credit he believed that coeducation could best be managed by someone less identified with the old regime. No president since the Civil War, when presidents were called superintendents, had confronted such turbulent times. That the school survived and prospered is a testament to him and to the resilience of the Corps and its alumni.

Chapter 12

SKIRTS CLIMB THE GATES

Major Wallace I. West, Jr. wrote his name into Citadel history when, as head of the admissions office, he approved the application of one "Shannon Richey Faulkner" of Powdersville, S.C. to become a member of the Class of 1999. As inevitable as it was that the school would eventually have to confront coeducation, West can rightly claim to have been duped by what amounted to a sleight of hand by the applicant and her guidance counselor, a woman named Martha Dolge.

At the applicant's request, Dolge doctored Faulkner's transcripts, using Wite-Out to eliminate what they both must have known would be fatal references to her gender. West, responsible for filling the class with 600 qualified applicants in an era of declining enrollment, can be forgiven for his failure to notice the lack of pronouns deliberately omitted from answers to questions posed on the form. A major point in applicant Faulkner's favor was his/her residency in South Carolina, as the school's policy mandated the admission of all qualified state residents. And, setting aside gender, Faulkner appeared qualified, with a high school GPA of 3.35, ranking him/her 40th in a Wren High School class of 234. In the furor that erupted after the ruse was discovered, Wren High's principal claimed in a press release to have disciplined Dolge for her role.[432] Faulkner, for her part, went on to fame or infamy, depending on one's point of view.

As dark a day as the Faulkner application represented in West's otherwise admirable career, a bright day occurring years earlier provided a counterpoint, a bookend high to the Faulkner low. When West reported to The Citadel in the fall of 1966 as a member of the Class of 1970, he fell under the considerable sway of a senior private, John Watts Bowditch. Bowditch carved his name in Citadel lore in the spring of 1967 during a food fight in the mess hall. The occasion was the change from winter to spring uniforms, meaning all seniors would be wearing wools for the last time at the evening mess. A tradition going back an arguable number of years required those wool pants to be destroyed while worn by those only too happy to be rid of them. Graduates might preserve field jackets for utility or store in a series of attics their dress blouse, but no one saved those black striped wool trousers.

Tradition notwithstanding, an order came down from the chain of command that no ripping of wools would be tolerated in 1967. Bowditch, who was no stranger to ignoring orders, ignored this one by ripping the wool pants off none other than the regimental commander, who had marched down to Fourth Battalion's mess area to put down the food riot. Bowditch's mortal sin had been preceded by many venial ones in his long cadetship, one of which was the making and selling of grill cheese sandwiches during ESP in Fourth Battalion, and it was the grill cheese enterprise that bonded Bowditch and West in an unholy business venture.

West roomed next door to Bowditch. In a nightly ritual, Bowditch banged on the wall at the beginning of ESP, the signal that West was to bring the hot plate Bowditch used to make his flavorful grilled cheese sandwiches. When the ritual began, the dialogue went like this:

> Bowditch: "West, I want you to take this hot plate to your room and hide it in your laundry bag. Bring it over when I need it."
>
> West: "Sir, Mr. Bowditch sir, permission to make a statement, sir."
>
> Bowditch: "What is it, West?"
>
> West: "Sir, it is against the regulations for me to keep a hot plate in my room."
>
> Bowditch: "That's true, West, but it is also against the regulations for me to keep one in this room. If a hot plate is discovered here during an inspection, I would get written up. I might have to walk tours and serve confinements. We wouldn't want that, would we West?"
>
> West: "Sir, no sir."
>
> Bowditch: "But if the hot plate is found in *your* room, it won't matter. Do you know why, West?"
>
> West: "Sir, because I'm a knob?"
>
> Bowditch: "Exactly. One of us must risk punishment if this contraband is discovered, and it is your duty as a knob to fall on your sword, so to speak. Is that clear?"
>
> West: "Sir, yes sir."
>
> Bowditch: "Excellent. And West, when I'm finished making the sandwiches, I'll need you to go door-to-door to sell them. Fifty cents each. We don't extend credit."

West became a fixture going door-to-door during ESP. He carried the inventory in a cardboard box suspended from some webbing around his neck, with a tee-shirt or towel covering the sandwiches to hold in the heat. Mercifully for his grades, the sandwiches sold quickly, allowing West to return to his room to study for what remained of the evening. Whether his parents ever learned that their tuition was providing Bowditch with spending money for weekends is unknown.

What is known is that in the spring of 1992, Bowditch had a son who was eager to attend The Citadel. Leland Bowditch had an impressive resume coming out of Gloucester High School in Virginia. He was an athlete, president of the student body, and well liked by his classmates. But his grades were average and his SATs somewhat below average, making an out-of-state application problematic. His father, John, anxious that he be accepted, decided to hedge his bets by calling the college to do a bit of ring knocking. When the switchboard answered, he asked to be put through to the admissions department. That conversation went like this:

> Bowditch: "My name is John Bowditch. I'm a 1968 grad even though I came in with the class of '67. I stayed an extra year for a little remedial work if you get my drift. Look, I've got a son who really has his heart set on being a Bulldog. His name is Leland Bowditch and he sent in his application last week. His grades aren't the best but he's a gifted kid who would make the school proud. Do you think there's anything you could do to help his application along?"
>
> Admissions Officer: "Mr. Bowditch, this is Wallace West, Class of 1970, and I've waited 25 years for this moment."

West was, in fact, both a reliable purveyor of grilled cheese sandwiches and an excellent admissions officer, Shannon Faulkner notwithstanding. In 1984, General Grimsley had singled him out for exceptionally outstanding work in managing the admissions and acceptance processes within the Admissions Department.[433]

The saga of women at The Citadel has eerie parallels to the Civil War. While that war indisputably began with South Carolina's secession from the Union in December 1860 and the subsequent firing on the *Star of the West* and Fort Sumter, most of the fighting took place in Virginia, at least in the early years, when First Manassas and Fredericksburg saw South Carolina troops in the front lines far from home. The same was true of the all-male admissions policies at the last two state-supported military colleges in America: VMI and The Citadel. Decisive battles in Virginia and Washington, D.C. eventually ended the coeducation conflict as surely as Appomattox ended the war.

But while the battle raged in Virginia, there was no shortage of action in Charleston, where litigation brought by Shannon Faulkner proved bitter and contentious. "We fought over every grain of sand," said her lead attorney, Valorie Vojdik.[434]

Arguably, the battle over coeducation ended before it began when the U.S. service academies admitted women. In 1975, President Ford signed into law the right of women to apply for admission, and in 1976 West Point admitted 119 (62 graduated four years later).[435] At the Air Force Academy, 157 entered in the Class of 1980 and 97 graduated.[436] At the Naval Academy, 55 graduated out of the 80 who initially reported.[437]

But, as is well known, tuition at the service academies brings joy to the hearts of all cadet and midshipmen parents, whose sons and daughters incur not fees and expenses but rather active duty obligations to their respective branches. Neither Virginia nor South Carolina were inclined to enact legislation comparable to that signed by President Ford, so not only would women seeking to attend VMI or The Citadel need to pay for their educations, but they would have to scale the walls of institutions that maintained policies against their admission and frankly did not want them there. In a 1994 survey conducted by the University of South Carolina's Survey Research Laboratory, 61 percent of men and almost 64 percent of women surveyed felt The Citadel should remain all male.[438] The fact that by then the service academies had each graduated 14 classes that included women would seemed to have deprived both state schools of the argument that women could not be accommodated. The issue was: should they be?

In April 1989, in one of General Grimsley's last reports to the board as president, he made members aware of a Justice Department inquiry to VMI based on a complaint of gender discrimination. One month later, he reported that the legal hand grenade had rolled all the way to Charleston; the Justice Department had received a similar complaint about The Citadel. Thus, by the early 1990s both schools found themselves in the legal crosshairs of a U.S. government agency with unlimited resources. The Justice Department could have as easily selected The Citadel and South Carolina as its target. Instead, it chose VMI and Virginia.

The following year, the Attorney General of the United States sued VMI and the Commonwealth of Virginia on behalf of a female high school student who wished to attend. The federal government alleged that VMI's male-only admissions policy violated the Equal Protection Clause of the 14th Amendment. A six-day trial ensued, during which the battle of experts was intense. At the close of the testimony, the trial court held in favor of VMI. The court was persuaded that single-sex education had value to either men or women and that VMI's status as the only all-male public college in Virginia provided a valuable diversity in education. It conceded that women were denied the "unique educational opportunity that is available only at VMI," but found three elements of the VMI experience that would not survive the admission of women: (1) personal privacy would have to be provided for the women where none existed for the men; (2) physical education requirements would need to be altered; and (3) the "adversative environment" would have to be modified. With these changes, reasoned the court, VMI would no longer be VMI, thus justifying the exclusion of women.[439]

On appeal, the Fourth Circuit disagreed. The problem, opined the appellate court, was that protecting the single-sex policy for men did nothing for women. It agreed that the changes cited by the trial court would have to made if VMI was to accommodate women, but found that "some women can meet the physical standards now imposed on men" and that "neither the goal of producing citizen soldiers nor VMI's implementing methodology is inherently unsuitable to women." On remand to the district court, the Fourth Circuit gave VMI three choices: admit women, forego state support by becoming a private college, or establish a parallel institution that would provide the opportunity for women that VMI provided for men.[440] This last option, the parallel institution, prompted Virginia to establish the Virginia Women's Institute for Leadership (VWIL) at Mary Baldwin College, a private, liberal arts school for women located in Staunton. It would also cost The Citadel the $5 million it paid Converse College to set up the Women's Leadership Institute in South Carolina.

The Fourth Circuit had articulated VMI's three options when Shannon Faulkner sued Wally West, General Watts and the Board of Visitors on March 2, 1993. The eight attorneys representing her included two from Greenville, one from Charleston, three from New York City's Shearman & Sterling law firm, and two from the Women's Rights Project at the ACLU based in New York. No one could accuse Shannon Faulkner of coming into legal battle under-lawyered. The suit was filed in the U.S. District Court, Charleston Division, which landed it in front of Judge C. Weston Houck. Charleston attorney Dawes Cooke represented The Citadel. When the litigation was over, Faulkner's lawyers sought $6.15 million in fees and costs. The cost to prepare their bill was $90,000. The school's lawyers claimed $3.8 million for over 25,000 hours spent on a case that lasted five years.[441]

Catherine S. Manegold covered the Faulkner trial for the *New York Times*. She later wrote a book about it, *In Glory's Shadow; Shannon Faulkner, The Citadel and a Changing America*. Published by the prestigious Alfred A. Knopf, the book makes a fair attempt to place the controversy into the larger social context of the feminist movement and the millennium's last years. For those who believe *Faulkner v. The Citadel* was wrongly decided, it promises to be a painful read. In the book's Acknowledgments, Manegold disclaims it as "a work of history in any traditional sense," and rather than provide a bibliography, she cites sources generally, though most quotes used in the text are attributed. Few of the college's warts, excesses or lapses in judgment escaped her notice (or mention), and a reader not familiar with the school might well wonder why Shannon Faulkner or any other sentient human being of either gender would go there. Faulkner herself, in testimony before Judge Houck, said she was drawn to the school "because of its alumni network, scholastic program and discipline."[442]

In the summer of 1993, Judge Houck ordered Faulkner to be admitted to fall day-classes with cadets, but the Fourth Circuit stayed the order until November. In January 1994 she began attending them. On July 22, 1994, the judge ordered her admitted to the Corps of Cadets, an order subsequently blocked by the Fourth Circuit Court of Appeals.

Meanwhile, back in Virginia, the District Court, on remand from the Fourth Circuit, examined VMI's option 3, the VWIL, and found that it passed constitutional muster. The court held that Virginia need not "provide a mirror image VMI for women" as long as the two single-gender programs produced "substantially similar outcomes." In language bordering on the poetic, the court said, "If VMI marches to the beat of a drum, then Mary Baldwin marches to the melody of a fife and when the march is over, both will have arrived at the same destination."[443]

Whether the Justice Department marched to a drum or a fife, it marched back to the Fourth Circuit to appeal. That court, in a split decision, affirmed the District Court's ruling in favor of VMI. To do so, it applied a standard it called "substantive comparability," essentially blessing the logic applied by the lower court. If the means were different, but the ends comparable, the Constitution required nothing more.[444]

Back in South Carolina, 22 women reported to Converse College to begin the SCIL, South Carolina Institute for Leadership. But Judge Houck did not recognize the SCIL as an alternative to The Citadel, and he again ordered Faulkner to be admitted to the Corps. Last minute appeals by the school urged a stay until the Supreme Court ruled on the VMI litigation. This time, the Fourth Circuit declined to block Houck's order. The Citadel's fight to keep Faulkner out ended.

On the night before she was to report as a knob, Faulkner, her parents and her legal team celebrated. She had waged an aggressive two-and-a-half-year battle and she had won. Noted Citadel alumnus Pat Conroy, who had supported coeducation in general and Faulkner in particular, joined the celebration as well but he left early, discouraged by what he perceived to be Faulkner's total lack of physical preparation for what Conroy knew awaited. He left thinking, "She doesn't stand a chance."[445]

With the court's blessing, she reported on Saturday, August 12, 1995 with her parents and two U.S. Marshalls. Unlike prior years, and not related to Faulkner's arrival, cadre did not take over until Monday. Saturday and Sunday were devoted to orientations. She tried out for the band and performed well. Assigned to I Company with 35 other knobs, she lived alone in Room 4433, with a whistle, a panic button and, outside on the gallery, two video cameras. She spent two nights in the barracks. On Monday, an exceedingly hot day, she became sick at lunch and that afternoon reported to the infirmary, diagnosed with heat exhaustion. She missed the swearing in ceremony Monday evening. She remained in the infirmary until Friday, when she announced she was leaving. To reporters she said it was hard for her to leave, that she had wanted it for so long, but that she had to think of her health. She could not keep her food down. The isolation as the only woman and the toll taken by the court battle were too much. She did not blame the school.[446]

To dwell further on her six days on campus serves no good purpose. It was a sad time for her and for the college. When word spread that she was leaving, some cadets embarrassed themselves and The Citadel with an unseemly celebration, photos of which made national news.

Shannon Faulkner's motivation in applying to The Citadel has been greatly (and hotly) debated. Some felt she did it for publicity. If she did, she succeeded beyond what could only have been her wildest expectations. General Poole, who as dean interacted with her when she attended classes prior to her admission to the Corps, came to believe she never expected to become a cadet.[447] According to Catherine Manegold, "It was a lark at first. She wanted most to make a point."[448] A Citadel spokesman at the time, Terry Leedom, speculated that she would "be here for a while, and then she'll cry 'sexual harassment' and get out and make her movie."[449] In her first deposition, Faulkner told Dawes Cooke, when asked why she thought she would like it there, that "graduates talked mysteriously about a 'brotherhood' that lasted all their lives. She liked the sense of that and saw in it a cushion for one's future." Cooke pressed her. "And could *she* be part of that brotherhood?" [emphasis in original] "I don't think it would be a brotherhood anymore," she replied. "It would be a family."⁴⁵⁰

Ten months after Faulkner's exit from the school, the U.S. Supreme Court handed down its decision. Understanding full well what was at stake in the VMI appeal, the state of South Carolina, working with Dawes Cooke, The Citadel's attorney, filed an *amicus curiae* brief urging the court to uphold the Fourth Circuit's ruling in favor of VMI. It did not. Writing for a 7-1 majority, Justice Ruth Bader Ginsburg's opinion highlighted the differences between VMI and the alternative proposed at Mary Baldwin College, which were indeed dramatic. At Mary Baldwin, a task force designing the curriculum and environment for the 25-30 women expected to enroll as an alternative to VMI concluded that for most women a military model such as the one at VMI would be "wholly inappropriate." As proposed by the task force, the VWIL would have a "largely ceremonial" Corps of Cadets, would not have a military format, would not require its students to eat together or wear uniforms. In contrast to VMI's adversative system, the task force favored "a cooperative method which reinforces self-esteem." In other words, the VWIL was to be what might be deemed "VMI-Lite," or as one Fourth Circuit judge called it, a "pale shadow" of VMI in terms of curriculum, faculty, funding, influence, alumni support and prestige. The real problem, in the court's view, was that while VMI was "wholly inappropriate" for most women, it was not inappropriate for all women, and Virginia's failure to provide a college for women capable of meeting all the individual activities required of VMI cadets was fatal to that school's desire to remain all-male. Virginia's contention that maintaining the single-gender policy at VMI as essential to educational diversity within the Commonwealth was undercut by the fact that it supported no all-female college, making diversity in essence a one-way street. The lone dissent in the case came from Justice Scalia, whose dependably conservative colleague, Justice Clarence Thomas, recused himself because he had a son at VMI. Scalia's opinion opened with the rhetorical flourish for which he was famous: "Today the Court shuts down an institution that has served the Commonwealth of Virginia with pride and distinction for over a century and a half."⁴⁵¹

The Virginia Women's Institute for Leadership at Mary Baldwin University recently celebrated its 20th anniversary. The 22 women who entered Converse in 1995 comprised the SCIL, which closed in 1999 due to lack of state funding and coeducation at The Citadel. There are three remaining all-male, four-year colleges in America — all private. There are currently no publicly funded all-male colleges.

Two days after the Supreme Court's VMI decision, The Citadel's Board of Visitors announced that the school would henceforth accept qualified female applicants. The skirts had successfully climbed the gates, with assimilation into the Corps still to be tested.

Chapter 13

A YEAR IN TRANSITION

The academic year 1996-1997 stands as one of the most transformative in the history of the college. In March 1996, when General Watts notified the board of his decision to retire at the end of August, the board confronted the challenge of finding new leadership when the stakes could hardly have been higher. Media attention devoted to Shannon Faulkner's entry and abrupt departure put the school in a public relations glare that threatened to adversely impact what it needed most to thrive: state funding, more and better applicants, alumni support, and a positive image throughout the state and nation. Finding just the right person seemed key to the future. Adding to that challenge was the uncertainty of coeducation, as the Supreme Court's decision was still two months away when the search committee was formed in April. The next man to occupy the president's office would need the judgment of a seasoned administrator and the flexibility to assimilate women should the court decide as many were predicting it would.

To lead the search for this critical selection, the board turned to one of its own: Frank Mood, who accepted the assignment on the condition he could pick the other committee members. He wanted individuals with experience and wisdom. Their fierce loyalty to the college would be a given. Mood described for the Advisory Council the characteristics that the right presidential candidate would possess; someone who could provide "inspired leadership to the Corps," support the direction chosen by the administration and senior leaders, and a man able to serve the myriad of constituencies it was essential to satisfy: the Corps, faculty, staff, alumni, legislators, donors, media and minorities.[452]

As is common practice among search committees, Mood's engaged a headhunter. Given the stakes, the committee expanded its horizons to such prominent Americans as Colin Powell, Sam Nunn and General Barry McCaffrey, all of whom were approached. Among those contacted by Korn-Ferry International that spring was Major General John S. Grinalds, USMC (Ret.), then in his fifth year as headmaster of Woodberry Forest, the prestigious prep school in Virginia. When asked by the headhunter whether he would have any interest in the Citadel position, Grinalds said no. He was quite happy where he was, but he agreed to come to Fredericksburg to share with the headhunter some thoughts on his transition from a military career to one in academia. Korn-Ferry's report back to the search committee prompted Mood to invite Grinalds to Charleston, not to interview for the job, as Grinalds had made it clear he wasn't a candidate, but to educate the committee on the military-to-academia transition Grinalds had so ably managed at Woodberry Forest and just as ably described to the headhunter.

The search committee's meeting with Grinalds took place in the Charleston home of General Seignious, a committee member. As he had with the headhunter, Grinalds talked about the unique challenges confronting a career military officer transitioning to an academic campus environment. Mood recalls being as impressed as the headhunter had been. Here was someone with his feet firmly planted in two worlds: education and military. His resume demonstrated rare levels of achievement in both. As a graduate of West Point's Class of 1959, Grinalds had competed for and won a Rhodes Scholarship. At Oxford he graduated with distinction, and at Harvard he finished with honors in pursuit of his MBA. He served as a White House Fellow. His time at Woodberry Forest had provided five years of experience in dealing with a faculty, a crucial component of any college president's role. For all his intellectual accomplishments, his military record was equally if not more impressive. Awarded a Silver Star for combat heroism in Vietnam, Grinalds also was inducted into the *Legion d'Honneur* by French President Mitterrand. Before retiring from active duty to accept the position at Woodberry Forest, he commanded the Marine Corps Recruit Depot in San Diego, which put him in charge of training 23,000 recruits. Upon learning of Grinalds' blend of talents and after meeting him personally, Mood sensed that perhaps they had found their man, but as Grinalds appeared unavailable, some courtship would be required.

By late spring 1996, it had become apparent that the search for Watts's replacement would not be completed by the time Watts retired and knobs reported in August. The man chosen to succeed Watts on an interim basis was Brigadier General R. Clifton Poole, USAR, elevated from his post as Vice President for Academic Affairs and Dean of the College to Interim President effective September 1, 1996.[453] General Poole, a member of the Class of 1959, brought a wealth of management experience when he returned to his alma mater in 1993. He received his Masters and Ph.D. from the University of South Carolina, then went on to do postdoctoral work at the London

School of Economics. He joined the faculty of the University of Richmond in Virginia in 1975, eventually serving as Dean of the E. Claiborne Robins School of Business there.

Upon Poole's elevation to interim president, Dr. Isaac "Spike" Metts became interim Vice President for Academic Affairs and Dean of the College, Poole's just-vacated position. The challenges associated with that position increased significantly when the state passed a law in May 1996 that would tie funding for all state supported colleges to performance criteria, a concept known as "performance funding." Prior to its passage, the amount of state support given annually to The Citadel and other colleges depended upon enrollment, program size, perceived need and legislative muscle. To call the method "imprecise" would be generous. Performance funding was seen as a way to measure schools based on 37 specific criteria that would, over time, reward schools that improved and, conversely, punish those that did not.

The concept of performance funding had been around since the 1970s as states sought more bang for their education bucks. The states that experimented with it generally employed it as one of a number of factors on which to base funding. But South Carolina, in the legislative equivalent of a "Hail Mary," decided to base 100 percent of its support for the state's colleges on performance funding. The criteria were phased in, with 14 used in 1997-98, followed by 25 used in 1998-99, and all 37 used in 1999-2000 to develop each school's "report card" for funding purposes. Anticipating the changes wrought by this new system complicated Poole's year as interim president and would vex the administration that followed.[454]

When, in late June, the U.S. Supreme Court ruled against VMI's all-male admission policy and the Citadel's board agreed that the school would henceforth accept applications from women, it must have seemed to General Watts that his tenure as president ended with a bigger hurricane than Hugo, the one that began it. A whirlwind of activity engulfed the school, as the administration had less than two months to find female applicants, admit them and prepare for their arrival.

But they did it. In August 1996, four women reported as knobs. They were Nancy Mace, Kim Messer, Jeanie Mentavlos and Petra Lovetinska.

Nancy Mace is the daughter of Brigadier General Emory Mace, Class of 1963, the most war decorated living Citadel graduate. He became Commandant during her tenure. Her older sister, Mary, graduated from West Point.

Kim Messer came from the crossroads of Clover, South Carolina. Her father was a retired Army sergeant. Reportedly, she was interested in a military career.

Jeanie Mentavlos had a brother who attended The Citadel and she had, the previous year, competed for the title of Miss Citadel. Her father had been a Secret Service agent.

Petra Lovetinska came from Washington, D.C., where her father transported diplomats as a driver for the Czech Embassy. Impressed with her, D.C. area alumni led by Ambassador Tony Motley, Class of 1960, funded her tuition.

The press and news media gave ample coverage to the matriculation of these pioneering women. A camera crew occupied the back seat of Nancy Mace's family car as she left her Goose Creek home to report. At the school's request, she had agreed to the filming of a "48 Hours" segment for CBS. As the Mace vehicle neared the college, she saw a front porch flagpole flying pink ribbons. She said she knew the ribbons were meant for her, and her spirits soared. Crowds of onlookers surrounded the gates, with television crews and cameramen seemingly everywhere.[455]

The women were housed in Padgett-Thomas Barracks. Mace and Messer roomed just down the gallery from Mentavlos and Lovetinska, with a recently installed female bathroom nearby. Their rooms were configured typically except for blinds installed in the windows and a sliding bolt on the inside of the doors. Except for media cameras relentlessly focused on the women, their orientation mirrored those of the other knobs who reported in the Class of 2000. The traditional haircut, a subject argued to exhaustion by Shannon Faulkner's attorneys, came early. College officials hovered over Mace as she became the first woman clipped. After a couple of unsatisfactory passes by a barber no doubt more nervous than she was, her hair reached the appropriate length; one-half inch on top and tapered at the sides. Lovetinska showed her game attitude by plopping into the barber's chair while instructing him to "cut it all off."[456] But her barber cut it to regulation, the same length afforded Mace.

In her book, *In the Company of Men*, Nancy Mace describes in detail her knob year. Except for the obvious differences any female would have experienced, it reads like the well-kept journal of a male knob, with all of the challenges, frustrations, intimidations, insecurities and rewards that the Fourth Class System has been demonstrated to deliver. As numberless other knobs have experienced, the school's random assignment of roommates is a lottery that can make a big difference in a cadet's life. Mace was paired with Kim Messer, and it proved an unfortunate match from Day 1, as Mace relates:

For starters, she [Kim] smoked. I asked her very politely not to do so in our room, and she promised she wouldn't, but when I returned to our room after an errand, I could smell smoke in the air. Clearly, Kim had no intention of honoring her promise. My mother had lost part of one lung to illness just a few years before, and I worried about breathing cigarette smoke day after day. Worse, it was only our first night in the barracks, and she got me in trouble. While I was gone to the restroom, Kim left our room for half an hour, leaving the door standing open. I returned to find an angry cadet officer in our doorway, who gave me heat for the open door. Even though I wasn't responsible for the infraction, I had no choice but to respond, "Sir, no excuse, sir." Kim just shrugged when I told her what happened . . .[457]

The Faculty Council commended the administration for its attitude toward its implementation of the new admissions policy. In the Council's view, "The board's prompt, decisive actions, bringing to an end a long and painful struggle, has enhanced The Citadel's reputation, given clear direction to the administration and faculty, and established an unambiguous framework within which the students of the Corps of Cadets could assimilate women into the previously all-male corps smoothly, and without rancor." *U.S. News and World Report* continued to acknowledge the school's ascendant trajectory by ranking it ninth overall of 15 regional universities in the South and tops for best value in education.[458]

General Poole may have experienced *deja vu* when he learned Hurricane Fran was headed to Charleston. Might his administration begin with the same logistical nightmares that ushered in the previous one? Knobs sent home in advance of the storm received a four-day reprieve from the plebe system, but more than a few decided to seek a permanent reprieve by not returning. The *Post and Courier* put that number at 15, citing figures released by the school, but General Poole reported a higher number, 22, to the board at its September 13, 1996 meeting.

Nancy Mace, whose family lived in Goose Creek, took two of her Band Company classmates home with her to ride out whatever Hurricane Fran had in store. She had survived her first two weeks, Hell night, her first menstrual period as a knob and Hell Week. In the car leaving school, laughing and telling stories with classmates Ryan and Mike, she felt euphoric. "I loved The Citadel," she said. "Going there was the best decision I had ever made."[459]

During that fall, Mace and Lovetinska demonstrated "can do" attitudes while proving they could meet the challenges of the Fourth Class System.

In late October, both Messer and Mentavlos were diagnosed with pelvic stress fractures, a condition not uncommon for shorter women attempting to match the longer strides of men. As a result, they went on XMD, Excused Military Duty, relieving them of physical training and many of the Fourth Class System rigors endured by their classmates, who grew resentful as the upper classmen grew cynical. Neither Mace nor Lovetinska were present for what became the most publicized controversy in the abbreviated cadet careers of Messer and Mentavlos, who claimed they were set on fire with a flammable nail polish remover. Upon learning of this episode on Thursday, December 12, school officials called in SLED and the FBI to investigate, and the women disgorged a litany of abuses they claimed to have suffered during the semester, most of the incidents alleged to have occurred after they went on XMD.[460] To the administration and the press they related a pattern of hazing and harassment, included unwanted sexual advances, shoving, being forced to drink iced tea until they became sick and being kicked. Messer said her company, Echo, was run by a "secret Fourth Class System" that was neither fair nor humane. She reported being shoved against a wall with a rifle butt and struck on her head. The school charged 11 cadets with violations of regulations, with two suspended pending further investigation and review. At the conclusion of its inquiry, the Justice Department declined to prosecute the male cadets alleged by the women to have been the cause of their distress, concluding that many male cadets were treated similarly.[461]

Here are the fictional recollections of two hypothetical cadets, the first a knob and the second a senior. There is enough public and documented evidence to support both accounts:

> Knob: I wasn't at all surprised they [Messer and Mentavlos] left. Their attitudes stunk. Those other two, Nancy and Petra, those girls had their s--- together, but Kim and Jeanie just never adapted. They went on XMD in what, October? Some kind of stress fractures, I heard. Yeah, stress. Tell me about stress, and about getting out of all the stuff your classmates have to do. They told people they weren't happy. Hello. This is The Citadel, and you're a knob. You aren't supposed to be happy. And that lighting-on-fire bull----? Man, they milked that for all it was worth. It's a party trick, like some magic act you do when you're half loaded. That nail polish or whatever it was burns off and nobody gets hurt. I heard they were all laughing, then those two saw their chance to get off the Cid train and bank some cash with a lawsuit. I liked

them okay, but I don't have any respect for either of them.

Senior: I saw it coming like a train wreck but there wasn't anything I or really anyone could do. The two who left, Mentavlos and Messer, had the misfortune of being compared with the two who stayed, Mace and Lovetinska. Those two — Mace and Lovetinska I'm talking about — were pretty much model cadets, at least for the one year I was here with them. I felt sorry for the other two. I've seen it happen a dozen times in my four years here, and it isn't pleasant. Once you stop caring, the corps smells blood, especially if you go on XMD. The law of the jungle hasn't been repealed, so weakness attracts unwanted attention. And they got plenty of attention just because they were women. Four women among 2,000 guys? A recipe for trouble. A few guys crossed the line, and the administration came down hard, but too late. They said those two didn't speak up soon enough, but I've been around this place long enough to know that a knob speaking up only attracts more attention. If you ask me, the school needed more time to prepare for women, and they needed more of them when they arrived. Hindsight is a wonderful thing.

Messer and Mentavlos left the barracks in December and did not return in January. Also gone by Christmas was Charlie Taaffe, the winningest coach in Citadel football history. Taaffe's head coaching record at the school from 1987 to 1995 was 55-47-1 with a Southern Conference Championship in 1992. He was suspended in August 1996 following his second DUI arrest in three years. The fact that he was acquitted on both charges added to the controversy over whether he should have been fired. On the night of the second arrest, Taaffe had been in Beaufort for a "Coach's Night" presentation. Testifying as to his sobriety when he left Beaufort were J. Thomas Mikell and William "Kooksie" Robinson, both members of the Class of 1964 and present for Taaffe's talk.

In announcing Taaffe's dismissal, President Poole said, "We are not buying out Mr. Taaffe's contract. This is a dismissal . . ." Responding to one of the coach's lawyers who raised the possibility his client would sue, Poole acknowledged that it wouldn't surprise him. "I've been in senior administration for 18 years and almost every major decision that is made is challenged in some form or another in a legal manner." Poole's instinct and experience proved accurate. Like Messer and Mentavlos, Taaffe sued.[462]

Tom Mikell, a lawyer in Beaufort, had more than a passing interest in

Taaffe's fate. Beginning in the late 1980s, Mikell had resolved to help the school recruit quality applicants. Working with Colonel D.D. Nicholson, he participated regularly in a loosely organized group Nicholson named CAPP, the Cadet Academic Procurement Program. As a volunteer in CAPP, Mikell visited Citadel clubs across the Southeast and sometimes beyond to spread the school's gospel, to recruit applicants, and to enlist others in the recruitment effort. Joining with him in this worthy volunteer endeavor were Bill Endictor, Class of 1959, Phil Menges, Class of 1948, Jim Moseley, Class of 1958, and Charlie Pearcy, Class of 1958. In 1992, during a meeting at Mikell's home, Moseley suggested they change the name to Citadel Volunteers. Mikell handled South Carolina, North Carolina and Georgia. During a particularly active year, he recorded $51,000 in otherwise billable time spent on recruiting. At the height of their efforts, The Citadel Volunteers enlisted 300 alumni in their small army. The Volunteers Conference now held annually in February is a direct result of their work. By the mid-1990s, the coordination required to keep it going had become so time consuming that they reached out to the administration for help. Generals Poole and Watts readily responded to their plea by assigning a staff person, Major Shamus Gillen, Class of 1996, who is currently Associate Director of Admissions. Known today as the Citadel Volunteer Recruiters, they visit hundreds of high schools across the country and in 2016 participated in 230 college fairs.

By the time of Taaffe's dismissal, Mikell had been elected vice president of the Citadel Alumni Association. Worries about filling the barracks persisted. Firing a winning coach only added to a drumbeat of negative press fueled by the seemingly endless parade of lawsuits, all of which assured a chilly reception among more than a few high school guidance counselors who recruiters depended upon to steer promising students toward The Citadel.[463] The school was entering into what Ambassador Tony Motley would later describe as "the nadir of our image."[464]

Between the Taaffe controversy and Shannon Faulkner, friction among alumni and within the CAA reached fever pitch. Part of the problem was an antiquated set of bylaws dating from the 1940s that gave all ex-presidents a vote on the CAA board. As CAA presidents served one-year terms, ex-presidents eventually outnumbered and therefore outvoted currently serving board members. Adding to CAA disgruntlement was the control asserted from Charleston and Columbia, real or perceived, which led to resentment by alumni in other parts of the state and region. As CAA vice president, Mikell and others wanted the old bylaws replaced by a set reflecting modern realities. At a contentious meeting in Summerall Chapel, the CAA adopted new bylaws at the same time it changed its name from the Association of Citadel Men to the Citadel Alumni Association. In addition to the name change, the new bylaws reduced ex-president votes to three and provided for out-of-state representation on the board.[465]

Meanwhile, as the search for a new president gathered momentum, Frank Mood had been recalling conversations with Major General John Grinalds on how this or that situation at The Citadel might be handled. With each "spot on" response from Grinalds, Mood became more convinced that he was the ideal man to become The Citadel's next president. As importantly, Grinalds began to feel the same; "a calling," as he was later to say. A deeply religious man, Grinalds knew about being called, as he had been called in 1974 to serve Jesus Christ. In the fall, he agreed to submit his name for consideration by the search committee, which would sift through over 160 resumes before making its selection.[466]

Grinalds was one of several quality candidates under consideration when the committee and the board met on campus during Christmas break, January 3, 4 and 5, 1997. The selection of the next president presented major challenges to the search committee and the board, in part because they knew what major challenges awaited whomever they selected. Stress on the school produced by female assimilation, some regrettable publicity, too many vacant rooms in the barracks, significant deferred maintenance, insufficient financial support from the State Legislature and an endowment still too meager to cushion the college from further setbacks all combined to bring to the decision makers the urgent need to get it right.

The field narrowed to four strong candidates: Lieutenant General Steven L. Arnold, USA; Lieutenant General Henry C. Stackpole, III, USMC (Ret.); Lieutenant General George Christmas, USMC (Ret.); and Grinalds. The fact that three of the four were Marines may have been coincidental, or it may have been an unconscious acknowledgement of the tough fight ahead. Members lobbied each other in favor of their preferred choice. There was comfort in knowing all were highly qualified, and after extended discussions two emerged on which the committee seemed equally divided. Like Mood, Billy Jenkinson had made up his mind to support Grinalds. Sensing that Colonel Harvey Dick was on the fence, Jenkinson took him out for a beer the night before the vote. "I leaned on him . . . hard," Jenkinson said. "But Harvey was tough and wouldn't commit. He said he'd go home and pray over it. He felt sure he would get a sign pointing him to the right decision." The next day, Dick told Jenkinson he had augmented his supplications to the Almighty with a phone call to General Carl E. Mundy, USMC (Ret.), a former Commandant of the Marine Corps who sat on the Advisory Council. Mundy's verdict was short and swift: "Pick Grinalds."

If other search committee members felt the need for divine guidance, Colonel Charles T. Clanton, the chaplain, was there to give it. Like Grinalds, Clanton had been awarded a Silver Star for heroism in Vietnam. He suggested that in light of the fact that it was Sunday, a church service would be appropriate. Members assumed he meant a mini-service to be conducted in the boardroom where they were gathered, but he disabused them of that notion. He meant Summerall Chapel, unheated over the holidays. So, the members walked to the cold, deserted chapel, where Clanton seated them in the front pew. He did not merely stand in front of them in a collegial fashion, but instead ascended into the pulpit to deliver his message from on high. "As fine a sermon as I've ever heard," Jenkinson said. Clanton spoke of the Old Testament's Book of Nehemiah, which tells of the rebuilding of the walls of Jerusalem. "We need a rebuilder," Clanton told the men shivering together in the front pew. When he finished, the board returned to the boardroom and elected John Grinalds unanimously.[467] Grinalds accepted the offer on January 5, 1997, his 59th birthday, subject to completing his sixth and final year at Woodberry Forest, where it was said he knew all 360 students by name.[468]

Grinalds did not wait to go on the payroll before opining on a subject as old as The Citadel itself. A month after accepting the school's offer, he said there were actually three Fourth Class Systems at The Citadel. There was an official system as contained in the Blue Book of regulations, the system as enforced by the administration, and what amounted to a hidden system that existed "behind closed doors and after hours." His goal was to meld those three systems into one.[469] Grinalds knew a thing or two about the Fourth Class System, having endured what he termed a "brutal" plebe year at West Point, where he reported at 175 pounds. An all-state tackle in high school, he went out for the football team, shrinking down to a mere 157 pounds by the end of the year. Food deprivation, an old issue at military schools, induced Grinalds to hide an orange under his raincoat on a particularly nasty day. On his march back to the barracks, it fell to the ground, but he managed to kick it along through rain puddles until he had a chance to pick it up unobserved. Back in his room, he quartered it to share with his three roommates, as famished as he. They devoured it peel and all.[470]

The spring of 1997 produced some of the worst publicity the school had endured since the Nesmith accounts in the mid-1980s, the *Sports Illustrated* article in 1992, and Shannon Faulkner's exit in 1995. Local news articles kept South Carolinians apprised of the drama surrounding the departures of

Messer and Mentavlos, but in March they drew national attention with two stories watched by wide audiences on ABC's 20/20 and CBS's 60 Minutes. The 20/20 piece aired on March 21 and featured Kim Messer. She alleged a pattern of taunting, screaming and harassment. The five glasses of iced tea she was ordered to drink made her throw up. Nail polish on her sweatshirt produced "flames up to my chin." A rifle shoved at her hit the brim of her head cover and caused her head to hit the wall behind her. She feared telling others, because "they target people who are different." On March 23, 60 Minutes aired "Cover-up at The Citadel," with Ed Bradley interviewing Jeanie Mentavlos, who recited her hazing and harassment allegations. She accused her cadet chain of command of knowing about and tolerating the abuse. Two senior cadets appeared on camera to insist the administration knew as well, a charge the college denied through its spokesman, Terry Leedom. The "devil's advocate" normally at work for 60 Minutes must have taken the night off, because about all Bradley could muster by way of questions was to ask her to repeat the most salacious allegations of hazing, torment and sexual harassment.

Viewers interested in The Citadel's point of view could justifiably ask why there was no mention whatsoever of the Mace-Lovetinska experiences. And it wasn't as if CBS was unaware of a competing narrative about the four female knobs because, as noted earlier, 48 Hours had filmed Mace's arrival at the school on the first day knobs reported. That piece aired on September 19, 1996. Also prominently featured was Bryant Butler, the college's second African-American regimental commander. At the end of the broadcast, host Dan Rather even went so far as put into perspective the annual knob attrition rate when he reminded his audience that the average rate for freshmen dropouts at colleges nationwide was 25 percent, above The Citadel's experience which is usually 16-20 percent.

By March, Brigadier General J. Emory Mace had been appointed Commandant. Mace, a member of the Class of 1963, served early notice as a cadet that he was not to be trifled with. He earned money by continuing his boyhood habit of poaching alligators in the swamps off the Ashley River. As company commander of F Company, he sent an unmistakable and highly unconventional message to a malingering knob by tossing a live alligator into the knob's room. He is a member of The Citadel's Distinguished Alumni list as one of the most highly decorated combat veterans in Citadel history. In Vietnam he earned a Distinguished Service Cross for extraordinary heroism. He was also the recipient of the Silver Star, three Bronze Stars for valor, three Army Commendation Medals for valor and a Purple Heart.

No doubt Mace values these well-earned testaments to bravery, but values even more his Citadel ring, according to a story told by his daughter, Nancy. As a young lieutenant in Vietnam, Emory Mace had been assigned as an advisor to a South Vietnamese paratrooper battalion. During a firefight in a rice paddy, his Citadel ring slipped off, a casualty to the 50 pounds he had lost in the 10 months he had spent there. In Nancy's words:

> When night fell, his unit fell back about a mile to friendly forces under the cover of darkness. He knew his ring was close to the enemy's location, but he had no intention of leaving it there. He asked his captain for permission to return and retrieve the ring. The captain was a VMI man himself, and he understood the importance of my father's ring, so he gave my father permission to return. My dad refused to take anyone with him, as he wasn't willing to risk any life but his own. … It took him two hours to make his way stealthily through the rice paddy, carefully retracing his path of the evening before. While moving quietly down the trails on the rice paddy dike, he encountered two North Vietnamese soldiers and killed them with his rifle. Finally managing to reach the spot where he had lain, he lay down and began to search. In the blackness of the moonless night, my dad searched the water, groping blindly through the silt for the familiar shape, his senses constantly alert for the approach of enemy soldiers. Finally, after searching for quite some time, he stumbled onto what he knew was his ring. Grasping the prize tightly, he slid the muddy ring onto the third finger of his right hand. Then, as silently as the alligators he once trapped, he made his way back to camp.[471]

The change of commandants, from Trez to Mace, in the spring of 1997 produced a significant change in style and philosophy. As Joe Trez himself stated, "Mace brought the hammer down on the Corps." Supporting Mace in his "get tough" approach were three professors of military science who went on record with the board by stating, "The Corps of Cadets leadership system is dysfunctional." Colonel J.M. Basel, USMC, Colonel John A. Folley, USAF, and Colonel William A. MacPherson, USA, issued that collective assessment in a memorandum dated February 11, 1997. "The current culture of the Corps places class over duty, which in turn has resulted in erosion of discipline within the upper three classes. In short we have evolved into a *fourth class system* instead of a *four class system*." [emphasis in original] In a refrain that echoes through generations of cadets, the colonels opined, "The Fourth Class System, as currently implemented, is largely a 'rite of passage.' It does not produce the basically trained, self-disciplined, motivated third classmen we expect. Fourth classmen are abused by immature members of the Corps, they know they are not receiving good leadership, and in the end many only want to hold rank so they can in turn repeat the abuse, and many more want to assume the role of third class 'senior privates.'"[472]

The solution proposed by the PMSs was leadership training on a class-by-class basis. In a number of their recommendations, they were fighting institutional lethargy, best illustrated by their recommendation that the Fourth Class System end at Corps Day. Here was a common-sense solution to the annual problem of knobs trying to study for final exams while their time and energy continued to be sapped. Ending the Fourth Class System by Corps Day had been recommended as far back as the Whitmire Report in 1968, being one of two recommendations General Harris took under advisement, in effect kicking the can down the road to a day that never came. The recommendation was repeated in the Mood Report (1980), affirmed by the Lane Committee in 1992, and endorsed by the PMSs and Mace in 1997. Ultimately, Commandant Captain Eugene "Geno" F. Paluso, II, USN (Ret.), made it happen in 2017. It took *48 years* to initiate a change that benefited everyone and for which the sole justification was the tradition of ending it at graduation.[473]

Introduction of General Mace was only part of the board's agenda in March. General Poole lamented the critical shortage of band members and pledged a renewed effort to recruit them. The Bulldog received the mascot equivalent of new wardrobe with the authorization of $3,000 to rebuild its costume, the cost to be reimbursed by the Brigadier Club. The report of a Cost Reduction Task Force was approved. To bolster enrollment in the Corps, the recruitment budget was increased from the current $928 per matriculant to $1,303 to bring it more in line with the national average of $1,595. Most importantly, incoming President Grinalds shared his vision for the future. That vision assumed a decline in the need for military service and a corresponding increase in the need for post-graduate leadership across a broader spectrum of society. Academic excellence, not military prowess, held the key to the future. He reaffirmed The Citadel's primary purpose: "To educate undergraduates as members of the South Carolina Corps of Cadets and to prepare them for post-graduate positions of leadership through programs of recognized excellence supported by the best features of a structured military environment." Given his stellar academic profile, General Grinalds was supremely qualified to accomplish that mission.

The spring of 1997 marked the first publication of *The Gold Star Journal*, meant to showcase outstanding writing by undergraduate cadets. Founded the year before by Dr. Suzanne Mabrouck of the Chemistry Department, it features cross-disciplinary nonfiction papers, an academic compliment to *The Shako* and *The Brigadier*.[474]

Presidential compensation was not greatly documented in Board of Visitors minutes during the school's first 150 years, but the Board addressed an element of Grinalds' package before his duties officially began. From the Ted Turner gift of $1 million in 1994 (he pledged a total of $25 million), the board agreed to pay $120,000 into a deferred compensation plan co-sponsored by Woodberry Forest, where Grinalds was headmaster when he accepted The Citadel's offer to become its 18th president.

As Mace and Lovetinska completed their first year, Dean Metts sought to find female cadets at Texas A&M who would transfer to The Citadel. Thirty-nine females had been accepted for the 1997-1998 academic year, and the presence of females in the upper classes experienced with the military environment was seen as a way to smooth the path for those reporting in September.

The public spotlight continued to focus on the college. On May 18, 1997, President Poole appeared on William F. Buckley's "Firing Line" to answer, "What Really Happened at The Citadel?" Poole denied any cover up of the Messer-Mentavlos matter, defended the school's handling of the situation once the administration became aware of the women's allegations, and alluded to some questionable editing of the 60 Minutes interview with two seniors who told Bradley the chain of command had knowledge of the hazing before the women came forward. Those seniors accused the school of threatening their ROTC commissions if they went public, but the account of one senior, Dan Eggers, had been thrown into doubt by a deposition response to Dawes Cooke, The Citadel's attorney. A spokesman for 60 Minutes stuck by its broadcast and The Citadel stuck by its contention that Eggers changed his story. Eggers went on to become a Green Beret and was killed on May 29, 2004, when his vehicle hit an IED in Kandahar, Afghanistan during Operation Enduring Freedom.[475] On March 20, 2005 (Corps Day), the Kabul Compound was renamed Camp Eggers in his honor.[476]

The following day, May 22, 1997, ABC's "Turning Point" posed a similar question: "The Citadel Women, What Really Happened?" Three of the four appeared on camera, Jeanie Mentavlos having originally agreed to appear but her lawyer later saying she would not. Mace and Lovetinska denied being hazed or witnessing any hazing of others. Messer repeated allegations of abuse and hazing, admitting she was a "bad cadet" but "that didn't give them the right to set me on fire." One of her comments must have struck alumni as telling: "The haircut completely broke me." As any graduate, male or female, will confirm, a person completely broken by a haircut on the first full day of activity is not likely survive their knob year. Messer also acknowledged tiring of the routine: "You're a college freshman and you had to get up and sweep." Bryant Butler, the regimental commander, had told the women repeatedly that they could consider him a resource if issues arose, an "open door policy." He stated both Messer and Mentavlos came to him several times to report their unhappiness, but they never claimed abuse or hazing. A Commandant's Board subsequently cleared Butler of any prior knowledge.

A day later, Mace and Lovetinska appeared on Good Morning America in dress whites. They confirmed the lack of any hazing and denied they ever felt threatened. Lovetinska said, in what may have been allusion to her former female classmates, "You get out of the system what you put into it."

What seems clear is that at some point in time not too long after matriculating, neither Messer nor Mentavlos wanted to be there. If the college made any error in handling them, it was encouraging them to stay after it became apparent they wanted to leave. General Poole acknowledged as much.

On June 8, 1997, Ed Bradley and Mentavlos were back, this time to brand the school for an allegedly skin-head, neo-Nazi culture. Company E, "Stalag Echo," and Company K, "Kappa Kappa Kilo," were singled out as breeding grounds for right-wing xenophobia.[477] General Poole acknowledged pressure from 60 Minutes to appear on the broadcast — an invitation he declined.[478] Perhaps he felt it futile in view of Bradley's agenda so clearly demonstrated in the earlier segment, or possibly he feared a repeat of Leedom's regrettable performance in March. In hindsight, Poole could hardly have made it worse than it was no matter what he said. The Post and Courier's Frank Wooten posed a question that must have been asked by too many others in Charleston and beyond: "How much deeper will the school's reputation sink?"[479]

Shortly after assuming his duties, Emory Mace set to work incorporating recommendations from the PMSs, correcting the perceived laxity and permissiveness that had crept into the system and, in Trez's phrase, bringing "the hammer down." He devised the "Mace Plan," which made significant changes to the Fourth Class System. A few of those changes included:

No one with a cumulative GPA below 2.0 eligible to hold rank;

Corporals on cadre serve in an administrative role only and not authorized to enforce the fourth class system;

Corporals, except clerks, not allowed unsupervised interaction with knobs;

Blazer uniform not authorized for Citadel functions like sporting events, chapel, awards banquets;

Civilian clothes authorized (1) to and from furlough (except knobs), (2) special orders such as job interviews, and (3) arrival at overnight and weekend leave destinations;

Seniors only authorized to have dates in cadet section of Johnson Hagood;

The 22:30 hours run privilege is revoked;

The Wednesday night Deas Hall privilege for seniors is revoked;

Reveille formation and breakfast mandatory for all cadets;

Charleston passes eliminated except for Gold Star, Dean's List, Commandant's List, President's List, and special purpose;

Sunday night Charleston passes authorized for proficient seniors until 22:30 hours;

Hell night eliminated;

"Knob showers" not authorized (were they ever?);

Knob messes retained until end of first semester with a senior mess carver and six knobs per mess;

Mess carvers will require knobs to serve themselves first;

Knobs authorized to remain at mess after second rest;

Push-ups may be assigned only by company commander, platoon leader or squad leader who must perform push-ups with knob. Sophomores not authorized to assign push-ups;

Push-ups limited to 20 in a 30-minute period, not permitted during ESP or general leave, and not in cadet rooms;

Violations of push-up regulations constitute hazing;

The Commandant will conduct SMIs every weekend where there is no conflicting requirement.

Although Mace's plan specified that the Fourth Class System would end at Corps Day, as had so often been recommended, it did not, with recognition withheld until close to graduation, as was the tradition.

An important feature of the Mace Plan provided that he establish a Citadel Leadership Development Center (CLDC), to include a formal program for instruction in positive leadership, with lesson plans and training materials for each block of instruction, the Citadel Leadership Development Program (CLDP). The CLDP began in July 1997 with athletic cadre training for the class of 2001. Between July 31 and August 7, fifteen cadre members received 72 hours of leadership training in subjects that included drill (8 hours), PT (9 hours), leadership/fourth class system (12 hours), Blue Book (7 hours), Honor (4 hours), sexual harassment (2 hours), sexual assault (1 hour), and "other" (29 hours). On August 7, 52 incoming freshmen athletes arrived. They received 16 hours of academic orientation and 100 hours of training, including subjects on which their cadre had trained the week prior.

On August 13, 1997, upperclass commanders and platoon leaders reported to spend three days in an intensive seminar in which they focused on coeducation and leadership issues and developed a Regimental Task List for the upcoming school year. That list included (1) enhancement of personal and collective honor and pride within the Corps of Cadets; (2) successful transition to coeducation; (3) achieve excellence in academics, leadership, physical fitness and military discipline; (4) enhance spiritual growth; (5) heighten awareness of negative effects of alcohol, drugs, and sexual harassment; and (6) increase community service.

The regular cadre, 325 strong, reported on August 15 to begin a week of preparation for the incoming knobs. Over the following week they received essentially the same 72 hours of training that the athlete cadre had received. It was enhanced by a number of guest speakers and, for 180 members, a trip to Parris Island for an orientation, Marine Corps style. On August 23, 559 members of the Class of 2001 reported. It included 15 females.[480]

Based upon the 1997-1998 school year experience, the CLDP was revised in the spring of 1998 to add additional requirements. It increased leadership training for knobs and added community service requirements for second class cadets (51 hours) and third class cadets (53 hours).[481]

It was in essence the approach implemented on a limited basis by Commandant Roy Zinser in the Watts administration, became ingrained in the Grinalds and Rosa administrations, and which ultimately culminated in the Krause Center for Leadership and Ethics. As Joe Trez observed, "Finally, after years of talking about it, we were going to put the resources into leadership development."

On June 27, 1997, General Poole attended his last board meeting as interim-president. He received a standing ovation for his administration and his dedication to the college, attested to by the fact that June 27 was his wedding anniversary.[482] His return to academia set the stage for the start of the Grinalds administration, with the stakes as high as they had ever been.

Chapter 14

INTO THE NEW MILLENNIUM

When Norwood Grinalds, the new president's wife, sent to the mothers of incoming freshmen in the Class of 2001 a letter addressed "Dear Citadel Mom," it introduced her and her husband to The Citadel family with charm, dignity and compassion. As the parents of four children, the Grinalds had faced some of the same anxieties in sending them off to schools. Citadel moms could not help but identify, and clearly the Grinalds were in it together.

"John Grinalds has a heart for young people and wants above all else to help prepare Citadel cadets for lives that are honorable, successful and selfless. I stand shoulder to shoulder with him in this effort," she wrote. After some negative press directed at the college in 1990s, it must have been reassuring to families receiving her letter, in which she not only offered her help but included the phone number of her residence at Quarters 1![483]

The most immediate challenge facing the school, arguably more pressing than improving its image off campus, was the assimilation of women on campus. Nancy Mace and Petra Lovetinska would be joined by 15 other women when the Class of 2001 reported, and the pressure to be ready was intense. Planning fell mostly on Colonel Joe Trez, recently named as Special Assistant to the President. Trez drew up an assimilation plan comprised of 80 items, a majority of which would have to be approved by Judge Houck and reported on periodically to the Justice Department. A small sampling of the 52 reportable items included:

> 10. Issue: What are the facilities problems associated with providing adequate security for female cadets in the barracks concerning locks on the doors?
> Recommendation: That inside latches be placed on the doors of female cadet rooms. [cost: $11 each].
> 20. Issue: Taking size measurements on a female cadet (as necessary).

Recommendation: Chest, waist and inseam measurements for female cadets should be taken by a female staff member.

21. Issue: Implementation of measuring and issuing Citadel Dress Uniforms to female cadets.

Recommendation: That The Citadel maintain the present uniform policy as outlined in the Blue Book. During the first year of admission female cadets will wear uniforms that look the same as their male classmates. The current Citadel dress uniform can be altered by The Citadel Tailor Shop to fit female cadets. Female patterned dress uniforms will be developed. Female unique uniform items will be addressed through the established Citadel Uniform Board.

28. Issue: Female cadet membership in current Cadet Activities.

Recommendation: Female cadet membership in current Cadet Activities will not require any changes to membership criteria.

34. Issue: Lack of privacy for the initial assessment of physical/emotional problems that may arise unique to a female.

Recommendation: The Citadel medical staff perform the initial medical assessment on female cadets and treat any general illness. Treatment requirements beyond capability of Infirmary should be referred off campus as with male cadets.

36. Issue: The Citadel policy concerning pregnant cadets.

Recommendation: That The Citadel develop a policy that precludes acceptance of pregnant applicants and dismisses pregnant cadets at an appropriate time considering academic, military and health considerations.

37. Issue: To determine the members of the upper class who will be allowed to discipline female members of the fourth class.

Recommendation: Apply the Fourth Class System equally to both male and female cadets in regard to which members of the upper class may correct and discipline them. Make no changes to paragraph K2, Chapter 16 of the Blue Book in terms of who may train, correct, counsel, or inspect members of the fourth class (male or female). Continue to emphasize that during the cadre training period that direct interaction between the fourth class and upper classes is limited to cadre only. Provide emphasis during cadre training that the use of sexually derogatory terms and references to gender in relation to fourth class cadets (male or female) presence, conduct, appearance or activities as a cadet is a poor leadership technique that will not be tolerated. Provide the same type of training to all upperclass cadets during leadership instruction to be received prior to the end of cadre training period and before the fourth class officially enters the Corps. Sensitize all cadet leaders, human relations officers, and tactical officers to be on alert for violations. Insure that on the spot corrections are made and report those cadets who do not comply for counseling and/or disciplinary actions as appropriate.

40. Issue: To determine if modifications are required to the current fourth class squad room procedures.

Recommendation: Modify squad room procedures so that both male and female fourth class cadets may equally participate. Eliminate the procedure of giving the traditional Citadel shirt tuck in the squad room. Require shirt tucks to be given in the privacy of the cadet's room prior to reporting to the squad room. Shirt tucks may be dressed within the squad room, however, trousers will not be lowered. Require the adoption of a procedure that requires a female to announce her presence before entering the squad room by sounding off with, "FEMALE ENTERING" and requiring the response of, "ALL DRESSED" from within the room before she enters. Above procedures will be outlined in a training memo that will be distributed during cadre.

49. Issue: What should The Citadel policy be toward the wearing of makeup by female cadets?

Recommendation: Upperclass female cadets can wear conservative makeup and clear fingernail polish. Fourth class female cadets may wear no makeup while wearing a uniform.

52. Issue: How should the physical fitness of women at The Citadel be evaluated?

Recommendation: Use the Army's women physical fitness standards for women at The Citadel. The important thing to incorporate is keeping the Corps fit according to acceptable published standards. The Citadel, in the future, may develop a fitness test for students which adequately measures all aspects of health related physical fitness.[484]

In addition to the 80 issues addressed by the assimilation plan, the board established a "Policy on Cultural, Racial, Religious and Sexual Harassment" as well as a "Policy on Cadet Senior/Subordinate and Inter-Gender Relation-ships."

The Sexual Harassment Policy is three pages long and quite detailed. Its essence is a prohibition on sexual harassment as defined by federal law and guidelines issued by the Equal Employment Opportunity Commission (the EEOC). The guidelines make clear that unwanted sexual advances can be verbal, nonverbal and, of course, physical.

Verbal prohibitions would include what the guidelines deem "sexist termi-nology"; "honey," "babe," "dear" or "sweetheart." Catcalls, offensive jokes, inquiries into one's sex life and repeated invitations to go out made to someone obviously not interested all qualify.

Proscribed nonverbal acts include "elevator eyes," blowing kisses, lip lick-ing, winking, displaying sexually suggestive visuals like cartoons or novelties, and sexually rubbing oneself around another.

Beyond the patently obvious physical acts, examples of harassment include "playing footsie" and unsolicited back or knee rubs. Less obvious, and more germane to life in the barracks, is cornering or blocking passage.

The policy on fraternization and dating is also three pages, but lends itself more easily to summation. Upperclassmen may date other upperclass-men, but not a member of his or her chain of command. Upperclassmen may not date knobs. Knobs may date each other. In all cases, those dating are expected to meet the high standards of discretion and good judgment expected of all cadets.

Fraternization is harder to pin down because subject to degrees. Frater-nization is prohibited between upperclassmen and knobs, but is common when cadets knew each other prior to coming to The Citadel or have been active together on a Corps squad or club sport. This is generally permitted for cadets in different companies. Whether dating or fraternization is at issue, the overriding concern is for conduct that may be detrimental to the maintenance of good order and discipline.[485]

With coeducation a reality, an alumni organization named The Associa-tion of Citadel Men since 1934 was out of step, so to speak. In April 1997 the board went on record favoring a change of name more in keeping with the times. The CAA, Citadel Alumni Association, resulted.[486]

Along with new rules came the personnel to help make them work. Dr. Suzanne Ozment served as the first Dean of Women. Selected over two other applicants from the faculty, she came to The Citadel in 1982 as an expert in 19th century British literature. From 1993 to 1994 she chaired the all-important institutional self-study for reaccreditation by SACS and served as a member of various SACS reaccreditation teams. In 1988 she received the James Self Outstanding Teacher Award and had been nominated as the South Carolina Professor of the Year.[487]

Commandant Mace selected Lieutenant Colonel Bonnie Houchen, USAF, as the first Assistant Commandant for Assimilation. Mace also chose eight new tactical officers from among 123 applications to serve at the battalion level, including three women: Master Chief Marilyn Knowles, USN; Lieutenant Commander Barbara Boyd, USN; and Command Sergeant Major Kay Wang, USA.[488]

President Grinalds lost no time in articulating his goals. At his first board meeting as president, he set June 2001 for achieving them. The first among them would surely have brought a smile to Admiral Stockdale's lips had he been advised of it: "Attain a national reputation for academic excellence."

The second goal listed by General Grinalds was no less worthy, and meeting it set the college on a path that has accounted for much of its success since: "Establish a formal four-year undergraduate program of leadership development based on achievement," which was to include community public service for sophomores and internships for juniors in Charleston public or private sector enterprises.

The remainder of the goals — athletic excellence, coping with facilities and deferred maintenance, increasing endowments — might well have been on the list of anyone selected to be president, but the first two proved visionary and would become hallmarks of the Grinalds administration.

The Class of 2001 reported with 559 cadets, but overall enrollment was down to 1,769 from 1,847 in 1995 and 1,821 the previous year. General Poole, who returned to his former position as Vice President for Academic Affairs and Dean of the College after his year as interim president, reported a national decrease in the population of 18-year-old males, with a projected increase in college-age students due largely to blacks, Hispanics and women, which The Citadel planned to increase its efforts to recruit. Efforts to recruit more female faculty were paying dividends, as 30 female Ph.Ds were now teaching. When Ms. Anne Pye and Ms. Allison Wright joined the board as advisory members, they broke the gender barrier.

The rare-book room at the Daniel Library got a $20,000 makeover courtesy of Colonel Thomas C. (Nap) Vandiver, Class of 1929. Vandiver was for many years the president of Southern Bank and Trust and served on the Board of Visitors for 33 years, retiring as Vice Chairman Emeritus. The school awarded him an honorary Doctor of Laws degree in 1979 and the prestigious Palmetto Award in 1986. Vandiver Hall, which houses facilities and offices for non-revenue sports, serves as his legacy on campus. He asked that the rare-book room be named in honor of Colonel William F. Prioleau, Jr., Class of 1943, a former chairman of the board with whom Vandiver served for many years. Funds for the room's refurbishment were transferred from the Vandiver Hall account. Today, the Prioleau Rare Book Room supplements the archives, housing volumes and collections that document our history in a pleasant, comfortable environment conducive to research and study.[489]

Commandant Mace, noting the absence of battalion flags within the Corps, proposed a design for one after research into the genesis of the Corps of Cadets flag and Big Red, adopted by the school as its official spirit flag in 1992. The flag he recommended was patterned after Big Red, with the addition of the battalion number and crossed rifles to indicate infantry. General Grinalds and the board approved.

General Mace notched another win when the board approved his recommendation that "extremism" be added to the college regulations as a class-one offense subject to expulsion. It prohibited participation in extremist organizations or activities, defined to include "any organization or activity which advocates violence, disruption or overthrow of the United States or State Government (Militiamen); denigrates others on the basis of race, ethnicity, religion or gender." It prohibited use of words, symbols, clothing, posters and decals from hate groups. Cadet company commanders were charged with the responsibility of counseling cadets alleged to be "racists, extremists, skinheads, or gang members" and ordering them to refrain from such unauthorized activities.[490]

But proving that you can't win them all, the board reversed a decision of the Commandant's Board to expel a cadet charged with possession of drugs and drug paraphernalia, and the board reduced the commandant's punishment for possession of alcohol. Grinalds and Mace would learn what Stockdale and other presidents and commandants before them had learned: In certain disciplinary actions, the Board of Visitors reserved the right to be the final judge and jury, and reversing a decision reached by the administration was hardly unprecedented. While Grinalds went on record as supporting the board in the particular case before it, he voiced concern "that the fallout from today's actions could be a perception among the Corps of Cadets that the Board of Visitors does not back the President and the Commandant in such a serious drug-related issue." Grinalds diplomatically covered his irritation, but it seems clear he felt it. The system was getting too legalistic, as Poole had expressed the year before. "Some cadets," said Grinalds, "will now feel that they can take advantage of the process, and if you have enough money to hire a good lawyer you can beat the system."[491] And a good lawyer is not the only means of beating the system. Board review of disciplinary decisions renders them open to political pressure. Perhaps the sole benefit of reduced state funding is the diminishing leverage of politicians to inject themselves into matters in which their only stake is a campaign contributor back home.

With the arrival of coeducation, the Advisory Council welcomed its first two female members: Rear Admiral Roberta S. Hazard, USN (Ret.), and Ambassador Roxanne L. Ridgway. For decades the Advisory Council to the Citadel Board of Visitors met twice a year to give advice and share perspectives that may not have been apparent to those serving on the board. Because South Carolina law requires board members to be South Carolina residents, the broader vision furnished by the Council was intended to act as a counterweight to any of the board's more parochial tendencies. It was established in April 1973 with General Clark as its first chairman.[492] He used his vast network of contacts at the highest levels of government and the military to recruit top-flight Council members. A list of those members over the years reads like a who's-who of the American armed forces. Among the notables who have participated are General Lyman Lemnitzer, Chairman of the Joint Chiefs of Staff under President Kennedy and Supreme Allied Commander of NATO from 1963 to 1969; Admiral Arleigh Burke, Chief of Naval Operations, 1955-1961; Frank Blair, longtime NBC newscaster, Today Show host, and a College of Charleston graduate; Admiral Thomas H. Moorer, Chief of Naval Operations (1967-1970) and Chairman of the Joint Chiefs of Staff (1970-1974); and General Andrew Goodpaster, NATO Supreme Allied Commander Europe (1969-1974), to name but a few. The Advisory Council remained a resource for the college until early in the 21st century, when it was disbanded in a cost-cutting campaign.

On October 25, 1997, the Council met jointly with the Board of Visitors. Alvah H. Chapman, Jr., Regimental Commander in the Class of 1942 and one of The Citadel's most successful graduates, chaired the meeting. In 1989 he retired as chairman/CEO of Knight-Ridder, Inc., at that time the world's largest newspaper chain. Chapman attributed his success to "my Christian faith; my wife, Betty; and the leadership training, education and sense of discipline I received at The Citadel."[493] For this meeting, Board of Visitors Chairman Frank Mood had given a "homework" assignment, asking each Council member to inquire of their respective constituencies how The Citadel was perceived and what might be done to reverse any negative perceptions. The collective wisdom of the group seemed to arrive at a consensus on several points: The school had come through a rough period made worse by negative publicity; The Citadel needed to define itself to the public and potential applicants through better public relations; an emphasis on academics and leadership was the path forward. Several council members, including the new female members, posed the basic question, "What is The Citadel?" Is it a military college with an academic component? Or is it a laboratory of learning and leadership with a military component? Answering that question in the public's mind held the key to the future, and it was critical that the school not be perceived, in the words of one council member, as "a 19th century military training school." Better public relations, particularly of negatives, would help, and better relations with the press and media was essential. But the real story was best told by cadets and alumni, defining the college by demonstrating the learning and values taught there.[494] The next 20 years would be an effort focused on precisely that. By 2017 most would agree that The Citadel is a college producing well-educated, principled leaders within a disciplined military structure.

General Grinalds had been a Rhodes Scholar, and in 1997 he was responsible for two cadets, Regimental Commander Brett Strand and Cadet Todd Garrett, being two of 12 Rhodes Scholar candidates from South Carolina. A "claim to fame" that has eluded The Citadel is that it has never had a Rhodes Scholar, a distinction we could do without and which some bright cadet will one day no doubt remedy.

At Homecoming 1997, Pat Conroy returned to Charleston for research connected to his upcoming memoir, *My Losing Season*. The essence of the book echoes the Stoic thought that Stockdale insisted got him through his long imprisonment, the idea that you can learn more from losing than from winning; that the road to success is often paved with failure. Conroy spent most of the weekend in a downtown hotel room peppering his former teammates with questions and pumping them for memories that were 30 years old. Basketball has been and remains an elusive quest at The Citadel, a frustration largely shared with VMI. Conroy habitually referred to the first day of the Southern Conference basketball tournament as "military elimination day," a joke but not by much. But even VMI has qualified for the NCAA tournament, while The Citadel and William & Mary remain two of a handful of teams never to be invited to "the big dance" of college basketball. Conroy's book is a favorite among many of his readers, making his teammates local celebrities when they appeared with him at book signings and public events. *My Losing Season* gave that team — Dan Mohr, Jim Halpin, John DeBrosse, Doug Bridges, Dave Bornhorst, Robert Cauthen, Bill Zycinsky, Alan Kroboth, Tee Hooper, Gregory Conner, Brian Kennedy and Conroy — a lasting legacy that will surpass that of many teams which enjoyed winning records.

General Grinalds spent three hours with Conroy during the author's visit to campus. They discussed a TV series that Conroy said might be in the works based on the book, which was published in 2002. Grinalds pledged his support provided it portrayed the school in the proper light. Board Chairman Frank Mood and Ambassador Motley also met with Conroy.[495] These meetings proved to be the beginning of a rapprochement between Conroy and his alma mater which would come to fruition when The Citadel awarded Conroy and The Boo honorary degrees in 2001.

Just prior to Christmas, Mood wrote to General Grinalds about the relationship between the Honor Code and fake IDs, commonly used by underage cadets in order to purchase or be served alcohol. The provision of the Honor Code that Mood found troubling was added in the 1980s, according to his recollection long after he served as Honor Committee chairman. His point is relevant today because the Honor Code still contains the language he referenced and fake IDs are still used. Paragraph 5(a)(2) of the Code states: "The use of any document, on or off campus, to misrepresent one's identity or status to gain a benefit that one would not have received without the misrepresentation will be considered and treated as a false official statement." The difficulty arises from the definition of an official statement, contained in paragraph 5(a). "An official statement is defined as a statement written or oral made to a commissioned or non-commissioned officer of the staff or of the faculty of the college, a member of the Guard on duty, or any cadet required in turn to use the statement as the basis for an official report in any form."[496] Since the bartender or bouncer to whom a fake ID would be presented is manifestly not a person identified in 5(a), a statement made to such person cannot by definition be an official statement, whether true or untrue. In the system as designed and implemented by General Clark in 1954, "[u]ntruths told to roommates, other cadets, campus personnel or the public at large did not fall within the jurisdiction of the Honor Code or Court." In Mood's view, the irreconcilability of the quoted paragraphs portended "a seemingly ever-expanding application of the Honor Code," which he considered bad policy. "While the desire for cadets to conduct themselves honorably under any circumstances is clearly laudable, I believe that as a matter of policy, the severe punitive sanctions of the Honor Code should be confined to their original purposes."[497]

The year 1998 began with heightened enthusiasm and focus within the Corps, according to General Grinalds' assessment. He placed his emphasis on three areas of need: admissions, fundraising and public relations. His interest in admissions furthered the goal of improving the quality of students, a key ingredient of raising the college's academic profile. Currently, 75 percent to 80 percent of applicants were accepted, and of those, 50 percent matriculated. Grinalds thought those percentages should be reversed, with 50 percent accepted and 75-80 percent matriculation.[498]

Controversy returned to the Summerall Guards when all 61 members pledged to abandon it rather than submit to new restrictions.[499] Crisis was avoided when General Grinalds and Commandant Mace stepped in, prompting board Chairman Frank Mood to praise them as an example to cadets of "leadership in action." The result was a constitution and bylaws for an organization that had never had them since the Guard's founding in 1932.[500]

A constitution and bylaws were also deemed to be the answer to the issues surrounding the Junior Sword Drill (JSD), if there were any answers. In dueling memos between board members Colonel Billy Jenkinson and Colonel Harvey Dick, the tension surrounding JSD was set out in black and white. Jenkinson favored revival of the JSD as a morale boost for the Corps and to enliven the Ring Hop, which in his words had degraded into a "'mom and pop show' without pomp, circumstance, dignity or the respect that should be shown on such a significant occasion." He granted the need for new safeguards and procedures, but preferred not to revisit the events which brought about the demise of the JSD in 1989. Dick very much wanted to revisit those events, reminding Jenkinson that, "I am the one who took the telephone call that infamous night from a cadet's father telling me his son was in the Naval Hospital with all of his front teeth knocked out and stitches inside and outside of his chin." As a result of that "infamous night," the JSD was disbanded in the spring of 1989, reinstituted that fall, only to be disbanded again in 1993 when the culture again proved unacceptable. Dick gave 11 suggestions for improvement in the event the board decided to resurrect the JSD.[501] In June, Jenkinson reported that the administration recommended that reinstatement of the JSD "not be considered at this time."[502]

Commandant Mace reviewed a Department of Defense memorandum that, in his words, put "the final nail in the coffin that will prevent active duty ROTC officers from ever being college tactical officers again." It applied to the six schools categorized under federal law as senior military colleges (The Citadel, VMI, Texas A&M, Virginia Tech, North Georgia and Norwich University). Henceforth, and continuing until present, active duty military can instruct ROTC but cannot serve as TACs, commandants or assistant commandants.[503] This change flowed through to The Citadel's bottom line, as it required the school to hire TAC officers as state employees and pay them as such with no corresponding revenue source.[504]

The Riverview Room at the mess hall benefitted from an effort by the Association of Past Regimental Commanders at The Citadel, which pledged $100,000 for both renovations and a permanent maintenance endowment. The pledged funds having been raised, the board authorized the renaming of the room to be known henceforth as "The Regimental Commanders' Riverview Room."[505]

Asked to identify problems the school might anticipate, two members of the Advisory Council specified "sex in the barracks." Ambassador Ridgway, one of the two female members, felt "consensual sex in the barracks should be punished by expulsion — period."[506] Indeed, the previous December a female cadet charged with that very offense had resigned in lieu of a Commandant's Board.[507] Alvah Chapman reported a conversation with two female members of Band Company. Not only did the women oppose relaxing the Fourth Class System to accommodate them but they went a step further by hoping the school didn't recruit female cadets in large numbers for fear it would "destroy what they came to The Citadel to get."[508] Evidently, for at least two women, a male-to-female ratio of 50 to 1 was more desirable than 2 to 1.

During 1998, much of the board's time was spent on appeals by cadets of disciplinary rulings, with cadets often represented by attorneys. The number of appeals heard by the board that year may have equaled or exceeded the number in the prior half-century. At times, the board sustained the administrative action, at times it reversed it, and occasionally it split. One such case was heard in June on a cadet's appeal of dismissal. He arrived with his attorney in tow, plus two character witnesses. He waived a closed hearing until a member of the press arrived, at which time his attorney asked that the hearing be closed. Following the board's debate in executive session, a motion to uphold the commandant department's punishment order was defeated by a vote of 6 to 5. Such a division was unusual on the board, but this one allowed the appealing cadet to graduate.[509]

Admissions again surfaced as a worry. The population of the Corps was down, impacting revenue and performance funding metrics. Had performance funding been in full effect for the 1997-1998 school year, the college could have lost as much as $2 million of its $15 million state appropriation, a whopping 13 percent reduction.[510]

There began about this time an effort by Chairman Mood and President

Grinalds to broaden the role of the Advisory Council and to take better advantage of the expertise possessed by its members. In the spring of 1998, Mood had asked the chairman of the Advisory Council, General Merritt, to consider expanding the Council to include members who could be counted on to help target solutions to problems considered by the Board of Visitors and General Grinalds as critical to the college's success. Mood had in mind organizational structures such as that used at Clemson, with its life-member program that allowed it to benefit from the talents of both non-graduates and out-of-state alumni. This broader collaboration would coalesce in task forces, led by members of the Advisory Council and aimed at a particular need. Examples given included the repair or replacement of Johnson Hagood Stadium, enhanced marketing and public relations, and recruitment of minority students and women, all goals articulated by General Grinalds early in his administration and a continuing concern to the Board of Visitors.

For his part, General Grinalds formulated the "Grinalds Matrix," a wire diagram intended to show the intersection of tasks with the organizations charged with accomplishing those tasks. The Matrix served to illustrate the necessary components of a successful task force: leadership, from Advisory Council members; academic support from the CDF (now TCF); athletic support from the Brigadier Foundation; operations support from the Citadel Trust, and alumni support from The Citadel Alumni Association. The process required involvement by college staff members who would have implementation responsibilities, and the board would retain ultimate approval authority.

On October 24, 1998, General Grinalds presented his Matrix Concept to the Advisory Council, having already received approvals from the boards of the Brigadier Foundation, The Citadel Alumni Association and The Citadel Trust. The Council gave the program a warm reception, agreeing that the time had come to broaden its membership and to more directly involve its members in solutions to the critical needs of the school. General Merritt praised the concept as "a reasonable way to overcome the restrictions of the laws of South Carolina as they related to membership on the Board of Visitors." In its wide-ranging discussion of the concept, the Council acknowledged its heavy concentration of military leaders and the need for a diversification of talents which the Concept envisioned. The idea that a Council member needed to lead each task force was discarded in favor finding the best person for that job, even if it meant recruiting a non-Council member who might serve on the Council for the duration of the task. On motion of Alvah Chapman, second by former president Seignious, the Council approved the Grinalds Matrix Concept. General Grinalds listed the priority tasks as (1) communications (internal and external, including marketing); (2) admissions, to both the Corps of Cadets and the College of Graduate and Professional Studies; and (3) fund raising, with a renewed focus on an annual fund drive. The Council endorsed the priorities as presented.[511]

On the day after the Council approved the Matrix Concept, Chaplin Sidney Crumpton celebrated his 90th birthday. Cadets from the 1960s and 1970s will never forget him standing near Lesesne Gate, in weather good and bad, waving goodbye to those departing on holiday leaves.[512]

Tensions surrounding the admission of women and litigation issues in the 1990s produced some predictable dissension within the alumni community, and that dissension spilled over into The Citadel Alumni Association (CAA), formerly the Association of Citadel Men. The CAA elected as its president in 1998 Colonel J. Quincy Collins, Jr., Class of 1953, the longest serving POW in Citadel history. Collins spent seven and a half agonizing years in the infamous Hanoi Hilton, having been shot down over North Vietnam on September 2, 1965. He suffered severe injuries upon ejection. Listed among the school's Distinguished Alumni, Collins received two Silver Stars and universal acclaim as a war hero. "He was labeled as 'incorrigible' by the North Vietnamese and was a 'cellmate' of John McCain, the 2008 GOP nominee for President. While a POW, and at the risk of extreme torture, he courageously wrote a patriotic song on bathroom tissue using blood as ink that was sung by all the POWs in 1972 during a prison uprising, and again at a Nixon White House reception for POWs in 1973."[513]

When installed as CAA president, Collins gave a rousing speech to those assembled for the annual meeting. He began by paying tribute to "this great military college for the training this system gave me in preparation for the 7½ tormenting years I spent in prison in Hanoi." After thanking his classmates and others "who never doubted my capacity to endure and to return home with honor," he acknowledged the challenges ahead. If the college hoped to realize Grinalds' dream for the school, "[i]t may mean we have to let go of some old, worn out, threadbare practices. It may mean we have to stop saying 'no' to anything new and different. But believe me, we have talked, debated, hated, sued and fought too long. Now is the time for positive action, and it begins with you and me."[514] Collins was right. The college's alumni banded together is a powerful force. Without their united efforts in the late 1870s and early 1880s, the school would never have reopened in 1882. Speaking with one voice is as critical today as it has ever been.[515]

General Grinalds continued to maintain his interest in Rhodes Scholars. In early 1999 he reported to the board the poor showing in the competition by South Carolina resident students over the past 10 years. The reason? Their failure to be "widely and deeply read."[516]

In April, the Advisory Council met for the first time since approving the Matrix Concept, which required amendment to the bylaws of the Council. The future composition of the Council continued to be debated. General Seignious, a Council member, reminded his colleagues that the Council had been originally conceived by General Clark "to counter the extreme parochialism which he had found on the Board of Visitors, the General Assembly, and other bodies close to the college." While no doubt true, we are left to wonder if the intense concentration of generals and admirals on the Council over the decades didn't contribute to a military parochialism slow to change with the times. The broadening of Council member expertise and experience then under consideration seemed entirely appropriate, and some would have said overdue.

A draft of the proposed bylaws had been circulated prior to the meeting. By way of discussing the changes, the chairman, General Merritt, asked Council members for their personal views on the role of the Council. General Andrew Goodpaster, USA (Ret.), a Council member for many years, felt the need for a "clearly articulated" purpose of both The Citadel and the Advisory Council, a need echoed by Rear Admiral Roberta Hazard, who thought it "essential to have a concise, gut-getter mission statement." General Carl Mundy, USMC (Ret.), made a similar point, insisting that "until we have identified what the institution is and intends to be it is difficult to nominate new members." Such comments would seem to indicate that the school's marketing image continued to be regrettably blurred, even among those quite familiar with the college.

On the second day of the council meeting, General Merritt attempted to summarize the observations of the day before. He described the Council's consensus as: (1) we need a strong statement of purpose; (2) the college "must initiate an aggressive approach to serving the citizens of South Carolina, the Lowcountry and especially the minority populations in our service area"; and (3) The Citadel's special nature "needs to be conveyed without being too narrow and too limiting."[517]

Performance funding was back on the board's agenda in May, as the coming school year, 1999-2000, would be the first in which all 37 performance funding criteria were to be used as the basis of the state's appropriation.

General Grinalds praised Colonel Metts for his outstanding work with the Commission on Higher Education. Because of his efforts and those of Colonel Holland, "we are coming out much better than we first feared we would." Three criteria used to determine performance funding — in-state enrollment, minority enrollment and SAT scores — continued to be concerns, and accordingly continued to spawn efforts at improvement.

On May 8, 1999, Nancy Mace became the first female cadet to graduate from The Citadel. By virtue of credits transferred from a community college, she was able to graduate three years after matriculating. During those three years, she served as Band Company clerk, cadet sergeant, company executive and academic officer. She earned Gold Stars every semester except one.[518] She had also gone the extra mile by making public speaking appearances and lending a hand to the school's recruiters to secure more female applicants. On May 19, 1999, a joint resolution of the State Legislature concluded thusly:

> That the members of the General Assembly of the State of South Carolina, by this resolution, hereby commend Nancy Ruth Mace of Goose Creek for her leadership, exemplary conduct, and outstanding achievements while a cadet at The Citadel, The Military College of South Carolina; congratulate Nancy Ruth Mace on becoming the first female cadet to graduate from The Citadel and for graduating magna cum laude; recognize Nancy Ruth Mace as the female cadet who set the standard to be emulated by all other females who become members of the South Carolina Corps of Cadets at The Citadel; and further recognize Nancy Ruth Mace as the prototype of The Citadel woman and a genuine source of pride to her alma mater, to South Carolina, and to women everywhere, as she takes her place in The Citadel's distinguished long gray line and as the first female cadet to graduate from this world renowned military college.[519]

The school took pleasure in the favorable publicity that Mace and her successful cadet career generated. On the day before she graduated, she made what General Grinalds described as a very favorable impact, when she appeared with her parents on "Good Morning America," additional rebuttal to the Messer-Mentavlos narrative.[520] And Nancy's late-night session with David Letterman was characterized to the Board of Visitors as having made a "tremendous impression," both on her own behalf and the school's.[521]

In her public appearances, which were frequent, Mace consistently denied the abuses alleged by Kim Messer and Jeanie Mentavlos, yet in her cadet career she experienced, by her own admission, loneliness, isolation and taunts ranging from thoughtless to downright cruel. Some of her biggest challenges stemmed from her unique circumstances. One such circumstance was her decision to graduate a year ahead of her class, which made her a member of the Class of 1999. That class had made a habit of boasting, prematurely as it turned out, that they were the last all-male class. As she wrote, "they did not want me graduating with them, did not want me wearing a ring with a '99 on it. I knew I would get my ring only over their loud objections." She was right.

At the Summerall Chapel ceremony, a chorus of hisses greeted her as she received her ring, a humiliation made worse because her parents sat with other parents attending the special occasion. At the ring hop, she dreaded the further embarrassment she would feel if those holding arched swords turned their backs as she and her father made the traditional walk beneath those swords. They did not, but hissing resurfaced.

Then came graduation, for which she had her "white skirt . . . sharply pressed for the last time." A photo of her in that skirt, taken on graduation day in front of her parents' campus home at Quarters 2, is included in her memoir. But as additional proof that nothing she did went unnoticed (as if additional proof was needed), there were complaints registered at a fall board meeting about her skirt not complying with regulations. Prior to Petra Lovetinska's graduation the following year, the board went on record as specifying the uniform for the graduation ceremony: full dress salt and pepper and "no ear rings."[522]

A key and obvious component of attracting women to The Citadel and in keeping them there involved athletics. The NCAA's gender equity committee, working with Joe Trez over a two-year period, devised a plan that promised to help both recruitment and retention. When the plan was adopted, the school sponsored 10 varsity sports for men in the NCAA's Division 1. Of these, five could offer competitive opportunities for women. Those were Cross Country, Indoor Track, Outdoor Track, Golf and Tennis. Given the infancy of coeducation at the school and the few women in the Corps of Cadets, one immediate hurdle was the NCAA's requirement that coeducational schools sponsor a minimum of seven sports for men and seven for women, though colleges that fielded football teams could remain Division 1 eligible with six teams for men and eight for women. As eight women's teams was a literal impossibility in 1998, The Citadel sought and received a NCAA waiver. The next hurdle was the Southern Conference, where all Citadel varsity teams competed. The SOCON granted a five-year waiver, which allowed women to compete in Cross Country, Indoor and Outdoor Track, Golf and Tennis as early as the 1997-1998 academic year.

Having the sports available wasn't much help without the women to compete in them, and to assure that, an aggressive recruitment effort was organized. The Athletic Department and the Admissions Office spread the word among high schools in its prime five-state recruiting area that a new athletic option was available for women at The Citadel. Those schools were asked to recommend students, and many did. A major attraction for those students were scholarships; a total of 13 full scholarship equivalencies were offered; two for Golf, two for Tennis, and three each in Cross Country, Indoor/Outdoor Track, and Volleyball. The cost to start the programs was estimated at $70,000, with $242,000 to fund them on an annual basis. Both the NCAA and Title IX imposed scholarship requirements, and the school committed itself "to make scholarship dollars available between men and women sports teams in proportion to the number of each gender in the Corps of Cadets and in relation to the interests and abilities of the eligible students." As far as coaches went, General Grinalds approved on October 28, 1998, the hiring of a full-time volleyball coach and part time coaches for tennis and golf. In the important area of coaches' compensation, the plan acknowledged that, "Initially, there may be a significant difference in the compensation received by female coaches as compared to Citadel male coaches. However, differences will only be due to different levels of experience, job descriptions and market forces."[523]

The 1998-1999 school year witnessed the formation of the first all-female team, Women's Cross Country. Members were Laurie Auger, Mandy Garcia, Patricia Giera, Sharon Hacker, Carol Hamlin, Peaches Hudson, Tosha Mitchell, and Amy Walsh. Jody Huddleston coached them. Lieutenant Colonel Bonnie Houchen coached the Volleyball Team, whose players included Laura Bristol, Deonn Crumley, Alicia Gabriel, Megan Gentry, Eileen Guerra, Carol Hamlin, Jill Lowery, Maggie Maisonet, Natosha Mitchell, Latrice Sales, Ryan Silver, Yaunna Thompson and Adrienne Watson. Mandy Garcia, a member of both squads, rose to become the second ranked cadet in the Class of 2001 and the first woman to serve as Regimental Executive Officer. In 2002, Women's Soccer joined the list of female teams and women competed with men in Cross Country, Golf and Rifle.[524]

The Strategic Plan adopted in January 1996 set goals and objectives Grinalds was committed to reaching. Not coincidentally, adequate performance funding depended on their realization as well. As The Citadel was still in the process of centralizing its fragmented fundraising, Grinalds pressed the CDF for (1) more money than would have been forthcoming under its "5 percent of net capital" policy; specifically, $988,000, and (2) an expansion of the purposes for which CDF money could be used. Two of the more critical needs, both of which were planks in the Strategic Plan platform, concerned merit pay for faculty and competition for new students.

Key to attracting more and better students were Intermediate-Value Renewable Scholarships, the scholastic equivalent of a bidding war. The Citadel had found these scholarships particularly effective and wanted to increase them. At stake were students with credentials impressive enough to warrant scholarship offers from other schools. By offering those students slightly higher scholarships, many came to The Citadel who otherwise would have opted for an alternative. The Citadel "won" the bidding war. To quantify its case, the school projected that the extra funds it was requesting from the CDF, used in part for Intermediate-Value Renewable Scholarships, would result in an entering class of 625 as opposed to one of 560 without those funds, for an increase of 65 incoming freshmen. As importantly, the projected average SAT score was 1088 with extra funding, and 1060 without it.

Faculty merit pay had an interesting history which Grinalds related to the CDF in support of his request. "The College has in fact had a detailed, comprehensive faculty evaluation process in place for more than thirty years, but throughout that period there has seldom been merit funding to address the consequences of these evaluations." Because the state allowed legally mandated cost-of-living raises to be dispensed as merit pay, The Citadel dispensed them as such until the mid-1980s, when the award to a deserving teacher reached a level bordering on insult, at which point the faculty said, in effect, thanks, but until there is some real money to distribute, we'll just accept cost-of-living. Grinalds sought that "real money" for merit pay, $440,000 for the 1999-00 academic year, noting that the college had been fortunate to have a loyal faculty over many years but that competition for the better instructors was increasing and the school needed the funds not only to maintain what it had but to be competitive in attracting new academic talent.

Another need identified by Grinalds was in the area of "assessment," a concept more nebulous than either student scholarships or merit pay but equally important. For years the school had lagged in assessment, a quality control of sorts designed to measure program success (or failure). The Strategic Plan called for the school "to make Assessment for Institutional Effectiveness the focus of The Citadel's operational approach for the future, especially in the area of resource allocation." And even if the Strategic Plan had not called for it, everyone else in the college world was. From SACS to the South Carolina Commission on Higher Education to the NCAA to even the Justice Department, everyone was assessing based on assessment. Grinalds requested $24,500 for "various assessment activities."

The school's Teacher Education Programs had been reviewed in 1997 by the National Accreditation Council for Teacher Education and been found deficient. Secondary teachers needed training in the use of information technology and they weren't getting it. NACTE gave the school two years to improve "or else." With another NACTE review looming in 2000, Grinalds made an urgent plea for the $50,000 needed to remodel a multimedia classroom and $55,000 for the essential technology and equipment. "Losing accreditation for a major academic program is simply unacceptable," he told the CDF.

The Class of 2003 reported with 639 members, 38 of whom were female. But before the administration dealt with whatever challenges the new class presented, it sought to deal with a holdover problem from the 1998-1999 academic year. Estimates ranged from 800 to 1,000 cadets who could not be accounted for at the start of ESP. They were on Corps squad, at club meetings, engaged in religious activities, and in the case of education majors, at academic internships. To address this issue, the administration and the Commandant sought authority for a one semester experiment which became known as the 24-Hours/ESP Test. They wished to move Retreat from 1800 hours (6 p.m.) to 1955 hours (7:55 p.m.), making it a mandatory muster formation before the start of ESP. The second change sought by the administration was to have upperclass cadets at evening mess eat buffet style within an open time frame. Knobs would continue to eat the evening meal family style at a set hour. A divided Board of Visitors went along with the experiment, and early in January extended it for the full academic year on the rationale that it had not been in effect long enough to assess its merits and that mid-year termination would be disruptive.[525]

In September, the administration began addressing the logistical complications and disruptions that would be occasioned by the impending demolition of Padgett-Thomas Barracks. Rebuilt Murray Barracks had been occupied in June, but housing was still needed for 114 cadets. The solution was temporary units to be constructed by the tennis courts at a cost of $1.4 million.[526]

Two separate incidents of hazing marred what was otherwise a smooth transition of the Class of 2003 into the Corps of Cadets. Both occurred in October. In the first, an upperclassman was alleged to have assaulted four cadets with his fists and a broom and put out cigarettes on the bodies of the two knobs. James Trabert was promptly expelled from school, arrested and confined to jail until he raised the $25,000 bond. The second took place at 3:30 a.m. on a gallery in Padgett-Thomas. An unknown assailant took a knob from his bunk, covered his face with sweatshirt, and "beat him bloody." Publicly and privately General Grinalds refused to blame the system, telling the *Post and Courier*, "I don't think you can, year after year, produce people like our graduates from a flawed system. But the system takes you to the edge, and if people aren't balanced it can lead them over the edge." To the Board of Visitors he praised the handling of the incidents by the cadet chain of command. All of the injured remained in the school.[527]

With the clock winding down on the 20th century, the school sought to find a solution for a problem that had vexed it since the 19th: fundraising. Board Chairman Mood used the October 14, 1999 meeting of The Citadel Trust to build a consensus for what he and others saw as the only viable vehicle, what Mood termed a "super foundation." The idea of a super foundation had been recommended in the final report of The Citadel Consolidated Fundraising Task Force, chaired by ex-governor John West. The task force had been composed of some veterans of the school's funding wars: Anderson D. Warlick and Brantley D. Thomas representing the CDF; Gerald D. Baysden and Rick M. Crosby representing the Brigadier Foundation; Alvah Chapman representing the Advisory Council; Mood and Doug Snyder representing the Board of Visitors; and General Grinalds representing The Citadel. Mood believed that the initial meeting of the Task Force "marked the first time in memory that all of the fundraising personnel on The Citadel campus had met together at one time." That observation echoed one made in 1992 when the Board of Visitors met with the CDF to implement the recommendations of George Brakeley, the consultant who had characterized The Citadel as a "startlingly undercapitalized institution."[528]

In the Task Force's concept, the super foundation would be developed using the CDF board as a nucleus. As with the Brakeley solution, the Brigadier Foundation would remain a separate entity to appeal to prospective donors who were not alumni, but TCBF would hold a seat on the board of the newly organized super foundation. The chairman of the Board of Visitors and president of the college would likewise have seats on the board. Mood articulated four essential functions for the new organization: (1) planning, needs assessment and the establishment of priorities in advance of an annual campaign; (2) combining the current CDF fund drive with the college's fundraisers in one location; (3) manage the endowment; and (4) allocate funds and grants (as the CDF was already doing). Mood put the amount needed to be raised annually for The Citadel to remain competitive at $10 million. At the close of the meeting, The Citadel Trust endorsed the concept, and on October 23, 1999, the board approved it and urged the affected organizations to revise their bylaws accordingly.

November of 1999 saw two burials, one literal and one figurative. The prior summer, a non-profit organization called the Confederate Heritage Trust (CHT), whose mission is to preserve Civil War historical sites, including graves, became convinced that soldiers and sailors from that era remained buried beneath the west side stands at Johnson Hagood Stadium. CHT pressed The Citadel for a chance to prove what its research showed, and ground penetrating radar confirmed the CHT contention. In June and July, dozens of volunteers dug out and sifted through 300 cubic yards of dirt to unearth bones and fragments of 23 sailors, marines and a child. In November, all were honorably interred in the Soldier's Ground at Magnolia Cemetery. Also found were the remains of four sailors who had served aboard the H. L. Hunley, the first submarine to ever sink an enemy ship in time of war. Their reburial took place the following March.

The figurative burial was the 1999 football season, when the Bulldogs struggled to a 2-9 record, their only wins coming over VMI and South Carolina State. Head coach Don Powers was on the ropes. But Powers had one year left on the five year deal he signed in 1996 and General Grinalds insisted the school honor its commitment for the 2000 season. Board member Col. Douglas Snyder, Class of 1982 and later Board chairman, recalls Grinalds slamming his fist down on the table at the idea that the college would renege on its contract. Said Snyder, "It was the only time I ever saw him lose his temper." It was not a popular decision. Grinalds acknowledged that Walt Nadzak, the Athletic Director, disagreed with it, and that more success on the field would help in recruiting and in building a new stadium. But there was a principle at stake, and Grinalds foresaw a longer term detriment to the school's values that overrode what he called the "short-term gain of a few more ticket sales." Publicly, the Board of Visitors supported its president, but privately the disagreement and grumbling were palpable.[530]

The computer phenomenon known by the shorthand "Y2K" caused the country and much of the world to hold its collective breath as the clock ticked down on the 20th century. Nostradamus, the 16th century soothsayer, could hardly have been expected to make predictions about a technology that would rule the 21st century, but plenty of his latter-day disciples foresaw disaster. Clocks would stop, nuclear reactors would shut down, hospital ERs would stand by helpless and ATMs would prove worthless, the money inside them equally so. The U.S. spent billions to prevent the chaos forecast by people now being described as "geeks."

As America confronted this digital Armageddon, the board wrestled with a problem not from the next century but from the last one. It took an action that would have been unthinkable and impossible one hundred years before. It urged the General Assembly to relocate the Confederate Battle Flag from the dome of the state capitol "according it appropriate display as a part of the history of this State."

Such a resolution would have been unthinkable in 1899 because of South Carolina's devotion to the Lost Cause, and it would have been equally impossible because the flag was not flown atop the state house until 1961, when it was hoisted in conjunction with Charleston's centennial celebration of the firing on Fort Sumter. The following year, a concurrent resolution of the General Assembly requested that it be displayed there, but by the time of that request it had already been in place for a year and the resolution contained no end date. So, the flag continued to fly beneath Old Glory and the State flag.

In the 1960s, mounting opposition within the state to the civil rights movement gathering steam in Washington and at lunch counters, bus terminals and other public places assured that no legislator would press for the flag's removal. By the 1990s, it had become a lightning rod for dissenting views about its significance. In 1999, many of the same legislators who supported the 1962 resolution had lived long enough to regret the entire episode. In a petition addressed to state officials and published in *The State* on December 10, 1999, "a majority of the surviving members of the 1962 South Carolina General Assembly . . . respectfully request the present South Carolina General Assembly to correct our omission . . ." The petition explained "our omission" thusly: "When this Resolution was adopted in 1962, the undersigned believe that no member of the General Assembly consciously intended for the Confederate flag to fly atop our state house for all times, but only as part of the Civil War commemorative activities, which ended in 1965. However, the Resolution failed to provide for the timely removal of the flag."

The issue came front and center at The Citadel when a meeting of the South Carolina Council of College Presidents was scheduled for December 7, 1999, with the flag listed as an agenda item. Potentially, presidents of the state's colleges would be put on the spot and on the record as to the controversy. In November, anticipating the meeting, Dr. John M. Palms, president of USC and a member of The Citadel's Class of 1958, sent a letter to his

Administrative Council, Chancellors and Deans "to explain my personal and professional views on this matter." That *personal* view favored "action to remove the Confederate flag to a more appropriate place of respect and to ensure that only the sovereign flags of our elected governments fly above the South Carolina State House." As to his *professional* view, Palms said, "As a public university, USC has responsibilities that other types of organizations do not have to meet. These responsibilities require us to take every precaution to protect it from being the subject of political pressures and to allow the intellectual, moral, and ethical judgments pursued here to have their voice." His "every precaution" dictated he remain neutral on December 7, when Clemson likewise declined to take a position.

Mood saw the duty of a public university, or at least The Citadel, differently, and he thought it unfair to put the responsibility of articulating The Citadel's position solely on the shoulders of General Grinalds. In a letter to the board dated December 3, 1999, Mood disclaimed any intent to "inappropriately impose my personal beliefs on The Citadel, nor to ask you to participate in doing the same." Nevertheless, he went on to say, "I believe that the mission which The Citadel has assumed, of instilling high principles, qualities of leadership, and a sense of civic duty in our students, imposes on us a greater burden than might otherwise be imposed on institutions." His personal and professional views were inseparable: the flag needed to go. By unanimous vote the Board of Visitors agreed, giving General Grinalds the high moral ground at the December 7 meeting. Their stance drew praise from the Citadel Faculty Council, which offered its "unanimous support" and wholehearted approval. An editorial in *The State* found the school's position to be consistent with its heritage. In a conclusion any college would be proud to claim, the paper noted:

> The Citadel's mission today is a broader and nobler one than ever. It serves a rapidly changing society, while never forgetting to uphold tradition. And no Citadel tradition looms higher than its devotion to serving the State of South Carolina. That's why, one week ago today, The Citadel drew its sword against the "divisive effect" that flying the flag over our Capitol is having on our state. All South Carolinians should be grateful that in these fractious times, we have an institution so devoted to duty, honor and the greater good.

The Citadel led, a good omen for the new millennium.[531]

Chapter 15

"WE PUT THE FUTURE OF THE CITADEL ON THEIR BACKS . . ."

O n January 1, 2000, Padgett-Thomas Barracks stood empty as it had for every New Year's Day in the 78 years it had been occupied, so it would have been impossible for cadets to gather there to toast the new millennium. Besides, alcohol was forbidden in the barracks, and what would a toast be without it? In February eight cadets raised a glass of something strong in a bar built beneath the floor of P-T. There is no record of the toast they gave, if any, nor any public record of the punishment orders handed down when they were caught. Trap doors cut into barracks' wooden floors had by then become a tradition. In 1963, seniors in T Company built a lounge beneath the southeast alcove of Stevens Barracks, complete with concrete floor, a press for civilian clothes, a television and of course a bar. Not only did it afford its members a place to get away from the above-ground rigors of cadet life, but it also allowed them to get away entirely with access to a manhole that opened into the fourth battalion parking lot. They were so proud of their creation that they couldn't resist taking a Polaroid photo found during an inspection and turned over to the The Boo. During the Christmas break, he pushed aside a press to reveal the trap door and that, as they say, was that.[532]

Tensions emerged early in 2000 over the structure of the super foundation that had been so warmly endorsed the previous fall. The issue was service on the Executive Committee of the new foundation by the chairman of the Board of Visitors. Mood, the man most immediately affected, had secured a verbal commitment that he and his successors would in fact sit on the Executive Committee, but the bylaws of the newly created foundation failed to specify it. That omission concerned some members of the Board of Visitors, four of whom opposed adoption of the new foundation's bylaws until the provision could be incorporated. A majority of six members were unwilling to delay, putting the board on record as being in favor. By its approval, the board performed the last act necessary to make The Citadel Foundation (TCF) a reality. The wisdom shown by all in consolidating the school's fundraising has been borne out in the stellar performance of that organization in the 17 years of its existence. Contemplating where the college would be without it is grim speculation. Thanks to TCF we are, to bury the George Brakeley description, no longer a "startlingly undercapitalized institution."[533]

In April, General Grinalds gave the board an upbeat report, describing himself as a happy president who continued to focus on communications, admissions and fundraising. In what proved to be an abundance of enthusiasm, he said he aspired to a term in office matching that of General Summerall's 22 years.

When in 2000 the General Assembly elected Allison Wright as a member of the Board of Visitors, she became both the first female voting member and a colonel, the honorary rank bestowed upon all board members. She had served as a non-voting member since 1997 and as of this writing is still serving as Allison Dean Love, having married Phillip E. Love, Jr. in 2004. She received her MBA from The Citadel in 1993. As the owner of Allison Dean Love Consulting, LLC, she has made valuable contributions to the board over many years in the fields of marketing and public relations. Her counsel served as particularly useful during the early years of female assimilation.

On April 4, 2000, Cadet Allen Brooks LaSure addressed the Customs, Regulations and Cadet Liaison Committee of the Board of Visitors on behalf of the African-American Society. In response to LaSure's impressive presentation, the Committee moved that in the future "Dixie" be played only at times deemed historically appropriate by the administration. The board gave the motion unanimous approval.

Also in April, plans to demolish the aging Padgett-Thomas Barracks hit a major snag when the Charleston Board of Architectural Review (BAR) denied the college's request to tear it down. But the BAR's nostalgia for the historic value of the property couldn't correct major deficiencies like collapsed ceilings, backed up sewers, falling concrete and general structural instability, all of which led to a decision to close it in September. In October the BAR relented, influenced by support for the school's request by three surrounding neighborhoods and by more than 100 letters sent in support. One such letter came from Alex Sanders: jurist, College of Charleston president and noted raconteur. Sanders equated the job of the BAR to that of a museum curator. In what was assuredly the sole letter written to BAR Chairman Charles Duell invoking the Ming Dynasty, Sanders said:

The Ming Dynasty produced the finest works of creativity, but the Ming Dynasty produced even more outright junk. The task of the museum curator is not to decide whether something is Ming but whether the thing has lasting value or is junk. Otherwise, the treasures in Ming museums would be crowded out by junk. Your task is precisely the same. In my considered opinion, the single word that best describes the Padgett-Thomas Barracks is junk.[534]

In the end, preservation yielded to reality. Samuel Logan, a BAR member who opposed the request in April but reversed his vote in October, said, "(To restore it), every structural supporting piece of that building will have to go. I'm sure there's a way to save it, but what have you gained if there's nothing left of it?" In May 2001, wrecking balls began doing what wrecking balls do. The venerable tower, the school's most identifiable landmark and visible from the Cooper River bridges to generations of cadets returning from Isle of Palms, Sullivan's Island, Mount Pleasant and points north, came down last, taking a demolition crane with it.[535]

For many years it was the policy of the board that only fathers and step-fathers who were Citadel graduates could present diplomas to their sons at graduation. This policy was followed but unwritten until 1980, when a motion approved by the board formalized it. That resolution made no provision for exceptions.[536] Thereafter, those eligible to present expanded to mothers, fathers, step-mothers and step-fathers who were Citadel graduates. Exceptions had been requested from time to time and were almost always denied. In the spring of 2000, the board felt the need to restate the policy. It had before it a request that Norman R. Knight, Jr., Class of 1960, be allowed to present the diploma to his grandson, Cadet John P. Jones. The extenuating circumstances justifying an exception to the policy seemed compelling. Jones's father was also a Citadel graduate, his father and mother had divorced when Jones was young, his grandfather had secured a Provisional Appointment shortly after Jones was born, and over many years his grandfather had provided "significant monetary, spiritual and parental support." In approving Jones's request that Knight be allowed to present his diploma in recognition of the parental role Knight had played in his life, the board restated the policy to require recommendation by the Committee on Honorary Degrees, Palmetto Awards and Special Recognition and approval by the Board of Visitors, with the caution that the granting of exceptions was extremely rare, as indeed they had been. In 2001 the policy was amended to expand those eligible to be presenters, from "only mothers, fathers, step-mothers or step-fathers who are Citadel graduates" to "only mothers, fathers, step-mothers or step-fathers who are Citadel graduates from the South Carolina Corps of Cadets or Veterans Program." The change coincided with the grant of an exception to a grandfather who stood as a graduating cadet's surrogate father. In that case, the grandfather was a Citadel graduate but the record does not disclose whether the cadet's father was also a Citadel graduate, as was the case with Knight-Jones.[537]

Presentation of diplomas was a minor drama at the Class of 2000 graduation when compared with efforts made on behalf of the school's second female graduate, Petra Lovetinska. In her four years, Lovetinska had endeared herself to cadets, faculty and administrators alike. Along with Nancy Mace, who graduated early the year before, she set a standard for the women who would follow. In her senior year, Lovetinska earned the honor of *Who's Who* and served as 2nd Battalion Executive Officer. Echo Company history, recited in the 2000 *Sphinx*, hints that she came about as close to being "one of the boys" as a girl could come. "Petra earned some tours for wearing PT's downtown . . . Petra would have drowned a knob had it not been for the Coast Guard." For her senior photo, she quoted H.T. Leslie, "The game of life is not so much in holding a good hand but in playing a poor hand well." She gave a shout out to the people most responsible for allowing her to get her college education, "Tony [Motley] and the Plank Holders." The Plank Holders were the 100-plus members of the Washington, D.C. area Citadel club that sponsored her.

The college owed both Mace and Lovetinska a debt of gratitude. Board Chairman Mood said of them, "We put the future of The Citadel on their backs, and they didn't miss a beat." The school got a chance to repay a small amount of the debt to Lovetinska just prior to her graduation when her ability to accept commission in the Marine Corps hit what was potentially a fatal snag: She wasn't a U.S. citizen. That unhappy realization produced a call to U.S. Senator Ernest "Fritz" Hollings, who introduced and rammed through a special act of Congress granting her citizenship. Only four others have been made a U.S. citizen by a special act of Congress: Mother Teresa, Winston Churchill, Raoul Wallenberg and William Penn. Once that was in place, federal District Judge Sol Blatt, Jr. convened his court to perform a naturalization service and administer the oath to one person, and one person only — Lovetinska.[538]

In May, the Board of Visitors devoted an entire meeting to consideration of the 24-Hours/ESP Test. Coming as it did in the opening months of the new millennium, the vote could be seen as a test of the old vs. the new, change vs. tradition. After the review of the pros and cons that follow, the reader is invited to predict the outcome of the board's vote, which appears in the footnote.

History: The 24-Hours/ESP test was commenced at the start of the 1999-2000 academic year, originally to last for one semester but extended to both semesters by a divided vote of the board in January. It was initiated on the recommendation of the administration and the Commandant as a way of addressing two principal concerns: First, the large number of cadets involved in Corps squad, clubs, academic internships and religious activities caused them to be absent from Retreat at the traditional time of 1810 hours (6:10 p.m.) and at the traditional start of ESP at 1930 hours (7:30 p.m.); and second, the rigidity of a system that required upperclassmen to eat the evening meal family style at a set hour.

Committee Proposal: After evaluating the results of the year-long test, the Committee recommended that between 1600 hours (4 p.m.) and 2000 hours (8 p.m.) on Mondays, Tuesdays and Thursdays only, the 24-Hour schedule be adjusted as follows:

Mandatory Retreat formation at a time set to achieve maximum attendance, but not later than 2000 hours;

Knobs required to assemble, march to mess, and eat supervised meals for both first and second semesters;

Upperclassmen have optional mess between 1600 and 1945 hours as specified by the administration.

Committee Recommendations: In the event the board adopted the proposal, the Committee made three recommendations to the administration in implementing the 24-Hour/ESP concept:

Family-style evening meals should be scheduled frequently, not just on Thanksgiving, Corps Day and special occasions, to reinforce "the camaraderie and unity of the Corps of Cadets;"

A summary of absences from formation, excused and unexcused, be sent to the board at the end of each semester;

Accountability procedures and advanced technology then being used at service academies to monitor students be researched and evaluated for use at The Citadel.

Committee Findings: The Committee acknowledged that none of its members were "totally and completely supportive" of the 24-Hour/ESP concept. As the Committee admitted, "The issue is not simple." The Committee's findings consume several printed pages and only the highlights are presented here in summary fashion.

The concept allowed cadets more free time for activities, individual tutoring, and self-directed use, despite the fact that ESP would be shortened by half an hour;

More time for club meetings, intramurals, and physical activity training;

The chaplin reported increased spiritual activity and strongly favored the concept;

The disruptions being experienced with Retreat at the traditional time would be eliminated. With a mandatory formation at which complete attendance was expected, the chain of command would spend less time accounting for absences and would therefore have more time to study.

Complaints from knobs and their parents had diminished due to the more relaxed mess hall environment. Calorie and nutritional needs of fourth classmen had been met and upperclassmen had benefited from the variety offered by the buffet-style mess.

The concept fit the needs of Corps squad athletes and had the full support of the athletic department. Athletes attending meals and Retreat with their classmates had "the remarkable effect of bridging the Corps-Corps Squad rift that has been a morale problem for many years." The concept allowed Corps Squad athletes a better opportunity to compete for and hold rank.

In presenting a complete picture to the board, the Committee acknowledged the negatives of the 24-Hour/EST concept. These include: The elimination of the time-honored tradition of the Corps marching from Retreat to the mess hall for the evening meal.

Vocal alumni had expressed disapproval. The departure from tradition would make the school less military, less difficult, and would defeat the essential purpose of a disciplined, military life.

The concept also noted that a cadet's schedule can be altered to fit the traditional time frames. But the camaraderie produced by the evening meal is lost.

So there it is. Compare your vote to the actual one held on May 12, 2000.[539]

Off-campus improvements became tangible proof of the college's improving fortunes. In September, Harbor Contracting Group, Inc. received a notice to proceed on construction of the Altman Athletic Center at the south end zone of Johnson Hagood Stadium. Funded primarily by a $1 million donation from the Altman family, it was named to honor Lieutenant Colonel William M. Altman, Jr., Class of 1931. On September 15, 2000, The Holliday Alumni Center opened across the street from the stadium. The Alumni Association had requested that it be named in honor of John M.J. Holliday, Class of 1936, a long-time supporter of the college and a former member

of the Board of Visitors and Chairman Emeritus.[540] Within the center, the
Courvoisie Banquet Hall, the "Boo Room," opened with 500 in attendance,
many of those his "bums" and "lambs" from the old days. More than 950
people donated over $367,000 to make it happen, with contributions still
coming in.[541]

In the fall, a couple of prodigal sons returned. Pat Conroy and Lieutenant
Colonel Courvoisie, The Boo, received honorary degrees at a Friday parade.
Conroy admitted to having been "shocked" by the gesture, but pleased to
be back in the school's good graces. "The past is the past," Board Chairman
Leonard Fulghum said. "The honorary degree is being presented to him for
his accomplishments as an author." The Boo also appreciated his honorary
degree and was especially pleased to be standing with Conroy when he got
it. "I owe him one because of his book," Courvoisie said.[542]

On November 7, 2000, Americans went to the polls to elect a president,
but it didn't get one until December 12, 2000, when the U.S. Supreme
Court halted a vote recount in Florida, thereby giving George W. Bush that
state's 25 electoral votes and the presidency in the closest election in U.S.
history.[543] Exactly one year later, Bush was back in Charleston, addressing the
Corps of Cadets. The world had changed dramatically three months before
when terrorists carried out a plot to attack America, hatched and funded by
al Qaeda and Osama Bin Laden. As Bush addressed the Corps, the ruins
of the World Trade Center in New York still smoldered, the open wound
at the Pentagon gaped, and the world was learning about the heroism of
passengers on United Flight 93 in bringing down the plane in Shanksville,
Pennsylvania, in all likelihood sparing the U.S. Capitol the fate of the other
buildings. Bush began by reminding his audience of comments he had made
on his previous visit:

> I have come to talk about the future security of our country, in
> a place where I took up this subject two years ago when I was can-
> didate for President. In September 1999, I said here at the Citadel
> that America was entering a period of consequences that would
> be defined by the threat of terror, and that we faced a challenge of
> military transformation. That threat has now revealed itself, and
> that challenge is now the military and moral necessity of our time.

In a decision that would impact many seated in front of him, Bush had
already sent troops into Afghanistan, where the enemy was the Taliban and
where, as of this writing, U.S. forces are still engaged in the longest war in

our history. Late in his speech, Bush addressed other known threats:

> One former al Qaeda member has testified in court that he was involved in an effort 10 years ago to obtain nuclear materials. And the leader of al Qaeda calls that effort "a religious duty." Abandoned al Qaeda houses in Kabul contained diagrams for crude weapons of mass destruction. And as we all know, terrorists have put anthrax into the U.S. mail, and used sarin gas in a Tokyo subway.

Bush ended his remarks by invoking the college's history and traditions:

> In all that is to come, I know the graduates of The Citadel will bring credit to America, to the military and to this great institution. In the words of your school song, you will go where you've always gone — "in the paths our fathers showed us. Peace and Honor, God and Country — we will fight for thee."[544]

The Class of 2001 brought The Citadel full circle in its love-hate relationship with alumnus Pat Conroy when it voted him as their commencement speaker. By the time he took the podium, he was considered one of the best public speakers around, the gold standard among authors called on to speak about their work. He always punctuated his message with humorous anecdotes and liberal self-deprecation. As he admitted in his opening remarks, "there were many years when I felt Saddam Hussein or Jane Fonda had a better chance of addressing this class than I did." Conroy told the Class of 2001 how much he appreciated their invitation to speak, so much so that they were all invited to his funeral, where their Citadel ring would be guaranteed admission. When Conroy died on March 4, 2016 of pancreatic cancer, at least 25 members of the class did just that, forming an aisle outside St. Peter's Catholic Church in Beaufort as his casket was carried into the church. Conroy's commencement speech is available on You Tube (https://www.youtube.com/watch?v=HcqzINxo8Tc).

When General Grinalds previewed the 2001-2002 school year, he found plenty of room for optimism despite the 9/11 attacks, which he believed held a kernel of positive prospects. Grinalds saw a new relevancy for the military and predicted better ROTC recruitment, more Police Corps scholarships and potentially more federal support for assets like the rifle range. He took particular encouragement from some metrics he and his predecessors kept watch over: a freshman class of 694, the largest in a decade and full barracks; applications higher than at any time in the past 10 years; higher GPAs of enrolled cadets; an increase in contracting and commissioning in ROTC branches; better SAT scores for those having placed admission deposits than at the same time the previous year; significantly more applications from women, minorities and South Carolina residents. In the closely watched *U.S. News and World Report*, The Citadel moved to sixth from seventh in Regional Universities in the South, with four of the five higher ranked schools being private.

Funding continued to be a major concern, exacerbated by a performance funding quirk that gave extra weight to improvement, meaning significant funding advantages for colleges that started out ranked near the bottom and improved their programs. This disadvantaged the schools at the top, where Grinalds placed The Citadel. To illustrate the disconnect, he pointed to the *U.S. News and World Report* ranking, where we ranked second in public colleges in the South, and the Commission on Higher Education ranking (using performance funding metrics), where we ranked next to last in the state.

The president's personal schedule reflected a man fully engaged in his work. He pledged to spend more time with the Corps, visit every classroom at least once and visit the barracks. As with all college presidents, more of his time was being devoted to fundraising, with personal visits to potentially large donors. With a FY 2001-2002 budget in excess of $59 million, such efforts were crucial to the continued growth and prosperity of the school because that budget would almost double in the next 15 years.[545]

Wallace Scarborough, Class of 1981, initiated another inquiry into the Fourth Class System with an October 5, 2001 letter to Commandant Mace containing some allegations that had come to Scarborough by virtue of his status as a graduate and his service in the South Carolina House of Representatives. Old complaints about the amount and quality of food allowed to knobs followed a well-worn path, but new ones included denial of knob access to the canteen and to the lounge in Mark Clark Hall. A final allegation concerned sleep deprivation for knobs in companies where all-night vigils were being practiced. Responsibility for responding to the Scarborough letter fell to Colonel Billy Jenkinson's Customs, Regulations and Cadet Liaison Committee.

Jenkinson's committee interviewed the school's physician, Colonel Clay Robertson; the Student Activities director, Colonel Richard Irby; the chairmen of the ROTC departments; a randomly selected cadet company commander from each battalion; a randomly selected cadet first sergeant from each battalion but from a company different from the commander selected; one TAC from each battalion; and one cadet specifically requested by a committee member. Interviews were conducted in November 2001, after which the committee scheduled interviews with selected fourth classmen in January 2002. The committee's pledge of confidentiality to witnesses prevented their identification in the final report.

The committee found that while the regulations contained no prohibition against knobs using the canteen, in practice they rarely did so. In some cases, they were ordered not to go or discouraged by upperclassmen from going. The other contributing factor was knob reluctance to spend time where upperclassmen congregated. To address this, the committee recommended printed and verbal reminders to upperclassmen, particularly cadre, that knobs were permitted access to the canteen, but as to knob reluctance to mingle among concentrations of upperclassmen, the committee essentially punted, suggesting that the canteen consider ways to segregate them.

A different solution was required for the Mark Clark Hall lounge because the regulations had been changed the year before to make the lounge off-limits to knobs except during general leave. Colonel Irby, whose domain was Mark Clark Hall, assured the committee that the rule would again be changed to permit knobs use of the room, but unwritten rules and congregations of upperclassmen effectively shut knobs out of the lounge and the poolroom. The committee recommended that the administration explore areas on the second and third floors where knobs could relax together.

Issues surrounding food and nutrition stemmed from complaints that knobs were allowed to chew only three times before swallowing and that they were being deprived of real food in favor of exotic things like hot sauce. Cadre, ever inventive, had developed the practice of stacking plates to conceal knobs' uneaten food. The committee found that a small group it called "the Fringe" purposely interfered with knob nutrition, while the majority of mess carvers and cadet officers were merely insufficiently attentive to the Fringe. There was even a finding of some self-imposed food denial from knobs who had been persuaded that it represented "Old Corps" tradition. The solution was an old one: better leadership training of those responsible to see that knobs ate full meals and better supervision by TACs and cadet officers in the mess hall.

As to the all-night vigils charge, the committee found no evidence to support it, leading one again to wonder if the only thing that truly never sleeps at The Citadel is the rumor mill. The committee reminded all that knobs should not be assigned tasks that would require ESP or sleep hours to accomplish.[546]

The April 2002 meeting of the board managed to set three precedents. First, General Grinalds delivered the President's Report in executive session due to what he described as the personal nature of his report. Next, in open session, Colonel Dennis Rhoad, chairman of the Education Committee, made a motion that his committee's report on the Veterans Program be accepted, but the minutes are silent on either a second or a vote.

Last, and perhaps most significantly, board member Colonel Harvey Dick, Class of 1953, brought to the surface tension between the board and the Commandant's Department in a letter openly critical of it. Dick had attended a March meeting of the Customs, Regulations and Cadet Liaison Committee. In a letter dated April 15, 2002, which Dick asked to be included in the minutes, he stated: "The following observations are submitted from the [March] meeting and cite several examples of the continued disregard the Commandant's Department has for the BOV policy." These are strong words from a BOV member to a senior administrator. Dick's ire had been aroused by two bugle calls he heard from his quarters at 1950 hours. He called the bugler, who confirmed that he was playing "call to quarters" to commence ESP. As the board had rejected in May 2000 the Commandant's recommendation that this be done, it appeared to Dick that the Commandant's Department was making an end run around official board policy. He further contended that the Corps was being hurt by double standards within it. One of those concerned female haircuts. According to Dick, Citadel barbers had instructions not to cut a female cadet's hair too short so as to make her look like a male. Even females asking for shorter cuts to mesh with her classmates were not getting them, while male knobs were "required to have their hair almost shaved weekly." Another double standard related to Corps Squad athletes. Dick cited a fourth class, non-scholarship female soccer player "who according to company commander has never marched in a parade or attended drill." Dick felt the dual standard between Corps Squad athletes and others deserved attention, as did "Corps' morale, excess punishments [and] the inability of the Corps to run the Corps." Evidence of differences between the board and the Commandant could be seen earlier in that same meeting, when the board had heard appeals from two cadets, voting in both cases to reduce the punishments handed down by the Commandant's Department.[547]

The year 2002 marked another milestone when six African-American women received diplomas: Toshika "Peaches" Hudson, Renee Hypolite, Natosha Mitchell, Geneive Hardney, Lesjanusar "Sha" Peterson, Adrienne Watson Jamey McCloud. The following year, Cadet Viann Bolick joined the groundbreaking by becoming the first female member of the Honor Court.[548]

In June, the board elected Colonel William E. "Billy" Jenkinson III as its chairman when Colonel Leonard Fulghum declined to seek re-election. The board rewarded 33 years of dedicated service by Tommy B. Hunter by naming the Cadet Store for him. It recognized departing Professor Suzanne Ozment's contribution as Dean of Women and Undergraduate Studies and the work done by Colonel Joe Trez as special assistant to the president. His job as such consisted almost entirely of managing litigation in which the school became embroiled, working with attorneys, giving depositions and responding to discovery requests. General Grinalds announced the arrival of the AFROTC program as "the largest in the country" and in a dead heat with Notre Dame for the largest USN/USMC ROTC. He expressed supreme pleasure with the past year's communications and public relations, which made the school a "nationally known entity." Some of that positive public relations had come from a visit to the campus by the cast of "Road Rules." The MTV series featured the Roadies in their Fleetwood RV for an episode called "The Campus Crawl."[549]

Colonel Dudley Saleeby, Jr., Class of 1966 and board member and chairman of the Strategic Planning Committee, presented for consideration a document two years in the making: a Strategic Initiative for 2002-2012, designed to "chart the course of this college over the next ten (10) years." Articulating a vision of "[a]chieving excellence in the education of principled leaders," the Initiative emphasized core values: academics, duty, honor, morality, discipline and diversity. Incorporating those core values, the Initiative committed the school to the preparation of "Citadel graduates to become principled leaders in all walks of life." To reach such an ambitious goal, the committee envisioned seven priorities:

• Continue to develop and formalize leadership programs.
• Character development and ethics education needed to be "fundamental components of The Citadel experience.
• Successfully raise funds to support programs aimed at academics, athletics and student life.
• Better facilities and technological support.

• Further develop and enhance the College of Graduate and Professional Studies.

• Ensure that the college has the leadership and talent necessary to accomplish its mission.

• Enhance the intellectual and academic learning environment for students and faculty.

In unanimous support of the Initiative, the board ordered broad dissemination of it, directed Saleeby's committee to work with the administration to assess and evaluate progress and to make periodic reports back to the board.[550]

The 2002-2003 academic year began with two far-reaching undertakings, both meant to put meat on the bones of the Strategic Initiative: the first, an academic reorganization of the college into schools headed by deans; and the second, a coordinated capital campaign under the auspices of The Citadel Foundation (TCF).

Academic reorganization anticipated the upcoming SACS review, but there were a host of compelling reasons for it not related to that review. Central to the concept was the role deans needed to play going forward. The plan created five new schools, though for two of those, business and education, the change was a name, from a "department" to a "school." The three new schools consolidated related departments under one dean. The School of Humanities and Social Sciences would now contain the departments of English, History, Modern Languages, Political Science/Criminal Justice and Psychology. The School of Science and Mathematics would now include the departments of Chemistry, Biology, Physics, Math/Computer Science and Health, Exercise and Sports Science. The School of Engineering combined the departments of Civil and Electrical. The advantages of the School Model were several: increased collaboration among departments within the same discipline; increased prestige and credibility for external support and partnerships; a decentralized budgeting process; and perhaps most critically, when coupled with the addition of deans, the best structure for program accreditation. The role of the deans was deemed critical to advocacy for their schools and the disciplines within them and to positioning the program for accreditation.

A significant metric in this reorganization was the diminished percentage of the school's budget expended for instruction from 45.9 percent to 37.4 percent. To reverse that troublesome slide, the TCF launched its Leadership Through Education Campaign to raise $100 million. This campaign was unprecedented in the history of the college. Never had so much money been sought from alumni, friends and foundations for such clearly identified needs.

The strength of the campaign lay in the case made for specific and identified needs and programs, academic enhancements for students ($30 million), faculty ($25 million), technology and equipment ($10 million), students and facilities ($25 million), and The Citadel Fund ($10 million in much-needed unrestricted dollars, the lack of which had plagued administrations past).

These broad categories of needs were further itemized for maximum effect. The $30 million requested for students would fund 40 Citadel Foundation Scholars at $250,000 each, 50 Citadel Leadership Scholars at $100,000 each, 100 Armed Forces Scholars at $75,000 each (to pay the difference between ROTC scholarships and the cost per year), and 50 Graduate Assistantships at $50,000 each. To supplement traditional academics with fine arts programs, lectures and specialized training, the Cadet Life Fund of $2.5 million promised to enhance the cadet experience outside the classroom. Not forgotten were the 2,000 students served annually by the College of Graduate and Professional Studies. The campaign targeted $2.5 million for financial aid, faculty support and related needs of the CGPS program.

Endowed faculty chairs, a venerable staple among the better schools, don't come cheap. The campaign sought to fund six of them at $1.5 million each. Named professorships carry prestige and also a price tag: $500,000 each, with 12 sought. To assure that members of the faculty remained at the forefront of their respective disciplines, the campaign set as its goal $7.5 million to fund continuous education and to promote academic scholarship through research and publications. For $2.5 million, a Visiting Scholars Program could become a reality.

A need critical for recertification by SACS was improvements to the Daniel Library. Five million dollars would fund cutting-edge information resources there. We had entered an age when technology changed daily, and keeping abreast of those changes with software and hardware upgrades took money: $5 million for immediate improvements to facilities and equipment.

Staying competitive in athletics presented a challenge for all schools in all conferences. Administrators stress the need for quality athletic teams for alumni support, student morale and as a recruiting tool to fill future classes. The Brigadier Foundation funds athletic scholarships, and in keeping with the unified fundraising to which the school was now committed, its allocation of $25 million was aimed at 10 fully funded Brigadier Foundation Scholarships, each carrying a $250,000 price tag. Also included in that request was $10 million for improvements to Johnson Hagood Stadium, $7.5 million for the Brigadier Foundation's annual fund and $2.5 million for its program fund.

The Leadership Through Education Campaign was ambitious and much was riding on it. The man chosen to lead the campaign was Steve Tobias, Class of 1967 and the chief financial officer for Norfolk Southern Railroad. The campaign exceeded its goal and its success made Tobias a logical choice to chair TCF.

General Grinalds continued to insist that increased emphasis be placed on ethics, which he viewed as impossible to separate from leadership. That emphasis received a major boost when Bill Krause, Class of 1963 and the chairman of TCF, committed $2 million to the cause. One million dollars of Krause's support would fund a "leader in residence" for 10 years and the other million an endowed chair in leadership and ethics.[551]

L. William (Bill) Krause's contributions to leadership development at The Citadel would be difficult to overstate. We are fortunate that the visions of Krause and Grinalds meshed in that vital area. Four years after graduating from The Citadel, Krause joined Hewlett Packard, eventually managing its General Systems Division with responsibility for worldwide sales of HP computers. In 1981 founders of 3Com Corporation, a venture capital start-up, brought him in as its president. As CEO he took 3Com to $1 billion in revenue. In 1991 he founded LWK Ventures, a privately held investment and advisory service, and remains its president.

In 2003 a key element of the Strategic Plan was put into place when the college established the Krause Center for Leadership & Ethics. As seen from prior chapters, pressure for formal leadership instruction and training had been building for a generation. Grinalds, with support from the board, and Krause brought it about. In February 2004, Grinalds introduced to the board Lieutenant Colonel Jeffrey Weart, USA (Ret.), the first Director of the Krause Initiative. Weart proved instrumental in implementing the "Mission, Goals, and Focus of Efforts" promulgated by Grinalds. From those early efforts emerged the blueprint for training principled leaders. Today, leadership courses comprise a part of every cadet's curriculum for all four years, and completion of courses is a prerequisite to graduate. The Center sponsors annually a Leadership Day in the fall and Principled Leadership Symposium in the spring. Through the Department of Leadership Sciences within the college, it is now possible to minor in Leadership and, at the postgraduate level, obtain a Master of Science in Leadership. When you consider that as knob in 1969, John Rosa learned leadership by watching those around him and deciding, "I want to be like him, but not that one," in reference to an earlier comment on leadership training — a new era has dawned.

In the spring of 2003, two combat deaths in Iraq served as a grim reminder that 35 percent of the 379 cadets who would graduate in May would be commissioned in the Armed Forces. Second Lieutenant Therrel Shane Childers, a 2001 graduate of the Marine Enlisted Commissioning Education Program (MECEP), became the first U.S. casualty in the Iraq war while serving in an infantry battalion.

USMC Captain Ben Sammis, Class of 1996, flew Cobra helicopters with General Grinalds' son, also a Cobra pilot. Sammis died April 5, 2003 when his helicopter crashed. At his funeral in Rehoboth, Massachusetts, Sammis's father urged mourners to follow the motto that meant so much to his son: Ben Sammis had engraved on his Citadel ring: "Thou Mayest."[552] More than 300 graduates were then serving in Iraq or the Iraq Theater.[553] Not all the lamentable deaths were combat related. Shortly after he was appointed to the Board of Visitors, Joe Shine, Class of 1971 and one of the first African-American graduates, died. General Grinalds attended his funeral in Columbia.[554]

In the spring of 2004, board member Colonel Glenn Addison, Class of 1979, visited the Air Force Academy, where he compared the campus ethos in Colorado Springs to the one he knew existed in Charleston. He learned they operated under a less stringent military system with less emphasis on their Honor Code. His time spent there would not have been especially notable except for the Superintendent who showed him around: Lt. Gen. John Rosa, Class of 1973, a man whose return to his alma mater was just over the horizon.[555]

General Grinalds maintained his intense interest in Rhodes Scholarships. The man put in charge of developing the action plan to make selected cadets competitive was, interestingly, Colonel Jack Rhodes. His plan called for promising sophomores to be identified and encouraged to pursue Truman Scholarships as juniors. The Truman, named for former President Harry S. Truman, carries a $30,000 award in the third year of undergraduate study. With about 60 awarded annually nationwide, the competition is intense. Winning a Truman can position a candidate nicely to reach for a Rhodes or a coveted Marshall Scholarship (named for former general and U.S. Secretary of State George C. Marshall), and to prepare they need special classes, seminars, off-campus internships and civic involvements, faculty mentoring and practice interviews. It is not generally appreciated how expensive it can be to compete successfully for a Rhodes, a Marshall Scholarship and other prestigious awards. Success brings prestige to the student but also to the institution at which he or she studied.[556]

On January 8, 2005, General Mace announced his retirement as of August

31, 2005. He took over as Commandant in March 1997, while General Poole served as interim president and two months after the selection of General Grinalds as the next president was made public. His retirement after eight years of dedicated service coincided with that of his boss. On January 18, 2005, General Grinalds announced his retirement, effective August 1, 2005. Grinalds disclaimed any relationship between the two retirements, but said their reasons for leaving were identical. Both men had assumed their duties at a time when the college was being battered in the media and when the pressure to successfully assimilate women raised the stress level on campus. One week later, Porter-Gaud School announced that Grinalds would become its new president after taking off for a year to write a book. Grinalds had served on the board at Porter-Gaud since 1999. Notwithstanding the prep school's enthusiasm in announcing the selection, it never came about for reasons undisclosed.[557]

In much the same way that the college had weighed "repair or replace" decisions on the deteriorating barracks in the 1990s, it confronted the same dilemma with the aging Johnson Hagood Stadium. For much of the Grinalds administration, one viable option considered was building a new stadium on Stoney Field across the street. So convinced was the board that a replacement stadium was the way forward that in September 2004 it had voted to proceed with its construction. The old stadium would be converted, when funds became available, to a facility for track and field, soccer and as a football field for Burke High School. By February 5, 2005, reality set in. A new 22,000 seat stadium on Stoney Field would cost $47 million, the cost escalated by soil and footprint issues. By contrast, refurbishing the old stadium with equal seating capacity would cost $36 million. The Stoney option meant refunding $1 million to the Altman family for Altman Center, obviously unnecessary if the cheaper option was exercised. Last among the major differences: Stoney couldn't be ready before the 2008 season, leaving football in limbo for four years, whereas the Johnson Hagood improvements could be made by kickoff in 2006. The board rescinded its September 2004 resolution and voted to repair and remodel Johnson Hagood.[558] Funding that decision required the school to incur significant debt and to defer maintenance that some viewed as more pressing, but the first-class facility that exists today and a winning football program have helped quiet the dissenters.

The Grinalds administration reversed the decline of the mid-1990s and helped build a foundation for his successor. His specific accomplishments reflect the talents and energies of a man fully committed to the mission of educating principled leaders within a military environment. They include:

• The successful assimilation of women. Asked to identify the key elements of that effort, Grinalds named three: (1) Joe Trez, for his formulation and management of the assimilation plan and for his competence in handling ongoing litigation and special projects as an assistant to the president; (2) Emory Mace, for the Mace Plan and the steady enforcement of rules by the commandant's department; and (3) superior senior cadet leadership in the class of 1998.

• Restoration of The Citadel's credibility with the press. Grinalds changed the policy of having a public relations employee speak for the school. *Post and Courier* reporter Sybil Fix took a particular interest in the school and "she had spies everywhere." With the proliferation of lawsuits, those who might otherwise have spoken refused to do so for fear of prejudicing some case. Worse, the few who did speak were not trustworthy in her view. Grinalds decided to speak for the college himself. His policy was simple. When Fix called, he told her all he knew about the subject in question. "Over time," Grinalds said, "she began giving the school the benefit of the doubt."[559]

• A renewed and enhanced focus on academics. Grinalds left the Marine Corps because he was committed to education, as his six successful years at the head of Woodberry Forest demonstrated. Almost everything he did as president of The Citadel was designed, directly or indirectly, to admit better students and to upgrade the quality of their education once they arrived. "He laid the groundwork for Rosa," in the opinions of board chairmen Frank Mood and Douglas Snyder.[560]

Rosa had big shoes to fill, but then John Rosa has big feet.

Chapter 16

PLANTING THE FLAG —
A BIG RED ONE

With the retirement of General Grinalds in August 2005 and the search committee having settled on a man whose selection was subject to his release from active duty, the board did what baseball Coach Chal Port had done in the lopsided Clemson loss detailed in Chapter 11. It went to the bullpen, signaling for General Poole to once again do duty as interim president. Given the turmoil surrounding his previous tenure in that position, the 1996-1997 school year, Poole could have been forgiven for asking, "Are you nuts?" But, of course, he accepted willingly and graciously. Poole was prepared to serve for the entire academic year had Rosa's release from active duty been delayed, but as it turned out his second stint in relief lasted only a few months.[561]

Again he dealt with a hurricane, this time Ophelia. He released the Corps on Saturday afternoon, September 10, and canceled classes for Monday and Tuesday. As storms go, Ophelia turned out to be something of a non-event, moving its way erratically up the coast before delivering its punch, such as it was, to the Outer Banks of North Carolina. Tragedy struck that day, but weather did not cause it. Cadets Clarke Russell, Brett Warren and Blake Campbell, headed to the Citadel-Florida State football game in Tallahassee, died when their car blew a tire on I-95. Their funerals drew large delegations of cadets, faculty and tactical officers.[562]

On September 16, 2005, the school welcomed back some war heroes on POW/MIA Recognition Day. Three living POWs from World War II, one from Korea, and six from Vietnam made up the school's 10 living POWs. Six of them attended, including Colonel Quincy Collins, USAF, Class of 1953; Commander Al Agnew, USN, Class of 1962; Lieutenant Colonel William Elander, USAF, Class of 1957; Captain Al Kroboth, USMC, Class of 1969; Captain Henry Lesesne, USN, Class of 1958; Lieutenant Colonel Glenn L. Myers, USAF, Class of 1964; and Lieutenant Richard H. Kellehan, USA, Class of 1944. All but Kellehan, a WWII POW, were imprisoned in Vietnam.

The Class of 1964 arranged for a POW/MIA flag to be flown and honored the men with a parade and a reception.[563]

In October, Mark Brandenburg, Class of 1990, came aboard as General Counsel to the college, a position he still holds as of this writing.

Having been released from active duty, Lieutenant General Rosa set the tone for his administration early in 2006. He spent his first month in office listening and asking questions. By the time he attended his first board meeting as president on February 4, 2006, he had engaged in his own style of "management by walking around," speaking with cadets, faculty, alumni and past presidents. He met with each of the school's vice presidents for full briefings on their respective areas of responsibility. Like the quarterback he had been in his cadet days, he could best employ his strengths by knowing exactly where the weaknesses were. He made one staff change during that first month, tapping Colonel Joe Trez as executive assistant to the president in place of Colonel Charles Reger, Class of 1967, who was retiring in April. Despite the well-thought-out initiatives Rosa inherited from his predecessor, he felt it key to have his own vision in place by his inauguration.

On Friday, April 21, 2006, Lieutenant General Rosa was installed as the 19th president of the college at a ceremony in McAlister. Attending were cadets, family, friends, public officials and, of course, alumni from Rosa's Class of 1973. Air Force General Lance A. Smith, commander of the U.S. Joint Forces Command, cited Rosa's personal integrity in praising the school's choice as a perfect match and lamenting his service's loss: "The Citadel Board of Visitors took a valuable asset away from the United States Air Force." He might have said two valuable assets because Donna Rosa came with her husband as part of the package.

Few general officers arrive alone at the military's highest ranks, as those who have made it there confirm. In an interview prior to his inauguration, Rosa said, "I don't see how a single college president could do it." He didn't hide his appreciation for what Donna brings to their partnership, extending far beyond the moral support of one spouse for another. Donna planned an active role, as was her habit at the Air Force Academy, particularly with engagement of female cadets. And, as the mother of the Rosas' two sons, John and Brad, she knew the needs of male cadets as well. Brad was in the Class of 2003. The entire Rosa family reunited for the ceremony.[564]

In his inaugural remarks, Rosa continued to set the tone, pegging character development as the most critical component of the four pillars of a Citadel education, with academic, physical and military achievement counting for nothing without character. And he addressed an elephant in the field house when he reminded those present that the school now had 96 female graduates and it was time to move forward in embracing diversity.[565]

One minefield Rosa knew awaited him was the one he had navigated at the Air Force Academy: sexual harassment. The issue had first surfaced there, but all the service academies were having to address it and Rosa wanted to get out in front of any new scandal that might be lurking. He had in mind his Values and Respect Program at the Academy, but needed a baseline against which to measure the results of an educational effort he intended to promote. To get such a baseline, he commissioned a survey, a Department of Defense tool modified for The Citadel. In April and May, 100 percent of the female cadets and 30 percent of the male cadets were asked to complete the anonymous online survey. Rosa expressed great satisfaction in the response rate: 96.6 percent for the women (114 of 118), 91.4 percent for the men (487). He was far less satisfied with the results. Nineteen percent of the women reported having been sexually harassed and/or assaulted during their cadetship, with sexual harassment defined as offensive remarks, jokes or unwelcome advances of a sexual nature. Unwelcome touching constituted sexual assault, from kissing to rape. Of the 27 incidents of assault reported by the women, 17 went unreported for fear of ostracism or peer ridicule. The comparable harassment/assault rate for men was 4 percent. Rosa blamed alcohol for 75 percent of the problem, which made it no less a problem but made a partial solution more obvious.

Publicizing the survey results drew praise from several quarters. Nancy Mace, the school's first female graduate, called Rosa's initiative brave and admirable, adding that she was not surprised by the results. She acknowledged incidents of sexual harassment during her time at the college, "but not sexual assault . . . I would send my daughter there." Gilbert Pohl, Class of 1976 and president of the Alumni Association, voiced overwhelming approval for the Values and Respect Program among the alumni, conceding that some few might cite the results to bolster their argument that women should never have been admitted in the first place. Jeri Cabot, Dean of Students at the College of Charleston, put the estimate of the number of college women nationwide who experienced rape or attempted rape at 20-25 percent. She agreed with Rosa that the source of the problem was usually alcohol, and praised The Citadel not only for taking the survey but for making the results public as well.[566]

The ideal size of the Corps of Cadets came under scrutiny. For the six plus decades since Stevens Barracks was completed in 1942, maximum capacity had been almost 2,000 cadets. With the completion of Watts Barracks, there was now the potential for five battalions. Two options were discussed. In the first, Murray, Padgett-Thomas, Law and Watts would house 16 lettered companies of 1,912 cadets. Stevens Barracks would be demolished, replaced by a multi-purpose barracks holding Palmetto Battery (100) and Regimental Band (126), with room for visiting teams, a quarantine area, TAC and computer rooms, and dormitory-style rooms for men and women on a temporary need basis. Capacity then increased to 2,138, with a net income advantage of $1.4 million as a hedge against declining state support.[567] By April, this multi-purpose barracks concept had been labeled Plan A as a Plan B emerged. Plan B was simplicity itself — five battalions of cadets with a Corps capacity of an additional 342 cadets and the additional revenues to be derived therefrom. At its annual meeting in June, the board opted for Plan A, but a multi-purpose barracks has never come to fruition and Stevens still stands, its future undecided.[568]

The first graduation of the Rosa era featured General Peter Pace, chairman of the Joint Chiefs of Staff, as commencement speaker. Pace, the first Marine to head the Joint Chiefs, told the 397 graduates in the Class of 2006 that their country needed them. "We are at war," he said, and reminded them on this day, when they felt they had climbed to the very top of the hill, that with all their hard work they had "absolutely earned the right to start at the bottom. There's nothing wrong with that. What you are about to do is simply going to be one heck of a ride." For 38 graduates, the occasion took on extra meaning when they received their diplomas from their parents and grandparents, including four female graduates whose alumni fathers had the honor. In June, Rosa told the board that Pace's presence had brought nationwide recognition to The Citadel.[569]

In September 2006, the college abolished the Citadel Summer Camp begun by General Clark in 1957. The camp had for decades provided boys, then boys and girls, a unique summer experience, as shown by the large number of repeat attendees. The board's rationale was sound enough. By 2006 many more residential camps had come into existence, giving boys and girls more options, and cadets who served as counselors likewise had more choices. Constant use of campus facilities during the summer reduced the time windows in which to perform critical maintenance. Unstated in the board's resolution was the trauma and expense caused by Michael Arpaio, a Marine captain who volunteered as a counselor at the camp. Arpaio, Class of 1997, pleaded guilty in a military court to various charges including indecent assault and providing alcohol to a minor. He received a 10-year sentence and was ordered to serve 15 months in a Navy brig. In August, the month before the board voted to eliminate the camp, the college had paid out $500,000 as part of $3.8 million in settlements to five of his victims.[570] Also unstated in the board's resolution, because unknown to the college at the time, was that another shoe would fall in 2007 when a former summer camper told a sordid tale involving Louis "Skip" ReVille.[571]

Academics came sharply into focus with a report that Citadel ROTC graduates were losing first choices of their branch assignments because of GPAs lower than the national ROTC average. Changing that would be a high priority for the new Provost as soon as one could be hired, with interviews scheduled to begin in December. A report from The Citadel Foundation by its chairman, Charlie Coe, offered encouragement that the funding essential to carrying out the Strategic Plan would be available. Its $100 million campaign was running well ahead of schedule with $85 million committed as of August 31, 2006. By the time the campaign ended, it had raised $108 million. Already TCF contemplated its next campaign, with the needs of the college at the forefront of that planning. Unfortunately for everyone in the planning business, the great recession about to engulf the country would require major revisions to all plans.[572]

Spring 2007 saw several changes. One of the most historically successful teams at The Citadel got a new home on February 2, 2007, when the Inouye Marksmanship Center was dedicated. Named for U.S. Senator Daniel Inouye (D. Hawaii), it brought state of the art technology to a sport in which the school excelled for decades. Grade results for the first semester showed three of the four classes attaining record GPAs. Dr. Samuel Hines joined the administration as the new Provost. The board received its first overview of The Citadel Development Model to be instituted for the 2007-2008 academic year. A key goal of the Krause Initiative, the model was designed to introduce defined leadership roles and requirements into the cadet experience. In October 2008, The Krause Initiative officially became the Krause Center for Leadership and Ethics. The board revived the Veterans Program and supported the administration's decision to install locks on all barracks doors. Lieutenant Colonel Ben Legare retired as Director of Governmental and Community Affairs after many years of representing the school's best interests in Columbia. A proposal made to change the name of the College of Graduate and Professional Studies to the Citadel Graduate College (CGC), was adopted several months later.[573]

On July 23, 2007, The Citadel hosted a Democratic presidential debate seen nationally. Over 2,500 filed into McAlister Field House to see and hear eight candidates answer 40 videotaped questions from Americans of various ages and hometowns. Hosted by CNN and moderated by Anderson Cooper, the audience heard from Hillary Clinton, Joe Biden, John Edwards, Bill Richardson, Mike Gravel, Dennis Kucinich, Chris Dodd and the eventual President, Barack Obama. Obama voiced his opposition to slavery reparations, but brought the argument home with the statement, "I think the reparations we need right here in South Carolina is investment in our schools." The program put the college in the national spotlight for an evening, a public relations success by all accounts and one that CNN expressed interest in repeating. It marked a good beginning for Colonel Cardon Crawford, the new legislative liaison who replaced Colonel Legare. Crawford led the ad hoc committee that coordinated the debate.[574]

In the year 2007, the other shoe fell on the Citadel Summer Camp. Camper "X" informed the college that five years before, when he was 14 years old and Louis "Skip" ReVille, Class of 2002, was a counselor at the camp, ReVille had lured him and another boy into ReVille's room, showed them pornography on his computer, and masterbated with them. After the Arpaio revelations and hefty settlements in 2005, this must have been the last thing the school needed to hear, but the allegations were shocking and it immediately undertook an investigation.

The college's General Counsel, Mark Brandenburg, met with Camper X and his family. He tried to interview the other camper allegedly present, but was rebuffed. When confronted, ReVille strenuously denied the allegation. Complicating Brandenburg's assessment was ReVille's stellar reputation at the time. Like Arpaio, ReVille had an impressive record as a cadet. His peers had elected him chairman of the Honor Court and at graduation services he received an award for excellence in public service. Another factor for Brandenburg to weigh was the concern for privacy expressed by Camper X and his family, who feared having their names linked to such a tawdry and criminal episode. In the face of ReVille's denials, with nothing to corroborate Camper X's account, and given the family's expressed need for privacy, the school concluded that it lacked sufficient evidence to report the matter to the police. And that, the school admitted in 2011, was a mistake. "Despite the concerns of the family, whose right to privacy was foremost in our minds, we regret that we did not pursue this matter further," said a joint statement issued by President Rosa and Board Chairman Douglas Snyder. ReVille went on to prey on others, eventually pleading guilty to molesting 23 boys. In June 2012 a judge sentenced him to 50 years in prison, seven years of supervision, and should he ever be released, a GPS ankle device for life. The State Law Enforcement Division cleared The Citadel of any criminal wrongdoing stemming from ReVille.[575]

As this history is written, a plaintiff identified as John Doe #2, one of ReVille's victims, has appealed a verdict in favor of the college in a civil suit brought against it. The suit alleges the school is liable for its failure to notify ReVille's subsequent employer, Pinewood Preparatory School, of Camper X's allegations against ReVille. In upholding the decision of the trial court, the South Carolina Court of Appeals ruled that "South Carolina law does not recognize a general duty to warn a third party or potential victim of danger or to control the conduct of another." More appeals are expected.[576]

In February 2008, Athletic Director Les Robinson announced his retirement after 24 years of dedicated service to the school. A major component of the Krause Initiative, the Leadership Symposium planned for Corps Day, promised an impressive lineup of distinguished speakers to include: Ms. Darla Moore, Vice President, Rainwater, Inc.; Coach Bobby Ross, former Citadel and pro football coach; and Lieutenant General Van Antwerp, Chief of Engineers and Commanding General, United States Army Corps of Engineers. Stevens Barracks clung to life with a $1.3 million renovation.

Exciting news came from Dr. Gary Durante, president of the Citadel Alumni Association, that the original Big Red battle flag may have been found. Within days after South Carolina became the first state to secede from the Union on December 20, 1860, a battery of about 50 cadets under the command of Major Peter F. Stevens, Class of 1849, was ordered to Morris Island to help defend Charleston from attack by sea. Word reached the battery that a Union ship would attempt to resupply and reinforce Union troops on Fort Sumter, under the command of Major Robert Anderson. As related in Chapter 2, by firing on the *Star of the West*, Citadel cadets unleashed the first hostile shots of the Civil War. The flag fluttering over the cadet battery on that early morning encounter became known as Big Red. It was made by a Charleston ship chandler named Hugh Vincent. Later that month, the government of the new Republic of South Carolina adopted as its official flag a similar design on a blue background, but until then, flag makers like Vincent felt free to use colors of their own choosing. He chose a red background. Not only was the war lost, but the flag was lost as well.

The banner suspected of being Big Red was then housed in the Iowa Historical Society Museum. The CAA needed to confirm its authenticity, but circumstantial evidence and historical records indicated a high probability that this flag was Big Red. Three months later, Durante reported that tests

260

on the flag had not been conclusive and additional testing appeared cost-prohibitive.[577]

A highly respected Citadel graduate made national news in March 2008 for humanitarian work in Iraq. Former Regimental Commander and USMC Major Kevin Jarrard, Class of 1994, commanded a company on patrol in Haditha, a farming town on the Euphrates River. Entering a home, Jarrard noticed that a 2-year-old girl, Amenah al-Bayati, seemed on the verge of medical distress when her hands and feet turned blue as she moved about the house. Jarrard had the battalion surgeon, Captain John Nadeau, examine the child. Nadeau diagnosed a heart condition familiar to him as a cardiologist. Because he also taught at Vanderbilt University's medical school, he contacted a colleague in Nashville, Dr. Karla Christian, who agreed to perform the necessary surgery at no cost. Jarrard led the effort to raise $28,000 to fly Amenah to Nashville with her mother. Aside from costs, numerous administrative obstacles had to be overcome, from visas to security clearances, female chaperones, culturally appropriate food and oxygen for the 14-hour flight. Her surgery proved far more complex than expected, but after three hours under anesthetic and four days of recovery, she headed home with a full life expectancy.[578]

At its June 2008 meeting, the board moved to correct what had been deemed a shortcoming in the Strategic Initiative as adopted six years earlier. The Strategic Initiative, as considered by the board in 2008, set seven initiatives:

1. Focus on the development of principled leaders;
2. Strengthen the college through institutional advancement;
3. Enhance Learning;
4. Develop the student population;
5. Enhance the facilities and technological support for the campus;
6. Improve institutional effectiveness;
7. Ensure that the college has the leadership and talent to accomplish these goals.

The key to successful implementation, as the board had come to realize, was what one member termed "institutional buy-in," requiring each goal to be assigned to a specific administrator to lead the effort toward it. The commandant was assigned 1; the VP of External Affairs 2; the Provost 3 and 4; the VP of Facilities and Engineering 5; the Associate Provost 6; and the VP of Business and Finance 7. Each of these administrators was in turn assigned a committee of the board to report to. This institutional buy-in made tangible what had previously been largely aspirational.

A report on deferred maintenance underscored just how critical it was becoming. The board learned that the majority of our buildings are ranked "poor" by the South Carolina Council of Higher Education and our deferred maintenance ratio was well above the college/university norm.[579]

Solving the deferred maintenance problem required money, the exact commodity that was increasing scarce. The United States entered a recession in December 2007 that wouldn't officially end, according to the Federal Reserve, until June 2009, but the woes brought on by the burst of the housing bubble lingered for years. The unemployment rate, which had been 5 percent at the recession's start, doubled by October 2009. Nationwide, home prices fell by an average of 30 percent, with three million homeowners receiving foreclosure notices.[580] This financial crisis occupied much of President Rosa's and the board's time and energy in 2008 and beyond.

The recession topped the board's agenda in February 2009. General Rosa predicted that the $70 million in deferred maintenance would get worse, despite the school's expenditure of $20 million on it in the previous five years. Capers Hall remained as the highest priority, a position to which it had become accustomed and would retain for most of the decade to follow. In much better shape than the economy was the Corps of Cadets, both physically and academically. He took satisfaction in the improvement in physical fitness over the past three years, with seniors now in better shape than knobs, a reversal of three years before. He expressed pleasure with GPAs of the athletes, higher than Corps', and with a 92 percent graduation rate, better by far than the 78 percent national average. Major General Arthur H. Baiden III, board chairman, paid tribute to the late Alvah Chapman, surely one of the most influential graduates in the school's history.[581]

That spring, Rosa reported excitement on campus and in the alumni community over the basketball team's win streak. New head coach Ed Conroy, Class of 1989 and Pat Conroy's cousin, brought the team up from the depths by notching 11 wins in a row and 20 wins in a season for only the second time in 98 years of Citadel basketball. It enabled the Dogs to secure a first-round bye in the Southern Conference tournament as the No. 2 seed in the South Division, with a chance to reach the NCAA's "big dance" for the first time ever. They fell short, but the effort pumped new life into a program that needed it. A bright note in the financial gloom was the Athletic Department's first budget surplus in a decade. Ted Curtis, Class of 1964 and historian for the Citadel Alumni Association, determined that Big Red was in fact the genuine article and reported on steps underway to get it from the Iowa museum where it was discovered.[582]

Following graduation of the Class of 2009, Rosa complimented the board on the completion of the Strategic Plan approved during the Grinalds administration. That plan had envisioned a road map for a decade, but financial realities dictated a new vision that Rosa was then formulating. He acknowledged the possibility of personnel reductions if state funding was again reduced below the level necessary to meet the 2009-2010 budget of $87.9 million. The economy was having its effect at The Citadel Foundation, with fundraising down by almost 50 percent in the first five months of 2009. Before adjourning, the board elected Colonel Douglas A. Snyder, Class of 1982, as chairman.[583]

Chairman Snyder is a CPA by profession, a handy background to have given the financial stress that characterized much of the 2009-2010 academic year. The state cut its appropriation almost 31 percent, from $16.3 million in FY 2009 to $11.3 million in FY 2010. By December the crisis threatened virtually all of the innovations Rosa contemplated, as he demonstrated in a Power Point presentation to the board. A series of state cuts led Rosa to remind the General Assembly that the school had gone from being state supported to "state assisted" (General Watts's term) to a point where a more accurate description was "state located." The combination of state cuts, rising debt, a growing list of deferred maintenance projects and reduced fundraising now threatened the school's viability. Dealing with the economic challenges was also being hampered by the time the board spent dealing with cadet disciplinary appeals, a situation Rosa sought to remedy in January 2010 when he urged the board to pass a resolution making him the final authority on suspensions, dismissals and expulsions. It passed, and though later modified to restore the board's authority in cases of expulsions, it represented a significant break in precedent. In another sign of the times, plans to build a much-needed campus parking garage, to construct some campus housing and to formulate a Campus Master Plan all fell victim to financial constraints. Colonel Fred Price announced there simply wasn't sufficient funding available to do any of them. The Veterans Program, reinstituted months earlier, was off to a slow start but showed good potential to grow. Another program with potential was the Citadel Success Institute (CSI), designed to orient incoming freshmen during the summer prior to their matriculation. A similar program had been running at VMI for some time, funded by its foundation. As many as 50 percent of VMI's incoming freshmen went through the program, while Rosa hoped for 150 the following summer. The fee later set was $2,450, and unlike at VMI, it would have to come from the future cadet's personal resources.[584]

Two football players brought the worst kind of notoriety to the college when they were arrested for two separate home invasions. Miguel Starks, the Bulldogs' quarterback, former Bulldog linebacker Reggie Rice, and a College of Charleston freshman broke into the home of assistant football coach Joshua Harpe on February 27, 2010. With the help of two female accomplices, also College of Charleston students, the masked trio, armed with handguns, bound Harpe with duct tape and stole valuable electronics. Three days earlier, the same offenders had burglarized a former Citadel cadet on James Island in much the same manner. Both Starks and Rice pleaded guilty to major felonies, including armed robbery and kidnapping. Just months before his spectacular self-inflicted ruination, Starks had come off the bench for injured quarterback Bart Blanchard to lead the Dogs to a 38-28 win over arch-rival Furman. Starks had what most would consider a career day, scoring four touchdowns and passing for a fifth. He will have a long time to reflect on the glory of that day, as both he and Rice were sentenced to 30 years in prison. At the first board meeting following the pair's arrest, Colonel Addison, representing the Brigadier Foundation, reported progress toward a record year of fundraising, $1.4 million, but worried about the impact Starkes' crime and the attendant publicity might have on future contributions.[585]

Corps Day weekend in 2010 saw the return of Big Red. According to Michael O. Smith, director of Iowa's State Historical Museum, the flag had been donated to the museum in 1919 by a Civil War veteran named Willard Baker, who found it in Mobile, Alabama at the end of the war. Extensive research and testing showed it likely to be Big Red.

The Alumni Association undertook an aggressive campaign to recover the flag. Ted Curtis chaired the committee charged with the responsibility of determining the flag's authenticity. In October 2009, the committee released a report making the case for the flag's genuineness, which spurred an effort to get the flag on loan from Iowa in time for the 150th anniversary of the firing on the *Star of the West*.

Bringing the 10' x 7' flag back was not going to be cheap. Transporting it from Iowa required a climate controlled truck, a security guard and a $1 million insurance policy. And once in Charleston, the flag that for nearly a century had been housed in a storage closet would now be displayed in a temperature and humidity controlled case in the Holliday Alumni Center, wired by a security system and watched by three cameras. The Alumni Association set out to raise the $75,000 needed, the Class of 2010 leading the way with a $5000 contribution.

Years before the flag's rediscovery, the school had adopted Big Red as its Spirit Flag, but with one detail awry, as it learned in 2009. The Spirit Flag adopted in 1992 showed the crescent facing away from the flag, as it is depicted in the David Humphreys Miller mural that hangs in the library. The board promptly adopted the inward facing crescent design — in modern parlance, Big Red 2.0.

Big Red 2.0 made it into space within a month of its return to Charleston when astronaut and Marine Lieutenant Colonel Randy Bresnik, Class of 1989, carried it with him on an Apollo flight to the International Space Station (ISS). He arrived at The Citadel from California on a scholarship. He majored in mathematics, earning Gold Stars, and upon graduation was commissioned in the Marine Corps. He became a Topgun Marine aviator, test pilot and flight instructor, with combat duty in Iraq as part of Operation Iraqi Freedom. In 2004 he and 10 others were selected from among 4,000 candidates for NASA's Astronaut Class 9. Aboard STS-129 in 2009, he became the first Citadel graduate to fly in outer space, logging two spacewalks totaling 11 hours and 50 minutes. In addition to a replica of Big Red, Bresnik carried into space with him his Citadel gear — an alumni sticker, a ball cap and a t-shirt, all donated to the college. He reentered Earth's atmosphere with one more child than he left it with, as his wife Rebecca gave birth to their second child, a daughter, while he was aboard the ISS. At the news from Earth, he passed out bubble gum cigars to the crew. When he came back to Charleston over Corps Day in 2010, he told *Post and Courier* reporter Prentiss Findlay that he learned leadership at The Citadel.

Bresnik's space travel allowed him to see firsthand how far technology and aerodynamics have come. If he could experience time travel, he could look back to March 20, 1843 to see how far The Citadel has come. With one of our graduates now a veteran of space, it was time for the college to ascend to new heights here on earth. The vehicle for that trip became known as LEAD 2018.

Chapter 17

LEAD 2018

I n the life of a school that will soon celebrate turning 175, there are only a few days that, viewed through history's telescope, deserve the label "pivotal." One such was obviously March 20, 1843, the original Corps Day. Another came on January 20, 1882, the day J.D. Kennedy, Lieutenant Governor of South Carolina and president of the state Senate, broke a 15-15 tie in that body that resulted in the reopening of the college. Our history likely would have been quite different had General Summerall not yielded to the many entreaties he received to remain as president after the insult he suffered in Columbia, as discussed in Chapter 3. The day he chose to remain proved pivotal. And a strong case can be made for June 9, 2012, for that was the date the Board of Visitors adopted the strategic plan campaign christened LEAD, for Leadership, Excellence and Academic Distinction. Because LEAD promised a road map for the school stretching out six years from its adoption in 2012, it became known as LEAD 2018.

To appreciate the importance of LEAD 2018, it is critical to understand the circumstances under which it was adopted. For several years prior, Rosa and the board's Strategic Planning Committee, chaired by Lieutenant General Michael Steele, experimented with planning efforts dubbed Blueprint I and Blueprint II. Elements of those Blueprints would eventually become the goals of LEAD 2018. But both men came to realize the futility of formulating strategic plans without the funding necessary to implement them. It looked for a time like LEAD 2018's great potential would fall victim to exactly the kind of thing George Brakeley had identified in 1992 when he concluded what General Watts already knew: that an administration which lacked discretionary funds was handcuffed when it came to projects like LEAD 2018.

Adequate funding for strategic planning faced the additional hurdle of a bad economy. The previous chapter discussed the major recession that began in 2007, when unemployment doubled and home values dropped precipitously. The recession's impact on the college was profound. South

Carolina tax collections plummeted, which in turn led to deep declines in state funding to The Citadel and other state colleges and universities. Faced with a deteriorating financial situation, Rosa reduced costs to the extent he could, but "knew that absent some supplemental financial support, he would be forced to cut into the core of The Citadel's academic enterprise."[586]

To avoid that, Rosa challenged TCF's Board of Directors to become the financial partner the state of South Carolina had once been. In point of fact, 2011 marked the year when TCF's financial support of the college surpassed the state's support, a reality that continues to today.[587] According to Claudius E. Watts IV, "Bud," Class of 1983 and currently chairman of TCF Board of Directors, "He [Rosa] asked TCF to step up to two challenges: 1) provide a multi-million dollar supplemental grant that would serve as an investment in growth programs that would put the college on a better financial footing, and 2) commit to working more closely with the college to increase funds available to The Citadel in the future."[588]

TCF's Board agreed, "but it wanted to understand in detail how the supplemental grant would be invested, what the outcomes would be and how those outcomes would be measured." To get those answers, Rosa hired the Boston Consulting Group (BCG), well regarded in higher education circles, and TCF agreed to cover BCG's costs.[589]

BCG spent substantial time and resources studying every aspect of the college's financial structure. It delivered its report in 2010 at a joint meeting of the administration, the board, the TCF Board, officers of TCBF, and the executive director of the CAA. BCG's assessment was grim: lack of funding threatened the school's existence. After that sobering presentation and a general discussion, Rosa spoke last. His message remains vivid in the memories of Steele and Bud Watts. Both recall how forcefully he expressed the need for teamwork.[590] That directive from the top seemed to convince the group to make the changes needed for more and better cooperation.

The closer cooperation sought by both The Citadel and TCF mandated an update to the existing Memorandum of Understanding (MOU) between them. Ultimately, they negotiated a new one executed by Rosa, BOV Chairman Doug Snyder and TCF Board Chairman Steve Tobias. Under it, The Citadel's president set fundraising priorities and sat on TCF's Board. TCF raised funds for the college by planning and executing capital campaigns. TCF was obligated to consult with the school on those campaigns, but independently managed its own staff and resources, including its Academic Endowment. To assure maximum coordination among the college's administration and TCF, TCBF, and CAA, TCF's chief executive officer became

The Citadel's Vice President for Institutional Advancement, with salary and benefits paid by TCF. In short, according to Watts:

> There was in concept to be one fundraising team, whose priorities were to be established by The Citadel President, in accordance with the BOV's strategic plans and priorities. Negotiation of the MOU had at times been difficult and when it was executed, there remained some skepticism on both sides about its ultimate effectiveness. Nonetheless, the MOU provided structure that gave closer cooperation a chance to succeed.[591]

This closer cooperation proved essential to any strategic plan Rosa and Board of Visitors could envision. Elements of the Plan had been in the making for some time before it was adopted. During the 2009-2010 school year, Rosa held a series of "Town Hall" meetings to make sure staff and faculty were fully informed on both the fiscal and operational circumstances that budget constraints were producing on them and on the college.[592] By way of assuring his faculty that they were not being asked to work at less than their worth, he cited data released by the Commission on Higher Education which showed Citadel faculty paid at competitive levels.[593] The message was, "We're all in this together," and the way forward was also together.

To the element of faculty buy-in was added that of administrative buy-in. The Grinalds era Strategic Plan benefited from matching its objectives to specific administrators who would be expected to lead in seeing them accomplished. That same matching carried over into LEAD 2018.

When fully developed, LEAD 2018 would require $49 million. Rosa thought he could find $1 million a year for the six-year life of the Plan, leaving it $43 million short for full funding. Even with a new MOU in place with TCF and the commitment for increased cooperation, that was serious money. But TCF, inspired by the LEAD 2018 initiatives, was determined to raise it. It quietly launched the Foundation for Leadership Campaign with a goal of $160 million. When early fundraising efforts met with success, TCF raised the goal to $175 million, a nice coincidence with the 175th anniversary approaching. Funding for Rosa's plan was thereafter largely assured. By early fall 2017, Foundation for Leadership had raised north of $218 million, 136 percent of its original goal, and was on track to fully fund LEAD 2018. With fundraising in high gear, the college's total endowment (TCF, TCBF, and Trust) reached an all-time high of over $281 million for the year ending December 31, 2016, the most recent figures available. Importantly, fundraising efforts were now being coordinated to assure a consistent message to alumni and potential donors. Just as importantly, the college and TCF were working hand-in-glove. A relationship that was strained for decades was no longer frayed. Bud Watts gives the lion's share of credit for this improvement in the working relationship to Rosa, to Board Chairman Steele, and to Steele's successor as chairman, Lieutenant General John Sams, USAF (Ret.). They, in turn, would be the first to credit Bud Watts with extraordinary skill in aligning the interests of two entities who have every reason to work together. "Raising that money wouldn't have been possible without Bud Watts."[594]

If Watts has any regrets regarding LEAD 2018, they center on timing of the fundraising objectives within it. "Ideally," said Watts, "we (TCF), with our fundraising insight and expertise, would have been in on LEAD planning at the outset. Frankly, when the BOV and administration initiated the planning for LEAD, we really hadn't figured out how to work together yet. I'm not sure we even knew we were supposed to. Since then, we've all learned a lot and for the next capital campaign, we'll have a seat at the table from the start."[595]

In that next campaign, "Foundation for the Future," TCF plans to boost its fundraising capacity to $40 million annually. It envisions an endowment of $300 million by 2018 and to $400 million by 2025. To meet those ambitious goals, TCF is placing major emphasis on increasing the percentage of alumni contributing, working to increase legacy giving, and strengthening its partnership with TCBF to significantly increase the funds available for athletic scholarships. Watts notes, "Getting there requires continued investment in TCF's fundraising capabilities and close coordination with the administration. It will also require replacing our retiring fundraiser extraordinaire, General Rosa."

The impact of a successful capital campaign like Foundation for Leadership can be measured it what it buys and funds. Not only did it fuel LEAD 2018, but as of this writing it has directed over $15 million to the Krause Center, over $10 million to the construction of Bastin Hall, over $10 million to the Baker School of Business Administration, more than $7 million to the Zucker School of Education, $4 million to the Daniel Library and $3 million to the Citadel War Memorial, to cite but a few examples. And there is still much more to come, with fundraising to support construction of a replacement for aging Capers Hall a significant ongoing priority.[596]

LEAD's timing was in several ways unfortunate. The uproar over ReVille in 2011 followed the school into 2012, when he dominated local news coverage in a way that wouldn't be repeated until Dylann Roof committed mass murder in 2015. Media coverage invariably mentioned The Citadel, either as the source of ReVille's college education or as the site of some of his atrocities. To that negative black ink must be added the red ink that threatened the college in the wake of the 2008-2009 recession. By 2012, the economy showed signs of rebounding, but additional state funding of colleges did not increase. Middle class families, the school's prime source for applicants, struggled to pay mortgages while their sons and daughters contemplated escalating student loan debt. Deferred maintenance persisted.

But as Dickens penned in *A Tale of Two Cities*, the worst of times can also be the best of times. And 2012 turned into the year that saw critical components of the college come together in LEAD 2018. Arguably, the key ingredients had been there all along, but like random horses hadn't been put together to pull as one team. Coaches remember the games when their team "put it all together," when offense and defense and special teams all played in sync at the highest level. They won those games, and LEAD 2018 was that kind of team effort.

At the risk of carrying the sports metaphor one step too far, former QB Rosa had called the play one year before when he listed for the board the priorities he viewed as critical to the college's long-term success: (1) Synchronizing the college's efforts with the S.C. Legislature, TCF and the BOV to ensure a coordinated effort by all to move the college forward. That meant a unified effort in funding. (2) Ensuring that staff restructuring is effective and results in increased efficiency. That meant lean and talented administrators. (3) Revenue growth to offset deficits. Raising tuitions had ceased to be the answer, if it ever was, and creative revenue streams needed to be found and fostered. (4) The college's development efforts must become more coordinated and ultimately responsible for increased giving to help offset the loss of state funding and provide financial support of the college's goals.[597] The strength of LEAD 2018 was, in Steele's words, that it "described what was to be achieved, who was responsible, [identified] resource requirements and prioritized how resources were to be applied. [The] Plan became part of John's management program for running the college . . . hope, method, responsibility and resources."[598]

In December 2011, the administration synthesized input and recommendations from its various campus constituencies, 258 in all, to formulate LEAD 2018. Of those 258, the plan incorporated 65 recommendations.[599]

When approved, LEAD 2018 set eight initiatives:

1. Develop principled leaders in a globalized environment.
2. Enhance the learning environment.
3. Strengthen the college through institutional advancement.
4. Develop the student population.
5. Enhance the facilities and technological support for the campus.
6. Improve institutional effectiveness.
7. Ensure the college has the leadership and talent to accomplish these strategic initiatives.
8. Provide outreach to the region and serve as a resource in its economic development.

Each initiative contained descriptors of what success looked like. For example, for initiative #1 to be met, the school's leadership model, embodied to a great degree by the Krause Center, would have to be nationally recognized, and for each class 75 percent of the graduates would have to be on their career path within six months, whether that path was military commissioning, graduate school or a job in their chosen field. An enhanced learning environment, initiative #2, required the school to maintain a four-year 75 percent graduation rate and sustain its excellent recognition in *U.S. News and World Report* rankings. Initiative #3, institutional advancement, required the athletic department to become financially self-sustaining. Developing the student population, initiative #4, required meeting diversity challenges with enough scholarship help to make The Citadel the go-to alternative to the service academies. Facilities and technological support, #5, mandated investment like the $3 million the college spent on the Banner program, its enterprise information system. Initiative #6, enhance institutional effectiveness, meant putting in place a secure financial plan and developing external funding sources. To meet initiative #7, each school within the college would need to distinguish itself through exceptional faculty and staff, including endowed chairs. Initiative #8 was designed to meet the educational needs of South Carolina and the region, with the college and graduate college furnishing the workforce needed.

For each of these eight initiatives, LEAD 2018 specifies a subset of objectives, and each subset contains "actions" toward the initiative and "key performance indicators" to measure success. As one example initiative #2, enhance the learning environment, has as one "objective" the enhancement of student retention. That means we need to keep the students who matriculate and graduate them on time. To do that, certain "actions" must be taken, including early identification of students who are struggling with challenging courses and bringing to bear the resources of the Academic Support Center. It also requires expanding the CSI, Citadel Success Institute, which has been shown prepare incoming freshmen for their knob year. When those "actions" have been taken, the "key performance indicators" measure success toward the goal. In this example, success means serving an additional 2 percent of the undergraduate population in the Academic Support Center, enrolling 400 incoming freshmen in CSI by 2018, and graduating 75 percent of our classes in four years by 2018. This structure of "objectives," "actions," and "key performance indicators" is in place for each initiative. A total of 31 objectives are identified to reach the eight initiatives, with 45 performance metrics to measure effectiveness.[600]

An increasingly obvious key to LEAD 2018 was Rosa, its primary architect. To make sure the school had his services, it structured a new contract in 2010 that assured his employment for an additional five years.[601]

Another five-year contract negotiated about this time committed the Balfour Company to supply class rings. LEAD 2018 didn't specifically cite the need for a symbol of progress to be prominently displayed, but Balfour's 3,500-pound replica ring turned out to be just that. Placed at the corner of Summerall Field facing Lesesne Gate, the Balfour Ring has become among the most photographed sites on campus, with alumni, families and guests posing around its distinctive design and the striking landscape on which it rests. Each year the numerals in the bezel are changed out to honor the senior class and, at homecoming, to honor the class celebrating its 50th reunion. To those driving onto the campus, the effect is immediate and positive.[602]

Core values don't change, but they can be restated in a more concise expression, which is what the board did in June 2011. "Honor, Duty and Respect" reduced to three potent words what the school stood for. LEAD 2018 wasn't going to succeed unless it could be marketed to the college's various constituencies, and a short, clear statement of values was yet another unifying element.[603]

The year 2013 began with a crucial hire. John Paul (Jay) Dowd, III, became the CEO of The Citadel Foundation and The Citadel Vice President for Institutional Advancement. Chairman Snyder gives Dowd much of the credit for putting the college on solid financial footing. "He led us through a transformation that was critical," Snyder said:

> We had completed our $100 million capital campaign relying primarily on alumni. Our strategic plan, which we called LEAD 2018, wasn't going to be much more than a document unless we

had the funding to match our goals and vision, particularly with less money from the state every year. Jay and TCF stepped up to meet the challenge. The guy has that rare ability to match a donor's legacy interest with the significant financial needs of the college. Whether he's in a boardroom in New York or hunting in the backwoods of South Carolina, Jay closes the deal."[604]

Bud Watts was equally complimentary of Dowd, calling him an honorary alumnus for his dedication to the college and what it stands for.[605]

Another building block to financial stability and to the objectives of LEAD 2018 were the assets of The Citadel Trust, which sprang to life in 1991 as a component of the complicated calculus which finances the college.[606] Until the Trust was established, the school relied on (1) tuitions and fees from students; (2) the state of South Carolina's annual appropriation; (3) contributions solicited by the school itself; (4) annual grants from TCF, then known as the Citadel Development Foundation (CDF); and (5) endowments such as the Daniel Fund, administered by the college. TCF operates under a Board of Directors separate from the Board of Visitors and for decades its annual disbursements funded only academic enrichment programs and cadet scholarships, though in some cases such as the renovations to McAlister Field House, it would loan the college money to get over some financial hump. Policies established by TCF determined how much of its income would be paid to the college and when. Those most familiar with CDF prior to 1991 describe it as an organization intent on independence and as much below the radar operations as it could defend, in perpetual fear that its corpus might influence the State Legislature to reduced its annual appropriation even more drastically.

Expenditures by The Citadel Trust, by contrast, fell within the exclusive control of the Board of Visitors, which elected the Trust's initial directors in June 1991 and gave the Trust full authority to manage the endowment.[607] By the end of its first year in existence, the Trust reported almost $20 million in cash.[608] Its income, corpus or both could be used to meet critical needs of the school. Because Trust bylaws allowed expenditures "to carry out the purpose of The Citadel as determined by the Board of Visitors," many of its assets were free of the straightjacket restrictions of those held by CDF. Not all funds held by the Trust were free of restraints. For example, a major funding source early in the life of the Trust was the sale of the home in Aiken that had been purchased for General Summerall's retirement. Those monies, designated the Aiken Fund, were specifically restricted to purchases of real estate by the college. In fact, after serving for many years as The Citadel's sole external source of unrestricted funds, the Trust's assets today, around $90 million, are largely composed of endowed funds like Aiken, expenditures from which are legally regulated and restricted to specific purposes, most often scholarships.[609]

With a Memorandum of Understanding in place for the college and The Citadel Foundation, it was time to bring the Brigadier Foundation (TCBF) into the fold. That was done in 2013 with execution of a MOU between TCF and TCBF, and the results were impressive. Larry Leckonby, Director of Intercollegiate Athletics, reported to the board that TCBF's partnership with TCF was working well, with integrated record keeping making a difference. TCBF had the best year ever raising $2.4 million, bringing its athletic scholarship endowment to $10.4 million, up from $6.4 million five years before.[610] Bud Watts confirms that from TCF's standpoint, the relationship is a good one. "We bring scale," he said.

Working together, TCBF and the combined athletic fundraising program benefit from significant resources and capabilities that would be difficult to afford on a stand-alone basis. TCBF manages its own operating funds as well as the Memorial Fund (the athletic portion of the endowment), but when it comes to fundraising, our TCF athletic fundraisers work together seamlessly with TCBF to maximize effectiveness. The proof is in the significantly increased fundraising numbers."[611]

A vibrant athletic program was yet another element of LEAD 2018, and this partnership was and is an asset to Citadel sports.

A major component of LEAD 2018 centered around community outreach, getting cadets involved in the greater Charleston area. This initiative not only benefitted the city and its citizens in tangible ways, but it gave the cadets a chance to further polish the leadership skills they were learning in programs structured by the Krause Center. The success of those efforts was acknowledged when the New York Life Foundation named The Citadel as one of five recipients of the Washington Center 2013 Education Civic Engagement Award. Lieutenant General Michael Steele, newly elected board chairman, had high praise for General Rosa, his staff, and the Krause Center for such national recognition, singling out the Krause Center's Professor Conway Saylor as having made an especially significant contribution.[612]

Measuring progress against LEAD goals and objectives was important to both Rosa and Steele. At a two-day board retreat at the Santee Cooper Camp Wampee Conference Center in Pinopolis, Steele sought to refine board governance by making more efficient use of the Executive Committee and by consolidating the board's eleven committees down to five. College regulations prohibited an immediate committee restructuring, so for the academic year 2013-2014 the board inactivated all except the Customs and Regulations Committee, which was necessary to hear cadet disciplinary appeals. From November through April, the board would "test drive" the new committees before putting them formally in place. The new committees proposed were Strategy, Vision and Governance; Education and Leadership Development; Communications and Community Relations; Operations and Risk Management; and the Executive Committee.[613]

Restructured committees played a key role in the success of LEAD 2018. Under the old structure, committees corresponded to vice presidents and chief administrators within the college. Time consuming committee reports at board meetings often merely parroted what the committee had been told by its administration counterpart. Compounding the inefficiency, many board members had little or no expertise in the areas their committee was expected to oversee, leading to acceptance at face value of whatever the administration chose to report. Rather than an active formulator of policy, the committee became a receptor of information, without the dialogue or exchange of ideas that would have made it more effective. In Steele's view, the streamlined committee structure, adopted in 2014, "offered the advantages of more effective use of Time and Talent."

First, it saved valuable BOV time by eliminating 11 routine committee reports and using the time for in-depth discourse on significant issues facing the board and college. Secondly, consolidating the board's talent and expertise into five committees and assigning members to multiple committees provided experienced leadership to lead each committee and an opportunity for personal, professional growth of all board members.[614]

In much the same way that LEAD 2018's need for $43 million coincided with TCF's plan for its Foundation for Leadership capital campaign, the board's restructuring happily coincided with the need to fulfill LEAD 2018's objectives. In Steele's words:

> The board provided the context for LEAD 2018 by focusing attention on strategic lines of effort — The Citadel ethos, shaping external environments, communications, advancement, development, compliance and risk assessment/mitigation, and establishing teamwork for vision, strategy, policy and governance. These lines

of effort established the college's strategic direction and provided the board and administration with the context for LEAD 2018 plan development and execution.[615]

The result was a relentless focus by the board, Rosa and the administration on the objectives of LEAD 2018. Without that focus and TCF's fundraising efforts, the plan would not have succeeded as it has and will when completed in 2018.[616]

Several chapters back, the importance of assessment was discussed in the context of measuring results. As the school strived toward the goals set by LEAD 2018, assessment became a watchword for nearly all administrative decisions. "Metrics" were studied and applied, particularly Citadel metrics when measured against peer organizations. As preparations continued for the critical SACS reaccreditation in March 2014, metrics became a focus. In his presentation to the board in October 2013, Lieutenant General John Sams reviewed the metrics used by *U.S. News and World Report*, telling his fellow board members that its ranking methodologies were superior to other rankings because of the focus on academic quality and success rather than campus amenities and student opinions. Five metrics topped his list: enrollment management, academic distinction, student learning, career placement and principled leadership growth.[617] The college actively worked to make progress in all five.

In 2015 TCF launched the public phase of its Foundation for Leadership campaign to support LEAD 2018. The effort was exceptionally successful. As a result of these coordinated efforts, historical annual fundraising increased nearly threefold, approximately 290 percent from 2011 to 2016.

LEAD 2018 is and always has been, as the name implies, a six-year road map. Its full impact won't be felt or measured until 2018 and beyond. But enough is known as this is written to pronounce it a transformative success. In the next chapter, The Citadel of today and tomorrow will harvest the fruits of this visionary program.

Chapter 18

THE CITADEL TODAY,
AND TOMORROW

I n 2014, The Citadel underwent its decennial SACS reaccreditation. These had been the source of institutional angst since 1924, when they began. Losing accreditation, a death penalty of sorts for a college, is fairly rare. Only 18 schools have lost it since 2000 according to the *Wall Street Journal*, and those had average graduation rates of 35 percent.[618] The SACS committee reviews self-assessment materials prepared by the college, conducts on-site inspections, asks for additional information and supporting documentation, and writes its report. That report lists shortcomings and makes recommendations, a bit like an in-law walking into your house, finding soiled carpet, and suggesting you get a more powerful vacuum. The college is asked to respond to the committee's concerns, and once the replies are exchanged and evaluated, the accreditation is renewed for another 10 years. A Citadel accreditation report, and General Grimsley's responses, appeared in Chapter 9. College administrators at schools like The Citadel don't worry so much about becoming unaccredited as they do about outsiders producing a laundry list of shortcomings that document weaknesses for which the administration is at least partly if not wholly responsible.

As rare as it is for a school to lose accreditation, it is rarer still to come through a recertification with zero recommendations for improvement, yet that was exactly The Citadel's experience in 2014. President Rosa was effusive in reporting the results. Tara E. McNealy, Associate Provost for Planning, Assessment and Evaluation, and her team were singled out for special praise. Formal and official notice of the results were to be announced in December at the SACS annual meeting.[619] Whoever is chosen as Rosa's successor will know that when 2024 rolls around, the accreditation bar has been set as high as it can go.

Notwithstanding the excellent SACS report, there was room for improvement, as a presentation by the commandant, Colonel Mercado, made evident. It is an interesting snapshot of the Corps in 2012 from the commandant's unique perspective:

• Alcohol use and abuse continues to be a challenge. Fourth Class infractions made up 38 percent of the incidents as compared to 8 percent for seniors. Infractions for minors were up 27 percent and on-campus use was up 24 percent.

• In regards to suspensions, dismissals and expulsions, if the board were to hear all cases there would have been a 68 percent increase in BOV hearings. In reviewing the five-year trend line, the BOV would have averaged 32 cases per year.

• Fourth Class Retention has improved to 85.69 percent; however, the Commandant will review Third Battalion, which leads the Corps in attrition to determine what the problems are.

• Five-year trend line for Fourth Class Retention shows gradual improvement.

• Random drug testing program has increased from 119 cadets tested in 2007-2008 to 650 in 2011-2012, which reflects a more aggressive approach.

• As to be expected, positive drug test results rose 17.4 percent attributed to increased number of cadets tested.

• Sexual harassment and sexual assault incidents are down this year, but the five-year trend is up due to two cadets in five separate incidents involving seven different victims.

• Nine percent of the Corps utilized the Counseling Center primarily for drug and alcohol, anxiety and depression situations.

• Unexcused class absences dropped this year due to increased due diligence by cadet academic officers.

Mercado then gave an assessment of the Corps from 2009 to 2012, insisting that 85 percent of the cadets were committed to achieving success and that his challenge was to motivate the remaining 15 percent to embrace what he called "The Citadel way."[620]

At the same meeting at which LEAD 2018 was approved, the board endorsed the concept for The Citadel War Memorial (CWM) to be constructed on campus.[621] Over 700 alumni have made the ultimate sacrifice, yet recognizing them has always had a haphazard quality about it. Plaques in Bond Hall and on the Summerall Chapel list some, with others sprinkled around the campus. Appropriate homage to alumni who have given all in service to the country would seem to be a awarded at a school like ours, where up to 35 percent of a given class might be commissioned in the Armed Forces upon graduation.

The Class of 1967 conceived the War Memorial project as its legacy gift to the school and funded for $1 million. With support from President Rosa and the board's Facilities and Engineering Committee, the college's resident architect, John Gardner, was entrusted with the design and project supervision. By agreement, approval from Rosa and the board would be required for the names appearing on the wall.

Evaluating the criteria for names on the wall fell to a committee overseen by the college's Senior Vice President for Operations and Administration, Colonel Thomas G. Philipkoski, USAF (Ret.), Class of 1982. His committee, composed of representatives of the alumni community, the administration, and TCF, tackled some thorny issues in a highly sensitive deliberation as to names entitled to appear on the walls. The committee opted for a policy of inclusion, recommending to the board that for this particular purpose an alumnus be defined as "A person who has graduated from The Citadel or has attended The Citadel provided that he or she left in good standing."

Colonel Harvey Dick died in 2012. A generation of cadets remember him as a gruff and thoroughly likeable human being who loved The Citadel and its Corps. Colonel Joe Trez recalls bugging his longtime friend to participate in The Citadel Oral History Project. "He wouldn't do it," Trez said, shaking his head in regret. "All those great Citadel stories were buried with Harvey at Magnolia Cemetery." Trez made sure he didn't make the same mistake, and has recorded hours of his recollections and insights for the Project.

As the Class of 2016 began its studies, a report General Rosa made to the board showed that the long shadow cast by ReVille remained. Early in 2012, Rosa had convened an Institutional Program Assessment Committee (IPAC), chaired by former University of South Carolina President, Dr. John M. Palms, Class of 1958. The report produced by the IPAC committed to the printed page a thought that had surely occurred to most within the Citadel family since the revelations about ReVille came to light:

> It would be difficult to overstate the degree to which The Citadel community was rocked by the arrest of our graduate, Skip ReVille, in the fall of 2011. As chair of the Honor Committee and cadet recipient of the Algernon Sidney Sullivan award, ReVille had seemed to epitomize our core values. The profound disconnect between who ReVille really was and who he had seemed to be caused many on campus to question whether there might be other instances in which our institution's realities are at odds with our ideals and values.

The short answer was yes, there were other instances, as the IPAC discovered and explored. In its 24-page Final Report, shortcomings were identified and solutions recommended. To condense the IPAC's work into a series of bullet points would not do justice to the thoroughness with which the committee appeared to approach its work, but the executive summary furnished here may suffice to provide a snapshot of the college's perceived weakest areas in the wake of the ReVille disgraces.

ReVille's perverse influence clearly drove the examination of protecting minors who came onto the campus. To enhance their safety, the panel concluded that employees, campus residents, students and volunteers should receive Darkness to Light Stewards of Children training, and these individuals should also be required to have SLED background checks. Darkness to Light is an international organization that seeks to protect children from sexual abuse by placing responsibility squarely on adult shoulders.

This history contains several references to institutional self-study, a term associated with SACS accreditation reviews and a part and parcel of the SACS protocols. IPAC also conducted a self-study, but on a far deeper, more personal introspection than those required for SACS. If a SACS self-study could be said to examine the institutional body, the IPAC examined its soul. It did so through six focus groups assembled in January 2012. Four of the focus groups were comprised of cadets (from all classes) and human resources personnel. TAC officers made up the fifth group and coaches and athletic administrators the sixth. Areas of focus came from two primary sources: (1) a list of topics developed by CEIT, the Citadel Experience Integration Team, based on cadet experience; and (2) an online survey of Citadel faculty and staff, with a 33 percent response rate from the 946 surveyed.

The major takeaways from the IPAC contain some surprises, plus a few that might have been greeted by veterans of the college with a rhetorical, "So what else is new?" These veterans would no doubt nod their agreement with the aphorism quoted in the IPAC report: "Culture eats strategy for breakfast."

High on the list of recommended changes to the honor system was a call for new Standard Operating Procedures (SOPs). Those would augment the efforts of the Faculty Advisor to the Honor Court (FAHC) with the addition of two Advisors for Investigations, one for prosecutions and an the other for defendants. This change was seen as a way both to relieve the FAHC of an increasing workload and to avoid any conflict of interest, or the appearance thereof, in the FAHC counseling both sides of an investigation and prosecution. A term limit of five years was recommended for the FAHC. Additionally, the current SOP by which the executive assistant to the president authorized investigations of a charge would be changed to place that responsibility on the deputy director of the Krause Center. The final decision to take a case to trial would remain with the FAHC after consultation with the Honor Court president, the two advisors for procecutions and for defendants.

A survey of the Corps of Cadets in 1996, taken immediately after the admission of women, might have shown as much as 90 percent of the Corps against it. Whatever the actual percentage, it would have been higher among the alumni. It was common knowledge that a large percentage of the pre-1996 Citadel family opposed coeducation, as years of bitter and expensive litigation confirmed. Viewed in that light, the 45 percent of the Corps who, when polled in a 2011 survey, believed that women do not belong in the Corps can be seen as progress — inadequate, too slow, but progress. IPAC sought to accelerate female integration by identifying factors contributing to the unacceptable rate and pace of assimilation: "only one of fourteen Greater Issues speakers in the past five years has been a woman"; only two TACS were female; the heads of all ROTC departments were males; there was a shortage of women among faculty and senior staff as well as within the cadet leadership and the Honor Court.

Closely related to progress on female assimilation was the issue of sexual harassment, "tied to a lingering resistance to having women in the Corps of Cadets." Taken together, hostility to women and harassment of them put at risk one of the college's core values: respect.

The IPAC examined diversity, where efforts to raise the female population of the Corps above 6.5 percent and the African-American population above 8.4 percent had failed. The IPAC attributed this to the school's consistent pursuit of unsuccessful policies and procedures. Acknowledging the problems, the committee came up short on specific suggestions, recommending new plans without defining those plans.

Easier to address, because more capable of correction, were issues related to security. Locks had been installed in cadet rooms, but doors remained unlocked. "Culture eats strategy for breakfast." Unlocked rooms permitted unauthorized access to M-14s, issued to all cadets without firing pins and selector switches. These, the committee learned, could be obtained from a gunsmith or gun show and the weapon made "fully mission capable" for about $100. The committee may have had Berra Byrd in mind when it addressed personal weapons brought onto campus, which was legal as long as the weapon was checked with Public Safety and stored in the college armory. It recommended improvement in security for both personal firearms and those issued for drills and ceremonies.

The IPAC study of alcohol abuse and illicit drug usage documented both the prevalence of binge drinking and the effectiveness of The Citadel's random drug testing. Survey results showed cadets drank more than their peers but used significantly less marijuana, with almost 46 percent of past drug users acknowledging that the random testing program deterred them from current usage. In an instructive footnote, the Final Report disclosed one barracks OC's field alcohol test: a cadet who arrived from leave able to walk and recite his or her name was allowed to proceed to their room, otherwise to the hospital.

The study concluded with 14 recommendations grouped around the core values of honor, duty and respect. Of those 14, ten can be said to recommend a new plan or revision of a failing plan or program. Four specific recommendations were (1) establish a fully staffed office to provide a more robust alcohol and substance abuse program for the college; (2) implement mandatory background checks and training programs for employees, students, and volunteers involved with youth programs; (3) improve weapons security on campus; and (4) enhance communications and the decision-making processes within the institution.[622]

The Fourth Class System was to be studied yet again by IPAC. The review of that committee is summarized here for the sake of continuity and as additional evidence that "the more things change the more they stay the same," at least where the Fourth Class System is concerned. The focus group studying the subject for IPAC concluded that "The Citadel's disciplinary system is broken." If that sounds familiar, it's because essentially the same assessment had precipitated the studies by Whitmire in 1968, Mood in 1980 and Lane in 1992. Before taking office in 1997, General Grinalds said as much when he talked about the three Fourth Class Systems operating simultaneously.

To its credit, IPAC declined to focus its primary attention on the usual suspects of sleep deprivation, undernourishment and violation of ESP's study time. Instead, it condemned the "350 pages of regulations," pronouncing them "far more elaborate than those of other military institutions such as VMI, Norwich and West Point. Testimony to the Panel indicates that 'very few (if any) people try to read, much less understand and follow, the intimidating volume of written rules.'" Because of this complexity and the need to document in writing nearly everything, punishment orders took two weeks to be administered and countless man hours to process.[623]

To press home IPAC's findings, six members of the Board of Visitors and the president of the Alumni Association signed a letter to their fellow board members urging "bold steps" to "change the approach and philosophy used for discipline at The Citadel." Missing were the names of the board's current chairman and the two members who would succeed him as chairmen.[624]

Following up on an IPAC recommendation to enhance the protection of minors from people like ReVille, The Citadel became the first college in the country to require Darkness to Light training for all staff, faculty and students. At the board's October meeting, Lieutenant Colonel Stephanie Hewitt of the School of Education administered the board's training on the program.[625]

The year 2013 saw the blossoming of the new Mechanical Engineering program. In October, the state Commission on Higher Education approved a Bachelor of Science in Mechanical Engineering. Three months later, faculty was hired and the facilities renovated to accommodate the new program. In a mere three years, Mechanical Engineering became the second most popular major at the college among entering freshmen, with 131 enrolled in the program in 2017. Only Business Administration, with 143, surpassed it.[626]

Discussion continued on the need for a parking garage, but location and funding remained problematic. Prospects dimmed in February 2014 when the board took a stance against increasing the school's debt by resolving to build any new facility with private funds or state-appropriated funds.[627] As neither was available for a parking garage, the project was back-burnered.

Early in 2014, the board toured Capers Hall for a firsthand look at what was arguably the most long-suffering building on campus. Proposals to repair, renovate and/or replace it had dotted board agendas for years. Funding never seemed to materialize, or some crisis erupted to require Capers grease to silence some other squeaky wheel. Professor Winfred "Bo" Moore, Dean of the School of Humanities and Social Sciences, gave board members a solid reason for addressing his rundown facility, pointing out that his departments taught 56 percent of the college's core curriculum and accounted for 42 percent of total credit hours. For half of the Corps of Cadets to spend their academic hours in a structure so in need of attention was unacceptable, making the case for kicking the Capers can down the road no longer. The tour of the building he conducted the board on "graphically pointed out the need for new construction to replace the current facility."

Older grads and jocks would be jarred out of their recliners by a program instituted by Commandant Mercado. The Corps Physical Fitness Test (CPFT) set a new standard by requiring every senior to pass it in order to participate in graduation exercises. Tied to it was a Physical Effectiveness Program for Cadet-Athletes, set for implementation in the fall of 2014. Corpswide physical fitness fit into the "one corps" concept touted by the school and the administration.[628]

Preparations for the 2014-2015 academic year included a visit from the South Carolina Superintendent of Education, Brigadier General Mick Zais, a former president of Newberry College. The board assembled at Camp Wampee for a planning retreat, as it had done the previous year. Zais' message contained some inconvenient truths, to borrow the Al Gore phrase. One of those was South Carolina's lamentable support for higher education — last in the nation, and this from a man whose department had turned down $50 million Race to the Top funds and another $144 million from the federal government for a teacher program. The cost of higher education continued to be a major concern, with college tuition up 350 percent during a period when family incomes rose 5 percent. College degrees were not just more expensive to obtain but in less demand, as 32 percent of the state's adults had them when only 17 percent of the jobs in South Carolina required them. He pronounced the long-term future of higher education in the state "grim," particularly for smaller colleges. On these upbeat notes, the board continued to plan, with Chairman Steele stressing the need to examine alternative educational models beyond 2018.[629]

General Rosa's recap of the academic year just concluded was as positive as the Zais report had been negative, though Zais had praised the school for steps taken to prevent sexual assault and protect children. Rosa cited as significant successes the SACS review. Steady progress in IPAC goals encouraged him as well. A still-developing financial model promised improved budgeting, assessment and predictability. His focus going forward would be the next capital campaign, a search for a new Provost, strategic marketing and communications (to include capitalizing on the upcoming 175th anniversary of the founding), and refining the business model for the college in light of the trends Zais and others had identified.[630]

At Homecoming 2014, the Citadel family learned that one of its illustrious alums, Mayor Joe Riley, would be returning to campus as the first occupant of the Joseph P. Riley, Jr. Endowed Chair of American Government and Public Policy. In addition to his teaching duties, Riley intended to produce his memoir, written by Brian Hicks and published in 2015 as *The Mayor*. He also promised to participate in the school's Oral History Project. In announcing his pleasure at being back at his alma mater, Riley told those gathered for the announcement that "The three major blocks in the early foundation of my personal and professional life were my family, my church and my education and training at The Citadel."[631]

Four days after Riley's announcement, billionaire philanthropist Anita

Zucker committed her family to a gift of $4 million to the School of Education. As of this writing, she is the CEO and chairwoman of InterTech Group, a Charleston based conglomerate founded by her late husband, Jerry Zucker, in 1982. Her reputation is one of passionate support for education and healthcare. Her attachment to The Citadel began in 1978 when she took classes there for two years, and was further cemented when her son, Jonathan Zucker, earned his MBA there. She credits her parents for her charitable instincts. The Holocaust interrupted their educations, but they put three daughters through college. Fundamental to her giving is one of Judaism's basic concepts, tikkun olam, Hebrew for "repair of the world." In funding the Zucker Family School of Education, the first school at The Citadel named after a major donor, she enabled it to "put on steroids efforts we have had in the past," said Dean Larry Daniel. Among other benefits, the gift enabled the school to establish an endowed chair for a national scholar in educational entrepreneurship and the Anita Zucker Institute for Entrepreneurial Education, which focuses on the local workforce so critical to the Lowcountry.[632]

The SACS experience became official in December 2014, confirmed by Provost Hines in a report to the board in January. Not only had the SACS Trustees approved full reaccreditation with no recommendations, but they had asked to use the college's Quality Enhancement Program (QEP) as a model for other schools in the accreditation process. Also receiving full accreditation with zero deficiencies noted were the computer science programs and the Civil and Electrical Engineering Schools from ABET (Accreditation Board for Engineering and Technology). As proof that LEAD 2018 was having its intended effect, Hines cited national recognition gained from an award from Carnegie, the 2015 Community Engagement Classification, as well as being named to the President of the United States Higher Education Community Service Honor Roll in the categories of Educational Community Service and General Community Service.[633]

Having already approved the transfer of various campus war memorials to the one to be built in 2017 beside the chapel, the board turned its attention to naming criteria for the new Citadel War Memorial.[634] It would list alumni, but who exactly is an alumnus? The board followed the War Memorial Committee's recommendation to define an alumnus as, a person who has graduated from The Citadel or has attended The Citadel provided that he or she left in good standing. Thus, any man or woman who matriculated, even those leaving after a week or a day, might be included.

Any Citadel alumnus who, while serving under competent authority in any capacity with one of the U.S. Armed Forces, or with the Armed Forces of their native or adopted state during the period 1861-1865, or with the Armed Forces of their native or adopted country, has been killed, or who has died or may die of wounds received under any of the following circumstances will be recognized:

> In action against an enemy of the United States.
>
> In action with an opposing armed force of a foreign country in which the U.S. Armed Forces are or have been engaged.
>
> While serving with friendly foreign forces engaged in an armed conflict against an opposing armed force in which the United States is not a belligerent party.
>
> As the result of an act of any such enemy or opposing armed forces.
>
> As the result of an act of any hostile foreign force.
>
> As the result of an international terrorist attack against the United States or a foreign nation friendly to the United States.
>
> As the result of military operations while serving outside the territory of the United States as part of a peacekeeping force.
>
> As the result of action by friendly weapons fire while directly engaged in armed conflict, other than as the result of an act of an enemy of the United States, unless as a result of willful misconduct of the individual.
>
> As the result of being held as a prisoner of war (or while being taken captive).
>
> As the result of illness or accident while deployed in support of operations where the above criteria might apply.[635]

The broad definition of an alumnus recommended by the War Memorial Committee and adopted by the board made eligible for inclusion anyone who matriculated, including the many who left voluntarily early in their knob year, provided he or she met one of the 10 service criteria formulated by the committee. While most alumni fell neatly into one of those, some did not, requiring the committee to debate and decide. There were, for example, alumni in combat theaters who died of natural causes, and Vietnam veterans who died (and are still dying) from exposure to Agent Orange decades before. Decisions as to who was or was not entitled to be named on the walls prompted extensive debates within the War Memorial Committee, which viewed as a sacred trust the fair and consistent application of the naming criteria.

The War Memorial plans set a time frame of five years for design and construction. It officially opened to the public at Homecoming 2017, the 50th reunion of the Class of 1967. At a dedication ceremony on October 27, 2017, Commandant Geno Paluso addressed a large crowd. The Citadel Chamber Choir sang the National Anthem and "Mansions of the Lord." To close the ceremony and open the gates of the memorial, Citadel graduate Mitchell Lee Wetherington, Class of 2010, sang "Long Gray Line," a song he composed several years earlier but which fit the occasion perfectly.

The nature of the memorial presented a golden opportunity for others to honor the school's many war heroes, and they did. Founding members contributed $500,000, and any class or organization wishing to qualify as a sponsor gave $100,000. The support given to this project is an acknowledgement by The Citadel family of the debt owed to patriots with whom we went to class, walked tours, shared a beer at Folly Beach or carpooled home for holidays.[636]

In July 2015, Dr. Connie Ledoux Book joined the administration as the new Provost and Dean of the college, the most senior position held by a female in the school's history. Her contributions in two years on the job made it obvious The Citadel was fortunate to have her. On March 1, 2018, she will assume the presidency of Elon University.[637] Showing that the board also felt fortunate to have General Rosa, it voted him a performance bonus of 30 percent of his annual salary for fiscal year 2014-2015.

Two members of the South Carolina General Assembly, Representatives James Merrill and Leon Stavrinakis, told the board in June that they foresaw a board of regents in the state's educational future. They stressed the need for the state's colleges and universities to structure their curriculums to prepare their students to meet the needs of the state's employers, something The Citadel has been focused on for some time. At the same session, a budget for FY 2016 was approved for $116.98 million. Two new acronyms entered the school's lexicon, CAS and SMART. CAS, Cadet Accountability System, had been the subject of a special request to the South Carolina Legislature, which funded it. It allows the administration to track cadet activities and maintain current information. CAS was implemented in the fall of 2015. SMART is an algorithm that identifies applicants who are more likely to matriculate, allowing the college to focus more resources on them and fewer on those likely to go elsewhere.[638]

The Citadel recorded a record number of graduates in 2015. They included 490 cadets, 21 veteran cadets, 6 active duty day students, 21 veteran students, and 344 from the Citadel Graduate College, for a total of 882. Over 30 percent of graduating cadets took Armed Forces commissions.

The city into which many of those graduates dispersed, enjoyed a renaissance few if any in the United States could match. For the third year in a row, readers of *Travel + Leisure Magazine* voted it the No. 1 city in the United States and Canada. It had a lock on ratings for People/Friendliness and Tourism, and was well on its way to one in hotels and restaurants. Graduates from the 1960s and 1970s hardly recognized major portions of it.

But for all the international accolades Charleston received as Ground Zero for Southern Hospitality, it took a body blow on June 19, 2015, when a young white supremacist, Dylann Roof, murdered nine African-Americans at Emanuel AME Church on Calhoun Street. The way the city came together in grief and forgiveness drew international recognition and praise. The Corps of Cadets had left for the summer when President Obama came to eulogize the dead and to lead the church's mourners in "Amazing Grace". In response, Governor Haley seized the moment to pressure the Legislature to remove the Confederate flag from the grounds of the capitol, a move long sought by civil rights organizations. The Citadel addressed its own flag issue. Since 1939, a Confederate Naval Jack had hung among the flags in Summerall Chapel. At a special meeting called for the purpose on June 23, 2015, the board and the administration went on record as favoring the relocation of the flag to an appropriate place on campus.[639]

As the academic year 2015-2016 got underway, the administration forecast state funding to be about 9 percent, a new low. Other than constant concerns over funding, there was substantial cause for optimism. The Regimental Commander set a goal for the Corps to perform 16,000 hours of community service, achieve a GPA above 2.0, and see zero failures of the Citadel Physical Fitness test.[640]

In September, the school rolled out the red carpet for ... a sword. The sword belonging to Col. Charles Courtenay Tew, CSA, the Citadel's first honor graduate in its first graduating class, 1846, came home. The sword had long been sought by Tew's family and was found in Canada. Following his graduation from The Citadel, Tew taught at the Arsenal in Columbia. When he left to found the Hillsborough Military Academy in North Carolina, his students gifted him the sword, which bears a faceplate, "The Cadets of the Arsenal Academy to Capt. C.C. Tew, November 25th, 1858." Tragically, Tew was killed on the Sunken Road in the bloody Battle of Sharpsburg in 1863. The sword's precise path from Sharpsburg to Canada is unknown. A delegation from the college journeyed to the battlefield in Maryland to retrieve it and to reunite it with other Tew memorabilia the school holds, including

Tew's Citadel diploma, his silver cup given to him by Hillsborough cadets, and some personal correspondence. Head Librarian David Goble counts the sword among the school's most significant artifacts.[641]

Later that fall it was announced that the Faculty Council, which had operated for decades, would be replaced by a Faculty Senate. Combining the Faculty Council, the Graduate Council and the Academic Board into a Senate allowed the faculty to speak with a unified voice on matters of common interest. It controls tenure and promotion, the curriculum including core curriculum and evaluations of academic programs. Senators are both elected and appointed, giving voice to both the administration and those most affected by it.[642] Major Joelle Neulander, a professor of history, was elected as its first president.[643]

The school received approval to establish a nursing program, yet another example of how it was moving to match education and training to jobs and careers in demand in South Carolina and beyond. By committing the $1.7 million required to start the program, The Citadel became the first college in the Lowcountry to offer a B.S. in Nursing.

Board member Colonel Allison Dean Love, one of the two females brought onto the board after the admission of women, was elected vice-chair of the important state Commission on Higher Education. It helps any college in the state to have a well-placed and articulate voice on that governmental body.[644]

Lightning struck again at Williams-Brice Stadium in Columbia on November 21, 2015, when the Bulldogs beat the Gamecocks 23-22. The win pushed the Dogs to an 8-3 record and earned them a berth in the FCS postseason tournament. As with the 1990 upset, the finish was dramatic, as USC appeared to have scored on a 94-yard pass play with 39 seconds remaining in the game. A penalty for illegal procedure brought it back. We all need a bit of luck from time to time, but The Citadel deserved the win. They rolled up 350 yards on the ground, with touchdown runs of 56 and 59 yards by Tyler Renew and Cam Jackson. The defense rose up when it had to by stopping USC on fourth down with seconds remaining. That defense included a tackle named Mitchell Jeter, the Southern Conference defensive player of the year in 2015. USC's streak of 22 straight wins at home against nonconference opponents came to a sudden halt. Those are the games that bring players back for reunions, but Jeter will be with them in spirit and memory only when they gather. Mitchell Jeter lost his life in a 2017 car accident.[645]

The year 2015 closed with a bizarre incident in the barracks that, at first blush, seemed to summon the ghosts of Kevin Nesmith's tormentors in 1986. Posted on social media — a term that had no meaning in 1986 —

were photos showing hooded freshmen cadets, prompting the immediate conclusion in some quarters that the KKK was in the barracks. Coming as it did six months after the Mother Emanuel massacre, nerves remained raw. An investigation prompted the question, "What were they thinking?", but also confirmed that the cadets, who were singing Christmas Carols at the time, meant no racial insult. The administration reacted quickly and firmly. Provost Book sent a letter to all accepted applicants to stress that the incident did not reflect Citadel values. The commandant and the president addressed the Corps, reminding them that poor judgement can yield some bad press. The school suspended two cadets and handed down tours and confinements for the other 12 involved, some of whom failed to stop what they knew or should have known was a decidedly bad idea. African-American community leaders initially called for Rosa's resignation, then relented in view of the steps he took to punish those involved and to form a task force for the advancement of diversity and inclusion. The *Post and Courier* praised Rosa's handling of the matter in an editorial entitled "Citadel steps up with honor."[646]

Some statistics provided to the board in January 2016 served as empirical proof that the school was doing some things right. Provost Book, comparing graduation rates, found that African-Americans matriculating at The Citadel stood an 18.2 percent better chance of graduating than those enrolling at USC and a 16.1 percent better chance than those entering Clemson.

For several years the museum and archives had been a victim of benign neglect. Not only was there no separate repository for General Clark's papers and memorabilia, as the board had committed decades earlier to provide, but the museum was, in the words of board chairman Sams, "just a room full of boxes." When long-serving archivist Jane Yates retired in 2011, she was not replaced until late in 2016. David Goble, mindful of the board's vote the previous June favoring relocation of the Confederate Naval Jack then hanging in Summerall Chapel, was understandably concerned that there was no museum to which it could be moved. Goble set up a committee to examine the problem. He also managed, with more dedication than resources, to reopen the museum in the summer of 2016. Located on the third floor of Daniel Library, the museum displays only a fraction of its holdings but still captures vital images and artifacts from the college's history.[647]

The board's desire to relocate the flag received the endorsement of the Charleston City Council in early March. The stumbling block was, and remains as this history is written, South Carolina's Heritage Act, which prohibits relocation of the flag or any artifact of or monument to the Confederacy to be moved without consent of the State Legislature. The controversy continues to swirl. Some Citadel alumni, including some former athletes, organized a "Take it Down Movement." Two Charleston legislators, State Senator Marlon Kimpson and Representative Seth Whipper, introduced bills to enable the college to legally do what it had gone on record as wanting to do, but as of this writing that legislation has not been acted upon.[648]

More controversy was about to arrive, but before the board took up the issue of whether an applicant could wear a hijab as a member of the Corps of Cadets, it took time to acknowledge Professor David Preston, winner of the prestigious Guggenheim-Lehrman prize for military history for his book *Braddock's Defeat — The Battle of the Monongahela and the Road to Revolution*. It also recognized Cadet James McManus, awarded a Fulbright to study in Norway.[649]

But back to the hijab. Sana Hamze of Fort Lauderdale, Florida, a 17-year-old Muslim woman, was accepted with those scheduled to report in August 2016. She requested an exemption to the dress code to enable her to wear a hijab, the traditional head covering for Muslim women. For a school that battled Shannon Faulkner in court over her haircut, the response was predictable: no. Hamze and her family reported being "heartbroken" and considered litigation before deciding she would matriculate at Norwich Academy in Vermont.[650]

More recognition came from *Forbes* magazine when it ranked The Citadel as the Best Value College in South Carolina. The Department of Mechanical Engineering was up and running and the new nursing program officially became named for the family providing the major support: The Swain Nursing Program. The diversity task force that grew out of the Christmas Caroling, hooded cadets incident had been formed in February, and Commandant Paluso expected the board to get its report in June.

Graduation exercises in 2016 would not include 24 seniors who failed the physical fitness test. One female who passed the test and therefore graduated was on her way to becoming a him. Keisha Pendery, a female knob, graduated as Kenton Pendery, a transgendered male. Critics of The Citadel, and there are some, accuse the school of a 19th century mindset. Pendery was yet another reminder that the college is no island, insulated from 21st century challenges. Keisha Pendery, adopted from South Korea as an infant, grew up as a tomboy in her small hometown in Michigan. She never outgrew her male tendencies, nor her attraction to girls. In her sophomore year at The Citadel, she came out as a lesbian. As she aged, she began thinking more about gender definition than sexual definition, which led to the decision to transgender. Over spring break of her senior year, she began hormone treatments. Kenton

Pendery still roomed with his female roommate, and by the time he did his student teaching at Wando High School, none of his students knew him as other than male. Of his experience at The Citadel, he said, "This school is a lot more accepting than people think. Cadets get a bad rap. They've been so much more accepting than I would have thought."[651]

The City of Charleston outdid itself in 2016. Not only was it recognized as the best city in the United States and Canada for the fourth consecutive year, but *Travel + Leisure* readers voted it best city in the world. The magazine crowned the Spectator Hotel, envisioned by Citadel alumnus Jay Keenan, Class of 1967, as the No. 1 best city hotel in the United States and the No. 2 best hotel in the world.

As recited in the chapter on LEAD 2018, we have entered the age of metrics, when everything is measured and assessed. That practice accounts for much of the progress the college has made under LEAD. A few of the more significant metrics merit mention. According to Colonel Weinstein of the Biology Department, the acceptance rate for Citadel students at medical schools is twice the national average.[652] Median annual income for Citadel graduates at age 34 is currently $62,800, ranking it 9th among 369 selective public colleges. Students who enter the school from the bottom fifth of the economic strata have a 45 percent chance of moving into the top fifth as adults, ranking us 15th out of those 369 colleges.[653] These are statistics that matter.

By August, the faculty apartments along Hagood Avenue had been demolished to make way for the new business school, Bastin Hall. Rick Bastin, Class of 1965, and his wife, Mary Lee, donated $6 million to make it happen. Rick earned an MBA at Emory, served in the Army, and eventually took over the family Mercedes-Benz dealership in Palm Beach, Florida. He attributes his business success to "the discipline I acquired at The Citadel." Construction will begin in 2018.[654]

With their time-honored passage through Lesesne Gate, 819 cadets reported in the Class of 2020 including 80 women, the largest female knob class to date. In comparing the entering class with freshmen from other colleges nationally, President Rosa reported that we lead in every category but two: critical thinking and civility and respect. Provost Book offered an explanation for the first; most colleges use an "integrated" curriculum model whereas The Citadel uses a model known as "distributive," which is less effective in driving critical thinking.

The Corps of Cadets stood at 2,331, with 100 percent of those housed in the barracks. In an era when 60 percent of colleges in the United States did not reach their projected enrollment, The Citadel filled the house. And they performed well. After first semester, GPA for the Corps averaged over 3.0 and for knobs it averaged 2.8.[655] In January, academics were again the focus, with new undergraduate degrees approved in Accounting, Construction Engineering and Intelligence and Security Studies.[656]

When Bastin Hall opens in 2019, it will house the Tommy and Victoria Baker School of Business. Charlestonians know Tommy Baker as an extraordinarily successful automobile dealer and entrepreneur. After service in the Marines, he enrolled at the college as a veteran student with the Class of 1972. "The education I received at The Citadel reinforced the discipline I learned in the U.S. Marine Corps, which together laid the groundwork for any business success I have experienced," he said. The Bakers' generosity will fund five professorships within the business school, make possible MBA and undergraduate programs in Principled Entrepreneurship and Innovation, and provide a host of other benefits.[657]

A notation in the Board minutes for March 1, 2017 may serve as a fitting end point for this history. Rosa told the Board that the Bastin Hall project is on track, but the college is running into issues with approvals for the Capers Hall Project. The irony of issues with Capers Hall will not be lost on a careful reader. For the 50 years that have been the focus of this work, the venerable old building has cried out for help only to see other and higher priorities intervene. The author of this work may be forgiven for exercising the "privilege of the pen," but he studied in Capers Hall from 1963 until graduation in 1967. He feels a fondness toward it the way he feels about Stevens Barracks, his home for four years. It is hard to pass either without saluting.

As we look forward, a new Capers Hall will arise, and one day the fate of Stevens Barracks will be finalized. The visitors side of Johnson Hagood will be rebuilt, the old stands having been torn down with structural and lead paint issues. Bastin Hall will rise, and near it a much discussed and needed parking garage will be built. Fishburne Avenue, from "The Joe" to Rutledge, is destined to become a major economic corridor. A museum that celebrates the school's history will expand, perhaps in a state-of-the-art library hopefully to be constructed.

As a college, we have been blessed with principled leaders dedicated to producing more of them. Colleges and people have this in common: A single event can damage a reputation overnight and, in today's social media world, minutes, while a record of excellence takes years to amass, built gradually a step at a time. In The Citadel's journey toward that goal, it had been essential to stop the bleeding caused by negative publicity, declining enrollment, anemic state funding and the other factors that have been detailed in this history. General Grinalds deserves the credit for bringing the school back from the "nadir of our image." He can rightly be said to have put the school on a path toward what it was destined to become under General Rosa. Both men had help along the way. Generals Harris and Duckett battled the most anti-military environment in generations. General Seignious turned around a dire situation in the 1970s almost overnight with his Spirit of '76 campaign. General Grimsley picked up the pieces in 1980 from a flawed administration and steered a steady course for the next decade. The nautical metaphor, The Citadel Ship of State, seems particularly apt when we consider General Watts, whose time at the helm saw a perfect storm of changes, controversies and setbacks that would have sunk most vessels and some colleges. But he brought us through. And, at the risk of mixing metaphors, General Cliff Poole served professionally and well as a much needed "relief pitcher" during changing administrations.

Challenges remain, as they always will. More change is inevitable, even at The Citadel. What will not change — what cannot be allowed to change — is what motivated the alumni and the Washington Light Infantry to press for the school's resurrection in 1882. If I may borrow my own words from those etched on the walls of the War Memorial, ". . . the institution we loved could not be allowed to die. We had found in its structure, its rigors, its *esprit de corps* something essential to preserve." May that "something" remain with us and among us, to "stand forever, yielding never."

• • •

Acknowledgments

W ith the 175th anniversary of the school's founding looming in 2018, it occurred to me that the half-century since Clark's retirement deserved a history, particularly in view of the momentous changes those 50 years encompassed.

The idea of producing such a history found a favorable reception at The Citadel Foundation, and a 50th reunion gift from my 1967 classmates made it financially feasible.

I am not a historian by training or profession, yet my long association with the college gives me perspective. My father was Class of 1930, my uncle class of 1919, and my eldest son, John C. Warley, III, Class of 1996. The bulldog roams on a long Warley leash.

The lack of a comprehensive history of the past 50 years does not mean those years have been ignored in print. Alexander Macaulay, Class of 1994, wrote *Marching in Step*, a fine book addressing some of the college's more controversial passages, such as integration and coeducation. I used his work as a valuable resource and, when encountering subjects he dealt with in greater depth, refer readers to his writings.

In *Marching in Step's* Acknowledgements, Macaulay honors the debt he claimed to owe Jane Yates, longtime archivist at the library. Unfortunately for me, she had retired by the time I began my study and the position stood vacant until December 1, 2016, when Tessa Updike filled it. Tessa is bright, energetic and dedicated. Given time, she will prove a major asset to any researcher, as she was to me.

David Goble, head librarian, and his fine staff at the Daniel Library could not have been more supportive. All were willing to lend a hand, but I would be remiss in not mentioning by name Elise Wallace, who seemed to put her finger on whatever was eluding me, and always with a smile.

Lt. General Michael Steele is a classmate, former roommate, teammate on The Citadel baseball team, and Chairman of the Board of Visitors from 2013 to 2015. From him I learned the backstory on a number of key events. As one of two early readers of this book, his observations and suggestions for improvement were prompt and spot-on.

The other early reader was Frank Mood, Class of 1960 and a longtime friend. He preceded me at both The Citadel and the University of Virginia School of Law, setting a standard at both schools that few could match.

We all had our favorite college professors whose influence extends far beyond Lesesne Gate and graduation. Larry Moreland, professor emeritus of Political Science, was such a man. He was a rare bird among the 1964-1967 faculty: an intellectual, a liberal, and a natty dresser. Those of us who sat riveted to his lectures in Constitutional Law marveled at how he got away with wearing civilian clothes and wondered if we might also assume that privilege. Larry provided needed encouragement when I began this project and furnished some faculty background I may never have uncovered without his guidance.

Mark Brandenburg, Class of 1990 and The Citadel's General Counsel since 2005, not only vetted the manuscript but provided some key background and context for a number of chapters.

Steve Smith is steeped in Citadel history and makes frequent contributions on the subject to various publications. He clarified my thinking on several points, for which I thank him.

Many thanks to the team at Evening Post Books: John Burbage, Gill Guerry and Kristen Milford. Louis Brems, who became The Citadel's official photographer in 2017, worked with them on photographs, including the excellent one that serves as the book's cover. It is a pleasure to work with professionals.

Researching and writing a book is a long haul, so I'm especially thankful for some folks who kept my spirits up and occasionally supplied spirits. Those include the gang at Johnson Hagood Suite 615: Jay and Jane Keenan; John and Suzie Sams; Mike and Pam Steele; John and Caroline McAleer. In Beaufort, classmate Scott Graber gave me some stories and stood as a reliable sounding board for mine.

My work reminds me of the stories and accounts which go untold, either because I didn't learn of them or they didn't fit into the narrative as I conceived it. Any omissions or factual errors are both regrettable and entirely my own.

ENDNOTES

1 - Unless otherwise noted, the contents of this chapter were derived from Lt. Gen. John W. Rosa, Jr., personal interview with the author, May 24, 2016.

2 - Herb Frazier, "New President Aims to Take Citadel Into the Future," *The Post and Courier*, April 22, 2006.

3 - Keith Roden interview with the author, April 23, 2017.

4 - Ken Burger, "New Citadel Chief has Lived Life in Uniforms," *The Post and Courier*, April 21, 2006.

5 - Diana Jean Schemo, *Skies to Conquer: a Year Inside the Air Force Academy* (Hoboken, NJ: John Wiley & Sons, 2010), e-book 48.

6 - Diana Jean Schemo, "Ex-Superintendent of Air Force Academy is Demoted in Wake of Rape Scandal," *New York Times*, July 12, 2003.

7 - W. Thomas McQueeney, *Sunsets over Charleston* (Charleston, SC: The History Press, 2012), 232.

8 - Laurie Goodstein, "Air Force Academy Staff Found Promoting Religion," *New York Times*, June 23, 2005.

9 - McQueeney, *Sunsets over Charleston*, 233.

10 - John Peyre Thomas, *The History of the South Carolina Military Academy* (Charleston, SC: Walker, Evans & Cogswell Co. 1893). Col.

O.J. Bond, *The Story of The Citadel* (Richmond, VA: Garrett and Massie, 1936). Col. D.D. Nicholson, Jr., *A History of The Citadel: The Years of Summerall and Clark* (Charleston, SC: The Citadel Print Shop, 1994)

11 - See generally Thomas, *History of the SCMA*; Bond, *The Story of The Citadel*; Rod Andrew, Jr., *Long Gray Lines, The Southern Military School Tradition, 1839-1915* (Chapel Hill, NC: University of North Carolina Press, 2001); Nicholson, *Years of Summerall and Clark*; Gary Nichols, *American Leader in War and Peace*.

12 - *Post and Courier*, February 14, 2014, "Denmark Vesey Monument unveiled before hundreds," Adam Parker. See generally Thomas, *History of the SCMA*; Bond, *The Story of The Citadel*; Rod Andrew, Jr., *Long Gray Lines, The Southern Military School Tradition, 1839-1915* (Chapel Hill, NC: University of North Carolina Press, 2001); Nicholson, *Years of Summerall and Clark*; Gary Nichols, *American Leader in War and Peace*.

13 - David Robertson, *Denmark Vesey* (New York: Knopf, 1999), 4-5.

14 - U.S. Census 1820.

15 - Thomas, *History of the SCMA*, 9, 12.

16 - Bond, *The Story of The Citadel*, 7-11.

17 - Schreadley, R.L., *Valor and Virtue; The Washington Light Infantry* *in Peace and In War*; The Reprint Company, Spartanburg, SC (1997), pp 27-28.

18 - Henry A. Wise, *Drawing Out the Man: The V.M.I. Story* (Charlottesville, VA: University Press of Virginia 1978) 9.

19 - Thomas, *History of the SCMA*, pp 20, 21.

20 - An Historical Sketch of the Washington Light Infantry, published November 1943 p.1.

21 - BOV Minutes September 14, 2002.

22 - *Colleges and Universities of South Carolina*, S.C. State Library Board, 1989; Walter Edgar, *South Carolina, a History* (Columbia: University of South Carolina Press, 1998) 260, 264; Nan Morrison, *A History of the College of Charleston, 1936-2008*, (Columbia: University of South Carolina Press, 2011) 1; Lawrence S. Rowland, Alexander Moore, George C. Rogers, Jr., *The History of Beaufort County, Vol. 1 1514-1861* (Columbia: University of South Carolina Press, 1996) 284-285

23 - Nancy Beadie and Kim Tolley, eds., *Chartered Schools: Two-Hundred Years of Independent Academies in the United States, 1727-1925* (New York: RoutledgeFalmer, 2002), 3, 21, cf Jennifer R. Green, *Military Education and the Emerging Middle Class in the Old South* (New York: Cambridge University Press, 2008) p 5.

24 - Bond, *The Story of The Citadel*, 215.

25 - Edgar, *S.C. A History*, 300.

26 - Rowland etc., *History of Beaufort County, Vol. 1* 285.

27 - Morrison, *History of College of Charleston*, p 3.

28 - Taylor, *Ante-Bellum SC*, 115-116.

29 - Bruce W. Eelman, "An Educated and Intelligent People Cannot be Enslaved"; The Struggle for Common Schools in Antebellum Spartanburg, South Carolina." *History of Education Quarterly*, 44 (Summer 2004), 250-70.

30 - Rosser S. Taylor, *Ante-Bellum South Carolina: A Social and Cultural History* (Chapel Hill, NC: University of North Carolina Press, 1942) 107.

31 - Eelman, *An Educated People*, 254-255.

32 - Taylor, *Ante-Bellum SC*, 107.

33 - Edgar, *South Carolina, A History*, 298.

34 - Taylor, *Ante-Bellum SC*, 107.

35 - Edgar, *South Carolina, A History*. Stephen R. Wise and Lawrence S. Rowland. *Rebellion, Reconstruction and Redemption, 1861-1893* (Columbia, SC: University of South Carolina Press 2015) 480.

36 - Green, *Military Education,* 1.

37 - Green, *Military Education,* 7.

38 - Green, *Military Education*, 145.

39 - Green, *Military Education*, 32.

40 - Thomas, *History of the SCMA,* 42.

41 - Edwin Heroit, *The Polytechnic School, the Best System of Practical Education* (Charleston: Walker and James, 1850) 5 cf Green, *Military Education*, 146.

42 - Green, *Military Education*, 8.

43 - Thomas, *History of the SCMA,* 25.

44 - Thomas, *History of the SCMA,* 31.

45 - Thomas, *History of the SCMA,* 38.

46 - Thomas, *History of the SCMA,* 35-36.

47 - http://www.in2013dollars.com/1840-dollars-in-2015?amount=200

48 - Thomas, *History of the SCMA,* 38.

49 - Green, *Military Education*, 39-40. The Citadel adopted this practice after it reopened in 1882. See Thomas, *History of the SCMA*, 339.

50 - Bond, *The Story of The Citadel*, 23.

51 - Picquet is French for picket.

52 - According to www.civilwartalk.com.

53 - Bond, *The Story of The Citadel*, 28.

54 - Bond, *The Story of The Citadel*, 29.

55 - Thomas, *History of the SCMA,* 44.

56 - Thomas, *History of the SCMA,* 39-40.

57 - J. Harold Easterby. *A History of the College of Charleston: Founded 1770.* (Charleston: Trustees of the College of Charleston, 1935), 130.

58 - Easterby. *History of the College of Charleston*, 53-54.

59 - Report of Stephen Elliot to the Trustees of Beaufort College, August 1, 1803 cf Lawrence S. Rowland address, "New College: New Nation," (delivered November 2, 2000, at Rededication of Beaufort College Building, Beaufort, S.C.)

60 - Daniel Walker Hollis, *University of South Carolina, Vol. 1, South Carolina College* (Columbia: University of South Carolina Press, 1951), 81.

61 - Thomas, History SCMA p 43.

62 - Andrew, *Long Gray Lines*, 1.

63 - Thomas, *History of the SCMA,* pp 74-75; Bond, *The Story of The Citadel*, pp 38-39.

64 - Morrison, *History of College of Charleston*, 14.

65 - *Citadel Cadets, The Journal of Cadet Tom Law*, PC Press (Clinton, S.C.) 1941.

66 - George Lee Simpson, Jr. *The Cokers of Carolina* (Chapel Hill: University of North Carolina Press, 1956), 47-50.

67 - http://www.sonoco.com/aboutus/history.aspx

68 - https://en.wikipedia.org/wiki/James_Lide_Coker

69 - Andrew, *Long Gray Lines*, 75.

70 - Bond, *The Story of The Citadel*, pp 42-43.

71 - Alexander Macaulay, "Discipline and Rebellion: The Citadel Rebellion of 1898," *South Carolina Historical Magazine*, Vol. 103, No. 1 (January 2002), 30-47.

72 - Gary Baker, Cadets in Gray pp 18-21. https://secure.citadelalumni.org/dcal/detail.php?id=136

73 - John Thomas, *History of The Citadel*, pp 108-109.

74 - Gary R. Baker, *Cadets in Gray* (Columbia, SC: Palmetto Bookworks, 1989).

75 - Bond, *The Story of The Citadel*, 99-102; Thomas, *History of the SCMA*, 325.

76 - Thomas, *History of the SCMA*, 339.

77 - Thomas, *History of the SCMA*, 339.

78 - "The Citadel Academy," *The News and Courier*, March 8, 1882, 1.

79 - Thomas, *History of the SCMA*, 571-72.

80 - Bond, *The Story of The Citadel*, 192.

81 - Thomas, *History of SCMA*, 423.

82 - Thomas, *History of SCMA*, 492-96.

83 - Bond, *The Story of The Citadel*, 149

84 - *The Sphinx*, 1900-1905.

85 - Bond, *The Story of The Citadel*, p 171.

86 - Bond, *The Story of The Citadel*, p 166.

87 - Bond, *The Story of The Citadel*, p 166, 192.

88 - The Citadel, Citadel History War Deaths, accessed May 16, 2016, http://www.citadel.edu/citadel-history/war-deaths/world-war-i.html.

89 - Bond, *The Story of The Citadel*, 193-198; Fraser, *Charleston, Charleston*, p 340.

90 - Bond, *The Story of The Citadel*, 199.

91 - *The Sphinx* 1923.

92 - Bond, *The Story of The Citadel*, 209

93 - Bond, *The Story of The Citadel*, 203-206.

94 - Remarks by Richard Hodges, November 3, 2016, "A Short Oral History of the Junior Sword Drill," Citadel Archives.

95 - Carmine Pecorelli interview with the author February 8, 2017.

96 - Bond, *The Story of The Citadel*, 219.

97 - Nichols, W. Gary, *American Leader in War and Peace*, White Mane Books, Shippensburg, PA (2011), p. 356-357.

98 - *Charleston Evening Post*, February 10, 1932, p. 1.

99 - Nicholson, *Years of Summerall and Clark*, p 42.

100 - Nichols, W. Gary, *American Leader in War and Peace*, White Mane Books, Shippensburg, PA (2011), p. 356-357.

101 - Nichols is emeritus professor, School of Humanities and Social Science in the History Department at The Citadel, where he taught from

1965 to 2007.

102 - Nichols, W. Gary, *American Leader in War and Peace*, White Mane Books, Shippensburg, PA (2011), p. 358.

103 - Nichols, W. Gary, *American Leader in War and Peace*, White Mane Books, Shippensburg, PA (2011), p. 360.

104 - Nichols, W. Gary, *American Leader in War and Peace*, White Mane Books, Shippensburg, PA (2011), p. 362-366.

105 - Nichols, W. Gary, *American Leader in War and Peace*, White Mane Books, Shippensburg, PA (2011), p. 362.

106 - Author interview with Brantley Harvey, September 16, 2016.

107 - Author telephone interview with Carmine Pecorelli, February 8, 2017.

108 - Nicholson, *Years of Summerall and Clark*, 294.

109 - Nicholson, *Years of Summerall and Clark*, 296.

110 - "Another Four-Star President," *The Charleston Evening Post*, October 24, 1953, 4.

111 - "General Mark W. Clark, USA, Ret. (1954-1965), www.The Citadel/home/office of the president/past presidents, accessed May 23, 2016.

112 - Alexander Macaulay, *Marching in Step*, (Athens, GA: University of Georgia Press, 2009) 36-37.

113 - Macaulay, *Marching in Step*, 38-42

114 - Col. D.D. Nicholson, Jr., *A History of The Citadel: The Years of Summerall and Clark* (Charleston, SC: The Citadel Print Shop, 1994), 328, 357. "Gen. Clark Will Retire as President of Citadel," *New York Times*, March 14, 1964, national edition 11.

115 - Nicholson, *Years of Summerall and Clark*, 348.

116 - Nicholson, *Years of Summerall and Clark*, 357.

117 - Since Clark's burial, a columbarium has been added inside the Thomas Dry Howie Memorial Bell Tower for alumni and specified others.

118 - Whitmire Report, p 42.

119 - General Summerall suspended the Fourth Class System between 1943 and 1946 because of the great influx of WWII trainees on campus. Demand by cadets and alumni brought it back. See Nicholson, *A History of The Citadel*, pp. 210-212; 215-220.

120 - *All American All the Way: The Combat history of the 82nd Airborne Division in World War II*, Nordyke, Phil, Zenith Press, St. Paul, MN, 2005, p. 19.

121 - *On to Berlin, Battles of an Airborne Commander 1943-1946*, Gavin, James M., The Viking Press, New York, 1978, p. 67.

122 - Gavin, p. 68. *Those Devils in Baggy Pants*, Carter, Ross S., Claymore Publishing Corp., Canton, OH, p. 59.

123 - Nordyke, p. 130.

124 - Nordyke, p. 412.

125 - *USA Today*, August 14, 2015 and May 5, 2017.

126 - National Study of Student Hazing, *Hazing in View: Students at Risk*, Dr. Elizabeth Allan and Dr. Mary Madden, 2006-2008.

127 - 2017 *Blue Book*, paragraph 1.5.2.

128 - South Carolina Statutes § 16-3-530.

129 - South Carolina Statutes § 59-101-200 (A) (4): "Hazing" means the wrongful striking, laying open hand upon, threatening with violence, or offering to do bodily harm by a superior student to a subordinate student with intent to punish or injure the subordinate student, or other unauthorized treatment by the superior student of a subordinate student of a tyrannical, abusive, shameful, insulting, or humiliating nature. (B) Hazing at all state supported universities, colleges, and public institutions of higher learning is prohibited. When an investigation has disclosed substantial evidence that a student has committed an act or acts of hazing, the student may be dismissed, expelled, suspended, or punished as the president considers appropriate.

130 - Willingham attended The Citadel for one year, 1940-1941. His best selling novel portrays life at a southern military school with sadistic, unflattering characters and scenes.

131 - As noted in Chapter 5, Charles Foster, the first black cadet, was purposely assigned to a company where the culture was less severe than the one to which his height would have led him.

132 - Rosa interview with the author, May 24, 2016.

133 - Calder Willingham, *End as a Man,* The Vanguard Press, Inc., New York (1947); https://en.wikipedia.org/wiki/Calder_Willingham

134 - 1953 *Sphinx*, "1949-1953 In Retrospect," p. 28.

135 - 1954 *Sphinx*, "Class History," pp. 66-69.

136 - 1955 *Sphinx*, "Class History," pp. 8-13.

137 - 1956 *Sphinx*, "Class History," pp. 80-83.

138 - Macaulay, *Marching in Step*, pp 20-21.

139 - Macaulay, *Marching in Step*, pp 38, 51.

140 - Remarks by Richard Hodges, November 3, 2016, "A Short Oral History of the Junior Sword Drill," Citadel Archives.

141 - *The Evening Star*, Washington, D.C., May 12, 1964, "Why?" p B-4.

142 - *The Sphinx* 1957, Vol. 57.

143 - The Citadel, Citadel History War Deaths, accessed May 16, 2016, http://www.citadel.edu/citadel-history/war-deaths/vietnam-war.html

144 - *New York Times*, May 13, 1954 p 1,3.

145 - *Charleston Evening Post*, Oct. 20, 1962 p 14-A.

146 - Nan Morrison, *History of the College of Charleston,* p. 78.

147 - In the summer of 1964, while a counselor at the Mark Clark Summer Camp, the author read a book on the recommendation of a classmate called *None Dare Call It Treason*. Alarmed by the McCarthyesque allegations, we interviewed General Clark in his office, pointing out the most sensational allegations of Communist intrigue at the highest levels of the American government. General Clark stated that sadly, it was all true. We were later asked by one of our political science professors if we had bothered to check the citations in the book. We admitted we had not. The professor had, and pronounced the entire book a right wing propaganda tract full of assumptions, innuendos and flat-out lies.

148 - Robert S. McNamara, *In Retrospect*, p 321.

149 - Walter J. Fraser, Jr., *Charleston! Charleston!* pp 414-417.

150 - BOV minutes March 1970, appendix "Facts on Cadet Enrollment" doc 328.

151 - Fraser, *Charleston! Charleston!* pp 427.

152 - Leamer, Laurence, *The Kennedy Men*, William Morrow, New York, 2001, pp. 176-179.

153 - McNamara, *In Retrospect*, p 39.

154 - *The Sixties*, Netflix documentary at about the 15:30 mark. *Reaching for Glory, Lyndon Johnson's White House Tapes, 1964-1965* (2001), Michael Beschloss editor, page 213.

155 - McNamara, *In Retrospect*, pp 190-191.

156 - *The Sphinx* 1965.

157 - Oct. 23, 2002 post by Brian Neal on Murphy's Vietnam wall page.

158 - *Charleston Evening Post*, Oct. 20, 1962 p 14-A.

159 - BOV minutes October 1, 1965.

160 - *The Brigadier*, November 6, 1965

161 - BOV minutes Oct. 1, 1965, Appendix II.

162 - Laurence W. Moreland, August 29, 2016 "Memo for John Warley," p 1.

163 - Laurence W. Moreland, August 29, 2016 "Memo for John Warley," Note 2.

164 - *The Brigadier*, October 8, 1966, "Rifle Team has Depth," Mike McCarter, p. 7.

165 - The College of Charleston did not admit its first non-white student until 1967, declaring itself integrated despite the widespread assumption that Sonja Ann Perey was Filipino, not African-American. Morrison, *History of the College of Charleston*, p. 87.

166 - Macaulay p. 84

167 - Email dated August 10, 2016, from James A. Probsdorfer.

168 - Macaulay pp 71-72. Charles

Foster died in 1986, making it impossible for him to be interviewed by Alexander Macaulay. Macaulay personally interviewed dozens of key alumni in researching his book *Marching in Step*, including most of the living black alumni. Our history is poorer for the lack of a Macaulay interview with Charles Foster, and the ranks of our alumni are poorer for Foster's absence.

169 - *The Brigadier*, "Rights Denied," Oct. 2, 1970, p 2.

170 - *The Brigadier*, "The Passing of a Legend," Grant Alexander, February 25, 1967, p 13.

171 - BOV minutes, February 11, 1967, Tab A.

172 - BOV minutes, February 11, 1967, Tab A.

173 - BOV minutes March 1967, Appendix 1.

174 - *The Brigadier*, May 1967, p 15.

175 - This was essentially the North Vietnamese negotiating position throughout the war. McNamara, *In Retrospect*, pp 181-182.

176 - *The Brigadier*, "6,766" April 8, 1967, p. 2.

177 - Myron Harrington interview with the author June 8, 2017; https://borinqueneers.com/content/soldier-3

178 - Myron Harrington interview with the author June 8, 2017.

179 - Karnow, Stanley, *Vietnam; A History*; Penguin Books, second revised and updated edition, 1997; pp 538-547.

180 - Myron Harrington interview with the author June 8, 2017.

181 - Karnow, Stanley, *Vietnam; A History*; Penguin Books, second revised and updated edition, 1997; p 546.

182 - http://valor.militarytimes.com/recipient.php?recipientid=4196

183 - Myron Harrington interview with the author June 8, 2017.

184 - B.T. Collins, "The Courage of Sam Bird," *Reader's Digest* May 1989, pp 49-54.

185 - Samuel R, Bird interviewed by William Manchester April 30, 1964, WMP [William Manchester Papers cited in Poole, Robert M., *On Hallowed Ground; The Story of Arlington National Cemetery* p. 330.

186 - *Miami Herald*, October 27, 2013; "Ted Bridis, well-known Vietnam vet and triple amputee, dead at - 67."

187 - Interview with William M. Steele, August 9, 2016; email from James A. Probsdorfer, August 10, 2016.

188 - *New York Times*, April 6, 1969, p.3, Murray Schumach.

189 - Zinn, Howard, *A People's History of the United States*, HarperCollins Publishers, 2003, pp. 483-501.

190 - *New York Times*, April 6, 1969, p.3, Ronald Sullivan.

191 - Macaulay p. 102.

192 - Frasier, *Charleston, Charleston* p. 422.

193 - Laurence Moreland email to author, February 21, 2017.

194 - Nan Morrison, *History of the College of Charleston*, p. 98.

195 - Fraser, *Charleston, Charleston* p 418-419.

196 - Telephone interview with J.T. Roe, August 5, 2016.

197 - Conroy, *The Boo*, Introduction to the 2005 Edition.

198 - Morrison, *A History of the College of Charleston,* p. 1

199 - Morrison, *A History of the College of Charleston,* pp 3, 43-44.

200 - Morrison, *A History of the College of Charleston,* pp 100-101.

201 - BOV September 27, 1968.

202 - Morrison, *A History of the College of Charleston,* p 3.

203 - Citadel Archives, Harris correspondence, Box 41, folder 1.

204 - Whitmire Report, pp 7, 18, 19, 20, Citadel Archives.

205 - BOV Minutes May 31, 1968, Appendix III.

206 - https://www.usnews.com/education/best-colleges/the-short-list-college/articles/2016-01-05/colleges-where-freshmen-usually-return

207 - https://www.usnews.com/best-colleges/rankings/regional-universities-south/freshmen-least-most-likely-return

208 - BOV Minutes January 27, 1968, Appendix II.

209 - BOV Minutes September 10, 1969.

210 - *Charleston Evening Post*, "79 Points in Five Years," Ron Brinson, September 4, 1970, p. 14.

211 - BOV Minutes March 20, 1970.

212 - BOV Minutes March 20, 1970.

213 - Minutes of August 21, 1970, executive committee meeting attached to BOV minutes May 29, 1970, BOV meeting (obviously misfiled).

214 - Appendix to May 29, 1970, BOV minutes.

215 - *Charleston Evening Post*, "79 Points in Five Years," Ron Brinson, September 4, 1970, p. 14.

216 - BOV Minutes March 15, 1974, Appendix III, which puts strength of Corps down to 1,570 with capacity of 2,000. In what can best be described as putting some "lipstick on the pig," a February 3, 1973, headline in *The News and Courier* proclaimed "Enrollment at Citadel Sets Record." Total enrollment of 2,799 included 1,723 cadets, evening and MAT students. BOV Minutes September 1, 1973, Appendix II.

217 - Seignious, George M. II, *A Grandfather Reports*, privately published memoir in possession of Frank Seignious, '68, pp. 22-23.

218 - *The News and Courier*, "Westmoreland Rumor Denied by Citadel," September 8, 1972.

219 - *The Brigadier*, October 23, 1970 p. 1.

220 - *Charleston Evening Post*, November 4, 1970 p. 2A.

221 - *The Brigadier*, February 1, 1974, p. 1.

222 - *U.S. News & World Report*, April 23, 1973, "Empty Seats in Colleges--End of a 20-Year Boom," page 43-47.

223 - Nicholson, *The Years of Summerall and Clark*, p. 241.

224 - Interview with David Goble July 26, 2017.

225 - Nan Morrison, *History of the College of Charleston*, p. 131.

226 - Post and Courier, February 27,1992, 1-B

227 - BOV Minutes March 15, 1974, Appendix III.

228 - BOV Minutes March 15, 1974, Appendix III.

229 - BOV minutes March 15, 1974, attached Exhibit 349.

230 - BOV minutes March 15, 1974, attached Exhibit 378.

231 - File Memo dated October 24, 1967, from Gen. Tucker, Archives, Harris correspondence, Box 50.

232 - BOV minutes September 17, 1976, attached Exhibit 182.

233 - See Pat Conroy's *A Lowcountry Heart*, pp 49-54, for a full account of incident.

234 - BOV minutes September 17, 1976, attached Exhibit 182.

235 - Seignious, George M. II, *A Grandfather Reports*, privately published memoir in possession of Frank Seignious, '68, p. 23.

236 - *The News and Courier*, January 1, 1978, "Citadel beset with Iranian problems," Fen Montaigne, pp. 1-C, 14-C.

237 - *The News and Courier*, January 1, 1978, "Citadel beset with Iranian problems," Fen Montaigne, pp. 1-C, 14-C.

238 - BOV minutes March 1978

239 - *The Brigadier*, April 28, 1980, p. 1; "Several Iranian students remain following Carter's deportation," Buddy Wilkes.

240 - Seignious, George M. II, *A Grandfather Reports*, privately published memoir in possession of Frank Seignious, '68, pp. 3, 65.

241 - Seignious, George M. II, *A Grandfather Reports*, privately published memoir in possession of Frank Seignious, '68, pp 8-9.

242 - Letter dated December 20, 1946, from Beatrice Patton to George Seignious, in possession of Richard Padgett, '68.

243 - Seignious, George M. II, *A Grandfather Reports*, privately published memoir in possession of Frank Seignious, '68, p 10.

244 - Inaugural 1975 address of Lt. Gen. Seignious as 14th president of The Citadel; Seignious, George M. II, *A Grandfather Reports*, Appendix III, privately published memoir in possession of Frank Seignious, '68, p 10.

245 - BOV minutes, Sept. 13, 1974.

246 - *The News and Courier*, August 29, 1974, p. 2-B.

247 - Hicks, Brian, *The Mayor; Joe Riley and the Rise of Charleston*, Evening Post Books, Charleston, SC (2015) pp 57-60.

248 - Hicks, Brian, *The Mayor; Joe Riley and the Rise of Charleston*, Evening Post Books, Charleston, SC (2015) pp 109-110.

249 - Minutes of the Advisory Committee to the Board of Visitors, April 5, 1975 (attached as an addendum to BOV minutes February, 1975.

250 - Minutes of the Advisory Committee to the Board of Visitors and the Board of Visitors, October 10, 1975.

251 - Gay Alliance of Students v. T. Matthews, 544 F.2d 162 (4th Circuit 1976).

252 - BOV minutes, March 1976.

253 - Seignious, George M. II, *A Grandfather Reports*, privately published memoir in possession of Frank Seignious, '68, p 24.

254 - Frank Mood, interview with the author February 14, 2017.

255 - BOV Minutes April 14, 1977.

256 - Seignious, George M. II, *A Grandfather Reports*, privately published memoir in possession of Frank Seignious, '68, p 25.

257 - BOV minutes March 1978; *The Brigadier* February 17 and March 3, 1978.

258 - Seignious, George M. II, *A Grandfather Reports*, privately published memoir in possession of Frank Seignious, '68, pp 25-26.

259 - Douglas A. Snyder interview with the author, August 24, 2017.

260 - BOV Minutes October 1978, December 1978.

261 - BOV Minutes July 1978 and May 1979.

262 - Richard Padgett interview with the author, May 3, 2017.

263 - James A. Grimsley interview by Jack Bass, October 2, 2008, Citadel Oral History Project.

264 - James A. Grimsley interview by Jack Bass, October 2, 2008, Citadel Oral History Project. Grimsley, James A. Jr., *A Soldier Reminisces*, personal memoir (2001), p. 16, Citadel Archives.

265 - Zeigler, Eugene N., *Refugees and Remnants*, Clio Press, Inc, Spartanburg, S.C. (2002), p. 199.

266 - 1942 *Sphinx*.

267 - James A. Grimsley interview by Jack Bass, October 2, 2008, Citadel Oral History Project; Grimsley, James A. Jr., *A Soldier Reminisces*, personal memoir (2001), p. 16, Citadel Archives.

268 - Emails dated March 16, 2017 from Mike McCarter to the author.

269 - For an excellent discussion of the Stockdale experience, see the chapter "Tampering with America," *Marching in Step* by Alexander Macauley, pp. 147-161.

270 - Stockdale, James and Sybil, *In Love and War*, revised edition, Naval Institute Press, 1990, pp 52,245.

271 - Stockdale, James and Sybil, *In Love and War*, revised edition, Naval Institute Press, 1990, p. 462.

272 - Frank Mood interview with the author, August 7, 2017.

273 - Frank Mood interview with the author, August 7, 2017.

274 - Stockdale, James and Sybil, *In Love and War*, revised edition, Naval Institute Press, 1990, p. 462.

275 - *The Sphinx*, 1960.

276 - Pat Conroy, *The Boo*, p. 170.

277 - Frank Mood interview with the author, August 7, 2017.

278 - BOV Minutes February 13, 1981, Appendix I.

279 - Minutes of the BOV May 1980, document number 401 E.

280 - Macaulay, *Marching in Step*, p. 149.

281 - Whittle interview with the author, March 28, 2017.

282 - Email dated May 8, 2017, from William C. Mills to the author; Mills interview with the author May 5, 2017.

283 - Eulogy by William C. Mills at the Memorial Service for Vice Admiral Stockdale, July 31, 2005.

284 - Stockdale, James and Sybil, *In Love and War*, revised edition, Naval Institute Press, 1990, p. 477.

285 - Mills interview with the author, May 5, 2017.

286 - BOV minutes, October 5, 1979.

287 - BOV minutes, March 21, 1980.

288 - James Rembert conversation with the author, April 19, 2017.

289 - Stockdale, James and Sybil, *In Love and War*, revised edition, Naval Institute Press, 1990, pp 472, 484-485.

290 - BOV minutes, August 23, 1980.

291 - Stockdale, James and Sybil, *In Love and War*, revised edition, Naval Institute Press, 1990, p. 485.

292 - Will Grimsley interview with the author, March 13, 2017.

293 - Whittle interview with the author, March 28, 2017.

294 - James Grimsley interview with the author, March 2017.

295 - BOV Minutes September 18, 1981 and October 30, 1981; Conroy letter to Frank Jarrell, *The News and Courier* October 25, 1981, p. 19-A.

296 - *The Brigadier*, March 18, 1983, p.2

297 - BOV Minutes April 3, 1981, President's report p. 5.

298 - BOV Minutes February 13, 1981, Appendix VI.

299 - BOV Minutes February 13, 1981.

300 - BOV Minutes February 8, 1985, Appendix III.

301 - BOV Minutes April 29 and May 14, 1981.

302 - Macaulay, *Marching in Step*, pp 167-170.

303 - BOV Minutes September 18, 1981, Appendix II.

304 - Greater Issues address by General William Westmoreland, January 28, 1982; Citadel Archives.

305 - *Charleston Evening Post*, January 29, 1982, p. 13-C.

306 - *The Sphinx* 1957. General Watts interview with the author, May 2017.

307 - Toledo *Blade*, June 7, 1983, "Potomac Mystery Hero Identified," p. 1.

308 - https://en.wikipedia.org/wiki/Arland_D._Williams_Jr., accessed May 19, 2017.

309 - BOV Minutes December 1985; https://en.wikipedia.org/wiki/Arland_D._Williams_Jr., accessed May 21, 2017.

310 - Commencement Address by President Ronald Reagan, May 15, 1993; Citadel Archives.

311 - BOV Minutes September 10, 1982; The Brigadier, September 24, 1982, p. 2.

312 - BOV Minutes September 10, 1982.

313 - The Brigadier November 12, 1982, p. 1; Seignious, George M., *A Grandfather Reports*, pp 24-25; Citadel Alumni Assoc. Website, Distinguished Alumni, Charles Daniel.

314 - The Brigadier November 19, 1982, p. 3.

315 - BOV Minutes February 18, 1983; BOV Minutes March 20, 1987, Appendix I.

316 - BOV Minutes September 6, 1985.

317 - BOV Minutes April 11, 1986.

318 - BOV Minutes September 12, 1986, Appendix II.

319 - BOV Minutes March 20, 1987.

320 - BOV Minutes January 29, 1988.

321 - BOV Minutes March 13, 1992, Appendix VII.

322 - https://en.wikipedia.org/wiki/1983_Beirut_barracks_bombings

323 - BOV Minutes March 13, 1992.

324 - *The News and Courier*, November 1, 1983, "Local, state Beirut victims arrive," Merle D. Kellerhals, Jr., p. 1-A, https://en.wikipedia.org/wiki/Invasion_of_Grenada

325 - *The News and Courier*, April 17, 1984, p 11-A.

326 - BOV Minutes May 11, 1984.

327 - BOV Minutes September 14, 1984.

328 - BOV Minutes November 9, 1984, Appendix I.

329 - *The News and Courier,* November 9, 1985, p. 1.

330 - *The News and Courier,* March 21, 1986. P. 1.

331 - *The News and Courier,* April 19, 1986, p. 5-B.

332 - BOV Minutes June 1986.

333 - *The Sphinx* 1986.

334 - *The News and Courier,* October 29, 1985.

335 - Tom Moore interview with the author, May 23, 2017.

336 - *Miami Herald* October 29 and November 8, 1985; BOV Minutes January 10, 1986.

337 - www.themiamiproject.org/about-us/, accessed May 18, 2017.

338 - BOV Minutes September 30, 2006.

339 - *USA Today*, September 19, 2006, Erik Brady, "Finally, Buoniconti, Citadel Reconcile."

340 - Charleston *Post and Courier*, October 1, 2006, "Citadel Crowd Cheers Buoniconti."

341 - Miami *Sun Sentinel*, October 21, 2015, Dave Hyde, "Thirty Years Later, Marc Buoniconti is the Face of Hope."

342 - *The Washington Times* October 26, 2010, Tom Canavan, "Marc Buoniconti Recalls Injury 25 Years Later."

343 - BOV Minutes June 27, 1986, Appendix I; BOV Minutes June 24, 1988, Appendix I.

344 - *The Washington Post*, "An American Sparta," Michael Weisskopf, October 26, 1985.

345 - Isaac Metts interview with the author, April 19, 2017.

346 - *The News and Courier*, November 16, 1986, "Demonstrators protest handling of racial incident," Charles Rowe and Frederick Horlbeck.

347 - *The News and Courier*, Dec. 19, 1986, page 1.

348 - *Sunday Post/Courier*, Nov. 9, 1986, page 1; report of the S.C. Human Affairs Commission, as reported in *Saturday Post/Courier*, Jan. 17, 1987, page 17; *The News and Courier*, January 24, 1989, "Hazing Lawsuit is settled against 5 ex-Citadel cadets," Herb Frazier.

349 - Letter from Joe Riley published in *The News and Courier* April 4, 1987.

350 - Harold Arnold interview with the author December 3, 2017, and email from Arnold to the author dated December 5, 2017.

351 - BOV Minutes September 9, 1988, Appendix IX.

352 - BOV Minutes September 9, 1988.

353 - BOV Minutes January 27, 1989.

354 - BOV Minutes March 17, 1989.

355 - BOV Minutes May 11, 1989.

356 - BOV Minutes May 19, 1989.

357 - BOV Minutes June 5, 1989.

358 - BOV Minutes June 23, 1989.

359 - Interview with Billy Jenkinson by the author, August 4, 2017.

360 - Interview with Frank Mood by the author, August 7, 2017.

361 - Lt. Gen. Claudius E. Watts III interview with the author, October 18, 2017.

362 - Hicks, *The Mayor*, p. 221.

363 - BOV Minutes November 3, 1989; *Charleston Evening Post*, December 14, 1989, "Grant will help Burke-Citadel pact," p 7-A.

364 - BOV Minutes November 4, 1989.

365 - December 6, 2017, memorandum "The History of How Big Red Became the Spirit Flag of The Citadel," from Scott Moore to the author; Citadel Archives.

366 - BOV Minutes October 16, 1992.

367 - *The News and Courier*, May 30, 1990, pages 1-D, 4-D.

368 - *The News and Courier*, June 6, 1990, page D-1.

369 - *The News and Courier*, June 13, 1990, page D-1.

370 - Ken Burger, *The News and Courier*, June 6, 1990, page D-1.

371 - College Park BAR 1, Office of The Citadel's General Counsel Mark Brandenburg.

372 - https://en.wikipedia.org/wiki/College_Park_(Charleston)

373 - *The News and Courier*, June 10, 1990, page 2-C.

374 - BOV Minutes January 29, 1988.

375 - BOV minutes, February 7, 1988.

376 - *The Post and Courier*, "Citadel Board Heeds Riley's Plea on Arena," February 8, 1988, p.1.

377 - BOV Minutes, September 7, 1990.

378 - *The News and Courier*, April 14, 1991,

"The best thing this nation has to give," Herb Frazier, p 20-D.

379 - http://www.citadel.edu/citadel-history/war-deaths/lebanon-grenada-persian-gulf-war.html'; *The News and Courier*, April 14, 1991, "The best thing this nation has to give," Herb Frazier, p 20-D.

380 - *The News and Courier*, October 21, 1990, "Citadel offense: From frustration to elation," Bob Lang.

381 - *The News and Courier*, October 22, 1990, "Poetic justice is a teacher for winners and for losers," Ken Burger.

382 - Morris Robinson 2017 commencement address, http://www.citadel.edu/root/ocm-videos/webcasts

383 - BOV Minutes May 10, 1991; BOV Minutes October 26, 1996, Appendix II.

384 - BOV Minutes June 1991.

385 - BOV Minutes November 21, 1991, Appendix I.

386 - *The Post and Courier*, December 5, 1991, "Port: 'It's been a great run,'" Bob Lang.

387 - *The Post and Courier* March 13, 1992 p. 1; *Post and Courier* March 17, 1992, p. 3-B; BOV Minutes March 13, 1992.

388 - BOV Minutes March 13, 1992; BOV Minutes June 26, 1992 (corrected copy).

389 - *The Post and Courier*, May 8, 1994, p.1.

390 - *The Post and Courier*, October 5, 1997, "Shooting Haunts Citadel Graduate."

391 - *The Post and Courier*, January 5, 1993, p. B-1.

392 - 1994 *Sphinx*, page 208.

393 - *The Post and Courier*, October 5, 1997, "Shooting Haunts Citadel Graduate."

394 - *The Living Church,* The Archives of the Episcopal Church, September 22, 1996, "Seminarian Admits to 1992 Shooting," p. 6.

395 - *The Washington Post*, "FBI Solves '92 Shooting at Citadel," August 28, 1996.

396 - *The Post and Courier*, October 5, 1997, "Shooting Haunts Citadel Graduate."

397 - BOV Minutes October 25, 1996.

398 - *The Post and Courier* October 26, 1996, "Citadel grad begs pardon CAMPUS SHOOTING: George Cormeny III asked the Board of Visitors to forgive his lack of integrity. 'We don't sit in judgment," was the reply."

399 - *The Post and Courier* October 25, 1997; "Ex-cadet gets Jail in Shooting."

400 - BOV Minutes January 31, 1992, Appendix I.

401 - BOV Minutes June 1992.

402 - Minutes of the July 30, 1992 joint meeting of the executive committees of the Board and CDF; BOV Minutes September 3, 1992-September 11, 1992, page 113.

403 - Notes from William Sansom's remarks to the Board and The Citadel Advisory Council on October 30, 1993, found in BOV minutes October 29, 1993 to November 11, 1993, at page 78.

404 - Notes from William Sansom's remarks to the Board and The Citadel Advisory Council on October 30, 1993, found in BOV minutes October 29, 1993 to November 11, 1993, at page 78.

405 - https://foundation.citadel.edu/document.doc?id=823

406 - Manegold, Katherine, *In Glory's Shadow*, p. 142-145.

407 - BOV Minutes September 3, 1992

408 - BOV Minutes November 13, 1992, Appendix III.

409 - BOV Minutes November 7, 1992, Appendix I.

410 - *The Post and Courier*, December 16, 1992, "Two Day Students Sue The Citadel, p. 3-B.

411 - *Sports Illustrated* September 14, 1992 issue; *The Sphinx* 1993, p 312.

412 - BOV Minutes September __, 1992 [first page with date missing]

413 - BOV Minutes January 29, 1993, Appendix I; Post and Courier December 6, 1992, "Proud seniors weren't ready for it to end," p. 9-C; http://www.ysusports.com/fan_zone/traditions/1993champs; *The Sphinx* 1993.

414 - Minutes of the joint meeting of the Advisory Council and BOV, September 12, 1992, Appendix V.

415 - *The Sphinx* 1993; *The Post and Courier* March 18, 1993, "Weekend great for children to see Citadel," p 15-D.

416 - BOV Minutes June 25, 1993.

417 - BOV Minutes June 25, 1993.

418 - BOV Minutes October 29, 1993, Appendix I.

419 - Thomas, History of SCMA, pp 39-40.

420 - BOV Minutes October 29, 1993, Appendix I; BOV Minutes January 28, 1994, Appendix II.

421 - BOV Minutes September 18, 2004.

422 - Minutes of the Advisory Council to the BOV, April 15, 1994.

423 - BOV Minutes May 1965.

424 - BOV Minutes April 1994.

425 - BOV Minutes May 13, 1994, Appendix IV.

426 - *TheWashington Post*, August 6, 1994, "Shannon Faulkner's Haircut," Ellen Goodman.

427 - Joe Trez, Oral History project November 7, 2016.

428 - 1994 SAC report, Reaffirmation Committee Recommendations & Institutional Responses, Citadel archives.

429 - BOV Minutes June 24, 1995; BOV Minutes April 11, 1997, Document No. 94.

430 - BOV Minutes August 20, 1995, Appendix V; BOV Minutes January 5, 1996, Appendix VI.

431 - BOV Minutes March 29, 1996.

432 - Catherine S. Manegold, *In Glory's Shadow*, pp 158-159.

433 - BOV Minutes March 16, 1984.

434 - Manegold, *In Glory's Shadow*, p. 147.

435 - http://www.usma.edu/corbin/sitepages/historypercent20ofpercent-20womenpercent20inpercent20the-percent20military.aspx

436 - https://en.wikipedia.org/wiki/United_States_Air_Force_Academy

437 - https://en.wikipedia.org/wiki/United_States_Naval_Academy#Women_at_the_Naval_Academy

438 - Minutes of the joint meeting of the BOV and Advisory Council, April 15, 1994, Appendix I. The Citadel faculty felt otherwise. In an October 1992 survey of tenured and tenured-track professors, 64 percent favored admission of women into the Corps. [Manegold, p. 145]

439 - *U.S. v. Virginia et al.*, 766 F. Supp. 1407 (WD Va. 1991).

440 - *U.S. v. Virginia et al.*, 976 F. 2d 890 (4th Cir. 1992).

441 - Manegold, *In Glory's Shadow*, pp 9, 166.

442 - *The New York Times*, May 27, 1994, Catherine S. Manegold, "Woman testifies that Citadel is unfair."

443 - *U.S. v. Virginia et al.*, 852 F. Supp. 471 (WD Va. 1994)

444 - *U.S. v. Virginia et al.*, 44 F. 3d 1229 (4th Cir. 1995)

445 - Pat Conroy conversations with the author, dates unrecorded.

446 - Manegold, *In Glory's Shadow,* p. 275.

447 - Cliff Poole oral history session No. 7, recorded October 4, 2017, Citadel archives

448 - Manegold, *In Glory's Shadow,* p. 10.

449 - Manegold, *In Glory's Shadow,* p. 211.

450 - Manegold, *In Glory's Shadow,* p. 177.

451 - *United States v. Virginia et al.*, 518 U.S. 515 (1996).

452 - Minutes of the Advisory Council October 26, 1996.

453 - BOV Minutes August 5, 1996.

454 - *The Post and Courier* May 10, 1996, "Legislators OK college funding bill," Sybil Fix; August 9, 1997, "Local colleges pass muster," Sybil Fix; http://www.governing.com/topics/education/gov-performance-based-college-funding-coming-stateside.html.

455 - Mace, Nancy with Mary Jane Ross, *In the Company of Men*, Simon and Schuster (2001), p 15-17.

456 - Mace, Nancy with Mary Jane Ross, *In the Company of Men*, Simon and Schuster (2001), pp 18, 34-35.

457 - Mace, Nancy with Mary Jane Ross, *In the Company of Men*, Simon and Schuster (2001), pp 25.

458 - *The Post and Courier* September 12, 1996, "15 Citadel freshmen gone with the wind," Sybil Fix; BOV Minutes September 13, 1996; BOV Minutes October 26, 1996, Appendix I.

459 - Mace, *In the Company of Men*, p. 75.

460 - BOV Minutes December 17 & 18, 1996, Appendix I.

461 - *The Post and Courier* January 24, 1998, "Justice won't pursue hazing allegations in Citadel case," Sybil Fix.

462 - *The Post and Courier* November 12, 1996, Andrew Miller, "Citadel Dismisses Taaffe"; BOV Minutes May 12, 1997.

463 - Interview with Tom Mikell by the author, August 17, 2017;

464 - "A Report to the Board of Visitors" by Langhorne A. Motley, February 1, 1999.

465 - Interview with Tom Mikell by the author, September 26, 2017.

466 - Interview with Frank Mood by the author on August 7, 2017, and with Major General Grinalds on August 10, 2017; *The Post and Courier* January 6, 1997, "Grinalds to lead Citadel," Sybil Fix.

467 - Interview with Billy Jenkinson by the author, August 3, 2017; BOV Minutes January 3, 4, 5, 1997.

468 - *The Post and Courier* January 6, 1997, "Grinalds to lead Citadel," Sybil Fix; *The Post and Courier* January 7, 1997, "Grinalds fans are already in Charleston," Elsa McDowell.

469 - *The Post and Courier*, February 13, 1997, "Grinalds seeks system revamp," Sybil Fix.

470 - John Grinalds interview with the author, August 10, 2017.

471 - Mace, *In the Company of Men*, pp 197-198.

472 - BOV Minutes March 14, 1997, Appendix VII.

473 - July 13, 2017 email from Col. Trez to author, confirming that first occasion for ending Fourth Class System and recognition of knobs at Corps Day occurred in 2017.

474 - BOV Minutes May 16, 1997; http://www.citadel.edu/root/goldstar, accessed July 9, 2017.

475 - http://thefallen.militarytimes.com/army-capt-daniel-w-eggers/262987

476 - https://www.globalsecurity.org/military/facility/camp_eggers.htm

477 - "60 Minutes," June 8, 1997.

478 - BOV Minutes 27, 1997.

479 - "60 Minutes" June 8, 1997; *The Post and Courier* June 10, 1997, "'60 Minutes plays rough — and Citadel asked for it," Frank Wooten.

480 - BOV Minutes September 6, 1997, Enclosure 2; Minutes of the Advisory Council April 4, 1998, Enclosure 7(d).

481 - Minutes of the Advisory Council April 4, 1998, Enclosure 7(e).

482 - BOV Minutes June 27, 1997.

483 - BOV Minutes August 9, 1997, Enclosure 4.

484 - "The Citadel Approved Plan for Assimilation of Female Cadets," attached to BOV Minutes July 27, 1996, Appendix I.

485 - "The Citadel Approved Plan for Assimilation of Female Cadets," attached to BOV Minutes July 27, 1996, Appendix I.

486 - BOV Minutes April 11, 1997.

487 - BOV Minutes August 9, 1997, Enclosure 5.

488 - BOV Minutes August 9, 1997.

489 - BOV Minutes September 6, 1997; https://secure.citadelalumni.org/dcal/detail.php?id=164; http://www.citadel.edu/virtualtour/#22.

490 - BOV Minutes September 6, 1997, Enclosure 10.

491 - BOV Minutes November 22, 1997.

492 - Minutes of the Advisory Committee to The Citadel Board of Visitors, April 6-7, 1973.

493 - https://secure.citadelalumni.org/dcal/detail.php?id=63

494 - Minutes of joint meeting of the BOV and Advisory Council, October 25, 1997.

495 - BOV Minutes Nov. 22, 1997.

496 - The Honor Manual of the South Carolina Corps of Cadets, 2015-2016, p. 2; http://www.citadel.edu/root/images/krause_center/honor-manual.pdf

497 - Letter dated December 18, 1997, from Francis P. Mood to MG John S. Grinalds, Citadel Archives.

498 - BOV Minutes January 17, 1998; Minutes of the Advisory Council April 3, 1998.

499 - *The Post and Courier* February 5, 1998, "The Evolution and Meaning of Tradition," Elsa McDowell;

500 - BOV Minutes April 3, 1998.

501 - BOV Minutes May 8, 1998; Enclosures 6 and 7.

502 - BOV Minutes June 27, 1998.

503 - Department of Defense memorandum March 25, 1994 at BOV Minutes April 3, 1998, Enclosure 6.

504 - Email from LTG Michael Steele to the author dated September 9, 2017.

505 - BOV Minutes April 3, 1998, Enclosures 8 and 9.

506 - Minutes of the Advisory Council April 4, 1998.

507 - Minutes of the Advisory Council April 3, 1998, Enclosure 7(d).

508 - Minutes of the Advisory Council April 4, 1998.

509 - BOV Minutes June 27, 1998.

510 - BOV Minutes October 6, 1998.

511 - Minutes of the Advisory Council October 24, 1998, Enclosure 2.

512 - BOV Minutes October 23, 1998.

513 - https://secure.citadelalumni.org/dcal/detail.php?id=75.

514 - CAA Annual Meeting Nov. 6, 1998, Remarks by J. Quincy Collins, Jr., President, 1999; BOV Minutes November 21, 1998, Enclosure 4.

515 - Email from LTG Michael Steele to the author dated Sept. 9, 2017.

516 - BOV Minutes January 29, 1999.

517 - Minutes of the Advisory Council, April 16 & 17, 1999.

518 - Mace, Nancy, *In the Company of Men*, p 208.

519 - Joint Resolution of the South Carolina General Assembly, May 19, 1999

520 - BOV Minutes May 7, 1999;

521 - BOV Minutes June 26, 1999.

522 - Mace, *In the Company of Men*, pp 191, 196-206; BOV Minutes April 15, 2000.

523 - Decision memorandum from Col. Joe Trez to President Grinalds dated November 2, 1998, with attached "Citadel Policy on Commitment to Gender Equity in Athletics."

524 - *The Sphinx*, 1998-2002.

525 - BOV Minutes August 24, 1999; BOV Minutes January 29, 2000.

526 - BOV Minutes Sept. 30, 1999.

527 - Minutes of the Advisory Council October 22, 1999; *The Post and Courier* October 20, 1999, "Citadel cadet beaten, suspect sought," Kristina Torres; October 23, 1999, "Citadel president says system is not flawed," Brian Hicks.

528 - Minutes of the Board of Directors of The Citadel Trust, October 14, 1999; BOV Minutes October 23,

1999; Letter from Chairman Frank Mood to BOV dated Feb. 3, 1999.

529 - Interview with Douglas Snyder by the author, August 24, 2017.

530 - *The Post and Courier* November 24, 1999, "Powers gets another year," Jeff Hartsell; *The Post and Courier* November 2, 1999, "Sadly, change is needed at The Citadel," Ken Burger; Interview with Frank Mood by the author, August 7, 2017.

531 - BOV Minutes December 3, 1999; H. 2261, South Carolina [Statutes?]; http://www.scpronet.com/point/9909/p04.html. Letter from Frank Mood to BOV December 3, 1999; Letter from Dr. John Palms to USC administrators, etc. November 19, 1999; The State, "Citadel honors tradition by call to move banner," December 10, 1999 editorial; Letter from Dr. Julie A. Lipovsky, chair, Faculty Council, dated December 21, 1999 to Chairman Mood.

532 - *The Post and Courier* February 18, 2000, "Eight Citadel cadets face charges over secret room," Charlene Gunnells; Pat Conroy, *The Boo*, pp 43-44. The author's recollection of the secret room is a personal one. As a knob in T Company, he was summoned from ESP to carry 100-pound bags of cement from the parking lot to the alcove.

533 - BOV Minutes February 23, 2000; Letter from Chairman Frank Mood to Anderson D. Warlick, February 29, 2000.

534 - September 28, 2000, letter from Alex Sanders to Charles H.P. Duell,

chair of Board of Architectural Review; files of The Citadel's General Counsel Mark Brandenburg.

535 - *The Post and Courier,* October 12, 2000, "BAR gives Citadel OK to raze, rebuild barrack," Charlene Gunnells; *The Post and Courier*, August 9, 2001, "And the tower comes tumbling down"; *The Post and Courier*, June 24, 2000, "Citadel closing barracks," Charlene Gunnells; BOV Minutes October 20, 2000.

536 - BOV Minutes June 20, 1980.

537 - Minutes of a joint meeting of the Advisory Council and the BOV, April 15, 2000, Enclosure 4; BOV Minutes Feb. 3, 2001, Enclosure 6.

538 - Interview with Frank Mood by the author, August 7, 2017; *The Washington Post*, October 27, 2016; "The Citadel didn't want to admit women. But once this woman got in, she was unstoppable," Petula Dvorak.

539 - BOV Minutes May 12, 2000, Enclosures 4 and 5. The Board voted 7-5 against the concept.

540 - BOV Minutes September 12, 2000.

541 - BOV Minutes September 29, 2001, Enclosure 9.

542 - *The Post and Courier,* October 18, 2000, "Citadel to honor one-time nemesis Conroy," Charlene Gunnells.

543 - https://en.wikipedia.org/wiki/United_States_presidential_election,_2000

544 - http://www.citadel.edu/root/presbush01

545 - BOV Minutes September 29, 2001; BOV Minutes June 10, 2016.

546 - BOV Minutes March 15, 2002, Enclosure 2. [the Scarborough letter is referred to as an attachment but is not attached]

547 - BOV Minutes April 20, 2002, Enclosures 2 and 3.

548 - http://www3.citadel.edu/pao/women/firsts.html accessed September 7, 2017.

549 - BOV Minutes June 14 and 15, 2002, Enclosures 1 and 2; *The Post and Courier,* "'Road Rules' to Feature stop in Charleston," June 15, 2002, Mindy Spar.

550 - BOV Minutes July 26, 2002, Enclosure 4; BOV Minutes February 1, 2003, Enclosure 4; BOV Minutes April 12, 2003, Enclosure 5.

551 - BOV Minutes Feb. 1, 2003.

552 - http://www.arlingtoncemetery.net/bwsammis.htm

553 - BOV Minutes April 12, 2003.

554 - BOV Minutes September 20, 2003.

555 - BOV Minutes May 7, 2004.

556 - BOV Minutes June 5, 2004.

557 - BOV Minutes January 18, 2005; *The Post and Courier* January 19, 2005, "Citadel president to retire," Deneshia Graham; *The Post and Courier* January 25, 2005, "New headmaster named for Porter-Gaud School," Seanna Adcox.

558 - BOV Minutes February 5, 2005.

559 - Interview with General Grinalds by the author, August 10, 2017.

560 - Interview with Frank Mood, August 7, 2017, and Douglas Snyder, August 24, 2017.

561 - Cliff Poole interview with the author on September 27, 2017.

562 - BOV Minutes September 24, 2005; *The Post and Courier,* September 11, 2005, "Lowcountry breathes sigh of relief," James Scott; "2 Citadel sophomores killed in crash on I-95," Adam Parker.

563 - *The Post and Courier*, September 16, 2005, "Citadel program honors POWS, MIA," James Scott;https://thecitadelmemorialeurope.wordpress.com/2015/11/29/experience-of-pow-lt-richard-h-kellahan/

564 - *The Post and Courier,* April 21, 2006, "School gets a team, not just a leader," Diane Knich.

565 - *The Post and Courier,* April 23, 2006, "Rosa, Citadel a 'perfect match'"; *The Post and Courier,* April 22, 2006, "Rosa surveys new command as 19th president of Citadel," Diane Knich.

566 - *The Post and Courier,* August 24, 2006, "Citadel snaps to attention over results of revealing survey," p 1-A; *The State*, August 24, 2006, "1 in 5 women assaulted at Citadel," Devon Marrow, p. B-1; BOV Minutes August 5, 2006.

567 - BOV Minutes March 11, 2006.

568 - BOV Minutes June 10, 2006.

569 - *The Post and Courier,* May 7, 2006, "Gen. Pace sends off cadets," Mindy Hagen; BOV Minutes June 10, 2006; http://www.cbsnews.com/pictures/commencement-2006/15/

570 - The balance, or $3.3 million, was paid by the IRF, the Institutional Reserve Fund.

571 - BOV Minutes Sept. 30, 2006. *The Post and Courier*, November 12, 2011, "Citadel warned, but did nothing," Glenn Smith; *Charleston City Paper*, June 14, 2012, "Skip Re-Ville was unstoppable until a mother found him out," Paul Bowers.

572 - BOV Minutes Sept. 30, 2006; BOV Minutes Feb. 8, 2008.

573 - BOV Minutes February 3, 2007; BOV Minutes April 21, 2007; BOV Minutes October 23, 2008.

574 - *The Post and Courier* July 24, 2007, "Candidates struggle to pull away from the pack"; BOV Minutes September 8, 2007.

575 - BOV Minutes April 28, 2012.

576 - *The Post and Courier*, Aug. 3, 2017, "Appeals court upholds dismissal of Citadel lawsuit," Paul Bowers, p A-3; *The Post and Courier*, Nov. 12, 2011, "Citadel warned, but did nothing," Glenn Smith; *Charleston City Paper*, June 14, 2012; "Skip ReVille was unstoppable until a mother found him out," Paul Bowers; *Charleston City Paper*, Nov. 23, 2011, "The Citadel's failure to act has tarnished its reputation," Paul Bowers.

577 - BOV Minutes February 8, 2008; BOV Minutes March 13, 2008; BOV Minutes June 14, 2008.

578 - *New York Times*, March 10, 2008, "Toddler returns to Iraq after life-saving surgery," Erica Goode; *Post and Courier*, August 10, 2013, "Student befriends Marine," Jennifer Berry Hawes.

579 - BOV Minutes June 14, 2008; Email from LTG Michael Steele to the author dated September 9, 2017.

580 - https://www.federalreservehistory.org/essays/great_recession_of_200709; http://money.cnn.com/2010/01/14/real_estate/record_foreclosure_year/

581 - BOV Minutes February 7, 2009.

582 - BOV Minutes April 18, 2009; *The Post and Courier*, March 3, 2009, "Dogs clinch bye," Jeff Hartsell; *The Post and Courier,* March 8, 2009, "Samford stuns The Citadel," Jeff Hartsell.

583 - BOV Minutes June 13, 2009.

584 - BOV Minutes December 5, 2009; BOV Minutes January 30, 2010; BOV Minutes April 17, 2010.

585 - *The Post and Courier*, March 1, 2010, "Citadel QB being held in jail," Jeff Hartsell; *The Post and Courier*, January 20, 2011, "Former athletes plead guilty," Diane Knich and David W. MacDougall; *The Post and Courier*, March 23, 2011, "3 given 30 years each for invasions," Schuyler Kropf; BOV Minutes March 1, 2010.

586 - Memorandum from Bud Watts to the author dated September 26, 2017.

587 - https://foundation.citadel.edu/document.doc?id=823

588 - Memorandum from Bud Watts to the author dated September 26, 2017.

589 - Memorandum from Bud Watts to the author dated September 26, 2017.

590 - Bud Watts interview with the author September 15, 2017; Michael Steele interview with the author September 16, 2017.

591 - Memorandum from Bud Watts to the author dated Sept. 26, 2017.

592 - BOV Minutes June 12, 2010.

593 - BOV Minutes April 29, 2011.

594 - Telephone conferences with Michael Steele, John Sams and the author, September 16, 2017.

595 - Bud Watts interview with the author, September 15, 2017.

596 - https://foundation.citadel.edu/document.doc?id=823

597 - BOV Minutes June 11, 2011.

598 - Email from Lt. Gen. Michael Steele to the author dated September 12, 2017.

599 - BOV Minutes June 8, 2012.

600 - http://www.citadel.edu/root/images/leadplan/theleadplan_forweb.pdf

601 - BOV Minutes December 16, 2010.

602 - BOV Minutes January 29, 2011; BOV August 19, 2011.

603 - BOV Minutes June 11, 2011.

604 - BOV Minutes January 4, 2013; Email from Doug Snyder to author dated August 19, 2017.

605 - Bud Watts interview with the author September 15, 2017.

606 - BOV Minutes March 15, 1991, Appendix IX; BOV Minutes May 10, 1991, Appendix II.

607 - Although venerable Citadel alumnus Leonard Fulghum is credited with originating the Trust, he was not among its first directors. Those were Thomas C. Vandiver, '29, Temporary Chairman; Keith Purcell, '44; William Burke Watson, '48; Charles L. Terry, Jr., '43; and Robert W. Scarborough, ' 50. BOV Minutes June 21, 1991; BOV Minutes June 26, 1992 (corrected copy).

608 - BOV Minutes November 1, 1991, Appendix II.

609 - https://foundation.citadel.edu/document.doc?id=823

610 - BOV Minutes June 7, 2013.

611 - Bud Watts interview with the author September 15, 2017.

612 - BOV Minutes August 1, 2013.

613 - BOV Minutes Aug. 29 and 30, 2013; BOV Minutes Oct. 26, 2013.

614 - Memorandum from Michael Steele to the author Sept. 29, 2017.

615 - Memorandum from Michael Steele to the author dated Sept. 29, 2017.

616 - Telephone interview with Mike Steele by the author on September 28, 2017.

617 - BOV Minutes Oct. 25, 2013; BOV Minutes Jan. 24, 2014.

618 - http://graphics.wsj.com/table/ACCREDITlost

619 - BOV Minutes April 2, 2014.

620 - BOV Minutes June 8, 2012.

621 - BOV Minutes June 9, 2012.

622 - BOV Minutes September 7, 2012; http://www.citadel.edu/root/images/oea/ipacreportnew.pdf

623 - http://www.citadel.edu/root/images/oea/ipacreportnew.pdf

624 - BOV Minutes October 5, 2012, and attachment.

625 - BOV Minutes October 5, 2012.

626 - BOV Minutes October 25, 2013; https://foundation.citadel.edu/document.doc?id=822

627 - BOV Minutes February 12, 2014.

628 - BOV Minutes January 24, 2014.

629 - BOV Minutes August 6, 2014.

630 - BOV Minutes August 6, 2014.

631 - http://www.citadel.edu/root/riley-chair-announcement

632 - *The Post and Courier*, November 12, 2014, Jennifer Berry Hawes; https://www.forbes.com/profile/anita-zucker/, BOV Minutes November 3, 2014.

633 - BOV Minutes January 23, 2015.

634 - BOV Minutes January 24, 2015.

635 - http://www.citadel.edu/root/war-memorial-naming-criteria

636 - BOV Minutes June 9, 2012.

637 - https://www.elon.edu/u/president-elect/

638 - BOV Minutes June 12, 2015.

639 - BOV Minutes June 23, 2015.

640 - BOV Minutes September 25, 2015.

641 - *The Post and Courier*, September 13, 2015, "Fallen Citadel alum's sword makes 153-year trip home," Robert Behre.

642 - http://www.citadel.edu/root/faculty-senate

643 - BOV Minutes April 15, 2016.

644 - BOV Minutes November 2, 2015.

645 - *The Post and Courier*, November 22, 2015, "Renew, Citadel hand USC its first FCS loss since 1990," David Caraviello; *The Post and Courier*, September 10, 2017, "Former Citadel player Mitchell Jeter killed in car wreck," Jeff Hartsell.

646 - *The Post and Courier*, January 27, 2016, "Citadel steps up with honor"; BOV Minutes January 12, 2016.

647 - BOV Minutes January 23, 2016.

648 - *The Post and Courier*, March 9, 2016, "Controversy heating up over Confederate flag at Citadel," Dave Munday and Diane Knich.

649 - BOV Minutes April 1, 2016.

650 - *The Post and Courier*, June 1, 2016, "Muslim student will attend another military college," Deanna Pan.

651 - *The Post and Courier*, May 13, 2016, "Becoming Mr. Pendery," Jennifer Berry Hawes.

652 - BOV Minutes June 10-11, 2016.

653 - https://foundation.citadel.edu/document.doc?id=822

654 - http://www.citadel.edu/root/bastin-hall-announcement

655 - BOV Minutes September 9, 2016.

656 - BOV Minutes January 9, 2017.

657 - http://www.citadel.edu/root/transformative-gift-names-tommy-and-victoria-baker-school-of-business

INDEX

3rd U.S. Dragoons 34
6th South Carolina Cavalry
    Regiment 35
"48 Hours" 199
82 Airborne 46, 76, 140, 166

-A-
Abrash, Dena 39
Academic Board 62, 130-131, 184,
    289
academic freedom 62-63
accreditation 62, 93, 142, 178, 184,
    230-231, 248, 277, 280, 285
ACDA 111, 116
Acenbrack, Steve 111
Adams, Bentley, III 109
Adamson, James B., Col. 95
Addison, Glenn, Col. 251, 264
Agnew, Al, Com. 254
Air Florida Flight 90 crash 135
al-Bayati, Amenah 261
Alfaro, Dan 130
Algernon Sydney Sullivan Award
    137, 279
Altman Athletic Center 241, 252
Altman, William M., Jr., Lt. Col.
    241
Alumni Courtyard 22
American Association of University
    Professors (AAUP) 62-63
American Eagle 42
American Leader in War and Peace
    40
An American Sparta 146
Anderson, Maxwell 115
Anderson, Robert, Maj. 34, 260
Anderson, Wallace E. 112
Anita Zucker Institute for
    Entrepreneurial Education
    269, 285

Antwerp, Van, Lt. Gen. 260
Appendix K 131-132
Arland D. Williams Endowed
    Professorship of Heroism 137
Arland D. Williams, Jr., Memorial
    Bridge 137
Arms Control and Disarmament
    Agency *See ACDA*
Arnold, Harold 150-151
Arnold, Martha 151
Arnold, Patricia 151
Arnold, Rebecca 151
Arnold, Victoria 151
Arpaio, Michael, Cpt. 257, 259
Arvad, Inga 58
Ashley River 36, 37, 79, 80, 110,
    163, 206
Ashmore, Henry, Dr. 141
Association of Citadel Men 142,
    175, 176, 204, 216, 225
attrition 47, 86-87, 95, 104, 108,
    121, 138, 206, 278,
Auger, Laurie 229

-B-
Baiden, Arthur H., III, Maj. Gen.
    262
Baker, Gary 35
Baker School of Business
    Administration 269
Baker, Tommy 133, 293
Baker, Willard 264
Baptist College 61
Barnwell, Ed. 15
Barr, Tom 49
Barrett, Michael 127
Basel, J.M., Col. 207
Bastin Hall 11, 269, 292, 293
Bastin, Mary Lee 292
Bastin, Rick 292

Battalion of State Cadets 34-35
Battle of Tulifinny Creek 35
Baysden, Gerald 232
Beamer, Frank 102
Bell, Theodore, S., Col. 67,116
Best System of Practical Education 26
Biden, Joe 259
Big Red (flag) 34, 159, 218, 254,
    260, 263 - 265
Billy Budd 125
bin Laden, Osama 242
Bird, Annette Blazier 74
Bird, Samuel R. 73-75
Blair, Arthur H., Col. 127
Blair, Frank 219
Blanchard, Bart 264
Blatt, Sol, Jr., Judge 239
Blumstein, Ted 178
Board of Visitors 12, 18, 25, 26,
    28, 31, 33, 36-38, 40, 42, 48,
    50, 58, 61, 63, 64, 66, 72, 76,
    82, 88, 90, 95, 102, 106, 108,
    109, 111, 119-121, 126, 128-
    132, 138, 144, 146, 152, 158,
    161-163, 169, 170, 172, 173,
    176, 185, 191, 195, 209, 217-
    219, 224, 226, 228, 231-233,
    235-240, 242, 251, 255, 266,
    268, 273, 282, 295,
Bolick, Viann 247
Book, Connie Ledoux, Dr. 287,
    290, 292
Bond Hall 38, 40, 47, 134, 157,
    278,
Bond, Oliver J., Col. 20, 32, 36-40
Bond Volunteers 39, 49, 111, 122
The Boo 80, 121
The Boo (nickname) 63, 80, 81,
    101, 107, 221, 242*See also*
    Courvoisie
Boo Room 242
Bornhorst, Dave 220

Bo Thorpe Orchestra 180
Bowditch, John Watts 187-189
Bowditch, Leland 189
Boyd, Barbara, Lt. Com. 217
Boyd, David 162, 163
*Braddock's Defeat-The Battle of
    Monongahela and the Road to
    Revolution* 291
Bradley, Ed 206, 209, 210
Brakeley, George A., III 173-176,
    232, 237, 266, 296
Brandenburg, Mark 178, 255, 259
Brennan, Joseph, Dr. 118
Bresnik, Randy, Lt. Col. 265
Bresnik, Rebecca 265
Bridges, Doug 220
Bridis, Sallie 76
Bridin, Ted, Lt. 76
*The Brigadier 39, 61, 63, 64, 67,
    68, 78, 88, 99, 110, 139, 209,*
Brigadier Club 160, 175, 176, 208
Brigadier Foundation 224, 232,
    249, 264, 274
Bristol, Laura 229
Brodie, Robert 170
Brown, Floyd 123
Buckley, William F. 209
The Bulldog (newspaper) 39

Bunch, Don 83, 85
Buoniconti, Marc 143-145, 173,
    178
Buoniconti, Nick 143
Burdock, David A., Jr. 171, 173
Burger, Ken 167
Burke, Arleigh, Adm. 219
Burke High School 150, 158, 252
Bush, George W., Pres. 242-243
Butler, Bryant 206, 210
Byrd, Berra Lee, Jr. 170-175, 177,
    181, 281
Byrd, Ralph, Col. 62

-C-

Caan, James 168
Cabot, Jeri 256
Cadet Company 35
Cadets in Gray 35
Callliopeans (debate society) 28
Campbell, Blake 254
Campbell, Carroll, Gov. 156, 180
Cantey Rebellion 32-33
Cantey, Samuel O., Sgt. Maj. 32-33
Capers, Francis W., Maj. 30-32
Capers Hall 11, 262, 269, 283, 293
Carter, Jimmy, Pres. 111
Cauthen, Robert 220
Cash, Carey 179
CDF 140, 174-176, 224, 230-232, 273
Chapman, Alvah H. 67, 115, 219, 223, 224, 232, 262
Chapman, Angela 177
Chapman, Betty 219
Charleston Air Force Base 79, 156, 183
Charleston, city of 161, 162, 292
Charleston Higher Education Consortium 135
Charleston Movement 57
Charles Naval Base 58, 79
Childers, Shane Therrel, 2nd Lt. 251
Christian, Karla, Dr. 261
Christmas, George, Lt. Gen. 204
Churchill, Winston 42, 50, 239
Citadel Alumni Association (CAA) 144, 153, 203, 204, 216, 224, 225, 241, 256, 260, 263-265, 282, *See also Association of Citadel Men*
Citadel band 36, 41, 64, 157, 180, 193, 200, 208, 223, 227, 257
Citadel baseball team 36, 142, 159-161, 163, 165-167, 169, 254, 295

Citadel basketball team 220, 262
Citadel Development Foundation *See The Citadel Foundation*
Citadel football team (Bulldogs) 14, 36, 38, 42, 60, 101, 102, 109, 143, 146, 160, 167, 179, 182, 202, 233, 252, 264,
The Citadel Foundation (TCF) 177, 182, 224, 236, 237, 248, 250, 258, 267-270, 273-276, 279
Citadel Leadership Development Program (CLDP) 211, 212
The Citadel Oral History Project 279, 284,
The Citadel Museum 142, 290
The Citadel Summer Camp 257-259
Citadel Volunteer Recruiters 203
The Citadel War Memorial 269, 278, 279, 285-287, 294
Citadel women's cross country 228-229
Citadel women's volleyball 229
Citadel Yacht Club 107,
City Station House 36
Civil War 11, 18, 21, 24, 25, 34, 35, 147, 148, 149, 185, 189, 233, 234, 260, 264,
Clanton, Charles T., Col. 205
Clark, Mark W., Gen. 10, 11, 12, 19, 20, 40, 42, 43, 54, 56, 58, 59, 60, 61, 62, 70, 72, 75, 78, 94, 97, 106, 128, 141, 142, 145, 153, 155, 156, 182, 219, 221, 226, 257, 290, 295
Clark, Renie 43
Clark, Walter 70, 72
Clawson, Andy 143, 144
Cleaver, Charles E., Lt. Col. 131,
Clinton, Hillary 259,
Clyburn, James, 50,

CNN 259,
Coe, Charlie 258
coeducation 11, 90, 168, 185, 187, 190, 193, 194, 196, 212, 216, 219, 228, 281, 295,
Coker College 31
Coker, James Lide 31
Colcock, Richard W., Maj. 30
College of Charleston 11, 12, 23, 28, 30, 56, 57, 61, 81, 82, 87, 95, 160, 219, 237, 256, 264,
College World Series 159, 160, 161, 165, 169
88Collins, B.T. 73-74
Collins, J. Quincy, Jr., Col. 225, 254
Collins, Robert C. 161
Committee on Customs and Traditions 88
company assignments by height 49, 63
Company of Men 199
Confederate Battle Flag 50, 147, 148, 149, 150, 159, 234-235
Conner, Gregory 220
Conroy, Ed 262
Conroy, Pat 80, 81, 121, 129, 130, 193, 220, 221, 242, 243, 262
Cooke, Dawes 178, 191, 193, 194, 209,
Cooper, Anderson 259
Copen blue 129
Cordell, Mr. and Mrs. J.D. 55
Cordell, Terry D., Cpt. 55, 59
core curriculum 122, 139, 151, 152, 283, 289
Cormeny, George F., III 171-173
Corps Day 10, 26, 27, 39, 58, 59, 111, 122, 144, 171, 179, 208, 209, 211, 240, 260, 264, 265, 266

Corps of Cadets 11, 12, 40, 43, 49, 58, 65, 66, 83, 92, 93, 96, 98, 103, 132, 133, 134, 137, 140, 146, 152, 167, 182, 185, 192, 194, 200, 207, 208, 212, 218, 225, 227, 228, 229, 231, 239, 240, 242, 256, 262, 281, 283, 288, 291, 292
Council on Higher Education 50
The Courage of Sam Bird 73
Courvoisie Banquet Hall 242
Courvoisie, Thomas Nugent, Lt. Col. 63, 80-81, 242
Cover-up at The Citadel 206
Coward, Asbury 32-33
Crabbe, William, Jr., Col. 94, 95, 121
Crawford, Cardon, Col. 259
Cronkite, Walter 78
Crosby, Rick M. 232
Crumley, Deona 229
Crumpton, Sidney 141, 225
curriculum, early 26
Curriculum Study Committee 139,
Curtis, Ted 263, 264
Custer, George Armstrong, Gen. 35, 46,
Cuttino, Col. 89,

-D-
Dallager, John R., Maj. Gen 13-15
Daniel, Charles 138
Daniel Construction Company 138, 139
Daniel Fund 273
Daniel, Hugh 138, 139
Daniel, Larry 285
Daniel Library 34, 142, 159, 217, 249, 269, 290, 295
Darkness to Light 280, 283
Davis, Emmett I., Jr. 176
de la Roche, Harry 110
DeBrosse, John 220

Decatur News 70

Democratic presidential debate 258

Department of Defense allocations 64

Dick, Harvey, Col. 159, 204, 222, 246, 279

Dickinson, Thomas R., Brig. Gen. 76

Discipline and Rebellion: The Citadel Rebellion of 1898 33

Dodd, Chris 259

Dolge, Martha 187

domino theory 56

Doucet, Norman P. 171

Douglas, Jack 166, 167, 179, 180

Dove, Robert 164, 165

Dowd, John Paul "Jay", III 272, 273

drug problems 93, 218

Duckett, James W., Maj. Gen. 86, 88, 89, 92, 93, 94, 95, 98, 99, 102, 106

Duell, Charles 237

Durante, Gary, Dr. 260

DuPont 79

-E-

Earthquake of 1886 35, 40, 155,

East Tennessee State University 143, 147

education in Antebellum South 24-25

Education Action Committee 66, 90

Edwards, John 259

Eggers, Dan 209

Eisenhower, Dwight D., Pres. 39, 42, 46, 56, 78

Elander, William, Lt. Col. 254

End as a Man 49, 52

Endictor, Bill 45-47, 203

Evening Post 78, 88, 90, 93, 296

expansion of The Citadel 37, 40, 66

-F-

Fajardo, Mario J., Cpt. 166

Faulkner, Shannon Richey 50, 131, 178, 180, 182-185, 187, 189-194, 196, 199, 203, 205, 291

Fennell, Edward 170

Fielding, Herbert, Sen. 147

Figg, Col. 89

Findlay, Prentiss 265

Fire of 1892 35

Fix, Sybil 253

Flock, John 170

Fluor International 138-139

Foley, Robert 183

Folley, John A., Col. 207

Forbes Magazine 291

Ford, Gerald, Pres. 190, 197

For the Boys 168

Fort Sumter 25, 34, 189, 234, 260

Foster, Charles D. 63, 64, 90, 99, 129

Fourth Class System 17, 30, 41, 44-54, 65, 83, 85, 87, 94, 95, 103, 115, 120-124, 127, 129, 134, 173, 184, 199-201, 205, 207, 208, 210, 211, 212, 214, 215, 223, 241, 244, 278, 282

Freda, Leon, Maj. 64

Freeman, Ricky 170

Free School Act 24

Free Schools 24, 26, 35

Freshman Academic Orientation Program 151

Friedgen, Ralph 102

Frost, Jack 38

Fulghum, Leonard 153, 161, 162, 163, 242, 247

Fuller, John 68

Fusilier Francaise 22

-G-

Gaillard, Palmer 107
Garcia, Mandy 229
Gardner, John 279
Gavin, James A., Gen. 46
Gay Alliance of Students 109
General Electric 50, 79
General Order No. 20 111
Gentry, Megan 229
Gibbes, John 37
Gibler, John K., Col. 111, 122, 127
Gibson, William, Dr. 147
Giera, Patricia 229
Gillen, Shamus, Maj. 203
Ginsburg, Ruth Bader, Hon. 194
Goble, David 94-95, 142, 289, 290, 295
Gold Lifesaving Medal (Coast Guard) 136
The Gold Star Journal 209
Good Morning America 210, 227
Goodpaster, Andrew, Gen. 219, 226
The Graduate 52
graduate program establishment 61, 66, 135
Graham, Billy, Rev. 141
Graham, William F., Cpt. 30
Gravel, Mike 259
great cricket caper 115-116
Great Depression 40
Greater Citadel 12, 36-38
Greater Issues program 42, 58, 67, 78, 135, 179, 180, 281
Green, Barth, Dr. 144,
Green, Jennifer R. 25-26
Greenberg, Reuben, Chief 147, 181
Grenada 140
Grice, George 56
Grimsley, James Alexander, Jr., Maj. Gen. 67, 86, 110, 112, 113-116, 120, 123, 128-129, 130-154, 157, 162, 189, 190, 277, 294
Grimsley, James A., Sr. 113
Grimsley, Anne Darby 113
Grimsley, Jessie 128, 146
Grimsley, Jim 128
Grimsley Plan 129, 132-135, 169
Grimsley, Will 116, 128
Grinalds, John S., Gen. 142, 196-197, 204-205, 208-209, 212-213, 217-218, 220-222, 224-227, 229-233, 235, 237, 243-244, 246-247, 250- 254, 263, 268, 282, 294
Grinalds Matrix 224-226
Grinalds, Norwood 213
Grunes, Rodney 62
Guerra, Eileen 229
Guggenheim-Lehrman prize 291
The Guidon 85

-H-

Hacker, Sharon 229
Hagood, Ben 153
Hagood, Johnson, Gov. 35
Halpin, Jim 220
Hamlin, Carol 229
Hampton Park 21, 37, 38, 57, 80, 120, 147
Hampton, Wade, Gen. 35
Hamze, Sana 291
Hanoi Hilton 118, 225
Hansen, Lance 179
Hardney, Geneive 247
Harpe, Joshua 264
Harrietta Plantation 110
Harrington, Myron 70-72
Harris, Hugh Pate, Gen. 59-62, 64-66, 78, 82-83, 85, 87-90, 92, 96-97, 106, 208, 294
Hartsville, SC 31
Harvey, Brantley, Jr., Lt. Gov. 41,

Harvey, Dick, Col. 159, 204, 222, 246, 279

Hayakawa, S.I. 78

Haynsworth, George 34

Hazard, Roberta S., R. Adm. 219, 226

Hazing 11, 47-48, 51-52, 65, 83, 86, 94, 120, 124, 183, 201, 206, 209-211, 231

Health, Education and Welfare (HEW) 89

Heriot, Edwin 26

Hewitt, Stephanie, Lt. Col. 283

Hicks, Brian 284

hijab controversy 291

Hines, Samuel, Dr. 258, 285

Holliday Alumni Center 22, 145, 241, 265

Holliday, John M.J., Col. 90, 93, 94, 241

Hollings, Ernest "Fritz", Sen. 67, 137, 239

Honors Program establishment 133, 139, 152

Hood, Col. 98-99

Hooper, Tee 220

hospital workers' strike 77

Houchen, Bonnie, Lt. Col. 217, 229

Huddleston, Jody 229

Hudson, Toshika "Peaches" 229, 247

Hue Citadel (Vietnam) 72

Humphrey, Hubert H. 77

Hunley, H.L., civil war submarine 233

Hunter, Tommy B. 247

Hurricane Fran 200

Hurricane Hugo 154-158, 160, 166, 198

Hurricane Ophelia 254

Hypolite, Renee 247

-I-

In Glory's Shadow: Shannon Faulkner, The Citadel and a Changing America 192

In Retrospect 59

Inouye, Daniel, Sen. 258

Inouye Marksmanship Center 258

Iowa Historical Society Museum 260

integration, racial 11, 43, 82, 148-149, 295

International Space Station 265

Inter-University Committee for Debate on Foreign Policy 67-68

Iranian students 102-104, 108, 140

Irby, Richard, Col. 244-245

Ivory City 37

-J-

Jackson, Andrew, Pres. 21

Jackson, Cam 289

Jacobs, Herman 143, 145, 173

James, George, Col. 144, 153, 162

James Self Outstanding Teacher Award 217

Jarrard, Kevin, Maj. 183, 261

Jarrell, Frank 129

Jenkins, Anthony 160

Jenkins Hall 81, 157

Jenkinson, William "Billy", Col. 18, 63, 180, 204-205, 222, 244, 247

Jennings, Gen. 89

Jesse Ball DuPont Fund 158

Jeter, Mitchell 289

John C. West Chair of International Affairs 138

Johnson Hagood Stadium 23, 60, 109, 134, 147, 157- 160, 163, 165, 211, 224, 233, 241, 249, 252, 293

Johnson, James P. 93
Johnson, Lyndon B., Pres. 58-60, 77-79
Johnson, Patricia 177
Johnston, Keith 111
Jones, James, Gen. 31
Jones, James, Col. 173, 176
Joseph P. Riley, Jr., Endowed Chair of American Government and Public Policy 284
Jumper, John P., Gen. 13-17
Junior Sword Drill 39, 49, 54, 107, 121, 122, 180, 222

-K-
Kappler, Edward S. 178
Karnow, Stanley 71
Keennan, Jay 292, 296
Kellehan, Richard H., Lt. 254
Kennedy, Brian 220
Kennedy, John D., Lt. Gov. 35, 266
Kennedy, John Fitzgerald, Pres. 48, 56, 57, 58, 59, 73, 75, 80, 219
Kennedy, Joseph P. 58
Kennedy, Robert, Sen. 77
Key, Sanford "Sandy" 159
Kimbrell, Harrison, W., Lt. Col. 96-101, 107-108
Kimpson, Marlon, Sen. 291
King, Martin Luther, Jr., Rev. 57, 77, 147
King, Robert, Dr. 142
Kissinger, Henry, Dr. 77, 92
Klene, Brian C. 110-111
Knight, Norman R., Jr. 238
Knowles, Marilyn, Mst. Chief 217
Krause, Bill 63, 250
Krause Center for Leadership and Ethics 48, 50, 134, 212, 250, 258, 260, 269, 271, 274, 281
Krause Initiative 18, 258, 260
Kroboth, Alan, Cpt. 220, 254
Ku Klux Klan 146, 148-149, 171, 290

Kucinich, Dennis 259
Kuralt, Charles 168

-L-
Lacey, Elizabeth 177
Lafayette, Marquis de 22
Lamotte, Charles O. 27
Lanham, Samuel T. 38
Lane Committee 184, 208
LaSure, Allen Brooks 237
Law, Thomas 31
Laycock, Jimmye 102
LEAD 2018 268, 270-276, 278, 285
Leadership, Excellence, and Academic Distinction See LEAD
Leadership Training Day 181
Leckonby, Larry 274
Lee, Robert E., Gen. 111, 149, 164,
Leedom, Terry 193, 206
Legare, Ben, Lt. Col. 258-259
Leland, James 161
Lemnitzer, Lyman, Gen. 219
Lesesne Gate 42, 56, 57, 101, 147, 295
Lesesne, Henry, Cpt. 254
Leslie, H.T. 239
LeTellier, Louis, Col. 42, 60
Letterman, David 227
Lilliewood, Chip 146
literary magazine See The Shako
Little, Allen H., Pvt., 34
Lockheed McDonnell-Douglas 79
Logan, Samuel 238
Lords of Discipline 129, 184
Love, Allison Dean 237, 289
Love and War 117
Lovetinska, Petra 198-202, 206, 209-210, 213, 228, 239
Lowery, Jill 229
Ludlum, Clay 159

-M-

Mabrouck, Suzanne 209
Macaulay, Alexander 33, 110, 295
Mace, Emory, Brig. Gen. 198, 206-213, 218, 222, 244, 251, 253
Mace, Mary 198
Mace, Nancy 256, 198-202, 206-207, 209-210, 213, 217-218, 227-228, 239, 256
Mace Plan 210
MacPherson, William A., Col. 207
Magill, William J., Lt. 34
Major General James A. Grimsley, Jr., Award for Teaching Excellence 151
Mahan, Thomas, W., Col., 153, 158
Maisonet, Maggie 229
The Man in the Water 136
Manchester, William 75
Manegold, Catherine 178, 192-193
Marching in Step 54, 295
Marion Square 12, 21, 28, 35-37
Mark Clark Museum 142
Marshall, George C. 251
Mary Baldwin College 191, 194
Masons of South Carolina 38
The Mayor 284
McAlister Field House 135, 161-162, 164, 167, 180, 259, 273
McCaffrey, Barry, Gen. 196
McCain, John 225
McCarter, Mike 116
McCloud, Adrienne Watson Jamey 247
McCombs, Cal 102
McDuffie, George, Gov. 23
McElwee, Les 160
McManus, James 291
McNair, Robert, Gov. 65, 77, 82
McNamara, Robert S. 59, 77
McNealy, Tara E. 277

Meenaghan, George 131, 158
Meeting Street Extension 36
Mehra, Jagdish, Dr. 180
Melville, Herman 125
Mendoza, Michael 146
Menges, Phil 203
Mentavlos, Jeanie 198-199, 201-202, 206, 209, 210, 227-228
Mercado, Col. 277-278, 283
Merchant Seamen's Club 79
Merrill, James, Rep. 287
Merritt, Gen. 224-226
Messer, Kim 198-199, 201-202, 206, 209-210, 227-228
Metts, Isaac "Spike" 139, 146, 177, 198, 209, 227
Mexican-American War 34
Miami Project to Cure Paralysis 144
Midler, Bette 168
Mikell, J. Thomas 202-203
Miller, David Humphreys 265
Miller, Timothy C. 93
Mills, William C., "Billy" 124-126
Milton, John 29
Miss USA Contest 110
Missar, Joe 60
Mitchell, Natosha 247, 229
Mohr, Dan 220
Mood Committee 121-123, 127
Mood, Dan 121
Mood, Francis P. "Frank", Col. 97, 121, 154, 185, 196-197, 204, 219, 221-225, 232-233, 239, 253, 282, 295
Mood, George, Dr. 120
Mood, Julius 121
Mood Report 122-124, 173, 184, 208
Mood, Rogers 121
Moore, Darla 260
Moore, Scott 159
Moore, Winfred "Bo" 283

Moorer, Thomas H., Adm. 219
Moreland, Laurence W. 62
Moseley, Jim 203
Mother Teresa 124, 239
Motley, Tony 199, 203, 221, 239
Mount Zion College 23
Mundy, Carl E., Gen. 204-204, 226
Municipal Guard 21-22
munitions 20-23, 35, 179
Murphy, Frank "Skip" 60
Murray Barracks 38, 231
My Losing Season 220
Myers, Glenn L., Lt. Col. 254

-N-

NAACP 57, 82, 146-148, 171
Nadeau, John, Cpt. 261
Nadzak, Walt 143, 161, 233
National Archives 44
National Liberation Front 67
National Organization for the Reform of Marijuana Laws (NORML) 109
National Sojourners Award 140
Neal, Brian 60
Nelson, John F. (Jack) 47
Nesmith, Alonzo 132
Nesmith, Amelia 147
Nesmith, Kevin 146-147, 154, 178, 205, 289
Nesmith, Larry 147
Neulander, Joelle, Maj. 289
Newport News Shipbuilding and Drydock Company 76
The News and Courier 78, 128, 141, 143
Nichols, W. Gary 40
Nicholson, D.D., Jr., Col. 20, 40, 203
Nixon, Richard M. 77, 92, 225
Nunn, Sam, Sen. 196

-O-

Obama, Barack, Pres. 259, 288
Ohio State University 11
Old Citadel 12, 21-22, 142, 179
Olmstead, Frederick 37
One-Eyed Jacks 52
Operation Enduring Freedom 209
Operation Urgent Fury 140
Ordinance of Nullification 21
Ozment, Suzanne, Dr. 216, 247

-P-

Pace, Peter, Gen. 257
Padgett, Richard 106, 112, 162
Padgett-Thomas Barracks 38, 49, 52, 164, 169-170, 172, 180, 199, 231-232, 236-238, 257
Palmetto Regiment 34
Palms, John M., Dr. 234-235, 279
Paluso, Eugene "Geno" F. 208, 287, 291
Paramount Pictures 129
Parker, Dean, Lt. 74-75
Parker, Red 15, 101
Parris Island 212
Pearcy, Charlie 203
Pecorelli, Carmine 39, 41
Pendery, Kenton 291-292
Penn, William 239
Pentagon 13-14, 116, 118, 135, 183, 242
Perry, Jack R. 138
Peterson, Lesjanusar "Sha" 247
Philipkoski, Thomas G., Col. 279
Picquet Guard 27
Pinewood Preparatory School 260
Plank Holders 239
Plunkett, Paul 14
Pohl, Gilbert 256
Policy on Cadet Senior/Subordinate and Inter-Genders Relationships 216

Policy on Cultural, Racial, Religious and Sexual Harassment 215
Pollock, Edwin A., Gen. 66, 92, 95
Polytechnics (debate society) 28
Poole, R. Clifton, Gen. 193, 197-198, 200, 202-203, 208-212, 217-218, 252, 254, 294
Popham, Roger, Col. 183
Port, Chal 159, 169, 254
Porter, Charles T., Jr. 112
Porter-Gaud School 252
Post and Courier 172, 200, 210, 232, 253, 265, 290
Potter, Terrence M. 93
Powell, Colin 196

Powers, Don 233
Preston, David 291
Prioleau Rare Book Room 218
Prioleau, William F. "Buddy", Col. 89, 112, 119, 153, 162, 218
private academies 24
Probsdorfer, James F., Lt. Col. 63, 76
Project Challenge 158
Pye, Anne 217

-R-
Raben's Tavern 64
Rather, Dan 206
Regulation 82 30
Rembert, James 126-127
Renew, Tyler 289
ReVille, Louis "Skip" 258-260, 268, 270, 279, 280-281
Rhett Farm 37
Rhoad, Dennis 246
Rhodes, Jack, Col. 139, 251
Rhodes Scholars 139, 197, 220, 226, 251
Rice, Reggie 264
Richards, Art, Col. 156
Richardson, Bill 259

Ridgway, Roxanne L. 219, 223
Riggs, William 63
Riley, Joseph P., Jr. 57, 107-108, 148, 150, 160-166, 179, 284,
Risher, William 162-165
Ritz, Michael F., Cpt. 140
Rivers High School 57
Rivers, L. Mendel 79
Riverview Room 223
Rizzo, Charlie 102
Robertson, Clay 244
Robinson, Les 260
Robinson, William "Kooksie" 202
Roden, Keith 14
Roe, James T. 79
Rosa, Brad 255
Rosa, Donna 18, 255
Rosa, John W., Jr., Lt. Gen. 13-19, 49-51, 212, 250-251, 253-257, 262-270, 274, 276-277, 279, 284, 287, 290, 292-294
Rosenblatt, Roger 136
Ross, Bobby 101, 102, 260
ROTC scholarships 98, 107-108, 249
Rusk, Dean 59, 63, 254
Russell, Clarke 254
Russell, Robert B. 164-165
-S-
SACS 38, 62, 93, 140-141, 184, 216-217, 231, 248-249, 276-280, 284-285
Saleeby, Dudley, Jr., Col. 153, 247-248
Sales, Latrice 229
SALT (Strategic Arms Limitations Agreement) 111
Sammis, Ben, Cpt. 251
Sams, John, Lt. Gen. 269, 276, 290, 296
Sanders, Alex 237
Sands, Everette 167, 179

Savas, Sam 63
Sayadchi, Easa J. 103
Saylor, Conway 274
Scalia, Antoine, Judge 194
Scarborough, Wallace 244
Schnorf, Charles J., 1st Lt. 139-140
Seignious, Anne 106, 109
Seignious, Dielle Fleischman 110
Seignious, George M., Lt. Gen. 67, 86, 92-93, 102, 104-116, 120, 130, 132, 135, 138-139, 197, 224, 226, 294
Seignious Hall 134, 138, 157, 161, 176,
Sexton, Chris 159
Shakespeare 44
The Shako 39, 209
Shine, Joe 64, 251
Silver, Ryan 229
Smalls, Robert 24
Smith, Lance A., Gen. 255
Smith, Lester 179
Smith, Michael O. 264
Snyder, Douglas A., Col. 111, 232-233, 253, 259, 263, 267, 272
Sonoco 31
Sossamon, Richard 111
South Carolina Commission on Higher Education 231
South Carolina Historical Magazine 33
South Carolina Interstate and West Indian Expedition 37
South Carolina Military Academy 33-34
South Carolina Professor of the Year 217
Spann, James 114
Spearman, Lewis 167
Spectator Hotel 292
The Sphinx (yearbook) 36, 107, 114, 128

"Spirit of '76" program 106, 108, 294
Sports Illustrated 179, 181, 205
St. John's Episcopal Church (Florence, SC) 114
St. Peter's Catholic Church (Beaufort, SC) 243
Stackhouse, George B. 171
Stackpole, Henry C., III, Lt. Gen. 204
Star of the West 34, 189, 260, 264
Star of the West medal 34
Star of the West mural 159
Star of the West scholarship 155
Starks, Miguel 264
The State 130, 234-235
Stavrinakis, Leon, Rep. 287
Steele, Michael, Lt. Gen. 76, 266-267, 269-270, 274-275, 284, 295-296
Stevens Barracks 157, 169, 256-257, 260, 293,
Stevens, Peter F., Maj. 260
Stiley, Joe 135
Stingley, Darryl 143
Stockdale, James Bond, Vice Adm. 86, 113, 116-128, 132, 153, 217-218, 220
Stockdale, Sybil 116
Strand, Brett 220
Student Army Training Corps 37
Summerall Chapel 58, 106, 125, 141, 203, 205, 228, 278, 288, 290
Summerall, Charles P., Gen. 39-43, 52, 58, 60, 85, 97, 128, 145, 237, 266, 273
Summerall Guards 39, 110-111, 121, 139, 180, 222
Swain's Department of Nursing 10, 291
Swift, John H. 27

-T-

Taaffe, Charlie 167, 179, 202-203
Tatum, Jack 143
Tangerine Bowl 42
Teachers' Committee for Peace in Vietnam 67
Tet Offensive 71, 77
Tew, Charles Courtenay, Col. 27, 288
Thomas, Brantley D. 232
Thomas, Clarence 194
Thomas, John P. 20, 29
Thompson, Joel 144
Thompson, Yaunna 229
Thurmond, Strom 108
Time Magazine 136
Tobias, Steve 250, 267
Tommy and Victoria Baker School of Business 133, 293
Trabert, James 232
Travel + Leisure Magazine 288, 292
Trevilian Station (Virginia) 35
Trez, Carmela Pinelli 49
Trez, Joseph W., Col 48-50, 183-184, 207, 210, 212-213, 228, 247, 253, 255, 279
Truman, Harry S., Pres. 251
Trump, Donald, Pres. 39
Tucker, David Bruce, Maj. 68
Tucker, Reuben H., Maj. Gen. 46-47, 68, 101
Turner, Ted 209
Twitty, Stephen M., Lt. Gen. 151

-U-

United States Air Force Academy 13, 255-256
United States Department of Defense 77, 132, 222, 256
United States Naval Academy 112, 116, 118, 125, 190
United States Navy Fleet Ballistic Missile Submarine Training Center 79

University of South Carolina 12, 23, 38, 63, 66, 166, 190, 197, 279
Updike, Tessa 142, 295
U.S. News and World Report 11, 18, 86-87, 93, 152, 158, 179, 181, 200, 244, 271, 276

-V-

Vandiver, Thomas C. "Nap", Col. 217-218
Venable, Louis 139
Vesey, Denmark 20-21
Vietnam: A History 71
Vietnam War 43, 49, 55-56, 59-60, 62-63, 67-71, 73, 75-79, 91-92, 96, 112, 116-117, 135, 168, 197, 205-207, 225, 254, 286
Vincent, Hugh 260
Vojdik, Valerie 190

-W-

Wallace, Buddy, Dr. 143-144
Wallace, Charles, II 159
Wallenberg, Raoul 239
Walsh, Amy 229
Wang, Kay, Sgt. Maj. 217
Warlick, Anderson D. 232
Warren, Brett 254
Washington Center 2013 Education Civic Engagement Award 274
Washington Evening Star 55
Washington Light Infantry 22, 35, 106, 110, 179, 294
Washington Post 146, 183
Washington Race Course 37
Waters, Wesley 178
Watson, Adrienne 229, 247
Watson, James M. 143
Watts Barracks 11, 257

Watts, Claudius E., III, Gen. 86, 131, 136, 153, 155-159, 167-169, 173, 176, 178, 181-182, 184-185, 191, 196-198, 203, 212, 257, 266, 268, 294

Watts, Claudius E. "Bud", IV, 267-269, 273-274

Watts, Claudius E., Jr. 155

Weart, Jeffrey, Lt. Col. 250

Weinstein, Col. 292

Welch, Jack 50

West, John, Lt. Gov. 67, 107, 232

West, Wallace I., Jr. 189

Westmoreland, William, Gen 77, 93, 135

Weston, Tucker, Dr. 142, 176

Wetherington, Mitchell Lee 287

Whipper, Seth, Rep. 291

White, Jerome 180

Whitmire, James M., Jr., Col. 83-85

Whitmire Report 45, 83, 85, 208

Williams, Arland D. 135-138

Williamston, SC 34

Willingham, Calder 49, 51-52

Wilder, Eugene, Corp. 34

Wilson, David 150

Winthrop College 60

Wood, Boyd L. 161

Woodberry Forest 196-197, 205, 209, 253

Wooten, Frank 210

World Trade Center destruction 242

World War I 36-37, 40, 70, 138

World War II 41-42, 46, 51, 58, 66-69, 75, 116, 183, 254

Wright, Allison 237, 289 *See also Love, Allison Dean*

-XYZ-

Y2K 233

Yates, Jane 142, 290, 295

Years of Summerall and Clark 40

yellow fever 27

Yonce, Leon 63

Zais, Mick, Brig. Gen. 284

Zaremba, Barbara A., Dr. 185

Zinser, Roy F., Jr., Col. 180-181, 183, 212

Zucker, Anita 284-285

Zucker Family School of Education 285

Zucker, Jonathan 285

Zycinsky, Bill 220